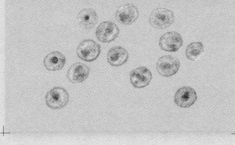

HIV Virus

Germs

THE
GENESIS
OF GERMS

Ebola

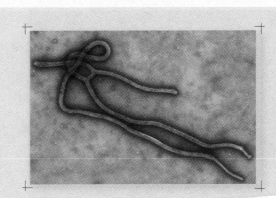

the origin of diseases

& the coming plagues

Smallpox

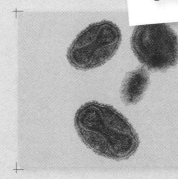

LAN L. GILLEN

Anthrax

First printing: January 2007
Second printing: November 2014

Copyright © 2007 by Master Books. All rights reserved. No part of this book may be used or reproduced in any manner whatsoever without written permission of the publisher except in the case of brief quotations in articles and reviews. For information write:

Master Books, Inc., P.O. Box 726, Green Forest, AR 72638.

Master Books® is a division of the New Leaf Publishing Group, Inc.

ISBN-13: 978-0-89051-493-1
Library of Congress Number: 2006937547

Cover Design: Rebekah Krall
Interior Design and Layout: Bryan Miller

All scripture quotations taken from the King James (Authorized) Version of the Bible unless otherwise stated.

Please consider requesting that a copy of this volume be purchased by your local library system.

Printed in the United States of America

Please visit our website for other great titles:
www.masterbooks.net

For information regarding author interviews,
please contact the publicity department at (870) 438-5288.

Master
Books®
A Division of New Leaf Publishing Group
www.masterbooks.net

Dedication
To the late Dr. Robert P. Williams, my mentor in microbiology and friend, and to the teaching assistants of microbiology at Liberty University.

Acknowledgments
I want to thank several people who made this book possible. They have offered useful suggestions and have given me support in this writing endeavor. The people who have helped me are: Jayne Gillen, Joy Khamvongsa, Dr. Paul Sattler, Dr. Charles Detwiler, Dr. Doug Oliver, Dr. Jay Wile, Elizabeth Paquette, Sarah Anderson, Su-Fern Tan, Hope Smith, and Racquel Sewell.

Table of Contents

The Genesis of Germs: The Origin of Diseases and the Coming Plagues

Preface

*How precious also are thy thoughts unto me,
O God! how great is the sum of them!
(Ps. 139:17)*

"I was merely thinking God's thoughts after him. Since we astronomers are priests of the highest God in regard to the book of nature," wrote Kepler, "it benefits us to be thoughtful, not of the glory of our minds, but rather, above all else, of the glory of God."

In past centuries, a number of the world's greatest scientists sought to integrate their biblical faith with science. In fact, it was Johannes Kepler who stated, as he used his telescope and astronomy research, that he was merely "thinking God's thoughts after Him." Kepler and many other great scientists were great because they started with God's Word as the foundation for their thinking. In a parallel manner, Anton van Leeuwenhoek, Louis Pasteur, and Joseph Lister used their microscopes and microbiology research to also view creation from a Christian world view. The meditation of "thinking God's thoughts after Him" becomes a problem when it is assumed that one can do this from nature (and science) alone without starting from God's revelation in Scripture.

The Genesis of Germs is a creation microbiology book. *The Genesis of Germs* describes the intelligent design of microbes in the original "very good" state of the original creation, while describing the fallen microbes that lead to disease. While writing this book on creation microbiology, I had the sense that I was actually working on several books at once. I wanted to capture the essence of the original good design of microbes by the Creator, the genesis of particular diseases and modern day plagues, as well as issues that are clinically significant.

The Genesis of Germs describes microbes in a fallen world. The book has numerous focus vignettes interwoven with evidence of creation, intelligent design, creation biographies, and contemporary disease issues. These explorations include disease aspects of body systems, current events, and classic (historic) and contemporary explorers. Although the evolutionary origin of microbes is now assumed among most professional biologists, this has not always been the case. Most of the foundation laid in medicine, microbiology and epidemiology *was done* by scientists who believed in creation.

Therefore, I have made it a goal to tell biographically about some of the famous explorers that were involved in microbiology, medicine, and disease discoveries. In addition, I also wrote with hope to convey an appreciation for the vast evidence that supports a creation or design view of the microbes by rendering medical facts in an appealing style.

This book, *The Genesis of Germs*, continues the approach I began in *Body by Design* and *The Human Body: An Intelligent Design*. It is not a sequel in the strictest sense because each volume stands alone and is written at different reading levels. *The Human Body: An Intelligent Design* emphasizes physiological evidences for creation and *Body by Design* emphasizes anatomical evidences for creation in the human body. It also follows a pattern that was begun in earlier books in that it gives credit to the Creator for forming and fashioning both microbes and man. It denies that microbes and men are products of evolution, and it shows that disease was not in God's original plan. All of my books focus on an in-depth treatment of biology and provide an apologetic for the Christian faith.

The purpose of *The Genesis of Germs* is to describe the world of microbes and how they cause disease. It explains the genesis of pathogens (i.e., germs), infectious disease, and microbiology from a creation, biblical perspective. The book was written to make the reader aware of the unseen world of viruses, bacteria, fungi, and protozoans. It challenges the reader to think of the unseen as relevant to his or her world and to be aware of the wondrous designs in microbes given by the Creator. A model of infectious disease is presented that incorporates creation, corruption, and the curse; it provides an alternative to the typical evolutionary model of disease origins.

Since Leeuwenhoek first declared that microbes were the most wondrous of the world's wonders, several hundred years of scientific discovery have only served to emphasize his words. The world of microbes is far more wondrous than Leeuwenhoek could have imagined. Up until the late 18th century, science was seen as a direct search for God. When Louis Pasteur, Joseph Lister, Walter Reed, and Ronald Ross made their discoveries, they believed their results taught humanity about God as well. The created world, they felt, revealed His nature. Not many people approach science that way any more.

The book should serve as a reference for microbiology students because it provides questions to study and definitions of basic biology terms. Many of these new terms can be found in a glossary included in the book.

Finally, after reading this book, the students should better understand the design of microbes and origin of infectious diseases from a creation perspective.

Finally, I believe that God, in Christ, is against disease. He is not against microbes per se, but rather against those that have become pathogens. Disease is an unnatural state. Through the Church (universal), He is working to restore creation, prevent infectious disease, treat patients with germs, kill pathogens, and to cure people who are sick. Although God had to pronounce a curse on the earth after man sinned because He is a Holy God, we see that very quickly He was looking for a method of redemption for all creation. This redemption and healing would happen through Jesus Christ. Jesus is our Great Physician and *Jehovah Rapha* in the flesh. We see Him throughout the gospels healing the sick and cleansing the lepers. Jesus was deeply concerned about the sick, which is evident by how He went about healing them. Although He was not a physician in the traditional sense of the word, and despite the fact that He did not leave a single prescription for a medication, nor author a book in medicine, disease, or healing, He has influenced the course of medicine more than any historical figure. The Apostle Paul tells us that the present distress and diseases of this life are temporary and that creation is waiting for restoration.

In my opinion, whatever we may have to go through now is less than nothing compared with the magnificent future God has in store for us. The whole creation is on tiptoe to see the wonderful sight of the sons of God coming into their own. The world of creation cannot as yet see reality, not because it chooses to be blind, but because in God's purpose it has been so limited – yet it has been given hope. The hope is that in the end the whole of created life will be rescued from the tyranny of change and decay and have its share in that magnificent liberty which only belong to the children of God! (Rom. 8:18-21, Phillips Version).

Someday, the Creator and Great Physician will rid the world of infectious disease and germs will be no more! This book covers the "genesis" and the "exodus" of germs.

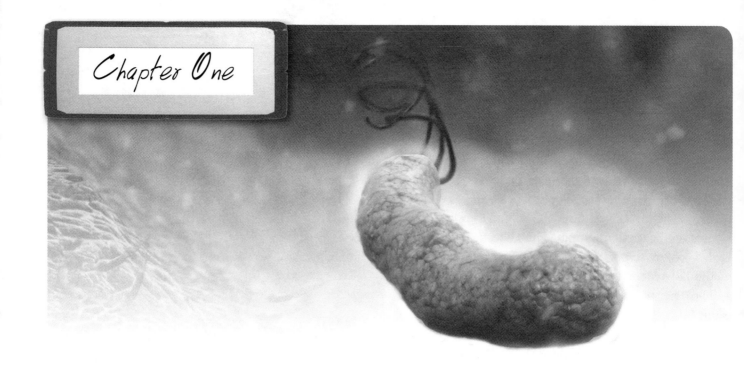

Chapter One

Microbes By Design

The news media writes frequently about the evolution of new microbe strains that can cause disease. New diseases such as hemolytic uremic syndrome caused by *E. coli*, flesh-eating *Streptococcus*, methicillin-resistant *Staphylococcus aureus* (MRSA), antibiotic-resistant malaria, and bird flu all capture the national headlines. With each passing year, news headlines reveal that some new disease outbreak or plague has "evolved" and it threatens thousands of lives. In the year 2005, the news flash "Bird Flu Threatens Globe" was broadcast across the nation, leading many people to become alarmed. The emergence of a new strain (H5N1) of flu may place millions at risk.

Another one of these prevalent and menacing diseases is MRSA, which is a new strain of *Staphylococcus aureus*; it is resistant to methicillin and therefore becomes very difficult to treat. Consequently, it becomes a huge nuisance and ailment to the one infected. The pace of the development of antibiotic resistance to emerging, incurable infections is faster than drug makers can keep up with and treat.

Are these examples of evolution? Are these facts of evolution? Did God make microbes by mistake? Are they accidents of evolution, out of the primordial soup? These timely questions are examined throughout this book.

First, these news headlines of bird flu and antibiotic resistance are not examples of Darwinian evolution. On the contrary, they are examples of variation, or change

within "kinds." Later in the book we will explore how and why these examples of minor changes (variations within kind) in microbes can cause disease. Second, microbes are not the Creator's mistake, nor are they random accidents of evolution. Not only were microbes originally created for our good (and the biosphere's), but their design also shows creativity, diversity, intelligence, and beauty. A few microbes (five percent of the bacteria) reflect decay and degeneration from the original plan. Disease was not the Creator's original plan, but rather a reflection of man's sin, the Curse placed on nature.

The Power Unseen

Microorganisms — this term is not new to the average layperson. These "animicules," "cavorting and wee beasties," and "minute eels," as Leeuwenhoek called them, are creatures of the unseen world. They may be introduced as harmless, beneficial, or even harmful bugs. No matter how efficient or awe-inspiring the presentation about microbes is, each person views them in a different way. Maybe you were not interested in microbiology and figured it was another subject no more significant than others. However, microbes are powerfully influencing our lives whether we acknowledge it or not. The purpose of this book is to show how life and microbes are inseparable. The microbial world is both surprising and stunning. It is surprising because it contains a wealth of diversity of life forms. The microbial world is also stunning because we rarely understand how these microbes affect our own world, and we also overlook the elegance of their design.

Bacteria are found throughout the earth, from the equator to the poles, and are presently the most common type of microorganism. It may be difficult to believe that creatures so minute can be so dynamic. They are surrounding us even as we speak. They are in our water, milk, yogurt, cheese, bread, and other foods. We never really realize their importance until something goes wrong with us. We get sick, and then we want to know something about the "bug." We want to take the first pill or antibiotic in sight to cure our sickness.

Fungi, protozoans, and viruses, like bacteria, make up the unseen world. They are also a part of our everyday life. We use yeasts in our daily bread. Protozoans are in our pond and aquarium water. Viruses are now responsible for a new and widely publicized epidemic, the bird flu. However, microorganisms also are inseparable from our world, and should be seen as relevant to our life. What would this world be like without the unseen? This book is designed to make the educated layperson and student aware of the unseen world of microbes. It also brings a creation and biblical perspective to microbiology. This book should challenge you to think of the unseen as relevant to your world and make you aware of the wondrous design in microbes given by the Creator.

BOOK OBJECTIVES

The objectives of this book are to:
• Describe the designed structures and purposeful functions for each of the microbial systems.
• Explain selective in-depth explorations for specific creative design components in bacteria, fungi, and protozoans.
• Explain the origin of disease from a creation, biblical perspective.
• Provide examples of microbiologists who have held a creation or intelligent design perspective.

What Is a Microbe?

The term microbe was first used in 1878 to describe "extremely minute living beings." At that time,

this definition was chiefly applied to one major category of microbes, the bacteria. Before 1878, scientists, including Louis Pasteur, used a variety of terms (examples: animalcules, infusoires, and germs) rather loosely to label the very small organisms that had interested them. It was not clear whether microbes belonged to the animal or plant kingdoms or to a completely different one. Early biologists also did not fully realize the extent of life on earth as we know it today. Visible effects of microbes on higher plants and animals, however, were commonplace and evident long before the existence of microbes was discovered in the 17th century. They were particularly obvious when the effects were deleterious, such as from an infectious disease, and were sometimes viewed as supernatural events or mysterious, "spontaneous" phenomena. Logical explanations of infectious disease and other manifestations of microbial life had to wait on two developments: the acceptance of the concept that invisible microbes existed and the tangible evidence of their reality. Several creation scientists, including Anton Leeuwenhoek, Robert Hooke, Louis Pasteur, and Joseph Lister, would play a role in developing the notion of their reality and in proving that those germs cause disease.

In the earliest observations of bacteria, fungi, and protozoans, *infusorium* was the most common term used for these creatures. This is because the first cultures of microscopic organisms were made with infusions, which consisted of water with added hay, straw, and soil. In 1879, a French scientist, Charles E. Sedillot, gave the term microbe. It included any living thing that must be magnified by a microscope. Traditionally, microbes have been described as free-living organisms that are so small (less than about 100 micrometers [μm]) that they are visible only under the microscope; however, a few microbes are large enough to be seen with the naked eye. The smallest bacteria are barely 0.2 μm long, but giant bacteria and protozoa can be 1 millimeter (mm) in length or even longer. Microbes are either prokaryotes (cells lacking a true nucleus), or eukaryotes (cells with a true nucleus). Eukaryotic microbes, other than algae and fungi, are collectively called protists. These include protozoans and slime molds. A complicating factor is that some microbes are especially hard to define, partly because they have large relatives. For example, yeasts are certainly microbes, but mushrooms are not — yet both are fungi.

Biosphere 2

How Small Are Microbes?

Microbes are very small. The volume of a typical bacterium is only about 1 μm³, roughly 1/1,000 that of human cells, such as cheek cells. However, there is a large range in size among bacteria; this illustrates that the Creator loves variety. Some species are considerably larger, while others are smaller than the average. One gargantuan species (*Epulopiscium fishelsoni*) that lives in the intestine of the surgeonfish is huge! It is over 0.5 mm in length and is visible to the naked eye. It is about three times bigger than *Paramecium*. The range in volume of the smallest to the largest known bacteria is well over one million-fold. Therefore, size is not always a good way to distinguish prokaryotes from eukaryotes. In addition, some marine algae are about 1 μm in diameter; they are the smallest known eukaryotes, well within the range of most prokaryotes. However, it is generally true that most prokaryotes are smaller than eukaryotic cells.

Why Microbes Matter

So why should we study microbiology? New and updated information about microbiology is continuously shaping our lives, especially concerning our society's healthcare. It helps us understand infectious diseases and the best ways to cure them. Microbes benefit our lives in the environment and provide the basis for many of our fermented foods. It also tells us about the Creator's handiwork; His intricate design extended down to the smallest creatures in our world. The icon for the intelligent design movement is the bacterial flagella. Furthermore, they help us recognize and understand various principles in the Bible.

Are Microbes the Creator's Mistakes?

Microbes have been designed as tiny, intricate machines that manufacture foods, vitamins, and essential materials for sustaining life. They are the Creator's provision for recycling valuable nutrients and making useful products for man. The news media publishes many articles about microbes that cause disease, but only a few discuss their usefulness. Many students have the impression that microbes are harmful and fear their hands-on study. We call this attitude microbe-phobia, or a fear of microbes. In reality, only about five percent of all bacteria are pathogenic. Most bacteria are beneficial and some are even essential for human life. Many microbiologists maintain that bacteria and other microbes have been maligned in the news media. Bacteria make products that are used every day; many foods, like yogurt, are created by microbe action. Barely a day goes by without using some of these products.

Without our intestinal flora, we would not survive very well. In fact, if intestinal microbes are not present early in our lives, the surface of the intestine does not develop normally. The surface would remain smooth rather than developing the carpet of projections called microvilli. We would have to adjust to living with a vastly reduced ability to absorb water and nutrients. Enteric bacteria supply our bodies with vitamin K, vitamin B12, thiamin, and riboflavin, which we need for normal body functioning. These intestinal microflora bacteria also stimulate lymph node-like structures, called Peyer's patches, which contain lymphatic tissue and provide the intestines with protection, even helping to prevent colon cancer. They maintain an intensely competitive and closed community, which makes invasion from pathogens a considerable challenge.

According to Dr. Jay Wile, additional evidence that microbes are not the Creator's mistake comes from a large experiment called "Biosphere 2." A team of scientists tried to design and build a self-contained system (i.e., Biosphere 2) for supporting life. Biosphere 2 was designed to be a microcosm of life on earth, containing a variety of animals and plants; it was to be completely self-supporting. These biologists spent seven years and $200 million designing and building this airtight, enclosed facility that spans 3.15 acres in Arizona. Despite the best that technology and science had to offer, Biosphere 2 could not support life for even two years! After about one year and four months, oxygen levels could not be maintained. They had to start pumping oxygen in from the outside. Many of the animal species that had been put in Biosphere 2 became extinct, while the populations of others boomed. In the end, Biosphere 2 was a failure. At least part of the reason behind this failure is that the scientists who designed Biosphere 2 did not take into account the incredibly essential role that bacteria and other microbes play in creation. Since these microorganisms were not present in the right amounts, Biosphere 2 could not sustain itself.

This outcome was not a surprise to microbiologists. The planet earth is an intricate web of hundreds of millions of processes that work together to support life. The best design, talent, and technology that humans have could never possibly mimic what the earth does naturally. Why? The answer is very simple. An awesome Creator and Sustainer of life designed the earth. He could foresee all of life's needs, even the tiny bacteria needed to support it. Limited human beings, on the other hand, just do not have the ability to design and create what God has designed and created, even on a very small scale. Biosphere 2 was a failure, and it stands in stark contrast to the grandeur and elegance of God's creation. So, in fact, microbes are not a mistake, they are made by design!

Magnificent Microbes

Bacteria have been receiving bad press since they were first discovered. People suspected the organisms that were so small must be doing something "bad." Many felt all these bacteria were "germs." The news that they caused disease was more than enough to keep the bad image going. The response of many people was "to kill all of the bacteria." Little did people know until later that destroying all the bacteria in our body could actually kill us. Humans are dependent upon bacteria for life, such as the *Escherichia coli* that help digest our food.

For many years, beneficial aspects of bacteria were either not known or not widely publicized. Today, we do know the beneficial aspects of bacteria. Bacteria are used to make and add flavor to dairy products, such as buttermilk, butter, and curds that are necessary to make cheese. Yogurt, a very popular health food today, is made as a result of adding *Lactobacilli* to spoiled milk. Other nondairy products made with the help of bacteria are vinegar, linen, rope, and antibiotics.

Another beneficial aspect of bacteria is that they have the ability to break down plants, animals, and other matter in nature. If bacteria did not recycle nutrients, there would be dead bodies of plants and animals lying around for hundreds of years. What a great stench that would be! Bacteria not only break down bodies, but also help to recycle such important elements as carbon, nitrogen, oxygen, and hydrogen through the biological community. Bacteria are necessary for balance in the ecosystem.

Industrially, bacteria are used in sewage treatment. In large tanks open to air, several kinds of aerobic bacteria break down the sewage. Also, bacteria are used in commercial production of amino acids. One of the important promises for use of bacteria is in the area of genetics. Using techniques that recombine DNA from different sources, bacteria have produced a variety of compounds such as insulin, human growth hormone, and vaccines against foot and mouth disease. What would the world be without bacteria?

Having a Recent Past

Any meaningful discussion of creation and evolution must include microbes. According to Darwinists, life started with microbes, and such unicellular organisms had the planet to themselves for about 80 percent of the time that life has existed on earth. Of course, evolutionists do not know the nature or location of the "primordial ooze" (or what Charles Darwin called a "warm little pond") where life began, but they think that microbes were the first cellular life forms to arise and thrive. Being so "ancient," microbes are said to have had a very long time to evolve and to develop the basic metabolic mechanisms that made all other life possible. The just-so story of evolution tells us that microbes have come to occupy a great variety of ecological niches, including some that seem improbable from a human point of view. Microbes grow in the frozen tundra, in waters whose temperature is over the boiling point (at high pressure), in strong acid and alkali, and in concentrated brine.

The microbial fossil record is scant, but together with genomic information, evolutionists tell us that microbes diversified early on into a great variety of shapes and lifestyles. Prokaryotes were supposedly alone on earth for some two billion years (according to evolutionists, about half the time there has been life on earth), after which eukaryotic microbes arose. According to Darwinists, multicellular organisms did not arise until some 750 million years ago. Prokaryotes are the so-called ancestors of all other life forms. All eukaryotes, from simple yeasts and algae to humans, arose from prokaryotic progenitors.

So, where do microbes fit into the creation account? Were they created along with the rest of the plants and animals in the first week of Creation, or were they created later after the Fall and are a result of the "Curse"? The Bible says, *"And God said, Let the earth bring forth grass, the herb yielding seed, and the fruit tree yielding fruit after his kind, whose seed is in itself, upon the earth: and it was so. And the earth brought forth grass, and herb yielding seed after his kind, and the tree yielding fruit, whose seed was in itself, after his kind: and God saw that it was good" (Gen. 1:11–12).* The word "plant" was used to describe microbes until the mid-1800s.

Focus1.1

Pasteur and The Origin of Microbes

The Theory of Biogenesis vs. Spontaneous Generation

The discovery of microorganisms raised an intriguing question: "Where did these microscopic forms originate?" For thousands of years, the idea of spontaneous generation suggested that organisms, such as tiny worms, could arise spontaneously from non-living material. This idea began to fall into disfavor after the findings of Francesco Redi. By a simple experiment, he demonstrated conclusively that worms found on rotting meat originated from the eggs of flies, not directly from the decaying meat as proponents of spontaneous generation believed. To prove this, he simply covered the meat with gauze fine enough to prevent flies from depositing their eggs. No worms appeared. Despite Redi's findings, the idea of spontaneous generation was difficult to disprove, and it took about 200 years more to refute this idea. Because the gauze used by Redi could not prevent the development of microorganisms, new experiments were needed to refute the theory.

The traditional experiment designed to determine whether microbes could spring from non-living material consisted of boiling organic material in a vessel to sterilize and then sealing the vessel to prevent any air from entering. If the solution became cloudy after standing, then one could conclude that microbes must have arisen from the organic material in the vessel, thus supporting the theory of spontaneous generation. Unfortunately, this experiment did not consider several alternative possibilities: that the flask might be improperly sealed, that microorganisms might be present in the air, or that boiling might not kill all forms of life. Therefore, it was not surprising that different investigators obtained different results when they performed this experiment.

Experiments of Pasteur and Biogenesis

One creation biologist who did much to disprove the theory of spontaneous generation was the French chemist Louis Pasteur, considered by many to be the father of modern microbiology. In 1861, Pasteur published a refutation of spontaneous generation that was a masterpiece of logic. First, he demonstrated that air is filled with microorganisms. He did this by filtering air through a cotton plug, trapping organisms that he then examined with a microscope. Many of these trapped organisms looked identical microscopically to those that had previously been observed by others in many infusions. Infusions are liquids that contain nutrients in which microorganisms can grow. Pasteur further showed that if the cotton plug was then dropped into a sterilized infusion, it became cloudy because the organisms quickly multiplied. Most notably, Pasteur's experiment demonstrated that sterile infusions would remain sterile in specially constructed flasks, even when they were left open to the air. Organisms from the air settled in the bends and sides of these swan-necked flasks, never reaching the fluid in the bottom of the flask. Only when the flasks were tipped would bacteria be able to enter the broth and grow. These simple and elegant experiments ended the arguments that unheated air or the infusions themselves contained a "vital force" necessary for spontaneous generation.

Pasteur's experiments on spontaneous generation

Biogenesis

The theory of biogenesis states that life can come only from other life. This idea sounds a lot like Genesis 1 principles: life begets life and like begets like. Yet, evolutionists imagine that at one time, life did spontaneously appear. It is a well-known fact that Louis Pasteur opposed the doctrine of spontaneous generation, and he brought telling evidence against it. Pasteur believed that the idea of spontaneous generation did not fit with the view of God as Creator of life. He suggested that to get new life, some kind of preexisting created life must be present. Read the translation of Pasteur's own words on this point:

Louis Pasteur

> *This is why the problem of spontaneous generation is all-absorbing, and all-important. It is the very problem of life and of its origin. To bring about spontaneous generation would be to create a germ. It would be creating life; it would be to* *solve the problem of its origin. It would mean to go from matter to life through conditions of environment and of matter. God as Author of Life would then no longer be needed. Matter would replace Him. God would need to be invoked only as Author of the motions of the universe.*

While giving a speech about his now famous experiment demonstrating that bacteria do not arise spontaneously in sterile culture bottles, Pasteur said, *"Never will the doctrine of spontaneous generation recover from the mortal blow of this simple experiment!"*

Pasteur not only refuted the idea that we can get something from nothing, but also proved that it must come from other life, or the Author of Life. This soon led to an understanding of both disease prevention (via aseptic techniques) and the germ theory of disease. Pasteur clearly demonstrated that infectious disease does not spontaneously appear as "miasmas," but rather was the outcome of germs causing disease. Later, Joseph Lister, Christian physician and creationist, developed the idea of using aseptic techniques in surgery. The idea of biogenesis was antecedent to asepsis, the germ theory of disease. Creation thinking, because it embraces truth (and God's blessing), frequently leads to practical applications, including in the world of medicine.

Magnificent and Miraculous Microbes

There are many extraordinary examples of design in the microbial world. In this chapter, two examples are given: the bacterial flagella and the production of a blood red pigment in *Serratia marcescens.* The molecular machinery of the bacterial flagella is magnificent. The amazing ability for *Serratia marcescens,* a rod-shaped bacterium, to produce a pigment that resembles blood is "miraculous."

Bacterial Flagella – Icon of the Intelligent Design Movement

We begin with Michael Behe who made the bacterial flagellum a popular argument for intelligent design in *Darwin's Black Box*, using them to illustrate the concept of irreducible complexity. The flagellum is a corkscrew-shaped, hair-like appendage attached to the cell surface acting like a propeller, allowing the bacterium to swim.

The bacterial flagellum is an irreducibly complex process. An irreducibly complex system is one that requires several interlacing parts to be present at the same time, where the removal of one or more parts causes the whole system to malfunction. Destroy one part and the whole system falls apart. The purported mechanism of evolution, on the other hand, is that a new trait will confer a selective survival advantage, and thus enable its possessors to compete better than organisms without the trait. In neo-Darwinian evolution, a new trait would have to be completely developed — no halfway measures would do. Given this requirement, new features are so complex that neo-Darwinian gradualism is very improbable because an incompletely developed trait would offer no selective advantage.

The Mousetrap Example

Dr. Michael J. Behe, biochemistry professor and author of the 1996 blockbuster book *Darwin's Black Box,* has challenged the classical neo-Darwinian explanation that intricate cell structures arose by chance. In the book, he uses the flagellum to introduce the concept of "irreducible complexity." If a structure is so complex that all its parts must initially be present in a suitably functioning manner, it is said to be irreducibly complex. All the parts of a bacterial flagellum must be present from the start in order to function at all. According to Darwinian theory, any component that doesn't offer an advantage to an organism (i.e., doesn't function) will be lost or discarded. How such a structure could have evolved in a gradual, step-by-step process as required by classical Darwinian evolution is an insurmountable obstacle to evolutionists. How a flagellum is used, however, adds an additional level of complexity to the picture.

Some bacteria have a single flagellum located at the end of a rod-shaped cell. To move in an opposite direction, a bacterium simply changes the direction the flagellum rotates. Other bacteria have a flagellum at both ends of the cell, using one for going in one direction and the other for going in the opposite direction. A third group of bacteria has many flagella surrounding the cell. They wrap themselves together in a helical bundle at one end of the cell and rotate in unison to move the cell in one direction. To change direction, the flagella unwrap, move to the opposite end of the cell, reform the bundle, and again rotate in a coordinated fashion. The structural complexity and finely tuned coordination of flagella attests to the work of a Master Engineer who designed and created flagella to function in a wonderfully intricate manner.

You might call it the Maker's molecular outboard motor. Its most interesting aspect is that it is attached to and rotated by a tiny, electrical "motor" made of different kinds of protein. Like an electrical motor, the flagellum contains a rod (drive shaft), a hook (universal joint), L- and P-rings (bushings/bearings), S- and M-rings (rotor), and a C-ring and stud (stator). The flagellar filament (propeller) is attached to the flagellar motor via the hook. To function completely, the flagellum requires over 40 different proteins. The electrical power driving the motor is supplied by the voltage difference developed across the cell membrane. This motor is one of the nature's best molecular machines!

Some scientists have called bacterial flagella the "most efficient machine in the universe" with its self assembly and repair, water-cooled rotary engine, proton motive-force drive system, forward and reverse gears, operating speeds of 6,000 to 17,000 rpm, direction-reversing capability, and hard-wired signal-transduction system with short-term memory.

Bacterial Flagellum: Paradigm for Design in *Yersinia*, Example 1

After Michael Behe made the bacterial flagellum a popular argument for intelligent design in *Darwin's Black Box*, Scott Minnich joined the ranks of the intelligent design movement. Dr. Minnich, a geneticist and associate professor of microbiology at the University of Idaho, takes the argument to the next level by describing how this design paradigm led to new insights in his research. Minnich has been studying bacterial flagella for over 15 years and has published work in the following areas: the structure and function of flagella in *Yersinia* and *Salmonella* species; assembly blueprints and genetic instructions; detail descriptions of the transcriptional and translational regulator genes; and integrating motility with signal transduction (chemotaxis).

In extensive research, Scott Minnich has discovered that bacterial flagella provide a paradigm for design. Minnich has been working with the genetics and flagella structure of *Yersinia enterocolitica* (cousin of *Yersinia pestis*, pathogen of bubonic plague) for more than a decade. *Y. enterocolitica*, a cause of food-borne infection (like *E. coli* or *Campylobacter*) is commonly found in the intestines of livestock. It causes food infections due to contaminated meat and dairy products. It causes enteric fever and may produce severe, life-threatening infections.

After describing over 30 individual proteins that make up its rotary-motor mechanism (close to 50 in the entire flagellum), Minnich noticed that the basal body of the flagellum produced a toxic secretion when the bacterium was under stress. If *Yersinia* was kept "happy" at 20°C (68°F) and in good environmental conditions (i.e., low osmotic saline), the basal body produced a hook and filament — the remaining portions of the flagellum. Minnich had predicted

from his genetic studies that a good design would be used for diverse purposes, like engineer-designed structures that serve dual functions. It is good genetic efficiency or optimal genetic design (minimum cost/benefit ratio). Even before observing this in humans, he predicted what would happen.

Yersinia was quite motile in its environment and could propel its rotary motor at up to 100 rpm. On the other hand, if *Yersinia* were incubated at 37°C (98.6°F) (or another stressful environment like high salt), the basal body acted as a "cannon," producing a harsh toxin. (Its technical name is a Type III secretion system. It is described in more detail in chapter 9, "The Origin of Infectious Disease".) In observing cells from the gastrointestinal tract, it was observed to avoid engulfment by macrophages. In its own defense, *Yersinia* produced a missile to avoid being eaten by human body defenses. The utility of a design model (instead of a Darwinian one) not only produced good science, but also has practical implications for medical microbiology and clinical medicine. Here we see evidence that design models accurately predict biological outcomes. Thinking God's thoughts after Him and openness to the idea that the Creator has made biological structures with purpose is the key to success in biological study. Evidence, not evolution. Creation, not chance. Design theory works. The bacterial flagellum is truly one of Providence's prokaryotic wonders!

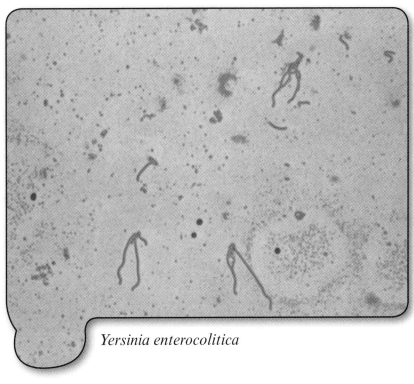

Yersinia enterocolitica

Biological Rotary Motor

The sensory and motor mechanism of the *E. coli* bacterium consists of a number of receptors, which initially detect the concentrations of a variety of chemicals. Secondary components extract information from these sensors that in turn is used as input to a gradient sensing mechanism. The output of this mechanism is used to drive a set of constant torque proton-powered reversible rotary motors, which transfer their energy through a microscopic drive train and propel helical flagella from 30,000 to 100,000 rpm. This highly integrated system allows the bacterium to migrate at the rate of approximately ten body lengths per second.

How fast do bacteria move with their flagella? Some have been "clocked" at up to 100 μm per second, or the equivalent of 50 body lengths per second. By comparison, bacteria move twice as fast as the cheetah, the fastest known animal. Cheetahs, which run up to 70 mph, go a mere 25 body lengths per second. Generally, bacteria with polar flagella move faster than those with peritrichous (many) flagella.

The complexity of the bacterial flagellum is direct evidence against neo-Darwinian evolution. All the interwoven parts of the body point to an intelligent Creator. In the early 1990s, Dr. Michael Behe argued for the intelligent design of the human body. His argument is called the principle of irreducible complexity. To illustrate the complex nature of this principle, one needs to look at the design in driving.

Driving by Design – *E. coli* Swimming Lessons

Microbiology is fun to study because the behavior of *E. coli* is increasingly being shown to be complex. Recent observation takes the argument of microbes by design to the next level by describing how new research has provided insight into how *E. coli* "drive" more orderly than some people. Harvard researchers have recently discovered that *E. coli* swim on the right side. The motion of *E. coli* is not random; it is directed, ordered, and reminds one of car traffic patterns (or even ant traffic patterns). When cells are confined to microchannels with soft agar floors made of hydrogels, they preferentially swim on the right hand side and closer to the floor of the gels. Bacteria are known to have clockwise, circular trajectories along surfaces; yet in free solution, they swim in random walk trajectories. All of these features seem to shout "design"!

In human terms, driving properly to avoid accidents takes driver's education school, intelligence, and practice. It is certainly not by random chance, nor accidental. This recent article shows *E. coli* driving on the right side, meaning that when placed in narrow forked tubes, they are more likely to swim up the right-hand fork, due to the anticlockwise direction in which the flagella rotate. This is more than just "fascinating fact" information; it may have clinical implications for urinary tract infections. *E. coli* can also cooperatively move over surfaces, called swimming. It is more than just congregating. During extended periods of migration, bacteria cells move better on gel surfaces than a solid surface. This observation, combined with the ability of directed traffic, may allow new explorations of behavior studies of factors that contribute to bacterial pathogenicity.

The sensory and motor mechanism of the E. coli *illustration*

Cilia and Flagella Structure
Outer Microtubule
Central Microtubule
Plasma Membrane

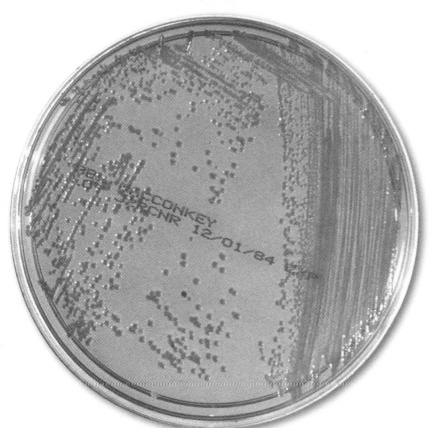

Serratia marcescens, *the "miracle" bacillus*

Microbes by Design, Example 2, *Serratia marcescens* – the Miracle Bacillus

Another example of design which can be seen in the microbial world is the production of a blood-red pigment made by *Serratia marcescens,* the "miracle" bacillus. *Serratia marcescens* is a rod-shaped, facultative anaerobic bacterium. It is a Gram-negative bacillus in the family Enterobacteraciae. This common microbe is found on plants and in soil, water, and animals. Most microbiologists are all too familiar with *S. marcescens,* one of the most frequent contaminants of Petri plates in the lab. This brightly colored bacterium also grows well on food that has been stored in a damp place.

The pigment production by microbes can impart color to contaminated food. *S. marcescens* has a long history in the church, as well as in microbiology. *S. marcescens* has a fondness for growth on starchy foodstuffs (e.g., bread and communion wafers), where the pigmented colonies have been mistaken for drops of blood. Indeed, in numerous historical incidents, the red pigment produced by *Serratia marcesens* growing in bread has been interpreted as a sign of blood.

Historical Focus 1.2

The "Blood of Christ" and the History of a Red Mystery

The history of *Serratia* goes back to the 6th century B.C., when Pythagoras reported on the blood substance that sometimes appeared on food. Then, in 332 B.C., soldiers of the Macedonian army of Alexander the Great, found that from time to time, their bread appeared to have blood on it. The Macedonian soldiers interpreted these bizarre phenomena as evidence that blood would soon flow in the city of Tyre and that Alexander would win. Later in the Christian tradition, since the time of the Middle Ages through the Renaissance periods, it was regularly observed to grow on communion wafers. This led many to think this was the blood of Christ, hence a miracle. For example, in the dark, damp churches of medieval times, sacramental wafers used in Holy Communion often became contaminated with *S. marcescens.*

On more than one substance, the "blood" on it was thought to be a miracle. One such event inspired the artist Raphael to paint his awe-inspiring masterpiece, the *Mass of Bolsena*. In 1263, four hundred years before Anton van Leeuwenhoek would observe bacteria under a microscope, a blood-like substance appeared on the communion bread.

The German priest Peter of Prague is shown breaking bread for communion at the Church of Saint Christina in Bolsena, Italy. When the famous priest broke the communion wafer, he thought that it had blood on it and that the bread had truly become Jesus' flesh!

In 1264, to honor of the miracle of Bolsena, Pope Urban instituted the feast of Corpus Christi ("Body of

15

Christ"). Neither the pope nor Peter the priest could ever have known that a red bacterium, *Serratia marcescens,* was the probable cause of this blood-like substance on the communion bread.

An important stimulus to the early development of microbiology came with attempts to discredit an infamous, alleged miracle. Bartholomeo Bizio, an Italian pharmacist from Padua, Italy, discovered and named *S. marcescens* when he identified the bacterium as the cause of a miraculous bloody discoloration in a cornmeal mush called polenta. He looked at the red spots under a microscope and saw what he described as a fungus. (Terms like fungus and virus were often used in the early microbiological literature to describe what we now classify as bacteria.) In 1817, he moistened some bread and polenta and left them in a warm, damp atmosphere. Twenty-four hours later, both the bread and polenta were covered in red growth. In 1819, Bizio named *Serratia* in honor of an Italian physicist named Serrati, who invented the steamboat. Bizio chose *marcescens* from the Latin word for decaying because the bloody pigment was found to deteriorate quickly. By 1823, he named the organism *Serratia marcescens.*

The Prussian microscopist Christian Gottfried Ehrenberg (1795–1876) also showed an interest in the red spots found on "bloody bread," and in 1848 he inoculated them onto potatoes, bread, and Swiss cheese kept in metal vessels, the atmosphere of which was kept moist with damp paper. In so doing he may have been the first person to cultivate bacteria. Ehrenberg is also likely to have been the first to use the term bacteria (meaning little rods). In 1836 he had described "infusoria" and named a number of bacteria, including *Bacterium* and *Spirillum.*

Irreducible Complexity of Prodigiosin Production

Serratia is most noted for its bright red pigment called **prodigiosin**. Over the years, it has certainly gotten the attention of churchgoers and scientists alike. It also is one of the few bacteria that produces bright pigments, and it comes in a variety of colors, including red, white, pink, and purple. Its color variation was noted as early as 1888. The first person to describe the biosynthesis of this pigment in the late 1940s was Dr. Robert

P. Williams, a Christian microbiologist. His interests in *Serratia* were many, including what controlled the expression of the red phenotype in *S. marcescens.* Pigment production in Serratia is influenced by several variables, including temperature, nutrient media, and exposure to ultraviolet (UV) light.

Some strains of *S. marcescens* are capable of producing prodigiosin, which ranges in color from dark red to pale pink, depending on the temperature, substrate, and age of the colonies. Most strains of *S. marcescens* are red under 27°C (80.6°F) and white above 28°C (82.4°F). (*Pigment and flagella production stops at approximately*

Chemical structures of prodigiosin

28°C.) The synthesis of prodigiosin is an irreducibly complex process. An irreducibly complex system is one that requires several interlacing parts to be present at the same time, where the removal of one or more parts causes the whole system to malfunction. Destroy one part and the whole system falls apart. In evolution, a new trait would have to be completely developed, no halfway measures would do. Given this requirement, new features are so complex that Darwinian gradualism is very improbable because an incompletely developed trait would offer no selective advantage.

Prodigiosin, a linear tripyrrole, is synthesized in a bifurcated pathway, in which mono- and bipyrrole precursors are synthesized separately and then couple to form the red pigment (above). (There are parallels in the way blood clots form — think of dominos in a Y formation — one falling upon and after another.) Prodigiosin is a secondary metabolite, which is constructed from several amino acids that may accumulate in the cell as a result of primary metabolism. The terminal stop in prodigiosin biosynthesis is by the condensing of the mono- and bipyrrole components and is temperature sensitive. Proline is incorporated intact in the prodigiosin molecule, histidine is used indirectly, methionine contributes a methyl group, and alanine is entirely incorporated except for a carboxyl group.

Prodigiosin Pigment Offers Protection

The functions of pigment have long been pondered, but only recently determined. Many texts say that there is no known function for prodigiosin. In the past, ideas range from prodigiosin associated with flagellar production to the enhancement of the aerosolization of *S. marcescens,* and the formation of prodigiosin allows the cell to remove toxic accumulation of metabolites such as amino acids. It appears that prodigiosin offers protection for *Serratia* in the natural environment. The red pigment offers protection against excessive UV in sunlight and serves as an antibiotic and has cytotoxic qualities. It appears that it is worth the energy investment to synthesize prodigiosin when it serves protection against UV light and when it has to compete with fungi in the soil and uses its red pigment as an antibiotic against neighboring molds.

Disease Focus 1.3

Serratia is an Opportunistic Pathogen

Only since the 1960s have microbiologists recognized *S. marcescens* as an opportunistic human pathogen. In the hospital, *Serratia* tends to colonize the respiratory and urinary tracts of adults, rather than the gastrointestinal tract. *Serratia* causes about two percent of nosocomial infections of the bloodstream, lower respiratory tract, urinary tract, surgical wounds, and skin and soft tissues of adult patients. Outbreaks of *S. marcescens* meningitis, wound infections, and arthritis have occurred in pediatric wards. In most cases, *Serratia* infections have occurred in people who have compromised immune systems or those who are aged.

The Creator's Signature, "Red-Lettered" Bacteria

So maybe *S. marcescens* was not the miracle that the pope expected, but this tiny organism does remind us of the wondrous invisible life that is all around. The pigment from *Serratia* may not be the blood of Christ, but it does in fact have a brilliant, blood-red color that attracts attention, and its natural production of variable bright colors testifies of the Creator's artistic abilities. When viewed in the Petri dish, or up close, it is a highly attractive microbe. Finally, ability of the bacterium to produce the pigment and adapt under varying environmental conditions suggests the Sustainer's foreknowledge of *S. marcescens'* need to survive.

The Creator formulated not only the plan for *S. marcescens,* but also produced the first working organisms. He is not only the Chief Architect of the red pigment, but is also the manufacturer of the prodigiosin components. He keeps everything going because He is the Maintainer. The predictable color of the prodigiosin at lower temperatures exists because the order of the precise plan was produced by an intelligent cause. These finely tuned and interdependent interactions are examples of what biochemist Behe calls irreducible complexity. It cannot be explained by Darwinian evolution. Most creation biologists would go a step further and say that it is clear, physical evidence of fingerprints from the Master's hand. Although an alleged miracle of communion, the blood of Christ may not have appeared as the church once declared; however, *Serratia* is still the miracle bacillus. The "miracle" is that an awesome artist would care enough to sustain and protect even His tiniest creations. He has left His signature on it — one of red-lettered importance.

Is Antibiotic Resistance Proof of Evolution?

Antibiotic resistance is one of the most important topics that a beginning biology student going into medicine should learn and understand. Antibiotic resistance is one of the so-called facts of "evolution." In this section, we will see that it is indeed a "fact" of change, but not one of real evolution (i.e., neo-Darwinian evolution). Antibiotic resistance has become one of the most serious problems to confront modern scientists. The first known antibiotics were produced by fungi, notably those from the mold *Penicillium chrysogenum* (see chapter 5 on fungi). An antibiotic is a substance produced by a microbe that, in small amounts, inhibits another microbe. However, today most antibiotics are produced by bacteria (esp. *Streptomyces*), not molds. Antibiotics have become the miracle drugs of the 20th century and have greatly reduced infectious disease and lengthened the life of man.

During the last 50 years, an alarming number of bacteria species have developed resistance to antibiotics. These resistant organisms are increasingly responsible for human diseases of the lungs, intestinal tract, blood, and the genitourinary tract. They are of special danger to those in burn and intensive care units, those with compromised immune systems, children, and the elderly. Among the most difficult diseases to treat are those that once succumbed to small doses of antibiotics, such as staphylococcal and streptococcal infections, bacterial STDs (e.g., gonorrhea), bacterial pneumonia, and tuberculosis (Table 1.1).

Table 1.1 Antibiotic resistance and major medical problems for:

1. *Enterococci* (vancomycin–resistant enterococci)
2. *Staphylococcus aureus* (methicillin–resistant *Staphylococcus aureus*)
3. *Streptococcus pneumoniae* (penicillin-resistant)
4. *Mycobacterium tuberculosis* (multiple-drug resistant to first-line drugs)

Microbes have acquired resistance to antibiotics in a number of ways (Table 1.2). With some antibiotics (e.g., penicillin) resistance arises from the microbe's ability to destroy the antibiotic before the antibiotic destroys the microbe. Resistance may occur in bacteria during the normal course of events, as happened with penicillinase-producing bacteria. Resistance can also arise from changes in the pathways of the microbial cell wall and membrane that restrict movement of the antibiotic into the cytoplasm. Alternatively, a microbe may alter the metabolic pathway on which an antibiotic normally acts and thereby bypass the drug inhibition. Resistance may also develop when a bacterium changes the target of the antibiotic (e.g., tetracycline), such as by changing the structure of its ribosome.

Table 1.2 Mechanisms that can lead to antibiotic resistance, including:

1. Enzymatic destruction of drug
2. Prevention of penetration of drug
3. Alteration of drug's target site
4. Rapid ejection of the drug
5. Resistance genes on plasmids or transposons that can be transferred between bacteria.

An alarming number of bacterial species have developed resistance to one or more antibiotics. The one of greatest concern over the past five years is *S. aureus*. The most notable feature of staphylococcal skin disease is a boil, or an abscess, a pus-filled lesion. More widespread staphylococcal diseases are pneumonia, septicemia, endocarditis, and meningitis. *S. aureus* is involved in over 250,000 infections per year, primarily in hospitals and nursing homes. Staphylococcal diseases are usually treated with penicillin, but over the years, strains of *S. aureus* have developed resistance to penicillin and numerous other antibiotics.

Multidrug-resistant *Staphylococcus aureus* (MRSA) has become a common problem in ambulances, emergency rooms, hospital wards, and clinics. Through those years, vancomycin remained a viable alternative for treating MRSA infections, even though it is a very expensive and somewhat toxic antibiotic. It was known as the drug of last resort. Then, in 1997, an MRSA strain emerged with partial vancomycin resistance. Although microbiologists and physicians have found useful treatment alternatives in drug combinations during the 1990s, they were grappling with the possibility that one day there will be no antibiotic to treat patients infected by MRSA. The concern was so acute because vancomycin-resistant enterococci exist in the human intestine, and gene transfers to *S. aureus* strains are possible.

The major drug that came in response to increasing MRSA infections is Synercid. Synercid is the first antibiotic approved for treatment of patients with serious or life-threatening infections associated with vancomycin-resistant *Enterococcus faecium* (VREF) bacteremia. Synercid is also approved for complicated skin and skin structure infections caused by *Staphylococcus aureus* (methicillin-susceptible) or *Streptococcus pyogenes*.

This drug helped to ease hospital concerns in 2005, but it has its limitations. The ongoing concern comes from the observation that antibiotic-resistance genes are frequently found on easily transmitted plasmids. Each year, pharmaceutical companies look for new and effective antibiotics to treat MRSA and other serious bacterial infections. There will always be a need for new antibiotics due to human activities (Table 1.3) and the ongoing change (variation) of bacteria.

Table 1.3 Misuse of antibiotics that selects for resistance mutants includes:

1. Using outdated, weakened antibiotics
2. Using antibiotics for the common cold and other inappropriate conditions
3. Use of antibiotics in animal feed
4. Failure to complete the prescribed regimen
5. Using someone else's leftover prescription

The most common mechanism of transfer is through the conjugative transfer of R plasmids. R plasmids frequently carry several resistance genes, each mediating resistance to a specific antibiotic. Thus, when a bacterium acquires R plasmid, it acquires resistance to several medications simultaneously. If a bacteria strain has multiple resistance factors, it is frequently known as a "superbug." These superbugs are troublesome in many hospital and clinical settings.

Resistance is not really new. Although reported only since the 1940s, resistance has existed in nature for thousands of years. There is "warfare" in the soil between bacteria and fungi and among bacteria. Most likely after the Edenic curse, such processes as intermicrobial transfer of plasmids containing resistance genes (R factors), conjugation, transformation, and transduction started to occur. One of the most convincing studies that demonstrate that bacteria become resistant to antibiotics through "old" genes present in the past was published in 1988. In that study, individual bacteria from the intestines of explorers

who had been frozen before the development of antibiotics were shown to already be resistant to several antibiotics that had not been developed until after the explorers were frozen. Thus the genes that produced resistance were already there. Thus, it is very likely that kind of antibiotic resistance has been in nature for a long time.

One Microbiologist Reported:

Scientists at the University of Alberta have revived bacteria from members of the historic Franklin expedition who mysteriously perished in the Arctic nearly 150 years ago. "Not only are the six strains of bacteria almost certainly the oldest ever revived," says medical microbiologist Dr. Kinga Kowalewska-Grochowska, "three of them also happen to be resistant to antibiotics. In this case, the antibiotics clindamycin and cefoxitin, both of which were developed more than a century after the men died, were among those used."
— Ed Struzik, "Ancient Bacteria Revived," *Sunday Herald,* September 16, 1990.

Antibiotic Resistance and Evolution

Exposure of a bacteria population to a specific antibiotic (e.g., penicillin, methicillin, etc.), whether in a person or in a Petri dish) will kill antibiotic sensitive bacteria (*S. aureus*), but not those that happen to have R plasmids to counteract that antibiotic. According to the theory of natural selection, biologists predict that under these circumstances the bacteria carrying genes for antibiotic resistance will increase. This event happens frequently and is declared by Darwinists as the "fact" of evolution. It is a fact of change, but it is not a fact of neo-Darwinian evolution. According to creation microbiologist and Director of the CRS Van Andel Creation Research Center, Dr. Kevin Anderson, "Evolutionists frequently point to the development of antibiotic resistance by bacteria as a demonstration of evolutionary change. However, molecular analysis of the genetic events that lead to antibiotic resistance do not support this common assumption. Many bacteria become resistant by acquiring genes from plasmids or transposons via horizontal gene transfer. Horizontal transfer, though, does not account for the origin of resistance genes, only their spread among bacteria. Mutations, on the other hand, can potentially account for the origin of antibiotic resistance within the bacterial world, but involve mutational processes that are contrary to the predictions of evolution. Instead, such mutations consistently reduce or eliminate the function of transport proteins, protein binding affinities, enzyme activities, and/or regulatory control systems. While such mutations can be regarded as "beneficial," in that they increase the survival rate of bacteria in the presence of the antibiotic, they involve mutational processes that do not provide a genetic mechanism for "descent with modification."

Anderson goes on to demonstrate how some "fitness" cost is often associated with mutations, although reversion mutations may eventually recover most, if not all, of this cost for some bacteria. A biological cost does occur in the loss of pre-existing cellular systems or functions. Such loss of cellular activity cannot legitimately be offered as a genetic means of demonstrating evolution, but is rather evidence of devolution.

Avian Flu Is Due to Genetic Reassortment and Variation of RNA

We frequently hear and read about microbes in the news. According to *Scientist* magazine, the number two story in all science for the year 2005 was about "bird flu." In all history, more deaths have been attributed to microbes than any other cause.

Influenza is an ancient disease that has infected humans at irregular intervals throughout recorded history. Symptoms of flu include fever (usually high), headache, extreme tiredness, dry cough, sore throat, runny or stuffy nose, and muscle aches. In some cases, gastrointestinal

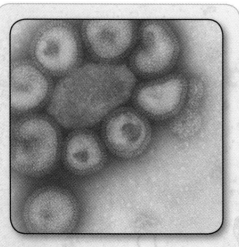

Influenza virus

symptoms, such as nausea, vomiting, and diarrhea, occur among children (very rarely in adults). Most related deaths are due to pneumonia and respiratory failure. While the 1918 "Spanish" influenza is the best-recorded catastrophic influenza pandemic, similarly severe pandemics occurred earlier, when the human population of the world was much smaller, and they will occur again. Our challenge is to understand all aspects of the influenza virus, the hosts and their response, and the virus's global impact so that we may be better prepared to face the inevitable next influenza pandemic.

The main reason for major changes in influenza is an antigenic shift. This means there has been a major exchange of chromosomes from one flu virus type to another type. Frequently, the domestic pig has been a "mixing vessel" for wild avian and human flu strains. New strains of influenza come to people after they are exposed. It is a genetic reassortment of genes (namely hemagluttin [H] and neuraminidase [N]) that get exchanged. It is not an evolution of new genetic material. The RNA gets dealt in different ways in birds, mammals, and people. Sometimes the changes are minor and sometimes they are major. These major ones are often the reason for threats of global pandemics. The same concept applies in domestic chickens — they have become a "mixing vessel" between wild birds and people.

The influenza virus that appears most threatening is the avian H5N1 strain that since 2003 has infected more than 130 persons in Vietnam, Thailand, and Cambodia, and has killed more than half of them. Nonetheless, the H5N1 influenza threat is viewed with disturbing complacency; a frequently heard statement is, "since the virus has not adapted to continuing human-to-human transmission by now, it is unlikely to do so in the future." Such complacency is akin to living on a geologic fault line and failing to take precautions against earthquakes and tsunamis.

According to Dr. R. Webster, "Ongoing outbreaks of H5N1 avian influenza in migratory waterfowl, domestic poultry, and humans in Asia during the summer of 2005 present a continuing, protean pandemic threat. We review the zoonotic source of highly pathogenic H5N1 viruses and their genesis from their natural reservoirs. The acquisition of novel traits, including lethality to waterfowl, ferrets, felids, and humans, indicates an expanding host range. The natural selection of nonpathogenic viruses from heterogeneous subpopulations co-circulating in ducks contributes to the spread of H5N1 in Asia. Transmission of highly pathogenic H5N1 from domestic poultry back to migratory waterfowl in western China has increased the geographic spread. The spread of H5N1 and its likely reintroduction to domestic poultry increases the need for good agricultural vaccines. In fact, the root cause of the continuing H5N1 pandemic threat may be the way the pathogenicity of H5N1 viruses is masked by co-circulating influenza viruses or bad agricultural vaccines."

The Unseen World Summary

Microbes are here by design. They are not God's mistakes. Microbes have not evolved; they were created with purpose. Microbes as "whole" organisms benefit the environment and mankind. Microbes, especially bacteria and their molecular motors and irreducibly complex processes, shout creative, intelligent design. Bird flu and antibiotic resistance are examples of variation, not neo-Darwinian evolution.

Microbiology is relevant to the educated layperson and to the health professional. Microbes affect our lives. Later chapters will explore bacteria, fungi, protozoans, viruses, microbial genetics, emerging diseases, and the origin of disease in more depth.

Disease is a consequence of the fall of man. The Edenic curse led to degeneration, corruption, disease, and decay. God has given man both the command to have dominion over the earth and to conquer disease — to heal the sick. These are topics for later chapters.

Eden Regained

There is hope for the Christian. Someday Eden will be regained. The Curse will be removed and there will be no more disease! Revelation 21:4 says, "And God shall wipe away all tears from their eyes; and there shall be no more death, neither sorrow, nor crying, neither shall there be any more pain: for the former things are passed away." Christ will provide the cure. This great deliverance from disease has been purchased by the Great Physician and Savior himself, Jesus Christ. In addition to the Curse being removed, in Revelation we read about healing from the Tree of Life. Still another noteworthy aside is that the leaves of the Tree of Life have great value also, serving to bring healing to the nations. Henry Morris believes that the Greek word *therapeia*, translated as "health" seems unlikely — that the immortal peoples of the new earth would actually need healing, either physical or spiritual is improbable. Henry Morris said the word basically meant "cure." In this case, the passage might be read, "The leaves of the tree were for the service of the nations." The chemical ingredients of the rich foliage of the trees might be available for innumerable uses in the pharmacies and industries of the nations of the ages. Possibly it is the pharmacy of the nations which is to be kept rich by the leaves of the tree. Not only will the curse be removed, but also any remnant of pathogens will be cured through the life-giving fruit from the Tree of Life.

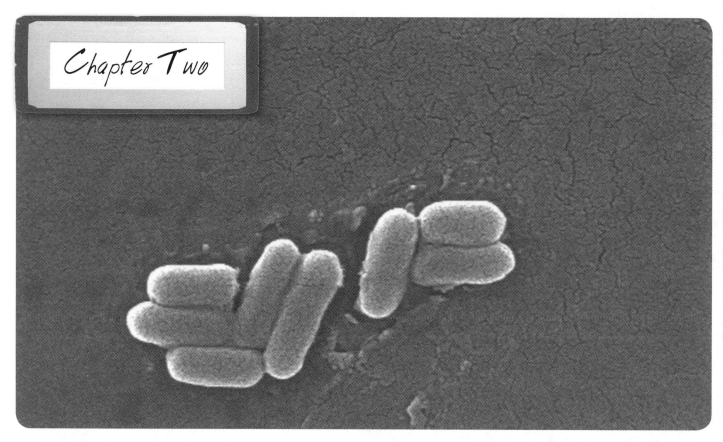

Chapter Two

Beneficial Bacteria (Bacteria, Part 1)

Magnificent Microbes

The term bacteria is a plural form of the Latin *bacterium*, meaning "staff" or "rod." Bacteria are prokaryotes and among the most abundant organisms on earth. The vast majority play a positive role in nature. Bacteria digest sewage into simple chemicals; extract nitrogen from the air and make it available to plants for protein production; break down the remains of everything that dies, recycling the carbon and other elements; and produce foods for human consumption and products for industrial technology. Many biologists believe that life on earth as we know it would be impossible without bacteria. They are the Master's magnificent microbes.

Bacteria have adapted to more different living conditions than any other group of organisms. They inhabit the air, soil, and water, and exist in enormous numbers on the surfaces of virtually all plants and animals. They can be isolated from Arctic ice, thermal hot springs, the fringes of space, and the tissues of animals. Some can withstand the searing acid in volcanic ash, the crushing pressures of ocean trenches, and the powerful activity of digestive enzymes. Other bacteria survive in oxygen-free environments, boiling water, and extremely dry locations. In short, they are ubiquitous (everywhere). The Creator must love them because they are the closest things to omnipresence on earth. Bacteria have so completely invaded the earth that the mass of bacterial cells is estimated to outweigh the mass of all plants and animals combined. They are Providence's prokaryotic wonders.

This chapter explains the importance of bacteria to our everyday lives. It also includes a discussion of their designed structures, size, classification, environmental functions, and their role in disease. Though most bacteria are beneficial, some are harmful. Certain species multiply within the human body, where they digest tissues or produce toxins resulting in disease. Other bacteria infect plant crops and animal herds. Disease-causing bacteria (i.e., pathogenic bacteria) are a global threat to all life forms, and in the 21st century, they have already been used as agents of bioterror. Bacteria have threatened human existence over the millennia through tuberculosis, bubonic plague, typhus, pneumonia, streptococcal infections, diphtheria, *E. coli*, and anthrax.

Design Focus 2.1
On Beneficial
Bacteria

Yogurt Aging Theory:
Does Eating Yogurt Prolong Life?

Yogurt, sometimes called Bulgarian milk, was popular among people of Eastern European countries. Dr. Elie Metchnikoff took note that many Bulgarian people lived to be over 100 years of age. He attributed their length of life to the yogurt they ate. He believed eating yogurt would neutralize a natural process that he called "autotoxication." The intestinal tract harbored great numbers of bacteria that Metchnikoff thought produced toxins that slowly poisoned the body and caused premature death. Metchnikoff believed yogurt bacteria were beneficial to the intestine and would replace other microorganisms that contributed to aging. Later, experiments by other scientists found Metchnikoff's aging theory was not supported by facts.

Metchnikoff's aging theory is no longer accepted among scientists. However, his research on microbes in the intestinal tract contributed to our knowledge about the human body. The body's internal and external surfaces support communities of microscopic allies. Populations of "normal flora," or friendly bacteria, live in the colon. Normal flora refers to the bacteria, yeasts, and molds that reside inside the body as friendly residents. Their presence prevents harmful organisms from attaching and multiplying. Any pathogen, or harmful microbe, trying to settle in the intestine must contend with a well-entrenched colony of the normal flora. In places, nearly 20 million microorganisms are present per square inch, some of which make life unpleasant for newcomers. Certain friendly bacteria produce chemicals that hinder the growth of other strains of bacteria and fungi. The bacterium *Escherichia coli,* which lives in the intestinal tract, simply uses up the nutrients that other, less favorable types of bacteria require to live — in effect, starving out their competitors.

Experience with antibiotics demonstrates the dangers of disturbing the microbial life that normally inhabits the body. Long-term use of these substances can wipe out the friendly, normal flora of microorganisms, as well as hostile ones. If the normal flora is eliminated, pathogens can establish themselves, sometimes causing intestinal problems. Given this potential for some pathogenic microorganisms to colonize the intestine, physicians often recommend that patients drink acidophilus milk or eat yogurt. *Lactobacillus acidophilus* occupies empty niches in the colon until the normal flora returns, thereby preventing attachment of pathogens.

After World War II, many people became health-conscious and, as a result, yogurt became a popular food among middle-class Americans. This growing appeal of yogurt stimulated further scientific investigation of its value in human health. The nutritional and therapeutic aspects of yogurt have long been debated in the scientific community. Several scientists assert that eating yogurt has no more positive effects than drinking milk. In fact, one writer reports that eating yogurt for health benefits is overrated because *Lactobacillus bulgaricus* will not colonize the intestine under normal conditions and cannot compete with normal flora. Some food scientists assert that yogurt may taste good and provide the same nutritional benefits as milk, but yogurt doesn't really help intestinal distress, nor will it prolong your life.

Recent scientific data provides evidence that yogurt does relieve intestinal distress during antibiotic therapy. In a controlled study, physicians reported that *L. bulgaricus* may not be able to compete with normal flora under ordinary conditions, but it does appear that *L. bulgaricus* will colonize the colon during and after the use of antibiotics. Bacteria in yogurt also may serve as a natural antibiotic. Evidence from this study indicates that not only will *lactobacilli* grow temporarily inside the intestine until the natural flora returns, but they will also prevent diarrhea that is associated with an antibiotic called erythromycin. These researchers report that the side effects of erythromycin, such as abdominal distress, stomach pain, and gas were less common among patients taking fermented yogurt during antibiotic treatment than patients taking pasteurized yogurt.

Another physician, in a review of animal studies involving yogurt and antibiotics, reported the nutritional and therapeutic value of *lactobacilli* in animal and human diets. Nutritionists have known for some time that yogurt is nutritious because of a high content of protein, riboflavin, and calcium. However, only recently have scientific studies shown that the *lactobacilli* increase the quantity, availability, digestibility, and uptake of nutrients.

This increase in nutrients can be explained by the finding that lactobacilli present in yogurt digest proteins to smaller, more readily assimilated substances. Yogurt bacteria also help the body to synthesize vitamins more efficiently. Physicians report therapeutic uses for yogurt bacteria, such as prevention of various intestinal infections caused by harmful microbes and diarrhea caused by antibiotics.

In 1992, studies by Dr. George M. Halpern at the University of California suggested that yogurt may boost the immune system. Eating yogurt may help you resist infections, such as colds and other upper respiratory infections. The study found that yogurt boosted the production of gamma interferon, a substance that helps fight infectious disease. A control group received no yogurt and two groups of people were given yogurt to eat. A second group ate yogurt with active bacterial cultures and the third group received yogurt that was heat treated to kill the active cultures. Only the group that ate yogurt with living *L. bulgaricus* and *S. thermopiles* had an immune system that was boosted. In this group, those who ate two cups of yogurt a day for four months had five times more gamma interferon than non-yogurt eaters. The *Houston Post*, reporting on this study, concluded, "To boost your immune system, increase your cultural exposure to yogurt."

In summary, eating yogurt has several nutritional and therapeutic benefits. Yogurt is nutritious because it is high in protein, riboflavin, and calcium. Yogurt also helps the body synthesize vitamins more efficiently. Eating yogurt is recommended during antibiotic usage to produce the same effect as acidophilus milk. Some antibiotics, during their administration, wipe out friendly bacteria, as well as the target pathogens. Bacteria in yogurt help the human body by temporarily occupying an empty niche during antibiotic treatment. These bacteria prevent unfriendly molds, yeast, and bacteria from colonizing the intestine. The value of yogurt to people trying to lose weight depends upon what type of yogurt is eaten. Yogurt made from skim milk and artificial sweeteners is low in calories, but yogurt made from whole milk with sugar and syrupy fruits is high in calories. The aging theory now is largely discounted, but many microbiologists believe that eating yogurt aids in good health by boosting the immune system, by providing the body with essential nutrients, and supplemental therapy during medical treatment. Although eating yogurt may not prolong your life, it may enhance the quality of your life. The chances of experiencing diarrhea, gas, and abdominal pain are reduced while taking antibiotics, not to mention the positive nutritional value and the enjoyment of eating good yogurt!

Prokaryota

The prokaryotic cells of bacteria are generally much smaller and simpler in structure than eukaryotic cells (Table 2.2). Their definitive feature is the absence of a nuclear envelope separating the genetic material from the cytoplasm. Today, bacteria still outnumber other organisms, thriving in almost every conceivable habitat, but because of their tiny size, they were the last major group of organisms discovered. Some of the larger bacteria were first observed and described by Anton van Leeuwenhoek in 1676. In the 1860s and 1870s, Louis Pasteur, Joseph Lister, and Robert Koch discovered the role of bacteria in causing food spoilage and many diseases. It is also interesting to note that Leeuwenhoek, Pasteur, and Lister were all creation scientists who sought God's thoughts (Ps. 139:17) in biology and in medicine. They sought not only to classify their newly found bacteria, but also to find useful applications to benefit mankind. Bacteria, like other living things, are classified by their morphology, molecular composition, staining characteristics, metabolic way of life, and growth characteristics. The table below (Table 2.2) gives the basic characteristics of prokaryotes.

Table 2. 2 Characteristics of Prokaryotes

1. Lack a true nucleus. DNA not enclosed within a membrane, but in a "nuclear region"
2. DNA not associated with histones like in eukaryotes
3. Cell structure simpler than in eukaryotes; Lack true membrane-bound organelles
4. Cell walls almost always contain peptidoglycan; Chemistry of the bacterial cell wall is unique
5. Usually divide by binary fission, some reproducing every 20 minutes

In the second edition of *Bergey's Manual*, prokaryotes are grouped into two domains, Archaea and Bacteria. Each domain is further divided into "clades," each clade into phyla, each phylum into classes, and so on. Bacteria are divided into five clades. Clades refer to distinct lines of phylogeny from a cladogram. This concept is based upon assumptions of common descent and neo-Darwinian evolution. Many creationists would refer to these unrelated, large, inclusive categories as polybaramins. Perhaps the largest collections of typical bacteria are the Eubacteria and the Cyanobacteria. Both possess "true" prokaryotic cells. Cyanobacteria have cells like bacteria, but form colonies and filaments like algae, with all being capable of photosynthesis. Hence, they were traditionally referred to as *blue-green algae*. Clearly they are a distinct kind, defying neat, clear classification according to modern taxonomic methods. Although some creationists still place them in the alga category, we are placing them in this chapter because most biologists today classify them with bacteria. We will focus our discussion of Cyanobacteria on their role in the nitrogen cycle and their overall importance to ecology. Archaea have unique attributes and are also difficult to classify. Archaea cells have many attributes similar to bacteria, but have some characteristics similar to Eukarya.

Domain Bacteria

Most of us have been conditioned to think of bacteria as invisible, potentially harmful little creatures. Actually, relatively few species of bacteria cause disease in humans, animals, plants, or any other organisms. Indeed, once you have completed a biology course, you will realize that without bacteria, the majority of life as we know it would be impossible. Evolutionists assert that all eukaryotic organisms probably evolved from Bacteria or Archaea. They believe that Archaea were some of the earliest forms of life on earth.

Metabolism and Ways of Life

We have already mentioned that bacteria are the most numerous organisms on earth. A handful of soil may contain billions of them. They occur in habitats as remote as the sea floor, icebergs, and hot springs, or as close as your mouth. They are before us even as we speak. This far-flung distribution is possible because many bacteria have metabolic abilities not found in any eukaryote. Some carry on

fermentation, others respiration. Aerobes require O_2 for respiration; obligate anaerobes are killed by O_2; facultative anaerobes can live in the presence or absence of O_2. Some anaerobic bacteria use nitrate (NO_3^-), sulfate (SO_4^-), or iron (Fe^{3+}) instead of O_2 in cellular respiration. Most bacteria that undergo aerobic respiration yield more energy than those that undergo anaerobic respiration or fermentation.

Because of their rigid cell walls, bacteria cannot take in large food particles. Rather, they absorb small molecules that filter through their walls. Many bacteria can make any organic molecule they need by starting with only one kind of organic molecule, such as glucose or fatty acids. Others require a more complex diet. The "picky eaters" are referred to as fastidious. When conditions are unfavorable for growth, some bacteria form thick-walled, resting spores resistant to heat and drying. Most bacterial spores are not a means of reproduction, because no increase in cell number occurs. Rather, spore formation permits cells to survive adverse conditions and disperse to new locations, where a new cell may develop from the spore.

Bacteria undoubtedly owe their biological success to their varied metabolic abilities, coupled with small size, rapid reproductive rate, and ability to form resistant spores. These features permit bacteria to live in many habitats that are here today and gone tomorrow. A raindrop on a leaf evaporates in a few hours, but by then a bacterium has divided several times, and its descendants have formed spores that can blow away to new habitats.

Bacterial Anatomy

Individual bacterial bodies have one of three basic shapes, but the shapes have many variations and arrangements (left). The cells of some bacteria are spherical; some are cylindrical or rod-shaped; and others have the form of a somewhat rigid, curved rod or of a short spiral. The spherical forms are called cocci (singular *coccus*); the cylindrical forms bacilli (singular *bacillus*); and the spiral-shaped forms spirilla (singular *spirillum*). Each of the many kinds of true bacteria is placed in one of these three morphological groups.

bacillus

coccus

spirillum

Bacilli. In Latin, *bacillus* means "a little stick or rod," and the bacilli have the shape of a little rod or cylinder. Individual kinds of bacilli show almost infinite variations on this basic shape. Some are so short and thick that they are nearly indistinguishable from cocci; others are long and slender. Their ends may be square-cut, rounded, or tapered to a blunt or fine point. Most of the bacilli are straight, rigid rods, but some are slightly curved and less rigid. Many species are motile, moving through liquids by means of delicate, whip-like appendages called flagella. Others lack flagella and are non-motile. Like cocci, bacilli are widely distributed, and numerous species are known. One common example of a bacillus is *Escherichia coli*, the common intestinal bacterium.

Cocci. The word *coccus* comes from a Greek word meaning "berry," and all cocci have a spherical form like a tiny berry. Many are not perfectly round, but are flattened on one side or more or less elongated. There are many species of cocci, and they are widely distributed. One common example of a coccus is *Streptococcus pyogenes*, the cause of strep throat.

Spirilla. In this group are bacteria having a helical shape like a corkscrew. Some spirilla are short, comma-shaped organisms with less than one complete spiral turn; these are classified in the genus Vibrio (e.g., *Vibrio cholera*). Other spirilla are longer, more delicately coiled threads; these are placed in the genus Spirillum. The body of a spirillum is rigid; its motility is due to flagella. Spirilla must be distinguished from spirochetes, which are delicate, flexible, filamentous forms, having the general shape of a rather long, more

or less tightly coiled wire spring. They are motile, but do not have special locomotive appendages (i.e., flagella). One common example of a spirochete is *Treponema palladium*, the cause of syphilis.

Size of Bacteria

As we have already learned, bacteria are so minute that they cannot be measured accurately by any familiar scale. A special unit of measurement, the micron (μ), is 1/1,000 of a millimeter, or about 1/25,000 of an inch. Most bacteria are smaller than eukaryotic cells but larger than the nucleus (Table 2.3). Two notable exceptions are *Epulopiscium sp.* and *Thiomargarita namibiensis*. These are quite exceptional and atypical. The first giant bacterium is over 0.6 mm long — 600 μ com-

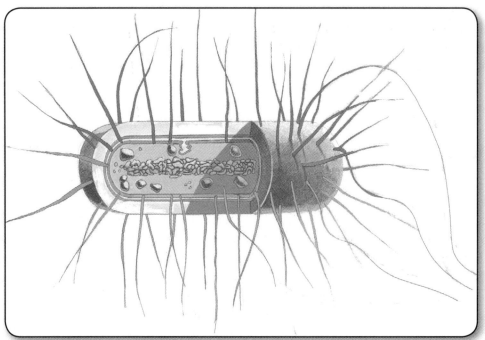

Illustration of a typical bacterial cell, sectioned to reveal its internal structures.

pared to 2 μ for *E. coli* dwarfing *Paramecium*. Found in the gut of surgeonfish near Australian reefs, the bacterium is the second largest. After the discovery of *Epulopiscium* in 1991, another "Goliath" bacterium was found in 1999. *Thiomargarita namibiensis*, meaning "sulfur pear of Namibia," was found in sediments off the coast of Africa. This bacterium is 750 μm, or a bit larger than the size of a period. Normally the fact that nutrients must enter the cytoplasm by simple diffusion limits the size of prokaryotic cells. In addition, they do not reproduce through binary fission. These observations present problems to evolutionary biologists; they cannot explain how such prokaryotic cells could evolve, and the giant prokaryotes cast doubt on current phylogenetic trees illustrating divergence of prokaryotes from eukaryotes. Table 2.3 gives examples of actual sizes of some of the best-known prokaryotes.

TABLE 2.3 SIZE OF COMMON BACTERIA Structure of Bacterial Cells

Name of Organism	Size of Individual Cells	Comments
Borrelia burgdorferi	11-25 μ long	Causes Lyme Disease
Clostridium tetani	2-4 μ long	Causes tetanus
Corynebacterium dipetheriae	1.5–6.5 μ	Causes diphtheria
Escherichia coli	2-3 μ long	Common intestinal bacterium
Neisseria gonorrheae	0.8–0.6 μ in diameter	Causes meningitis
Mycobacterium tuberculosis	2-4 μ long	Causes tuberculosis
Salmonella typhi	1-3 μ long	Causes typhoid fever
Staphylococcus aureus	0.8–1.0 μ in diameter	Causes boils
Streptococcus pyogenes	0.4–0.75 μ in diameter	Causes sore throat
Streptococcus pneumoniae	0.8–1.2 μ in diameter	Causes pneumonia
Treponema pallidum	8-14 μ long	Causes cholera
Vibrio comma	1-2 μ long	Causes cholera

The basic elements of bacterial anatomy include (1) the cell wall and (2) the inner cell body, or cytoplasm. The latter is surrounded by a cytoplasmic membrane just inside the cell wall, and commonly contains various granules, other cell inclusions, and vitally important nuclear material. In addition, the entire bacterium may be enclosed in an envelope or sheath of slimy, viscous or gelatinous material, forming a more or less definite capsule. There may be organs of locomotion called flagella, and some bacilli have pili. Certain bacteria may develop internally special structures called spores.

Cell Walls and Gram Stain

Since the majority of bacteria are not spherical, instead maintaining distinct shapes, such as that of a long rod, it is obvious that there must be an outer wall of considerable rigidity. Such a wall cannot ordinarily be seen in preparations of bacteria colored with commonly used stains, but at times the cytoplasm of a bacterium becomes contracted, pulling away from the wall, revealing the latter clearly. The existence of this cell wall, distinct from both the outer slime layer (capsule) and the cytoplasmic membrane, has been clearly demonstrated by special staining and electron micrographs. From the behavior of living bacterial cells in motion, it is inferred that the cell wall is rather rigid, with little elasticity. The Gram stain was named for Danish physician Hans Christian Gram, who discovered a technique that could differentiate all known bacteria into two categories. The staining technique, utilizing various dyes, would leave Gram-positive cells a deep purple and Gram-negative cells bright red. During the late 1800s and early 1900s, the reason for this distinction was unclear. By the mid-1900s, electron microscopy of bacteria revealed differences in the fine structure of cell walls of Gram-negative and Gram-positive bacteria. Gram-negative walls are not continuously associated with the underlying cytoplasmic membrane, have a thick layer of peptidoglycan, and usually are multi-layered. In Gram-positive bacteria, the walls are usually closely associated with the cytoplasmic membrane and can consist of a single, amorphous layer or of several layers — the structure varying in different species.

Through the impetus of investigating the mechanism of antibiotic action, great advances have been made in understanding bacterial cell-wall chemistry. Both Gram-positive and Gram-negative cell walls contain the same chemical substance forming the backbone of the rigid structure. This material, peptidoglycan, is a complex polymer containing two amino sugars, glucosamine and muramic acid (Latin *murmus*, "wall") and several amino acids. The muramic acid in bacterial cell walls is unique; no other type of cell is known to contain this sugar. These simple components join to form a complex, cross-linked chemical structure, Peptidoglyca.

These simple components join to form this complex and interwoven cross-linked chemical structure. Peptidoglycan is responsible for the rigidity of bacterial cell walls. Some Gram-positive organisms contain teichoic (Greek *teichos*, "wall") acids important for pathogen specificity. Other bacteria have special attached carbohydrates or proteins, such as the M-protein of streptococci, contributing to its virulence. Gram-negative bacteria contain lipopolysaccharides in their cell walls that sometimes contain an endotoxin. The cell walls of Gram-negative bacteria are more complex chemically than those of Gram-positive organisms. They contain lipoproteins, lipopolysaccharides, and phospholipids, but contain no teichoic acid. Only four or five different amino acids are found in Gram-positive cell walls. Their lipid content is minimal, but they can contain teichoic acid.

Cell Membrane and Membrane Systems

The plasma membrane (or cell membrane) of eukaryotic and prokaryotic cells is similar in function and basic structure. There are, however, differences in the protein types of the membranes. Eukaryotic membranes contain carbohydrates that serve as receptor sites, assuming roles in such functions as cell-to-cell recognition. These carbohydrates also provide attachment sites for bacteria. Plasma membranes carry enzymes for metabolic reactions such as nutrient breakdown, energy production, and synthesis.

Bacteria contain a network of interconnected, membranous structures in their cytoplasm. Mesosomes are invaginations of the cytoplasmic membrane into the cytoplasm (right). They are irregular infoldings of plasma membrane artifacts, but not true cell structures. These structures serve not only as sites for respiratory enzymes, but also as regulators of orderly division of bacteria. Mesosomes provide a continuous membrane linking together nuclear fibrils at one end with the cytoplasmic membrane at the other. Since division involves both of the latter structures, mesosomes may be the means for their coordination during division.

A bacteria cell membrane. In some bacteria that cause strep throat (i.e. Streptococcus pyogenes*), their cell membrane and envelope components have M-proteins that make the throat feel scratchy and sore.*

Ribosomes of bacteria are thought not to exist in the cytoplasm as discrete particles, but arranged in linear fashion on interconnected membranes attached to the plasma membrane.

The Nuclear Region

The nuclear apparatus in bacterial cells is obscured when cells are stained by basic dyes because of the presence in the cytoplasm of relatively large amounts of RNA, which has affinity for these dyes. These structures are sometimes called chromatin bodies, but in reality are nuclei and are also seen through the electron microscope. They have been shown to divide just before the whole bacterial cell divides. Chemically, the nuclei contain DNA bound to a basic protein. Bacterial "nuclei" are not surrounded by a membrane, as in true eukaryotic nuclei. The nuclear substance consists of DNA arranged into bundles of fibers. These bundles can rapidly change from compact arrangements into long, tape-like forms, depending on the environment.

Capsules, Glycocalyx, and Biofilms

A distinct layer often surrounds many bacterial cells beyond the cell wall. In some cases it is referred to as a capsule, and at other times it is a less defined, adhesive layer called a glycocalyx. This layer often releases a sticky, gelatinous, enveloping slime layer. The slime layer serves as an adhesive and growth medium for more bacteria to reproduce. This enveloping sheath is too thin to be seen in most species, but in some it regularly develops into a clearly visible capsule external to the cell wall, with a sharply defined outer edge following the contour of the cell body. Often the capsule is much wider than the bacterial cell itself. Chained or paired organisms are often enclosed within a single, continuous capsule.

The capsular material may arise from a modification

of the cell wall, or may be secreted by the living bacteria, remaining attached as a firm, mucilaginous structure. Some bacteria secrete glycocalyx into their surroundings without forming a definite capsule. Capsule formation is markedly influenced by environmental conditions; it can be induced, in special circumstances, in strains of bacteria ordinarily showing no evidence of any slime layer or biofilm. These biofilms can form not only on natural environmental structures like rocks in a stream, but also contact lenses, food bowls, used syringes, catheters, urinary-tract tissue, and human skin and tongues. Biofilm microbes are estimated to be 1,000 times more resistant to microbiocides. Disease experts estimate that 65 percent of human bacterial infections involve biofilms.

The bacterium that causes anthrax, *Bacillus anthracis*, has generated much interest recently. The capsule of the anthrax bacillus is a polypeptide, consisting mainly of D-glutamic acid. Among pathogenic bacteria, the phenomenon of capsule formation is of prime importance. Species that also develop large capsules include *Streptococcus pneumoniae*, *Klebsiella pneumoniae*, and *Bacillus anthracis*. Most pathogenic bacteria develop at least a small amount of capsular substance when growing in body tissues, and the most conspicuous capsules are seen on organisms freshly obtained from the infected host. The capsules seem to act as a defense against bactericidal factors in body fluids. Therefore, they contribute directly to the disease-producing power, or virulence, of the organisms. These capsules are lost by most species after cultivation for some time in the laboratory, usually resulting in markedly lost capacity to produce disease.

Encapsulation is also significant in another respect. The chemical structure of the capsular material determines the specificity of protective antibodies formed by the infected individual. The numerous "types" of pneumococci, for example, differ from one another in the chemical composition of the polysaccharides making up their capsules. Consequently, each type stimulates the formation of a different antibody. Immunity to a particular type of pneumococcus requires an antibody that will react with the capsulated organisms of that type.

Motility and Flagella

All known spirilla, and about half the more familiar species of bacilli, possess the power of locomotion through liquids; that is, they can move independently from place to place. Bacteria possessing this capacity are said to be motile; those that cannot move about independently are non-motile. The movement of motile bacteria can be plainly seen when examined under the microscope. For their size, these mighty microbes are some of the fastest swimmers in the Designer's creation. At top speed, an *E. coli* can swim nearly 50 times the length of its body in one second inside your urinary tract; the equivalent of a six-foot man swimming at 200 mph. Yet *E. coli* devotes less than two percent of its energy to swimming from your bladder toward the kidney inside the ureters. It achieves this remarkable feat through a special propulsion system, a speedboat-like "motor" turning spiral propellers at up to 100,000 revolutions per minute. The reversible motors are controlled by a complex feedback system that monitors the concentrations of food and/or toxins outside the bacteria, adjusting the motors accordingly. Bacteria do not run on gas or electricity the way man-made outboard motors do; the Master Engineer must have constructed these incredible microbes in motion. (See Design Focus 2.2 on flagella function.)

The organs of locomotion are delicate, hair-like processes extending from one or more parts of the cell bodies of the motile bacteria. These are called flagella (Latin for "little whips"). They do not have a lashing movement, however. Instead, the organisms appear to be propelled by wavelike, rhythmical contractions passing along the length of the flagella (10 to 20 μ). The flagella filament arises from the cytoplasm, anchored by a basal region consisting of a hook-like structure and a basal body. The basal body has a central rod and set of enclosing "O rings." They are usually somewhat coiled and often much longer than the bacterium from which they arise. They are remarkably thin, having a width of only about 0.013μ, and are easily broken off. Apparently, when the bacteria are in motion, the flagella often entwine to form a tail-like locomotor organ. The pattern of flagellar attachment to bacterial cells, as well as the number of flagella, is distinct to each species. In *Pseudomonas*, a single flagellum, or a tuft of flagella, is located at the end of the bacterium as polar flagella; *E. coli* has multiple flagella projecting from all around the cell known as peritrichous flagella.

Chemical analyses indicate that flagella are composed mostly of fibrous protein subunits termed flagellin. This protein is contractile and similar to the contractile proteins in muscle tissue. There are nearly 50 proteins making up all the subunits associated with flagella, and most of these are highly interdependent. The subunits of flagellin aggregate into long strands that twist about each other in a helical fashion to form the flagella. Two, three, or as many as five strands, depending on the species of bacteria, can form the helices. Flagellin apparently undergoes elastic contractions and expansions to account for flagellar movement. Bacterial flagella are unique structures not equivalent to the cilia or flagella of protozoa or higher organisms.

Focus on Flagella Function

Antony van Leeuwenhoek, using a single-lens microscope, was intrigued by "animalcules" (little animals) that he saw in his well water. He wanted to know whether they might survive exposure to pepper, so he ground up some and added it to a sample. The number of animalcules waxed and waned until August 6, 1676, when he made a discovery: "*I now saw very plainly that these were little eels, or worms, lying all huddled up together and wriggling; just as if you saw, with the naked eye, a whole tubful of very little eels and water, with the eels a-squirming among one another: and the whole water seemed to be alive with these multifarious animalcules. This was for me, among all the marvels that I have discovered in nature, the most marvellous of all; and I must say, for my part, that no more pleasant sight has ever yet come before my eye than these many thousands of living creatures, seen all alive in a little drop of water, moving among one another, each several creature having its own proper motion.*"

When Leeuwenhoek described little or "minute eels," he was looking at a spirillum, probably *Spirillum volutans*, the large bacterium shown in the accompanying sketch. Leeuwenhoek never saw its flagella. Flagella, the organelles of locomotion were first seen on *Chromatium okenii*, another large bacterium, by Christian Ehrenberg in 1836, and later on *S. volutans* by Ferdinand Cohn in 1872. The role that flagella play in that response was examined in detail after dark-field condensers were developed, beginning in 1909 with work done by Karl Reichert and culminating in 1920 with the work of Paul Metzner, who described the motion of flagellar bundles of *S. volutans* in stunning detail.

S. volutans has two flagellar bundles, each composed of about 25 flagellar filaments. Here, the cell is swimming from left to right. Its body is helical. The bundle on the left is in the tail configuration; the one on the right is in the head configuration. When the filaments change their directions of rotation, the bundles switch their configurations and the cell moves in the opposite direction. An *Escherichia coli* bacterium is shown below the *S. volutans* for comparison. As many as six flagellar filaments arise at random from the sides of the *E. coli* cell and form a bundle that appears near one pole. Rotation of the filaments in the bundle pushes the cell forward. When the bundle changes its orientation, the cell goes off in a new direction.

Bacteria may have one flagellum or many, displayed on the surface in a variety of patterns. Polar flagella come off the ends of bacteria, whereas peritrichous flagella are distributed randomly over the entire surface (peri means "around"; trichous means "hair"). Bacteria with polar flagella may have one, two, or even a tuft of hundreds of flagella at one or both ends of the cell. A few bacteria, call spirochetes, have internalized flagella that lie beneath the cell wall and coil around the cytoplasmic membrane.

The way bacterial flagella move is completely different from the action of eukaryotic flagella. Bacterial flagella neither flex nor whip; they rotate like the propellers on a boat. If a bacterium with a single polar flagellum were held by its flagellum so that the flagellum did not move, then the body of the whole bacterium would rotate. Rotation is accomplished by a basal body and the hook that connects the flagellum to the bacterial cell. The basal body attaches the base of the flagellum to the cytoplasmic membrane and cell wall and acts as a motor to turn the flagellum. The hook transfers the rotation from the basal body to the external flagellar filament.

Flagella rotate counterclockwise to propel bacteria forward, and the motion is driven by chemotaxis, which is the movement of bacteria in response to chemicals in the environment. Especially important are chemicals that can be used as energy sources, and bacteria have receptors on their surface to detect these molecules. When such a molecule interacts with the receptor, a signal is sent to the basal body, the flagellar motor starts, the flagellum rotates, and the bacterium moves toward the energy source.

Bacteria with a single polar flagellum move simply back and forth. They move forward by rotating their flagellum counterclockwise, and in reverse by rotating their flagellum clockwise. How do bacteria with a tuft of polar flagella or flagella distributed peritrichously over their entire surface move? Won't the flagella get all tangled up? In order for bacteria like these to move, the action of all the flagella must be synchronized.

Bacteria with peritrichous flagella or tufts of polar flagella show an overall pattern of movement consisting of a series of "runs" (or "swims") and "tumbles" (or "twiddles"). During a run, all of the flagella are brought together into a functional bundle and rotated synchronously in a counterclockwise direction to propel the bacterium toward the energy source. During tumbles, the flagellar bundles disassemble. The relative proportion of time spent in runs determines how fast the bacterium moves in a specific direction and depends on the concentration of the energy source. The greater the concentration of molecules

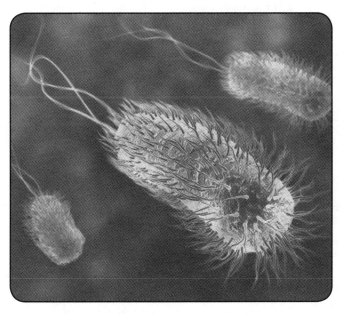

Computer artwork of E. coli *bacteria showing flagella*

of energy source, the more interaction there is with the receptors, the more time the flagella rotate counterclockwise and the farther the bacterium moves. As the concentration of the energy source decreases, there is less interaction with the receptors, the flagella are engaged less, and the bacterium does not move as far. Instead, the bacterium tumbles more often. During a tumble, flagella turn clockwise, but rather than reversing the direction of the movement, this causes bacteria to cease forward motion and randomly jiggle about. Every time a bacterium finishes a tumble, it moves randomly away from the site where the tumble occurred. Thus, the more a bacterium tumbles, the greater the chance that it will not move in a definite direction. Motility requires that more time be spent in runs than in tumbles.

Pili and Fimbriae

A number of species of Gram-negative bacilli possess surface, hair-like structures distinct from flagella. These are sometimes called pili or fimbriae. A single hair or a few long hairs are usually referred to as pili, while multiple, short, hair-like structures are called fimbriae. Pili have no relation to motility, occurring in both non-motile and motile organisms. They are very thin fibrils shorter than flagella, numbering several hundred on a single bacterial cell. They can be visualized only in electron micrographs. Pili may serve as a means for obtaining nutrients and attaching bacilli to surfaces. In liquid media cultures, pili may aid in forming a surface skin, or pellicle, of growth. Pili apparently are composed of subunits of a protein called pilin. These subunits probably aggregate into fibers that in turn wind about each other to form a hollow, helical, tube-like structure.

Design Focus 2.2

E. coli — "Superbug" and Evidence of Extraordinary Engineering

Just how simple are bacteria? For decades, biology students have learned the unscientific concept that prokaryotic cells are "primitive." Creation scientists counter that if it is alive, it is necessarily complex. Only those with a Darwinian world view maintain that microorganisms such as bacteria are simple or basic. For more than half a century, *Escherichia coli* has been the tireless workhouse of biological research. In the 1940s, it was used as a host organism to determine the life cycle of viruses. Many of the important metabolic pathways, including the renowned Krebs cycle, were first worked out in this organism. In the 1950s, biochemists used *E. coli* to discover the three forms of microbial recombination. In the 1960s, it was the major research organism for deciphering the genetic code and learning how genes work. In the 1970s, *E. coli* became the guardian of public health as a valuable indicator of water pollution. It also emerged as an industrial giant, producing enzymes, growth factors, and vitamins. Since the 1980s, biochemists have used it as a living factory to produce an array of genetically engineered pharmaceuticals. In the 1990s, *E. coli* continued to illustrate how bacteria can be put to work in the interest of science and for the betterment of humanity.

E. coli is a testament to complexity. After its genome was completed, a technical review of the microbiology literature on its genetic and DNA design inferred that its systems were irreducibly complex in nature. *E. coli* has intricate regulation and transport systems, and other complex cellular processes. It is an important bacterial species normally found in the large intestine (unless one is taking antibiotics). It is one of the most thoroughly, intensely studied of all microorganisms and is found anywhere there are people.

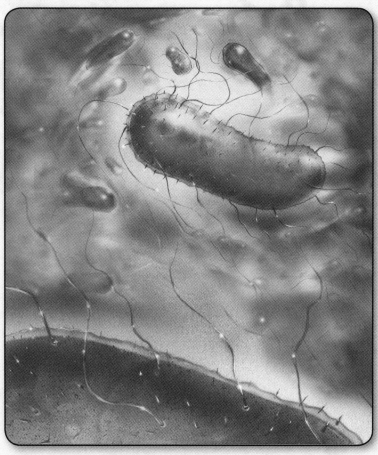

Illustration of E. Coli

Then along came *E. coli 0157:H7*. To be sure, this strain has caused much human misery because of its propensity to invade intestinal tissues, pass to the blood, and cause serious kidney damage. It has made us more careful about what we eat, causing us to think twice about having a rare hamburger. Along the way it has become the "germ of the week" on various news programs, portrayed as the chief villain in a world of villains. Unfortunately, this has made us forget all the good things *E. coli* has done for us. What a shame! Perhaps one bad apple can indeed spoil the whole barrel. Unless we are

very hygienic, non-lethal strains can be found even on our hands.

Evolutionists traditionally have viewed bacteria as simple forms of life. These single-celled organisms, so the story goes, were one of the first life forms to have naturalistically sprung from the primeval oceans several billion years ago, and therefore have to be of simple construction. However, contrary to evolutionary assumptions, research has shown bacteria to be highly organized. We have also witnessed the discovery of new phenomena, such as autoaggregation of chemotactic bacteria and coordinated behaviors in complex-colony morphogenesis.

Bacterial cells are highly ordered, with communication and decision-making capabilities enabling them to coordinate growth, movement, and biochemical activity. Are these not amazing processes for a "simple" organism?

Just how "primitive" is *E. coli*? Biologists still are not sure. Even five years after the E. coli genome was announced, microbiologists are still far from knowing all the details of how the cell operates, lives, replicates, coordinates, and adapts to changing circumstances. There are tens of thousands of journal articles on *E. coli,* and new biological information continues to accumulate. New metabolic capabilities are discovered, connected to underlying genes. There are new regulation systems, new transport systems, and more information on cellular constituents and processes, but how many regulators are needed to maintain coordination of expression of the genes and proper interaction among gene products? Regulation systems are not the same in all bacteria, and we still do not have all the information for the regulatory networks of even one bacterial species. The minimal set of genes and proteins necessary to sustain an independently replicating cell does not have an easy answer.

Experimentation into details of the biology of *E. coli* continues to grow, yet not all enzymes and pathways in *E. coli* are known. Besides data for genes for unknown enzymes, we have data for enzymes that don't have genes. There have been 55 enzymes of *E. coli* isolated, purified, and characterized over the years, but many of their genes have never been identified. The advent of DNA-sequencing technology and the completion of more than 50 microbial genomes now available to the public have not yet brought us to a complete understanding of exactly how a single, free-living cell functions and adapts to changing environments. Creation scientists cheerfully predict that if and when science does have a complete understanding of how a free-living cell functions and adapts, evolutionism will have nothing to do with it!

Conclusion

Autoaggregation? Regulatory networks? Transport systems? Coordinated behavior? Communication and decision-making capabilities? Enhanced export abilities? Is this why we should believe bacteria evolved from non-living chemicals? One could just as easily be speaking of a massive, high-tech automated factory — a sophisticated organization that certainly doesn't spring up by chance, time, and natural processes! This is another example of how evolutionary theory contradicts science.

Why do evolutionists insist on preaching that bacteria (prokaryotes) are simple or primitive, when empirical research shows the opposite? Worse, how can they say that "simple" life evolved from non-life, using nothing but chance and time? As one creation biologist has said, when people make things smaller and smaller, it's considered a wonder of modern technology (nanotechnology). When "nature" does it, it's primitive. The Christian microbiologist can look through a creation lens in his microscope and observe an awesome, distinct design in *E. coli!*

Spore Formation by Bacteria

Certain kinds of bacilli are capable of changing into resistant bodies called spores (or endospores). Each individual bacillus becomes converted into a single spore, except in a few rare species where two spores appear to form in a single cell. The spore can withstand comparatively high temperatures and other unfavorable influences, keeping the organism alive when it would otherwise perish. When suitable conditions are supplied, the spore germinates and returns to the original bacillus form. This remarkable property is confined to a few species of bacilli only, but has great practical importance. The aerobic, spore-forming bacteria make up the genus Bacillus, and the anaerobic species are classified in the genus *Clostridium.*

Some spore-bearing bacilli change to the spore form more readily than others, and certain types of culture media or other environmental conditions tend to favor sporulation, while other circumstances suppress it. Sporulation is always preceded by a period of active multiplication, and nearly all the organisms in the same culture begin to form spores at about the same time. The conversion of the bacilli into spores preserves the life of individual organisms subjected to an unfavorable environment, thus perpetuating the species under circumstances that would destroy non-spore-bearing organisms. It is important to note, however, that sporulation is clearly a regular habit of spore-forming bacteria and part of their normal cycle of development, irrespective of any special need for protection from injurious influences.

Spore formation may be suppressed by cultivation under unusual conditions — for example, at abnormally high temperatures (as Pasteur showed with anthrax vaccines), on deficient media, or when sufficient access to oxygen is denied. In general, endospore formation is favored by the same conditions favoring active growth, though it may be inhibited by factors that do not measurably influence the amount of growth.

Creation Focus 2.3

The ABC's of Anthrax: Its Anatomy, Bioterror, and Creation

In 2001, we witnessed the greatest terrorist attack in the United States, including the release of anthrax in mail envelopes. Prior to 9/11, the few people acquainted with anthrax were microbiologists. Most Americans wondered if anthrax was a new disease; it actually dates back to the plagues described in Exodus. Anthrax derives its name from the Greek word for "coal," *anthrakis*, because the disease causes black, coal-like skin lesions. It is caused by *Bacillus anthracis*, a Gram-positive, spore-forming, rod-shaped bacterium. Anthrax spores germinate upon entering an environment rich in nutrients, such as found in animal or human tissues. The rapidly multiplying bacilli have poor survival rates outside their hosts, dying within 24 hours. This contrasts with the environmentally hardy properties of the spore that can survive for millennia.

Since ancient times, anthrax has played major roles in history, including the plagues recorded in Exodus 9. When the Lord visited Egypt with a "a very grievous murrain" upon Pharaoh's cattle (Exod. 9:1–6), the severe plague was most likely anthrax. Tough *Bacillus anthracis* spores can persist for years in alluvial soil like in the Nile Valley, ravaging herds that venture near the aerosol. In this case, the Israelites were probably spared because they camped on sandy ground above the river's flood plain.

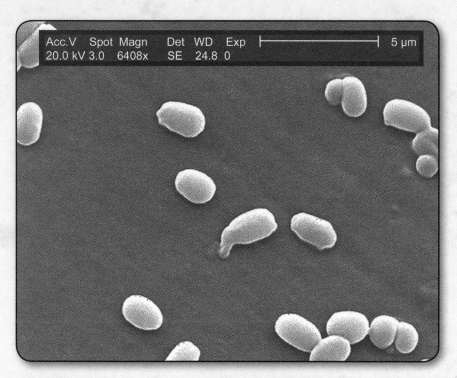

An electron micrograph of spores from the Ames strain of Bacillus anthracis *bacteria.*

A miracle of highly directed winds (from the Creator) could have stirred up alluvial soil in Egypt, affecting only those in the immediate area. Stricken livestock dying in the grip of anthrax's gruesome spasms and convulsions would definitely seem cursed.

Anthrax is known as a zoonotic disease because people catch it from animals — mostly cattle, sheep, horses, etc. — and not from other people. Spores enter humans through cuts, tainted meat, or inhalation. The spores multiply, producing enough toxin to injure surrounding cells and tissue. In a subsequent plague (Exod. 9:7–11), Moses was instructed to release "ashes," and boils came upon the Egyptians. These ashes may have contained anthrax spores, serving as the Creator's biological warfare agent for judgment, with death coming quickly.

In Europe during the 1800s, anthrax ravaged livestock workers. Robert Koch formulated his famed postulates in 1876 by developing methods to grow pure cultures, testing them in guinea pigs, and proving the germ cause of anthrax. Since anthrax was concurrently devastating sheep flocks, Louis Pasteur was summoned to produce a vaccine against it. Pasteur's vaccine not only saved millions of animals, but also led to a human vaccine as well. Today, government agencies are expanding technologies for anthrax detection because it is quite probable that anthrax will be used again in biological terrorism.

Since, as a rule, only one spore is formed from a single bacterium, spore formation is not a method of multiplication. Certain conditions must be maintained for bacterial growth. Temperature is one important factor. Some bacteria can be active at temperatures as warm as 100°C (212°F) or as cold as 0°C (32°F). The desired temperature for parasites in humans hosts is 37°C (98.6°F) body temperature, which is normal. Another factor affecting bacterial growth is moisture. Relatively active bacteria contain approximately 90 percent water. Dryness will destroy most species. Another important factor in bacterial growth is proper atmosphere. Aerobic bacteria require free oxygen for respiration. Anaerobic bacteria (those not needing free oxygen) may dwell at the bottom of a pond, lake, or ocean.

Like us, food is necessary for survival of bacteria. Their diet varies from living tissue to agar. Some bacteria are autotrophs; they can make their own food. The breakdown of inorganic sulfur, iron, or nitrogen compounds often secretes energy. Few bacteria undergo photosynthesis. The majority of bacteria are heterotrophs, unable to make their own food. This majority enjoins the fight for survival between human beings and bacteria. Bacteria need sources of vitamins, minerals, sugars, salts, and sometimes protein.

Growth Characteristics of Bacteria

The life of a bacterium or other microorganism is, of course, profoundly influenced by the character of the other organisms present, and by the moisture content, pH, temperature, and other factors in its immediate environment. Hence, the number of living individuals of one species likely found in any one place fluctuates greatly and unpredictably from time to time. In the highly artificial conditions of a pure culture growing in a liquid medium, however, we find that the development and decline of bacterial populations follow a definite, predictable course. By counting the number of living bacteria in the culture at different time intervals during incubation, then plotting these data in relation to time, we may derive a growth curve.

It is customary to divide the growth curve into several parts, but these may be combined into four chief phases: the lag phase (A to B), the logarithmic growth phase (B to C), the stationary phase (C to D), and the death or decline phase (D to E). The lag phase usually lasts no more than a few hours. During the first part of this phase there is no apparent increase, and even a reduction, in the number of living organisms, for some of the bacteria may die while others are unprepared for active multiplication. The bacteria are adjusting to a new environment, synthesizing enzymes and actively metabolizing, though cell division is not yet occurring. The lag phase ends when the organisms finally begin dividing with increasing rapidity.

During the logarithmic (log) growth phase, organisms multiply at a constant, maximum rate. The bacteria increase in number by geometrical progression (two divide to make four, four to make eight, eight to make sixteen, etc.), and if the logarithms are plotted in relation to time we get a straight, steep line as in the chart below (B to C). With a number of bacteria, for example the colon bacilli and the cholera spirilla, the generation time (i.e., the time between the formation of a new bacterium and its division to form two new cells) may be as short as 20 minutes. Organisms such as staphylococci and streptococci are said to multiply almost as rapidly, whereas other species, such as diphtheria bacilli, increase at about half this rate. A few bacteria apparently always multiply, even during this logarithmic phase, at a markedly slow rate; the generation time of tubercle bacilli in laboratory media, for example, is said to be about 18 hours.

Whatever the species of organism, the logarithmic growth phase is brief. The reduction in available food substances, accumulation of waste products, and lack of sufficient oxygen force the culture into the stationary phase, when organisms are less active and divide less frequently. The total number of living organisms remains practically constant, the death rate balancing the multiplication rate. The bacterial population reaches its greatest density within 24 to 48 hours when incubated at 37°C. The death or decline phase then sets in; the organisms gradually cease multiplying entirely. The death phase may be as rapid as the growth phase. The bacteria eventually die as nutrients decline and waste products build up. Not all the bacteria in a culture are in the same phase at the same time. Some organisms proceed to the next phase before others, and some lag behind. Thus, a gradual rather than abrupt transition generally occurs from one phase to the next.

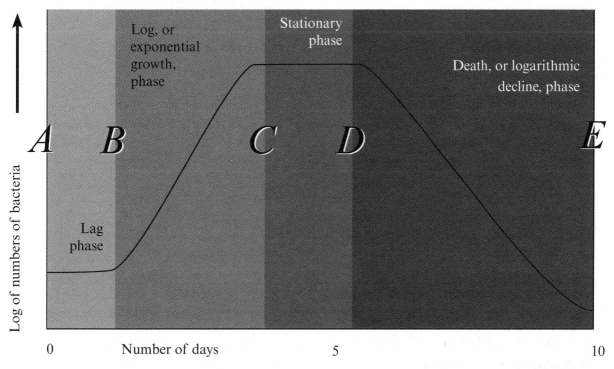

A bacterial growth curve, showing the four typical phases of growth.

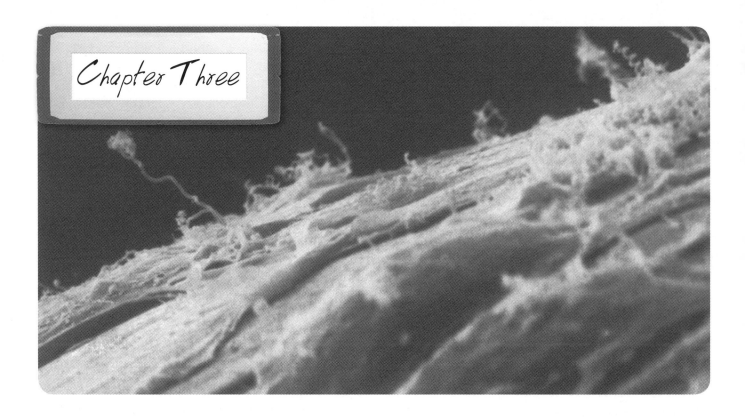

Chapter Three

Bacteria In A Fallen World (Bacteria, Part 2)

Koch's Postulates and TB

For several decades during the 1800s, bacteria were suspected of causing disease. Men like Pasteur and Lister had provided increasing evidence that specific bacteria caused certain diseases, like anthrax, yet they could not provide the conclusive evidence needed to prove the developing theory. They did, however, lay the groundwork for Robert Koch to develop a logical series of observations and experiments that would prove the specific element of infectious diseases. The series of steps worked out by Koch and others has become known as Koch's postulates. He completed the famous postulates with anthrax, but the next important disease that made it famous was tuberculosis. TB is a lung disease consuming alveoli and other neighboring tissues. At the turn of the 20th century, it was the leading cause of death in the United States. It is still the number one killer worldwide; about two billion people (one-third of the world) test positive for antibodies against the bacterium causing TB.

In the early 1880s, Robert Koch was working with the bacterium *Mycobacterium tuberculosis*. The organism was of great interest because researchers suspected it caused the widespread, often-lethal infection. Koch made two important discoveries. He found a way of staining human tissue for microscopic examination that showed *M. tuberculosis* cells as thin blue rods on a brown background of human cells. He also found that *M. tuberculosis* — a slow-growing, highly fastidious bacterium— would grow on coagulated blood serum. With these tools, Koch set out to prove that tuberculosis was caused by *M. tuberculosis*. In the 1880s, not only was there no proven connection between the two, there was also no proof that any particular microorganism caused any particular disease.

Koch began by examining tuberculosis patients for the presence of *M. tuberculosis* cells. He found the bacterium in every patient — blue rods against brown tissue. Then Koch cultured the tuberculosis cells on coagulated blood serum, isolating pure *M. tuberculosis* cultures he injected into guinea pigs. They succumbed to tuberculosis. Unequivocally, *M. tuberculosis* caused tuberculosis. Koch's work with *M. tuberculosis* provided absolute proof of the microbial etiology (cause) of an important infectious disease. Moreover, he enunciated a valuable principle. Fulfilling Koch's postulates provides absolute proof that a particular microorganism causes a particular disease:

1. The causative microorganism must be present in every individual with the disease.
2. The causative microorganism must be isolated and grown in pure culture.

3. The pure culture must cause the disease when inoculated into an experimental animal.
4. The causative microorganism must be re-isolated from the experimental animal and re-identified in pure culture.

Of course, Koch's postulates cannot be met if there is no way the pathogen can be grown or if it only infects humans. Koch himself faced this dilemma later in his career when studying cholera. He discovered that a batch of *Vibrio cholera* was present in all the intestines from all the patients he examined and was able to culture the organism. But he could not find an experimental animal susceptible to the disease. The third postulate was ultimately fulfilled when a physician working with Koch accidentally swallowed cholera bacteria and developed the disease. Koch's postulates are not the only route to determining infectious etiology. They are, however, the best time-tested models for determining specific cause and effect in bacteriology.

techniques were fairly basic: isolate the microorganism, grow it in pure culture, and examine human and microbial cells under the microscope.

Until relatively recently, most of our knowledge about microbial virulence and pathogenesis was based on the same techniques. Clinicians observed the manifestations of a disease, pathologists examined diseased tissue grossly and under the microscope, and microbiologists used Koch's postulates to prove that a given microorganism was the etiologic agent of a given disease. One character sketch of Dr. Robert Koch by Sir Arthur Conan Doyle (*Review of Reviews*, December 1890, p. 552) said:

Never, surely, could a man have found himself in a position less favorable for scientific research — poor, humble, unknown, isolated from sympathy and from the scientific appliances which are the necessary tools of the investigator. Yet he was a man of too strong a character to allow himself to be warped by the position in which he

Koch's Postulates Applied Today

The study of microbial pathogenesis — the relationship between pathogenic microorganisms and the diseases they cause — began little more than 100 years ago, when Robert Koch conclusively proved that a specific species of bacterium caused a specific human disease. Koch's success, along with Louis Pasteur's at about the same time, initiated a period of intense research. This period — from the late 1800s through the early 1900s — became known as the Golden Age of Microbiology. Most major bacterial pathogens were isolated during this time. The

Table 3.3. History of Disease Discovery During The Golden Age of Medical Microbiology

Date	Disease	Bacterium	Date	Disease	Bacterium
1876	Anthrax*	*Bacillus anthracis*	1886	Pneumonia	*Streptococcus pneumoniae*
1879	Gonorrhea	*Neisseria gonorrhoeae*	1887	Meningitis	*Neisseria meningitidis*
1880	Typhoid fever	*Salmonella typhi*	1887	Brucellosis	*Brucella spp.*
1880	Malaria	*Plasmodium spp.*	1892	Gas gangrene	*Clostridium perfringens*
1881	Wound sepsis	*Staphylococcus aureus*	1894	Plague	*Yersinia pestis*
1882	Tuberculosis*	*Mycobacterium tuberculosis*	1896	Botulism	*Clostridium botulinum*
1883	Cholera*	*Vibrio cholerae*	1898	Dysentery	*Shigella dysenteriae*
1883	Diphtheria	*Corynebacterium diphtheriae*	1905	Syphilis	*Treponema pallidum*
1885	Tetanus	*Clostridium tetani*	1906	Whooping cough	*Bordetella pertussis*
1885	Diarrhea	*Escherichia coli*	1909	Rocky Mountain spotted fever	*Rickettsia rickettsii*

* Discovered by Koch

found himself or too diverted from the line of work which was most congenial to his nature.

After Robert Koch opened the way for precise methodology in epidemiology, other microbiologists and physicians discovered other specific disease-causing germs. Table 3.3 lists the history of some of these discoveries. The contributions of creationists Louis Pasteur and Joseph Lister had paved the way for proof of the Germ Theory of Disease. The application of Koch's Postulates in working out the specific element in disease would mark the pinnacle of the Golden Age of Microbiology. Many bacteriologists have considered 1876 to be the formal introduction of medical microbiology as a scientific subdiscipline. The importance of Koch's Postulates lies in its demand for rigorous logical proof of cause and effect. Good science is marked by keen observation, repeatability of experiments, falsifiability, and predictive power. Koch's Postulates provided epidemiologists and physicians with a framework to diagnose and treat infectious and parasitic diseases. If only more biology subdisciplines, like the study of origins, required such rigorous proofs before wild speculations about phylogenic trees, cladograms, and vestigial organs took place, the world of biology would be a better place. It is the observable evidence in biology, not evolution, that leads us to cause-and-effect relationships. Here's how Carl Fliermans, a modern creationist and excellent microbiologist, investigated the cause of Legionnaire's disease and fulfilled the requirements of Koch's Postulates.

Creation Scientist Focus 3.1

Carl Fliermans and His Research on *Legionella*

Dr. Carl B. Fliermans is a microbial ecologist with DuPont and is on the technical advisory board at the Institute for Creation Research. He holds a Ph.D. in microbiology from Indiana University, and a post-doctoral fellowship at the National Institutes of Health. Dr. Fliermans is the scientist who first isolated the "Legionnaires' Disease" bacterium. He has published over 60 works, and is a member of the American Society for the Advancement of Science, the American Institute for the Biological Sciences, and the American Society for Microbiology, among others. Dr. Fliermans is a Christian who believes the Creator guided him in his discovery of *Legionella*.

August 1976 Newspaper Headline: "Mystery Illness Strikes Legionnaires"

In one of the most dramatic entrances of any disease into the public-health arena, Legionnaires' disease appeared at the U.S. Bicentennial Convention of the American Legion, July 21-23, 1976, in Philadelphia. Nearly 5,000 Legionnaires attended the three-day meeting, with over 600 staying at the elegant but aging Bellevue Stratford Hotel. Even before checking out of the hotel, several Legionnaires began to feel ill with flu-like symptoms. On Tuesday, July 27, only four days after leaving Philadelphia, an Air Force veteran who had stayed at the Bellevue Stratford during the convention died at a hospital in Sayre, PA. He was the first of more than 30 Legionnaires to eventually succumb to a lethal pneumonia that the news media quickly named "Legionnaires' disease." What was the cause of this new disease?

- Was it biological or chemical?
- Where did the pathogen, if there was one, come from?
- How was the disease spread?
- How could the disease be prevented?

These key questions and more became the focus of an intense investigation that resulted in the discovery in January 1977 that a Gram-negative, rod-shaped bacterium caused the disease. The bacterium was named *Legionella pneumophila*. Good microbiologists like Dr. Joseph McDade and later Dr. Fliermans considered pathogenic sources in nature, routes of transmission to susceptible persons, and means of preventing the spread of pathogens. Their process illustrates how classical techniques are used to prove the cause of a specific disease.

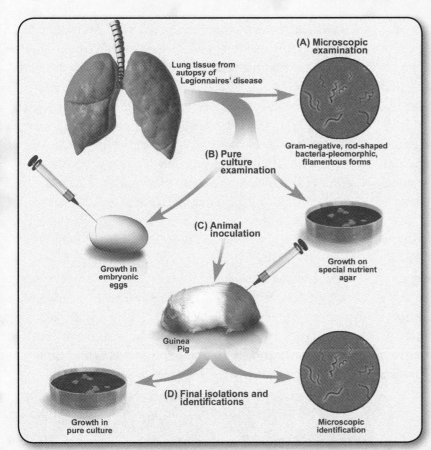

Lung tissue from
autopsy of
Legionnaires' disease

**(A) Microscopic
examination**

Gram-negative, rod-shaped
bacteria-pleomorphic,
filamentous forms

**(B) Pure
culture
examination**

**(C) Animal
inoculation**

Growth in
embryonic
eggs

Growth on
special nutrient
agar

Guinea
Pig

**(D) Final isolations and
identifications**

Growth in
pure culture

Microscopic
identification

*Investigation of the etiology of Legionnaires' disease and
summarizes Koch's postulates.*

The illustration above traces the investigation of the
etiology of Legionnaires' disease and summarizes Koch's
postulates. Legionnaires' disease was first recognized in
August 1976. It was more than six months before Koch's
postulates were fulfilled and *Legionella pneumophila* was
pronounced the etiologic agent of the disease. First, if the
etiological agent were biological, then the agent had to be
found to be regularly associated with the disease. Tissues
from lung biopsies and sputum samples were examined
for a recurring microorganism. A Gram-negative rod with
a tendency to form long, looping filaments was consistently detected in specimens. Second, the newly discovered
bacterium was isolated in pure culture in the laboratory.
This necessitated learning *L. pneumophila's* nutritional
requirements and designing special growth media that
would meet these requirements, supporting the bacterium's growth. Third, a susceptible animal was needed to
demonstrate that *L. pneumophila* could produce disease,
particularly a respiratory disease similar to Legionnaire's
disease in humans. The guinea pig proved to be the animal
model of choice. Finally, *L. pneumophila* was recovered
from infected guinea pigs to verify that it had established
an infection.

Initial Isolation of Causative Agent

Through a series of experiments, Dr.
McDade and his team first discovered from
clinical specimens in January 1977 the evidence for the existence and pathogenesis of the
bacterium that causes Legionnaires' disease.
The first step was to remove lung samples
from a deceased Legionnaire. These cells were
ground up, injected into chicken eggs, and
incubated. After the incubation period, the
eggs were cracked, and the yolk sacs extracted
and injected into the footpads of guinea pigs.
These animals then developed the typical
symptoms of Legionnaires' disease. McDade
then drew blood samples from disease sur-
vivors, assuming they contained antibodies
against the causative agent. He then mixed the
samples with the yolk-sac isolates, and they
reacted, confirming that the agent in the yolk
sacs was the same agent causing disease in the
33 people.

McDade explained that his team had
been stumped for months by several unusual
characteristics of the bacteria: The bacteria
did not grow under typical conditions. The
scientists tried to culture the bacterium from the Legionnaires' blood and tissue samples in a solution filled with
standard media fluid used to grow other bacterial varieties. However, nothing grew. This lack of growth led the
team to think that the agent was a virus or "Andromeda
strain" never seen before. It was not until samples not
treated with antibiotics were injected into the eggs that
evidence of biological activity was determined.

Another delay was caused by the use of mice in
experiments. It was not until the team switched to guinea
pigs that their efforts were productive. Though mice are
often used as animal models, it turned out that *Legionella*
replicate primarily inside macrophages. Mice macrophages
are very inefficient at ingesting this bacterium, so they
never got infected from samples from the Legionnaires. In
contrast, guinea pigs were susceptible to *Legionella* and
got infected.

The next step for McDade was to determine why this
bacterium was so difficult to culture. They soon discovered that the *Legionella* bacterium has peculiar physiological needs. Standard culture media does not promote
growth because it requires high levels of the amino acid

cysteine, inorganic iron supplements, low sodium concentrations, activated charcoal, and elevated temperatures. Dr. Fliermans was the first to recognize that the lipids of *Legionella* were very similar to the thermophilic bacteria he discovered in the thermal areas at Yellowstone National Park. Also, the bacterium tends to live in a nutrient-rich, dark environment as a biofilm (scum) associated with selected algae species. These conditions contributed to the difficulty in viewing the organism in its environment using standard microscopy and other techniques.

McDade asked Fliermans to help complete Koch's postulates for Legionnaires' disease. Since 1969, Fliermans has been conducting research on microorganisms associated with natural thermal habitats like those at Yellowstone and man-made habitats coming from thermal streams near electrical and nuclear facilities. The microorganisms associated with these habitats were often mesophilic and thermophilic in their physiological response in that their optimal growth temperature was between 30° and 90°C (86° and 194°F). The second characteristic unusual for these thermopiles was the large number of branched-chained fatty acids they contained, just like the clinical isolates of *Legionella*. Armed with this information, Fliermans began looking in aquatic habitats, both natural and man-made, both ambient and thermal, for the presence of *Legionella*. Fliermans' seminal work demonstrated that *Legionella* could be isolated from natural habitats not associated with an outbreak of the disease. These findings opened a new area for thinking, experimentation, and understanding. For Fliermans, the question now became: How and where does *Legionella* fit in the ecological setting?

Although many at the Centers for Disease Control were puzzled as to the origin of *Legionella*, the epidemiological data lead Fliermans to focus on aquatic niches as the bacterium's natural habitats. This hypothesis came from examining the fact that initial clinical presentations demonstrated a seasonality of infection. Such a cyclic pattern was very similar to that observed for the growth of aquatic bacteria. Theories as to the cause of the illnesses ranged from nickel carbonyl intoxication and viral pneumonia to a pharmaceutical conspiracy against American veterans. At the CDC, many hypothesized that *Legionella* may have been genetically engineered as an "Andromeda strain" by the

Soviets or as some other Communist plot. After all, it had primarily affected veterans. Reading his Bible one day, Dr. Fliermans observed Ecclesiastes 1:9: "The thing that hath been, it is that which shall be; and that which is done, is that which shall be done: and there is no new thing under the sun." Dr. Fliermans believed this was true, and soon altered the way his laboratory looked for the organism, since the bacterium was probably not new under the sun. After praying, planning, and exploring, Dr. Fliermans found the bacterium in thermal waters (initially isolated at 45°C [113°F] at Savannah River Laboratory) discharged from a nuclear reactor and subsequently from natural hot springs in both the Eastern and Western United States. Once isolated from the environment, the next task was to culture it. At first, it grew only in guinea pigs. Koch's postulates were initially fulfilled in Dr. Fliermans' daughter's guinea pig in the summer of 1977 with samples drawn from cooling towers. He was able to develop and deploy a fluorescent antibody test for detecting *Legionella*.

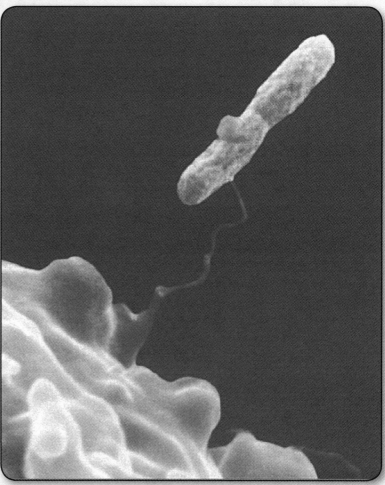

This electron micrograph depicts an amoeba, Hartmannella vermiformis *(lower left) as it entraps a* Legionella pneumophila *bacterium (upper right) with an extended pseudopod*

Legionella was now easily identified in situ, in vivo, and in vitro. Knowing the molecular and ecological basis of a pathogenesis helps one develop new ways to prevent and cure illnesses. For one thing, one can predict conditions under which pathogens are likely to thrive, spread, and cause illness. With improved techniques and molecular tools, fluorescent antibodies aid in diagnosis. A similar medical detective story is also true for the discovery and diagnosis of the agent causing Lyme disease. (See *Body by Design*, 2002, p. 145, for details.) Being a medical Sherlock Holmes helps one synthesize the diversity of facts into a unity.

Like Daniel in the Bible, one still seeks the Creator for guidance, direction, and solving enigmas. Detecting design in the world of biology is also like this. Design theory and order provide one with assumptions leading to the One who made us and the world around us. He can be a very present help in time of trouble, as in the day of Legionnaires' disease. God can work through people like Dr. Fliermans to help solve practical problems. In the footsteps of Robert Koch, Fliermans successfully isolated a suspected pathogen from the wild and grew it in pure culture, proving beyond all doubt the specific element (*Legionella*) in an infectious disease (Legionnaires'). Like scientists of the Reformation era (e.g., Kepler), Dr. Fliermans sought to think after God's thoughts (*Ps. 139:17*), being confident in God's Word. His Word is true, and there is no final conflict between God's world and God's Word, as He is the author of both.

Life's Extremists: An Introduction to Archaea

The domain **Archaea** was not recognized as a major domain of life until quite recently. Biologists distinguished between **prokaryotic** bacteria and the four **eukaryotic** kingdoms. The distinction recognizes the common traits shared by eukaryotic organisms, such as a true nucleus, a cytoskeleton, and various internal membranes. The scientific community was shocked in the late 1970s by the discovery of an entirely new group of organisms — the Archaea. Dr. Carl Woese and his colleagues were studying relationships among prokaryotes using DNA sequences, and found there were two distinct groups. Those "bacteria" living at high temperatures or producing methane clustered together as a group well away from the usual bacteria

and eukaryotes. Because of this vast difference in genetic makeup, Woese proposed that life be divided into three domains: Eukaryota, Eubacteria, and Archaebacteria. The term was later simplified to Archaea because microbiologists wanted to distinguish this group from "true" bacteria.

The three domains shown below illustrate each group's different cell traits. To the molecular biologist, cells from Bacteria, Archaea, and Eukarya are vastly different, having distinct biochemical make-ups. It is true that most archaeans look similar to bacteria under the microscope, and that the extreme conditions under which many species live has made them difficult to culture. For years, their unique place among living organisms went unrecognized. However, their rRNA sequences (coding for various proteins) are distinct from bacteria. For example, near nucleotide 910 (out of 1,500), this difference in RNA sequence has been found:

Bacteria AAACUCAAA
Archaea AAACUUAAAG

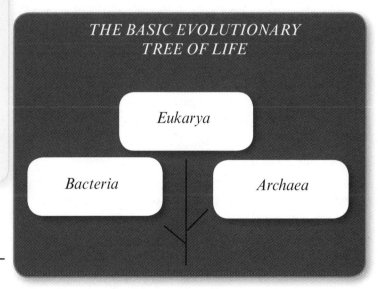

THE BASIC EVOLUTIONARY TREE OF LIFE

Eukarya

Bacteria

Archaea

The sequences of Archaea are more similar to Eukaryotes than to bacteria. Early classification of bacteria depended on individual shapes, the appearance of colonies in laboratory cultures, and other physical characteristics. The classification of bacteria underwent changes in the 1980s, when it became possible to sequence their DNA rapidly. The nomenclature shift came because Archaea are not bacteria in the traditional sense. Their cell walls do not contain peptidoglycan, their cell membranes have unusual lipid composition, and the RNA in their ribosomes has a unique chemical composition.

Because ribosomes are so critically important in the functioning of living things, Darwinists feel they are not prone to rapid evolution. A major change in ribosome sequence can render the ribosome unable to fulfill its duties of building new proteins for the cell. Because of this, evolutionists say the sequence in the ribosomes is conserved — not changing much over time. By comparing the slight differences in ribosome sequence among a wide diversity of bacteria, groups of similar sequences were found, then recognized as a related group by secular microbiologists.

Another reason for separating Archaea from other prokaryotes is the extremely harsh environments in which many species live. Archaeans include inhabitants of some of the most extreme environments on the planet. Indeed, the new word *extremophiles* has been coined for organisms like these. One group is the thermoacidophiles, which live under extremely acidic, hot conditions, including near rift vents in the deep sea at temperatures well over 100°C (212°F). Others live in hot springs, or in extremely alkaline or acidic waters. Still other Archaea have been found inside the digestive tracts of cows, termites, and marine life, producing methane and referred to as methanogens. These live solely on carbon dioxide, nitrogen, and water, and are found in the anoxic mud of marshes, at the bottom of the ocean, and even in petroleum deposits deep underground. Another group of Archaea can survive the desiccating effects of extremely saline waters, such as Utah's Great Salt Lake and ponds near San Francisco Bay. One salt-loving group of Archaea includes *Halobacterium*, a well-studied Archaean (opposite page). These are called extreme halophiles. It's interesting to note that the red light-sensitive pigment giving *Halobacterium* its color, a simple photosynthetic system providing *Halobacterium* with chemical energy, is known as halorhodopsin and is chemically similar to rhodopsin, the light-detecting pigment found in vertebrate retina. This is a case of parallel design by the Creator.

Archaeans may be the only organisms that can live in extreme habitats like thermal vents or hypersaline water. They may be extremely abundant in environments hostile to all other life forms. Many secular biologists speculate that Archaea represent the oldest life forms; they postulate that early earth conditions were harsh when life first started to evolve. However, Archaea life forms are not restricted to extreme environments. New research shows Archaeans to be quite abundant in the plankton of the open sea. These findings suggest Archaea are just variations of the Creator's plan for bacteria-like life forms, created at the same time as "typical" bacteria, fungi, and other microbial life forms. There is still much to be learned about these microbes, but it is clear that the Archaea are a remarkably diverse, successful group of microbes.

Creation Focus 3.2

Yellowstone's Hidden Biological Resources

For over 100 years, the large populations of big animals like elk, moose, buffalo, and bear have fascinated visitors to Yellowstone National Park. However, these beautiful animals represent only a tiny fraction of its significant biological resources. Visitors might be surprised to learn that the living organisms in Yellowstone with the greatest economic impact on society are quite invisible. These are the microorganisms living in the boiling waters and runoff channels of the geysers and hot springs. Though their color is visible to the naked eye, individual microbial cells are completely invisible. It is only because of their vast numbers that we know they are there. The microorganisms of the hot springs are mostly bacteria, but at lower temperatures, algae and protozoa are also present. Why are these tiny creatures of Yellowstone's hidden depths so important? Since their discovery in the 1960s, they have been found to have major uses in the biotechnology industry. The most important discovery was the Taq polymerase, an enzyme used in PCR (see chapter 19), isolated from a hot spring bacterium called *Thermus aquaticus*. Because these unique bacteria can survive such hot temperatures, their enzymes work extremely fast, therefore greatly accelerating other biochemical reactions in the wild or in the laboratory. Yellowstone has been a wonderful resource for researchers from biotechnology companies worldwide looking for new kinds of bacteria to be used commercially.

The Creator's Watercolor Mosaic at Yellowstone

Although Yellowstone is famous for its geysers, the beautiful colors associated with them are often a surprise. One sees hot water flowing over patches of brilliant yellow, orange, red, and green; hot pools lined with color; and even steam appearing to be colored. The geologists who mapped the thermal basins in the late 1800s recognized that the colorful deposits were microbial. The presence of living creatures in water too hot to touch is amazing. But even more impressive is that these organisms are not only living, but also thriving. In fact, they are so perfectly adapted to their environments that they can live nowhere else. Such organisms, called thermophiles, are found in hot environments worldwide — not only in hot springs but also in volcanoes, deserts, and man-made thermal environments like power plants and hot-water heaters. But nowhere else are they in such obvious, brilliant profusion as at Yellowstone.

Many living organisms and their parts can best be visualized as mosaic patterns. Mosaics in nature mirror artwork. The architectural designs of Escher represent a mosaic, blending mathematical principles with artistic vision. Likewise, biological mosaic patterns show contrasts between colors, pigments, and structures. Biological mosaics are most readily seen in cell pigments. Like a master painter splashing colors to paint a sunset, we see equally beautiful colors at Yellowstone and in other features. What causes these colors? In Grand Prismatic spring, and others of similar character, the orange color is due to pigmented bacteria of microbial mats, and the blue color to refracted skylight. The principal pigment for photosynthesis is chlorophyll, which is green. However, chlorophyll is sometimes masked by carotenoids, pigments related to vitamin A, and which are orange, yellow, or red. Carotenoids protect the cells from the bright sunlight occurring at Yellowstone, especially during the summer.

The color of a mat depends principally upon the ratio of chlorophyll to carotenoids. In the summer, the chlorophyll content is often low, so the microbial mats appear orange, red, or yellow. In the winter, the mats are usually dark green, because then the sunlight is subdued, and chlorophyll dominates over carotenoids. In fact, even a few cloudy days in mid-summer can lead to an increase in chlorophyll and a darkening of the mats. Thus, it is not only the kinds of bacteria but also their response to sunlight that determines the colors.

Temperature is one of the most important environmental factors, and organisms differ strikingly in their ability to adapt to high temperatures. Biologists recognize three major categories of living organisms: Eukarya, Archaea, and Bacteria. Complex organisms (plants and animals) are Eukarya, so called because their cells have true nuclei and undergo cell division by mitosis. We call these organisms eukaryotic. Archaea and Bacteria are much simpler, seldom occurring multicellularly, and lacking true nuclei and mitosis. They are called prokaryotic.

The upper temperature limits for bacteria are very high. Note that the eukaryotes are unable to adapt to high temperatures, their upper limit being about 60–62°C (140–144°F). The upper temperature limit for plants and animals is even lower — less than 50°C (122°F). Note that very few eukaryotes are able to adapt to these upper limits, the majority being restricted to much lower temperatures.

At temperatures above 60–62°C (140–144°F), the only organisms present are prokaryotes. Photosynthetic bacteria have upper temperature limits lower than in non-photosynthetic bacteria. The upper limit of photosynthetic bacteria, is about 70–73°C (158–163°F). At higher temperatures, only non-photosynthetic bacteria can grow. At the highest temperatures, over 100°C (212°F), the only bacteria found are a few unusually heat-adapted Archaea called hyperthermophiles.

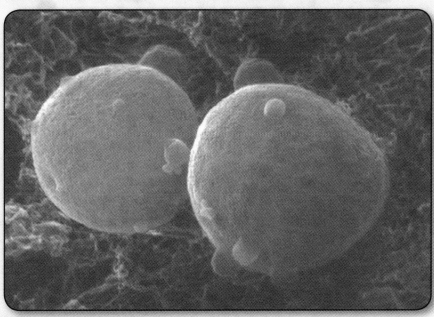

Scanning electron micrograph of Halobacterium mediternaei *bacteria.*

Water boils in Yellowstone at about 92°C (198°F). These bacteria thrive in boiling water!

The Upper Temperature for Life

When microbiological researchers first began studying the Yellowstone hot springs in the 1960s, one of the biggest surprise discoveries was that prokaryotes were thriving even in boiling water. These prokaryotes were not obvious, such as the microbial mats, living attached to the rock-like walls of the springs or to pebbles. Sometimes their long, intertwined filaments accumulated on the bottom of the channels. Even if the source pool looks white and sterile, microscopic study usually reveals large numbers of prokaryotes. Such prokaryotes are found not only in Yellowstone, but also in hot springs worldwide, even in springs at lower altitudes where water boils at higher temperatures. It is amazing that, in addition to living in boiling water, these prokaryotes are growing surprisingly rapidly; a population can double in as little as two hours.

The presence of prokaryotes in boiling water (100°C, 212°F) makes us wonder if there is an upper temperature for life. Temperatures even hotter than 100°C occur in the thermal vents found on ocean floors. Because of the high pressure in ocean depths, temperatures of over 300°C (572°F) are found. Careful study has shown that at such high temperatures, no living organisms are present, but evidence exists of prokaryotes living at temperatures as high as 115°C (239°F). In fact, cultures have been obtained that can be easily grown at this temperature in the laboratory. Interestingly, 115°C (239°F) is near the temperature at which hospital sterilizers operate, yet here are prokaryotes that actually prefer such temperatures! Prokaryotes can grow over the complete range of temperatures in which life is known possible.

Thermophiles and Evolution

How is it possible for living organisms to survive at such temperature extremes? Actually, this only surprises us because of our anthropocentric orientation. Humans and other animals are very heat-sensitive, but the biological world is much more diverse than we realize. Life, especially prokaryotic life, is able to adapt to environmental conditions deadly to humans.

In fact, many Darwinists believe that life as we know it might first have arisen three billion or so years ago in high-temperature environments, and that the first organisms on earth might therefore have been thermophiles. Such thermophiles would then have continued to exist in the intervening period, finding refuge in the hot springs continuing to dot the earth. In addition, these thermophiles would have been the forerunners of all other life forms, including, eventually, humans.

Beneficial Aspects of Bacteria: The Magnificent Microbes

As Pasteur first pointed out, it would be difficult to overemphasize the importance of the activities of saprophytic microbes in decomposing the bodies of dead animals, plants, and non-living organic matter of all sorts. The final result of all the activity of this "rotting" bacteria is the conversion of entire complex organic material into simple, inorganic substances. The process of decomposition itself is not pleasant to contemplate. A piece of putrefying meat or a rotten egg, with its disagreeable appearance and foul odor, is a disgusting object, but it takes little imagination to realize the vital importance of the rotting process. Suppose the dead bodies of plants and animals, and fecal matter and other waste materials excreted from man and animals, accumulated where they fell and never decomposed! There would soon be no room on the earth's surface for living things. As Pasteur said, the earth would soon be "encumbered with cadavers." In decomposing lifeless, organic remains, bacteria make the earth fit for the living. Pasteur was able to comprehend the Creator's wise plan for recycling the "dust of the earth."

The decomposition of non-living materials by bacteria not only rids the earth of useless waste but also accomplishes an even more important result. It releases from dead or lifeless matter the elements needed for the growth of plants, returning these essential elements to the soil. The activities of saprophytic bacteria furnish the link between the dead and the living. All-important nitrogen is locked up in the bodies of dead plants and animals in the form of organic compounds. Nitrogen is released from its complex combinations by the action of putrefactive bacteria, passing into the soil in the form of nitrates — simple, inorganic compounds that plants use for food. Thus, nitrogen, really the master element of living substances, passes through a perfect cycle from the soil into the growing plant, then to the animal body when the plant is eaten, and back again to the soil through the agency of bacteria when the plant or animal dies. Other elements necessary for life, such as carbon, phosphorus, and sulfur, pass through a similar cycle in which bacteria play an important part. The supply of these chemical elements on earth is limited, and soon would be exhausted if not for the necessary work of bacteria. The fertility of the soil is, therefore, largely a result of bacterial activity.

The Nitrogen Cycle

Certain kinds of bacteria have an especially marked influence on soil fertility because of their participation in the nitrogen cycle (below). These are the nitrifying, denitrifying, and nitrogen-fixing bacteria. Nitrifying bacteria bring about the oxidation of ammonia (NH_3) to nitrites ($-NO_2$) and of nitrites to nitrates ($-NO_3$). This is called nitrification. Since nitrates are the most useful form of nitrogen for the nutrition of plants, the amount of nitrates in the soil largely determines its fertility. The action of the nitrifying bacteria thus directly enriches the soil. These organisms are strictly autotrophic and non-spore-forming. Some are bacilli; others are cocci or spirilla. Nitrosomonas oxidizes ammonia to nitrites, and changing nitrites into nitrates is accomplished by Nitrobacter. A few other types of bacteria and fungi can also bring about the oxidation of ammonia or nitrites.

Denitrifying Bacteria

The action of the denitrifying bacteria is to bring about the reduction of nitrates ($-NO_3$) to nitrites ($-NO_2$), and the release of free ammonia (NH_3) and sometimes free gaseous nitrogen, as the final steps in the microbial decomposition of lifeless organic matter. Various anaerobic soil organisms utilize nitrates as hydrogen acceptors, thereby reduced from nitrates to nitrites. Proteins and other organic nitrogenous compounds are decomposed to amino acids, and the amino ($-NH_2$)

groups are split off in the form of ammonia (NH_3). Urea, a metabolic waste product found in the urine of man and animals, is decomposed by various microorganisms, with liberation of ammonia. These elementary, reduced nitrogen compounds — nitrites and ammonia — are useless to growing plants. They would be largely lost to the nitrogen cycle if not for the oxidizing capacity of the nitrifying bacteria.

Nitrogen-Fixing Bacteria

A most important contribution to soil fertility is made by still another group of bacteria — the nitrogen-fixing bacteria. These organisms can fix nitrogen from the air; i.e., capture atmospheric nitrogen gas and cause it to combine with other chemical elements to form organic compounds in the soil, eventually becoming available in a form useful for the nourishment of plants. Thus, free nitrogen in the atmosphere is put to work. This remarkable nitrogen-fixing property is possessed by two groups of soil bacteria.

The members of one group live free in the soil. An example is the organism named *Azotobacter*. These free-living organisms utilize carbohydrates in the soil as a source of energy and obtain nitrogen directly from the air. The nitrogen is combined into their protoplasm and later released in the form of nitrates, or other usable compounds, when the organisms die. Bacteria are themselves decomposed by other soil microbes.

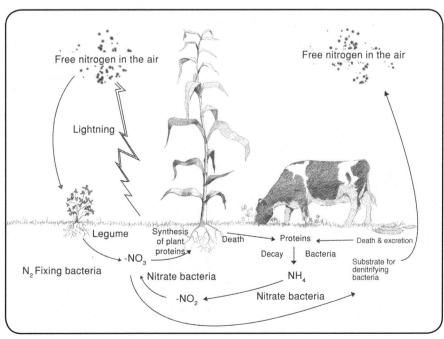

The Nitrogen Cycle

The growth of *Azotobacter* also enriches the soil with another needed element — phosphorus — which, like nitrogen, is built into the growing cells. Bacteria of some other genera (e.g., *Clostridium* and *Aerobacter*) also can fix atmospheric nitrogen.

The second group of nitrogen-fixing organisms is composed of root-nodule bacteria, which live symbiotically in nodules on the roots of certain plants (below). The plants that bear the nodules on their roots are called legumes. They include clover, peas, beans, and alfalfa. It has been known for centuries that plants of this kind enrich the soil. Farmers have long rotated crops on a particular field, sowing clover, soybeans, or some other leguminous plant every so often. When the clover is plowed under and the field planted again, the land is found to be more fertile. It is a common practice to inoculate soil or seeds with these organisms before planting to be certain that active development of the root-nodule, nitrogen-fixing bacteria occurs.

Rhizobium leguminosarum is a principal species of root-nodule bacteria. The rhizobia enter the tips of the root hairs of leguminous plants. They become surrounded by a kind of gelatinous coating or capsule and penetrate further into the roots. The organisms extend their growth into the tissue cells of the plant, and these cells respond by proliferating to form a protective nodule. The organisms in these root nodules utilize carbohydrates and other nutrients from the plant juices, simultaneously fixing nitrogen directly from the air. The end result of this remarkable symbiosis is the addition of large amounts of nitrogen to the soil.

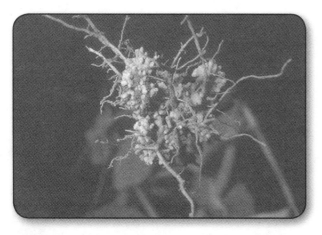

Rhizobium leguminosarum

Creation Scientist Focus 3.3

Microbiologist Joseph Francis

The Biomatrix of Life: A Creationist Perspective of Microbes and Viruses

Dr. Joseph W. Francis

Dr. Joseph W. Francis is a cellular immunologist and currently an associate professor of biology at The Master's College in Santa Clarita, California. He taught biology at Cedarville University in Ohio for ten years prior to his position at Master's. While at Cedarville, he was named faculty scholar of the year in 2000. He has a B.S. degree in microbiology from Michigan State University and a Ph.D. in biology from Wayne State University. After graduate school, he accepted an appointment as a post-doctoral fellow at the University of Michigan in the department of pediatric hematology and worked in cellular immunology. Dr. Francis has published over 20 scientific papers and given numerous presentations at scientific meetings. He has also authored and teaches an online, college-level biology course. He is a member of the Society for Leukocyte Biology, as well as the Baraminology Study Group, a society of creation biologists dedicated to developing a creation model built upon the truth claims of the Bible.

In his baraminology studies, Dr. Francis is developing models attempting to explain and describe how microbes and viruses may have functioned in the perfect pre-Fall environment as described in Genesis. Dr. Francis has discovered that a remnant of the original "very good" creation can be observed in microbes and viruses today. For instance, only a small fraction of microbes and viruses cause pathology and disease. In fact, a large percentage of microbes appear to beneficially interact with and positively affect biological life in numerous ways. For instance, microbes are involved in all major biogeochemical cycles, including the carbon and nitrogen cycle. Dr. Francis has referred to this pervasive functional population of the microbes on earth as a "biomatrix" or "organosubstrate" (below, right).

Dr. Francis proposes that microbes and viruses were created as a link between macroorganisms and a chemically rich but inert physical environment, providing a substrate upon which multicellular creatures can thrive and persist in intricately designed ecosystems. Consistent with this perspective, microbes and viruses are abundant in all ecosystems, separated by the discontinuity from macroorganisms that separates the major groups of viruses and microbes, designed for symbiotic relationships with both macroorganisms and other microbes and viruses, extract inorganic minerals from earth minerals, participate in the cycling of all elements and compounds important in macroorganismal biology, and effect bioremediation. This concept explains the organelle/bacterial similarities used as evidence of evolutionary endosymbiosis theory. The organosubstrate concept also suggests that pathogenesis is a relatively recent and rare deviation from original created function. Evidence of this includes the rarity and lower fitness of pathological forms, and the late addition to and modification of symbiotic design features in microbes and viruses. The organosubstrate concept is imminently testable and well-supported.

Furthermore, all living creatures harbor microbial symbionts. These microbial symbionts are primarily involved in providing nutrition for organisms, and also may be involved in reproduction control and host defense reactions. It also appears that microbes were created to interact with biological organisms, including humans. Dr. Francis is working on a theory that would show that microbes and viruses possess design features consistent with extracellular or extraorganismal organelles. We certainly have no problem accepting the fact that our cells have intracellular organelles, therefore we shouldn't be surprised about the existence of extracellular organelles. There are many potential advantages to possessing such organelles. For instance, they perform many functions that would be burdensome or energetically costly to their hosts. Because of their independent nature, they could leave the host but be picked up from the surrounding environment, possibly providing information promoting the host's adaptation to it.

This new way of looking at microbes and viruses also raises many questions about the immune system. If there was no death, disease, and putrefaction in the garden, what was the original role of the immune system? We certainly cannot rule out the idea that God knew about the fallen environment in which we would live, and therefore in His foresight and mercy created this system. However, it appears the immune system possesses specific, complex mechanisms that recognize and adhere to microbes and viruses. They are so complex that we can hypothesize that the immune system could have been created for more than just host defense. Perhaps the immune system was created to aid in the uptake and harboring of microbial and viral symbionts that God intended to be part of human bodies, animals, and plants. Modern

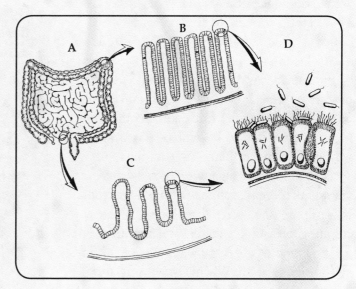

The Biomatrix of E. coli *and human intestines*

medicine has recently shown that we experience many health problems when the normal flora bacteria in our intestines are compromised. In fact, the intestinal tract does not develop correctly in animals in which bacteria have been removed. Recent studies have shown that the immune system interacts with normal intestinal flora, and may control its population and promote its maintenance there. In this association between the immune system and normal flora bacteria in the intestine, we may be witnessing a snapshot of the original purpose of the immune system.

Cyanobacteria

The Cyanobacteria (blue-green algae) are microscopic — the simplest and most bacteria-like of the algae. Cyanobacteria are incredibly tolerant to harsh environmental conditions, thriving in waters high in nutrients or fertilizer runoff. Some can fix atmospheric nitrogen from the environment in cells called heterocysts. One example is *Anabaena* (below, right), which contains enzymes that fix nitrogen (N_2) into ammonium (NH_4) for use by the growing cell. Species growing in water usually have gas vacuoles that help the cell float in favorable environments. It is therefore not surprising to find among them forms adapted to growth in almost every sort of environment, including places in which no other kind of vegetation can exist. They occur not only in fresh or brackish water at ordinary temperatures, but also in hot springs at temperatures of up to 80°C (176°F), in cold mountain streams, and even in water with a salt concentration as high as 27 percent. The bright colors of the terraces and "paint pots" around the hot springs at Yellowstone are due to the blue-green algae in the outer layers of this calcareous deposit. Other varieties may be visible to the naked eye as a moss-like film on virgin or cultivated soil, and still others are found as parasites, or in symbiotic association with various higher plants and animals.

The blue-green algae may grow as individual microscopic cells somewhat larger than bacteria, but they often form long, filamentous colonies consisting principally of multiples of just one kind of algal cell held together within a gelatinous sheath. When a heavy spreading growth of these algae develops, as, for example, over the surface of a pond or reservoir, or over a

sizable area in the sea, this is called a bloom. There are no organs of locomotion, but the cells can glide forward or backward parallel to the long axis of the filaments. There is no morphologically distinct nucleus, and reproduction is most commonly by simple asexual cell division. These traits suggest a design similar to true bacteria. Some Cyanobacteria have internal membranes, or lamellae, along the periphery of the cells, and apparently are extensions of the external cell membrane. These apparently have a function connected with photosynthesis. The cell walls of the blue-green algae are similar to those of bacteria.

Cyanobacteria are recognized by their blue-green color, hence the name, but among the approximately 2,000 species now known, there is a wide range of colors. Most species have three pigments: chlorophyll (green), phycocyanin (blue), and phycoerythrin (red). The pigment particles are dispersed throughout the cytoplasm, especially along the peripheral lamellae, and in the sheath as well. The majority of these organisms are autotrophic and aerobic. They require no pre-formed organic matter for growth, but only oxygen, inorganic substances, and light, and photosynthesis utilizes the energy of light to build their protoplasm from the water and carbon dioxide in the air.

Cyanobacteria are agriculturally important. Activities of the blue-green algae are economically significant on several counts. First is the contribution of some species to soil fertility through the fixation of atmospheric nitrogen. For example, in the waterlogged soils of the Far East, where rice has been cultivated for centuries, an abundant bloom of blue-green algae develops,

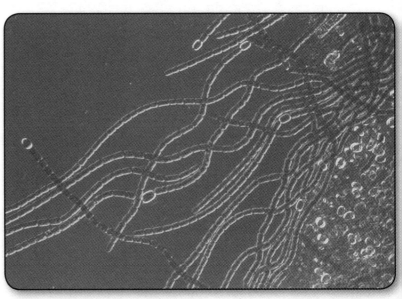

Blue-green Algae

contributing to the nitrogen content of the soil and permitting good crops every year even without addition of manure or chemical fertilizers. Also, the oxygen liberated by the algae in photosynthesis may be beneficial. Artificial inoculation of soil with blue-green algae has been successful in improving certain crops.

Blue-green algae are usually the first organisms to colonize barren rocks and arid soils. This surface growth may result in an accumulation of organic matter of such thickness that bacteria and fungi, and eventually complex plant forms, may live there. In the sea, algae are important food sources for fish and other marine life. Overgrowths of algae often develop around the intake pipes of water-supply systems and in reservoirs or cisterns of fresh water, imparting disagreeable odors. Algal blooms are likely to occur around collections of sewage-polluted water. The water consequently becomes depleted of oxygen, and fish cannot survive in it. Most of these difficulties in sanitation are controlled, however, by treatment of affected areas with copper sulfate or similar algaecides.

Summary and Conclusions

In summary, the Eubacteria, Cyanobacteria, and Archaea are tiny but very successful, judging from their ability to live in virtually every habitat on earth. Bacteria have adapted to more different living conditions than any other group of organisms. They inhabit the air, soil, and water, and exist in enormous numbers on the surfaces of virtually all plants and animals. Their diverse nutritional processes and complex genetics and cellular structure are not as different from so-called higher organisms as once believed. The Creator must have deemed bacteria important because of their ubiquity in the world, contributing to nutrient cycles and energy flow. Bacteria are also important in the body's normal flora, and many, like *E. coli*, produce vitamins for the body. Bacteria are clearly made of designed structures and perform purposeful functions.

Of course, some bacteria are harmful. Certain species multiply within the human body, digesting tissues (e.g., tuberculosis) or producing disease-causing toxins (e.g., anthrax). Other bacteria infect plant crops and animal herds. Disease-causing bacteria are a global threat to all life forms in their natural state, and in the 21st century they have already been used as agents of bioterror. Bacteria have threatened human existence over the millennia with bubonic plague, typhus, tuberculosis, pneumonia, streptococcal infections, diphtheria, *E. coli,* and anthrax. These diseases are likely to remain until the Lord comes back and establishes a new heaven and earth.

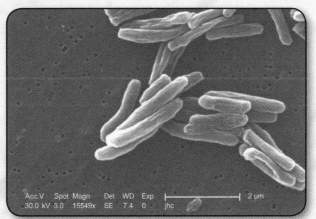

Under a high magnification of 15549x, this scanning electron micrograph (SEM) depicted some of the ultrastructural details seen in the cell wall configuration of a number of Gram-positive Mycobacterium tuberculosis *bacteria*

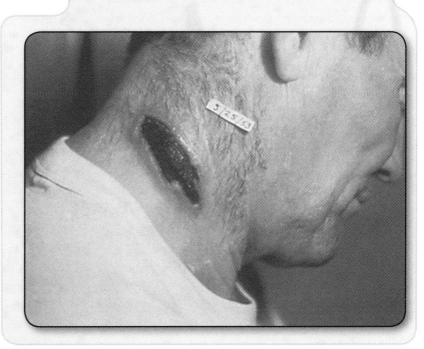

Cutaneous anthrax lesion on the neck.

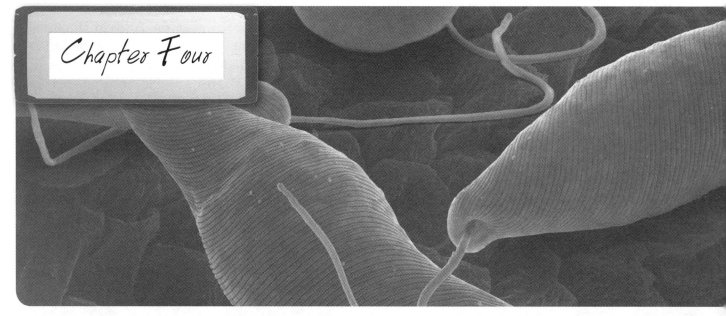

Chapter Four

Protista: A Zoo in Pond Water

Protists make up the most diverse life forms in one large kingdom in terms of size, shape, color, and composition. They are the Master's jewels brightening the natural world. Protists provide food for animals, recycle valuable nutrients, and dazzle observers with their tiny locomotor machines. Protists are found in soil, ponds, lakes, rivers, and oceans. They were first described by Anton van Leeuwenhoek (see Creation Scientist Focus 4.1) and include protozoans, slime molds, and algae. Leeuwenhoek considered them to be the Creator's "little animalcules" (little animals). Most are microscopic, but the largest among them (kelp) can reach several hundred feet. This chapter surveys the significance of the protists and describes some of their complex structures.

Protists: A Microbial Grab Bag

The protists are a kingdom of eukaryotic microbes lumped together for classification convenience, yet clearly unrelated in terms of ancestry and morphological features. They are a mixed group of miscellaneous organisms grouped together in categories not fitting clearly in other well-defined kingdoms. They are groups assigned to Whittaker's Protista kingdom by default even though they do not share broad taxonomic similarities. Unlike Bacteria and Archaea, the members of kingdom Protista have eukaryotic cells, most having a true nucleus, mitochondria, and other organelles. Most protists are unicellular, but like the bacteria, there are filamentous and colonial forms as well. The existence of Protista testifies to the difficulty taxonomists have had in classifying the vast array of creatures. The fact is that protists have no unique characteristics distinguishing them from other kingdoms. For instance, almost every manner of nutrition found in other kingdoms is found among protists, and some individual protists, like *Euglena*, may be both autotrophic and heterotrophic in the presence of light, but heterotrophic in darkness.

Classification of Protists

Kingdom Protista is divided into 14 taxonomic groups (Table 4.1), including six autotrophic divisions (botanical equivalent of phyla) commonly referred to as "algae" or "algae-like protists," three divisions representing slime molds and water molds, and five phyla of heterotrophic or "animal-like protists" — protozoa. Protists are a complex group; major phyla are clearly unrelated. Because most textbooks assume evolutionary origin, protists' taxonomic systems often differ vastly because biologists differ widely in how they evolved. Evolutionists have difficulty establishing phylogenetic lines for protists because of the lack of transitional forms among protistan fossils. Perhaps biologists should be asking, "Are there any missing links we have yet to see and understand?" Indeed, a classification system based upon phylogeny can hinder fresh thinking and hypotheses if its limitations are not recognized.

We will not belabor classification within Protista but simply introduce a few representatives of the more notable groups. This chapter presents a simplified taxonomic system based upon historic groupings of locomotion and morphology, and assumes a creation origin. Table 4.1 provides a traditional classification of Protists.

Creation Scientist Focus 4.1

The Unseen World of Anton van Leeuwenhoek

Anton van Leeuwenhoek found God's great glory in His tiny creations. The Dutch cloth merchant retained a boyish delight in discovery from his younger years, when he first discovered protists, until his death at age 91. He lived to grind and focus a new lens on a world formerly unseen. Leeuwenhoek spent his days grinding pinhead-sized lenses and peering through them, hour after hour, by candlelight. For this Christian layman-scientist, the astonishing array of tiny life forms revealed under his homemade lenses glorified God as much as the brightest stars. Born in Delft in 1632, Leeuwenhoek became a draper, only taking up scientific study as a hobby after seeing micrographs while visiting London in 1660. He did not invent the microscope, but took it to new levels of power. In the process, he opened human eyes to the world of microorganisms, founding a new branch of science: microbiology. By 1673, Leeuwenhoek was discovering things with his superior microscopes that no human eye had ever seen. He began sharing them in letters to the natural philosophers at the Royal Society of London. The British scientists were skeptical of the claims by this untrained layman. When in 1676 he described finding microorganisms so small that "ten thousand of these living creatures could scarce equal the bulk of a coarse sand grain," they requested corroboration from other eyewitnesses. Several friends sent letters that they also saw these microbes through Leeuwenhoek's microscope. As his observations were found to be accurate, his reputation grew, and he was soon elected a fellow of the Royal Society. The amateur microscopist kept up a lively correspondence with the British scientists, who translated and published hundreds of his letters.

Leeuwenhoek's letters sparkle with the excitement of discovery. Describing the "wee animalcules" and "cavorting beasties" (protozoa and bacteria) he observed in a drop of fresh water, he wrote, "The motion of most of them in the water was so swift, and so various, upwards, downwards, and roundabout, that I admit I could not but wonder at it. I judge that some of these little creatures were above a thousand times smaller than the smallest ones which I have hitherto seen. . . . Some of these are so exceedingly small that millions of millions might be contained in a single drop of water." Leeuwenhoek investigated almost anything he could mount, exemplifying technical skill that became a model for others. He was the first to observe bacteria, rotifers, and protists like *Vorticella* and *Volvox*. He observed blood cells and was the first to see the whiplike action of sperm cells. He advanced proofs against spontaneous generation, a popular doctrine in his day. This taught that living things emerge spontaneously from inanimate matter: shellfish from sand, maggots from meat, and weevils from wheat. He observed the complete life cycles of ants, fleas, various insects, and other small animals, proving that all organisms have parents.

Born into the Dutch Reformed tradition, which encouraged man's investigation of God's handiwork in nature, Leeuwenhoek shared with Robert Boyle and other "new philosophers" of science a concern to glorify God and benefit humankind through research. He was one who *"sought God's thoughts after Him"* (Ps. 139:17). He laced his writings with exclamations of the greatness and wisdom of the God who created the wonders he saw through his lenses. He marveled at the perfection the Creator had built into even the tiniest, most hidden facets of creation. His stand against spontaneous generation was also a defense of creation against the incipient materialism that was starting to enter science. The Dutch microscopist believed it foolish to think his "animalcules" could have formed by chance, and he worked diligently to prove that all things reproduce after their kind, as Genesis asserts. After working for weeks observing the propagation of insects, for example, Leeuwenhoek stated confidently, "This must appear wonderful, and be a confirmation of the principle that all living creatures deduce their origin from those which were formed at the Beginning." Leeuwenhoek died in 1723, shortly after dictating a final set of observations to the Royal Society. Microscopy has come a long way since then; scientists now use electron microscopes magnifying more than a million times, investigating wonders more amazing than Leeuwenhoek could have imagined, like DNA, molecular motors, and the machinery of the cell.

Table 4. 1 Classification of Kingdom Protista: Subkingdom Protozoa and Its Phyla Archaezoa:

Protozoans lacking mitochondria; typically spindle-shaped and having flagella (e.g. *Trypanosoma*)

Ciliophora	Ciliated protozoa (e.g., *Paramecium*)
Euglenozoa	Flagellates that have mitochondria (e.g., *Euglena*)
Rhizopoda	Amoeboids, radiolarians, foraminiferans (e.g., *Amoeba*)
Sporozoa	Spore-bearing, parasitic protozoa (e.g., *Plasmodium*)

Subkingdom Myxobionta: Slime Molds and Water Molds and Their Phyla

Acrasiomycota	Cellular slime molds (e.g., *Dictyostelium*)
Cyxomycota	Plasmodial slime molds (e.g., *Physarum*)
Oomycota	Biflagellate water molds (e.g., *Phytophthora*)

Subkingdom Phycobionta: Algae and Algae-like Divisions*

Chlorophyta	Green algae (chloro = green)
Chrysophyta	Golden algae, diatoms (chryso = golden)
Phaeophyta	Brown algae (phaio = brown)
Pyrrophyta	"Fire algae," dinoflagellates (pyro = fire)
Rhodophyta	Red algae (rhodo = red)

* Division used for the plant and plant-like phyla.

Subkingdom Protozoa

The complicated, purposeful activities of single-celled protozoa are among the most wondrous of all the many-sided manifestations of life found anywhere in nature. Free-living protozoa are found in fresh or salt water, in the soil, and in decaying organic matter everywhere. Some varieties, such as the common amoeba, are widely distributed, while others are restricted to particular habitats. The universal occurrence of free-living protozoa in common materials may be demonstrated by a simple infusion of hay in water. After such an infusion has stood in an open vessel for a few days, it will be found to contain an abundant population of microbes. There will certainly be some bacteria present, and probably some molds, but the most conspicuous microbes will be the large, actively motile "slipper animalcules" (*Paramecium*) and other varieties of protozoa.

Parasitic protozoa are found in association with practically every kind of living animal, and there are even kinds that parasitize other protozoa. These parasitic forms are naturally more limited in distribution than the free-living organisms, occurring only in the particular animal or human hosts to which they have become adapted. The majority of these microbes exist as harmless commensals.

The science of **protozoology** is one of the most valuable and fascinating fields of study. The activities of protozoa are of considerable economic importance. Since they feed on bacteria, the number of protozoa in a particular soil or water determines in part the size and character of the bacterial population there. Protozoa are common parasites of fish, so their growth in reservoirs often concerns sanitation authorities. A high abundance of certain undesirable species may add distasteful odors or tastes to the public water supply. Though not as frequently encountered as bacterial diseases, parasitic protozoan infections can be found in man and in domestic animals. Malaria, caused by the protozoan *Plasmodium,* has probably killed more people than any other infectious disease in history; only tuberculosis afflicts more people in the world today.

Classes of Protozoa

Protozoans might be called Providence's one-unit power cells because all the free-living ones have remarkable locomotion abilities. Some move by pseudopodia, some by cilia, and some by flagella. Each has been equipped by their Creator to move freely in their environments and seem to have lots of energy. The basic classification system, in fact, is based largely upon locomotion. Only the Apicomplexa parasite group does not have motor organelles; they "bus" to locations chosen by the host. There are four traditional categories of protozoa (below, center):

1. **Sarcodinines** ("fleshlike" organisms): The most important subgroup is the Amoebae. These exist as naked globules of protoplasm characterized by the use of pseudopodia as organs of locomotion and capture of food.

2. **Flagellates, or Mastigophorans** ("whipbearing" forms): These swim about by means of flagella, long, whip-like projections from the cytoplasm.

3. **Ciliates:** These have the most elaborate internal structure of all protozoa. They move about actively, propelled by the sweeping movement of innumerable short, delicate, hair-like cilia on their surface.

4. **Sporozoans:** These protozoa are relatively small, living as parasites in the cells or tissues of animals or man. At some stage in their life cycle they reproduce by forming multiple spores (merozoites or sporozoites). The immature forms inside red blood cells show limited amoeboid movements. The male sexual form (gamete) is flagellated and capable of independent locomotion.

Characteristics of Protozoa

Most protozoa are readily distinguished from other types of microorganisms. They differ from bacteria in several aspects. They are usually larger, eukaryotic cells, with a more complicated internal structure, and often have complex life cycles, including both sexual and asexual reproduction. Some of their outstanding anatomical features are illustrated (above). All protozoa have at least one nucleus, distinct from the cytoplasm. The hundreds of different species vary greatly in size. Some parasitic forms have the dimensions of the smallest bacteria, while others measure 20, 50, 100, or even 400 μ in length and 30 to 50 μ in width.

These creatures include the largest and most complicated of all single-celled organisms. Although their whole organism is a single cell, many protozoa have complex internal structures, including an arrangement of organelles for capture, digestion, and storage of food; excretion of liquid and solid wastes; protection and support of the body; and reproduction. These organelles function like the organs of complex animals.

The nucleus, which may take many different forms, is not always clearly visible in the living organism, but when the protozoan is dried on a slide or fixed in a section of tissue, then stained, the nuclear material becomes prominent. It stands out from the cytoplasm because of the presence of chromatin, which colors deeply with basic stains.

Outside the nucleus proper, other masses of chromatin material are often present, some appearing to have definite physiological functions. For example, flagellated protozoa, such as trypanosomes, have at the base of the flagellum a small chromatin body usually called the **kinetoplast**, or **blepharoplast** ("eyelash former").

Physiological Properties

The great majority of protozoa, both free-living and parasitic, are distinctly animal-like in their nutritional habits. They take solid food particles into their bodies, digest them, and then cast out the indigestible residue. The parasitic organisms of the class Sporozoa, however, are nourished only by direct absorption of soluble food material through the cell wall. Despite their specialized physiological needs, many protozoa, including pathogenic varieties, may be grown in test tubes on media enriched with blood and other complex protein substances similar to the enriched agar used for cultivating pathogenic bacteria.

The wide occurrence of free-living protozoa is due in part to their ability to encyst — to form resistant resting cells called cysts. Most parasitic protozoa also can encyst when their immediate environment is drying up or otherwise becoming unfavorable. Cysts of intestinal protozoa form in the lower intestines and are voided in the feces. Fecal material thus becomes the source of infection for new hosts.

Asexual Reproduction

A simple form of multiplication — seen, for example, in *Paramecium*, other ciliates, and amoebae — consists of simple fission of the nuclei followed by a splitting of the cytoplasm across the short axis into two approximately equal parts. In another form of the reproductive process, common in flagellates, the nucleus first undergoes more or less complicated changes, similar to the mitosis regularly occurring when cells of plants and animals multiply. The organism then splits into two parts by longitudinal division of the cytoplasm.

In malaria parasites and other Sporozoa, the characteristic reproduction method is multiple division (sporulation). The mature protozoan growing within a body cell divides throughout into a number of daughter forms, each with its own nucleus, thus making a mass of new cells that finally separate and develop individually. When this process is entirely asexual, occurring without preliminary formation of a cyst, it is called **schizogony**, and the new cells are called **merozoites**. A similar process occurring within a cyst (usually after previous union with a male cell has fertilized the encysted female cell) is called **sporogony**, and the new cells are called **sporozoites**.

Sexual Reproduction and Life Cycles

At some time in the development of practically all varieties of protozoa, the asexual multiplication processes mentioned above are interrupted, and sexual phenomena intervene. Sexual reproduction among protozoa involves the fusion of individuals of the same species in such a manner that nuclear material is exchanged or fused. When this union is temporary, it is called **conjugation**. The individuals concerned, after attaching themselves to each other for a time, during which nuclear matter is exchanged, separate completely, and each then grows and multiplies independently. The individual cells are sometimes morphologically alike, but more

commonly differ in size and form in a manner comparable to the spermatozoon and ovum of the multicellular animals. In the highest development of this sexual type of multiplication, the entire process is amazingly similar to reproduction among vertebrate animals.

The series of changes a protozoan undergoes from one act of fertilization to another constitutes that organism's life cycle. Many parasitic protozoa pass through complicated life cycles, assuming quite different forms and multiplying in different ways. Many pathogenic species pass the sexual part of their cycle exclusively in one host and the asexual part in another host. For example, in the sexual phase of their cycle, malaria parasites develop only in the bodies of malaria-carrying *Anopheles* mosquitoes, multiplying by sporogony; but within the red blood cells of human hosts, they multiply asexually by schizogony.

Amoebae

The amoeba is the best-known protozoan, having a remarkably flexible body that can change shape at will. Its single-cell body is a tiny mass of living matter with-

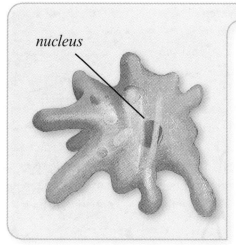

nucleus

in a thin, flexible, semi-permeable membrane. There are no visible internal structures except a nucleus. The cytoplasm, however, has numerous vacuoles and various other inclusions.

Free-living, harmless amoebae, such as *Amoeba proteus*, reach large proportions, some having diameters of about 400 μ or more. These organisms may be found in infusions made with dead leaves or grass, or in the material scooped from the bottom of shallow, quiet ponds.

Amoebae are characterized by their curious method of locomotion. They continually send out, first from one and then from another part of their surface, blunt projections called **pseudopodia** ("false feet"). Some of the semifluid cytoplasm of the amoeba flows into each new pseudopod, while the older pseudopodia go back into the general mass. Thus, the animal moves about slowly and irregularly, continually changing shape and never progressing long in any one direction ("amoeba" is derived from a Greek word meaning "change"). Amoebae capture bits of solid food by surrounding them with a pseudopod, thus enclosing the food particle within a vacuole in the organism. Digestive enzymes are secreted into the vacuole. If the particle is not acceptable food, it is expelled from the cell.

Parasitic amoebae are regularly found living in association with all kinds of animals, and also with man. *Entamoeba histolytica* is the amoeba that causes amebic dysentery and other forms of amebiasis in humans. Amebiasis is a severe diarrhea infecting over 50 million people each year, killing over 40,000. Perhaps five percent of the U.S. population are asymptotic carriers of *E. histolytica,* and ten percent of these infections progress to a more serious stage. *Entamoeba* is transmitted between humans through the ingestion of the cysts excreted in the feces of an infected person. *Acanthamoeba* is an emerging parasite in the United States, and can grow in swimming pools and tap water. *Acanthamoeba* infects the cornea and may cause blindness.

Flagellates

Organisms of this class of protozoa swim about by means of long, delicate processes, called **flagella**, extending from the cell surface. By the whip-like lashing of these flagella, the organisms are propelled along, usually rather slowly and irregularly. In addition to flagella, some species possess an undulating membrane that also assists in locomotion. There are numerous distinct varieties of flagellates, showing great differences in size and structural details. Each kind has a definite, characteristic shape, usually basically oval, and the front end always bears the flagella. Free-living flagellates include some distinctly plant-like forms containing chlorophyll and making their own food by photosynthesis. One example is *Euglena* (above). Other flagel-

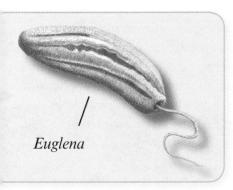

Euglena

lates, whether free-living or parasitic, are animal-like, capturing and ingesting their food in the fashion of typical protozoa.

Barnyard pools and sewage-treatment ponds often develop a rich, green bloom of *Euglena*. Superficial microscopic examination of water from such a pool usually reveals large numbers of active green cells, and closer inspection may reveal any of the more than 750 species of flagellates, of which *Euglena* is the best-known example. Many botanists classify these with the algae, while zoologists classify these amazing flagellates with protozoans. *Euglena* has been included with the protozoans rather than algae because more species of euglenoids are animal-like (two-thirds lack chlorophyll) than plant-like (one-third have it).

A *Euglena* cell is spindle-shaped, has no rigid wall, and changes shape even as the organism moves. Just beneath the plasma membrane are fine strips spiraling around the cell parallel to one another. The strips and the plasma membrane, together called a **pellicle,** are devoid of cellulose. A single flagellum, with numerous tiny hairs along one side, pulls the cell through the water. A short second flagellum is present within a reservoir at the base of the long flagellum.

Other features of *Euglena* include the presence of a **gullet**, or groove, through which food can be ingested. The food of most of the 500 *Euglena* species is ingested, with only about a third having mostly disc-shaped chloroplasts permitting photosynthesis. A red **eyespot**, which along with the short flagellum is associated with light detection, is located in the cytoplasm near the base of the flagella. A carbohydrate food reserve called **paramylon** normally is present in the form of small, whitish bodies of various shapes.

Reproduction is by cell division. The cell starts dividing at the flagellar end, eventually splitting lengthwise and forming two complete cells. Sexual reproduction is suspected, but has never been confirmed. Some species of *Euglena* can live in the dark if appropriate food is present. Others can reproduce faster than their chloroplasts under certain circumstances, with some chloroplast-free cells being formed. As long as a suitable environment is provided, these cells can survive indefinitely. In the past, when only two kingdoms were recognized, *Euglena's* capacity to satisfy its energy needs through either photosynthesis or ingestion of food resulted in it being treated as a plant in botany texts and an animal in zoology texts.

Parasitic flagellates include several species found in

the digestive tract or on the genitalia of man and animals. The best known of these belongs to the genera *Giardia* and *Trichomonas*. The most important pathogenic flagellates are the trypanosomes and the *Leishmania*. Many trypanosomes are parasites in the blood streams of horses, cattle, and other vertebrates, in man causing African sleeping sickness and Chagas' disease of South America.

African trypanosomiasis, or **sleeping sickness,** is a protozoan disease affecting the nervous system. The disease affects about one million people in Central and East Africa, and about 20,000 new cases are reported each year. The disease is caused by two forms of *Trypanosoma brucei*, flagellates injected by the bite of a tsetse fly. Animal reservoirs for the two trypanosomes are similar, but occur in different habitats and are spread by different species of tsetse-fly vector. During the early stages, a few trypanosomes can be found and the pathogens move into the cerebral spinal fluid, causing a decrease in mental and physical activity. The host enters a coma, and death is almost certain. Some

moderately effective agents, such as suramin and eflornithine, block the proliferation of the parasite. A vaccine is being developed, but the trypanosome can change at least 100 times and thus evade antibodies aimed at only one or a few of the proteins. Trypanosomes are very successful at evading the body's immune system. The population of each trypanosome clone multiplies as the immune system suppresses its members with a different antigenic surface. Each time the body's immune system successfully suppresses the trypanosome, a new clone of parasites appears with a different antigenic coat.

Giardia is a pathogenic protozoan causing a gastrointestinal illness called giardiasis, characterized by severe diarrhea that can last several weeks. **Giardia** is a distinguished ciliate in that it has four pairs of anterior flagella and two nuclei that stain darkly, giving the appearance of having eyes in its **trophozoite** (vegetative) stage. Many believe that Anton van Leeuwenhoek described *Giardia lamblia* as early as 1681 in his stool samples. Giardiasis is commonly transmitted by drinking water cross-contaminated with sewage. It is also known to exist in clear-running streams due to wildlife depositing their wastes in the water. To drink water from trout streams without boiling it or adding iodine tablets is unsafe. Many unsuspecting campers and fishermen have picked up giardiasis when returning home from an outing. Instead of enjoying fresh,

home-cooked fish, they instead experience diarrhea, gas, and abdominal pain. The moral of the story is don't drink untested waters from the wild — it may have *Giardia!*

Ciliates

This class of protozoa grows well in infusions of hay, dead leaves, grass, and similar materials generally used for laboratory study. These organisms are all characterized by hundreds of short, hair-like processes on their body surfaces known as cilia (see Design Focus 4.2). The rhythmical, sweeping movement of these cilia propels the organism rapidly and smoothly through liquids. The ciliates have the most elaborate internal structure of all protozoa.

Paramecium caudatum is among the best known of the free-living ciliates. Its slipper shape (above) makes *Paramecium* easy to recognize. *Paramecium* are the Creator's ciliated, one-celled wonders. *Paramecia* has a primitive gullet, a "mouth" into which food particles are swept, a single large **macronucleus,** and one or more micronuclei. During sexual recombination, two cells make contact, and a cytoplasmic bridge forms between them. A **micronucleus** from each cell divides, forming four micronuclei, with one remaining alive and undergoing division. Now a "swapping" of micronuclei takes place, followed by a union re-forming the normal micronucleus. This genetic recombination is somewhat analogous to what occurs in bacteria. It is observed during periods of environmental stress, suggesting the formation of a genetically different and perhaps better-adapted organism. Reproduction at other times is by mitotic cell division.

Sexual recombination in *Paramecium* involves the following steps (opposite page, top):

1. Two cells make contact, and a cytoplasmic bridge forms between them.

2. A micronucleus in each undergoes two divisions to form four micronuclei per cell.

3. Three micronuclei disintegrate, and the remaining one divides by mitosis.

4. An exchange of micronuclei takes place.

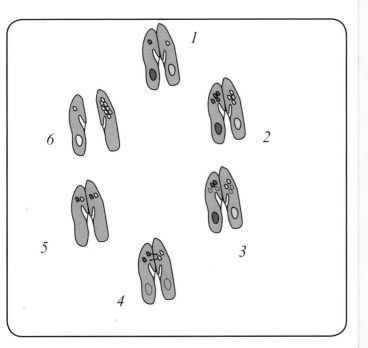

5. The cells separate, the micronuclei fuse, and the macronuclei disintegrate.

6. A new macronucleus forms in each cell from the dividing micronucleus.

Another feature of *Paramecium* is the genetic **kappa factors**. These nucleic-acid particles are apparently responsible for synthesizing toxins that destroy ciliates lacking the factors. *Paramecium* also possess **trichocysts**, organelles discharging filaments to trap prey. A third feature is the contractile vacuole that "bails out" excess water from the cytoplasm. These organelles are present in fresh-water ciliates but not in salt-water species, because little excess water exists in the cells.

Ciliates have been the subject of biological investigation for many decades. They are readily found in almost any pond or gutter water; have a variety of shapes; exist in several colors, including light blue and pink; exhibit elaborate, controlled behavior patterns; and have simple nutritional requirements, making cultivation easy. The only species of ciliate at all common as a parasite in human beings is *Balantidium coli*. This organism is responsible for mild dysentery.

Design Focus 4.2

Cilia: Molecular Machines of Movement in *Paramecium*

Cilia and flagella are molecular machines in the respiratory system. Bacteria and *Euglena* are single-celled creatures that move about by means of flagella, whereas *Paramecium* move by means of cilia. Cilia are tiny, hair-like projections extending from the cell membrane and also found in human cells lining respiratory passageways. These ciliated cells secrete mucus that traps heavy particles and microbes. The cilia of mucous-membrane cells move particles along the respiratory tract and up the throat to be swallowed. This mechanism is called the **mucociliary escalator**. Motion sweeps foreign particles out of the lungs and up the windpipe to be swallowed or expelled.

A human cilium is a structure looking like a hair and beating like a whip. In contrast, the cilium in *Paramecium* moves the cell much as an oar moves a boat. If the cell is stuck in the middle of a sheet of other cells, the beating cilium moves liquid over the surface of the stationary cell. The Creator made cilia for both jobs. The stationary cells lining the respiratory tract each have several hundred cilia. The large number of cilia beat in synchrony, much like the oars handled by slaves on a Roman galley ship, pushing mucus up to the throat for expulsion. The action removes air pollutants, cigarette particles, and pathogenic bacteria that, when inhaled, stick in the mucus.

Both cilia and flagella are complex molecular machines consisting of bundles of several microtubules and motor proteins encased in a flexible membrane. The pull of the motor proteins slides the microtubules past each other, causing the entire assembly to bend. They have both power strokes and recovery strokes that propel *Paramecium* in water. By beating rapidly back and forth like a fish's tail or a row of oars, a cell can swim rapidly through the water. Light microscopes have revealed thin hairs on some cells for over 200 years. The intricate, interlacing details of cilia, however, were not noticed until the advent of scanning electron microscopes. Micrographs revealed that the cilium is a complex structure of motor proteins and **microtubules,** which lie stiff and motionless without motor proteins, such as **nexin** and **dynein**. Furthermore, it requires linkers to tug on neighboring strands, converting the sliding motion into a bending motion, preventing the structure from falling apart. All these parts are required to perform one function: ciliary motion. Just as a mousetrap does not work unless all its constituent parts are present, ciliary motion does not exist in the absence of microtubules, connectors, and motors. Therefore, we conclude that a Darwinian explanation of chance mutations and natural selection is extremely inadequate to explain the origin of such a highly interdependent, intricate apparatus.

The cilium's molecular machine is a highly complex system, giving evidence of creation in its interwoven system of proteins. A swimming system requires a paddle to contact the water, a motor or energy source, and a connector to link the two. All systems that move by paddling, from protozoans to ships, will not work if any one of the interdependent parts is missing. The cilium is a member of this class of swimming systems. The microtubules are the paddles, contacting the water and pushing against it. The protein arms are the motors, supplying the force to move the system. The protein arms are the interlacing connectors, transmitting the force of the motor from one microtubule to its neighbor. The complexity and apparent design of the cilium is inherent in the task itself. It does not depend on the size of the system, whether it has to move a cell or move a ship — in order to paddle, several common parts are needed. This irreducibly complex system is strong evidence for intelligent design and an omniscient Creator.

Sporozoa

All members of this class are relatively small, non-motile organisms adapted to an exclusively parasitic life. Many have complicated life cycles, involving existence in two quite different hosts in succession. They all form reproductive spores at some time in their development — hence their name. Sporozoa may be found in practically every type of animal, living in blood cells, other tissues, or body cavities. Some produce no evident illness in their hosts, whereas others are responsible for some of the most severe and widespread of protozoan diseases. By far the most important pathogenic varieties are classified in the genus *Plasmodium*. These cause human malaria. Similar organisms infect monkeys and birds. The human disease is carried from person to person by the bite of infected *Anopheles* mosquitoes.

Malaria

Malaria literally means "bad air." This comes from the notion that people who lived near swamps breathed in foul-smelling air, later developing malaria. This concept was not far from the truth, in that mosquitoes are most abundant near swamps and shallow water. It would not be until the late 1800s that man would finally know the truth behind the cause of malaria. Sir Ronald Ross, physician and committed Christian, uncovered the mystery behind the connection between swamps, mosquitoes, and the *Plasmodium* parasite (Design Focus 4.3).

Malaria is an acutely infectious disease caused by protozoa of the genus *Plasmodium* (center) and transmitted from man to man only by *Anopheles* mosquitoes. It is one of the most common and widespread of all parasitic diseases. It would not be an exaggeration to call it the most important parasitic disease now suffered by humans. Malaria is especially frequent and severe in tropical and subtropical countries, but occurs in localized endemic areas throughout most of the world, annually responsible for an estimated one million deaths among children. Perhaps one in every ten people worldwide has had the disease sometime during life.

Malaria has played an important part in the history of nations, and is still so common that it constitutes one of the most serious drawbacks to the development of mankind in many places. Malaria, according to the latest research, has been around throughout recorded history. Secular biologists believe that malaria infections have been around for about 8,000 years, when agricultural practices began providing sufficiently sunlit pools for mosquito breeding and sufficient population densities for human hosts. Perhaps malaria proliferated after the global flood of Noah's day, a time period with more available standing water. There are an estimated 500 million cases of malaria worldwide, and about two million people a year die from it.

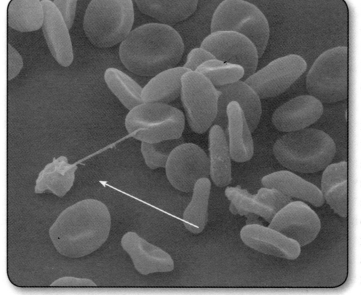

Scanning electron micrograph (SEM) of the gametocyte form of the Plasmodium falciparum protozoa

Symptoms and Forms of Malaria

Within human red blood cells, the merozoites undergo another series of transformations resulting in several gametocytes and thousands of new merozoites. In response to a biochemical signal, thousands of RBCs rupture simultaneously, releasing the parasites and their toxins. Now the excruciating malaria attack begins. First there are intense chills, with shivers and chattering teeth. The temperature then rises rapidly to 104°F, and the sufferer develops intense headache and delirium. After two to three hours, massive perspiration ends the last stage, and the patient often falls asleep, exhausted.

During this quiet period, the merozoites enter a new set of red blood cells and repeat the cycle of transformations. Malarial classification is based upon disease symptoms. The different time intervals between successive attacks of chills and fever in infections caused by different species of malaria parasites reflect the time required for the organisms to complete a cycle of development within the red blood cells. Four different species — *Plasmodium vivax, P. ovale, P. malariae,* and *P. falciparum* — cause malaria. *P. vivax* is the most common in the United States, and *P. falciparum* is the most severe form.

In the Human Host

Plasmodium grows by sexual reproduction in the *Anopheles* mosquito. When an *Anopheles* carrying the infective stage of *Plasmodium*, called a sporozoite, bites a human, sporozoites can be injected into the human. The blood carries the sporozoites to the liver, undergoing **schizogony** in liver cells and producing

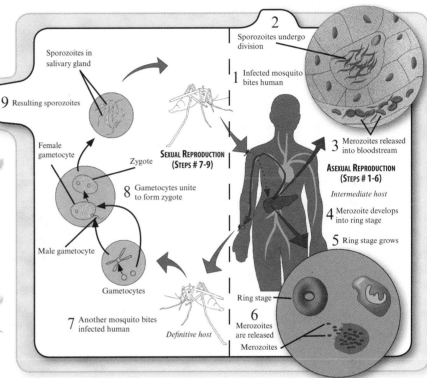

Life Cycle of Malaria Parasites

thousands of progeny called merozoites. Merozoites enter the bloodstream and infect red blood cells. The young trophozoite looks like a ring in which the nucleus and cytoplasm are visible. This is called a **ring stage**. The ring stage enlarges and divides repeatedly, and the red blood cells eventually rupture and release more merozoites. Upon release of the merozoites, their waste products, which cause fever and chills, are also released. Most of the merozoites infect new red blood cells and perpetuate the cycle of asexual reproduction. However, some develop into male and female sexual forms (gametocytes).

The Life Cycle of Malaria Parasites

All species of malaria organisms pass through the same life cycle. *Plasmodium* has a complex life cycle involving transmission between several hosts. This complex life cycle makes it difficult to develop a vaccine against malaria. There are two distinct phases: in the mosquito, where *Plasmodium* undergoes sexual reproduction; and in the human body, where *Plasmodium* undergoes asexual reproduction. A diagram summarizing the life cycle is given above right. The life cycles of the malarial parasites have three important stages: the **sporozoite**, the **merozoite**, and the **gametocyte**. Each is a factor in malaria. The mosquito sucks human blood and acquires gametocytes, the form of the protozoan found in red blood cells.

In the *Anopheles* Mosquito

Even though the gametocytes themselves cause no further damage, they can be picked up by the bite of another *Anopheles* mosquito; they then enter the mosquito's intestine and begin their sexual cycle. Here the male and female gametocytes unite to form a **zygote**. The zygote forms an oocyst, in which cell division occurs and asexual sporozoites are formed. When the oocyst ruptures, the sporozoites migrate to the mosquito's salivary glands. They can then be injected into a new human host by the biting mosquito. The mosquito is now a deadly vector of malaria.

The mosquito is the **definitive host** because it harbors the sexually reproducing stage of *Plasmodium*. The host where the parasite undergoes asexual reproduction (in this case, the human) is the **intermediate host**. It takes from 10 to 15 days for the development of the parasites within the mosquito; until these changes are complete, the insect is unable to infect human beings. Once the parasites have reached the salivary glands, however, a mosquito may infect many persons in succession over several weeks. The mosquito does not seem to be harmed in any way by the presence of the malaria parasites. A definite diagnosis of malaria is made when the parasites are found microscopically in blood smears. The malaria parasite is most easily identified by an "O" signet ring inside a red blood cell.

There is an amazing synchrony to the invasion and bursting of red blood cells. For reasons not fully understood, it seems that millions of infected blood cells burst simultaneously, releasing merozoites. It is this timed, en-masse slaughter of red blood cells that brings about the shakes. In all four kinds of infection, the symptoms are reccurring chills, fever, sweating, malaise, headache, and muscle pain — all looking like and often misdiagnosed as the flu. Rapid diagnosis followed by treatment with chloroquine or sulfa drugs, or both together, usually has excellent results, although some resistant strains are now developing in Asia, Africa, and the Amazon basin. In cases of high concentration of parasites or neurological dysfunction, intravenous quinidine gluconate is used, requiring hospitalization in an intensive care unit. Otherwise, oral chloroquine is usually enough to wipe out the disease after a week of treatment. Fear of malaria should not interrupt your plans for outdoor activity in the summer, at least if you live in the United States. Missionaries, beware!

Prevention of Malaria

The insecticides DDT, lindane, and dieldrin were of great value in controlling *Anopheles* mosquitoes during the mid-1900s. They were outlawed in the 1970s due to environmental concerns. They were efficient as pesticides when distributed as an oil spray from boats, as a dust or aerosol from airplanes, over water where the larval forms of the insects grow, and as agents for destroying or repelling adult mosquitoes within houses.

The success in controlling malaria in the United States and several other areas of the world has led to the hope of soon eradicating this disease worldwide. However, many problems remain, including those posed by the development of malaria parasites resistant to therapeutic drugs and mosquitoes relatively insensitive to available insecticides. The genomes for *Anopheles* and *Plasmodium* have been completed. There is hope that knowing the precise genetic code for both the vector and the parasite will lead to an effective vaccine against malaria. There is now a portfolio of approaches to controlling and treating malaria. Many scientists have hailed the genome work as a breakthrough in the war on malaria, predicting that data mined from the parasite, mosquito, and human genomes will yield new, effective drugs, insecticides, and vaccines. One new antimalarial, fosmidomycin, has already been developed by using *P. falciparum* genome data, and the preliminary results in animal tests have been promising.

Creation Scientist Focus 4.3

Ronald Ross: The Microbe Hunter That God Used to Discover the Cause of Malaria in Mosquitoes

Malaria may be responsible for more human suffering and death than anything in history. Only infectious diseases like tuberculosis, measles, plague, influenza, and smallpox compare with the deaths caused by malaria. For centuries, however, its mode of transmission was unknown. Although ideas were rampant in the 1800s, few agreed with Patrick Manson, who favored the hypothesis of transmission by mosquitoes. While on leave from the Indian Medical Service, Surgeon-Major Ronald Ross met Manson and got the idea that malaria was caused by a protozoan parasite. For several years, Ross worked during every spare minute, searching for the mosquito stages of malaria that he had become certain existed.

He dissected mosquitoes at random and also after allowing them to feed on malaria patients. He found many parasites, but none proved to be what he was searching for. Ross's first significant observation was that exflagellation normally occurs in the stomach of a mosquito, rather than in the blood as then thought. In his early efforts, he continued searching for further development of the parasite within the mosquito. Failing in this effort, he concluded that he had been working with the wrong kinds of mosquitoes (*Culex* and *Stegomyia*). After two years of work, he nearly gave up the cause. Though soon eligible for retirement, he was determined to try "one more desperate effort to solve the Great Problem." He toiled far into the nights, dissecting mosquitoes in a hot little office. One late evening, he dissected some "dapple-winged" mosquitoes (*Anopheles spp.*) that had fed on a malaria patient, and found some pigmented, spherical bodies in the walls of the insects' stomachs. The next day he dissected his last remaining specimen and found that the spheroid cells had grown. They were most certainly the malaria parasites! That night he penned in a notebook, "This day relenting God hath placed within my hand a wondrous thing, and God be praised. At this command, seeking His secret deeds with tears and toiling breath, find thy cunning seeds, Oh million-murdering Death."

He reported his discovery to Manson and immediately set about breeding the correct kind of mosquito in preparation for transmitting the disease from the insect to humans. Manson found similar organisms (*Plasmodium relictum*) in birds. He repeated his feeding experiments with mosquitoes, finding similar parasites when they fed on infected birds. He also found that the spheroid bodies ruptured, releasing thousands of tiny bodies that dispersed throughout the insect's body, including into the salivary glands. Through Manson, Ross reported to the world how malaria was transmitted by mosquitoes. Only a single experiment remained to prove the transmission to humans. Ross never did it. The authorities were so impressed with his work that they ordered Ross to work out the biology of Kala-azar in another part of India. This transfer seems to have broken his spirit, for he never really tried again to finish the study of malaria. The concentration had made him ill, his eyes were bothering him, and his microscope had rusted tight from his sweat. Besides, he was a physician, not a zoologist, and was most interested in learning how to prevent the disease, not in determining the finer points of the parasite's biology. This he considered done,

and he retired from the army. He was awarded the Nobel Prize in Medicine in 1902 and was knighted in 1911. He died in 1932 after a distinguished post-army career in education and research.

Several persons who were working on the life cycle of the parasite claimed credit for the discovery that pointed to the means of controlling malaria. There were many scientists who all made important contributions to the solution to the problem, but it was Ross who found the crucial clue that made all subsequent research on the subject "mere child's play which anyone could do after the clue was once obtained." Ronald Ross was a Christian physician who, through original investigation, earned high distinction and the Nobel Prize. His work traced the cycle of malaria through mosquito to man and back again. Though several parasitology books tell the story of Sir Ronald Ross, few tell that it was the Creator who led him to discover the cause of malaria. Few biologists and physicians today would use Ross's methods and say, "He is the Lord of light; He is the thing that is – He sends the seeing sight; And the right mind is his" (Graves, 1999, p. 153).

Yet more scientists might benefit if they, too, turned to the Creator to solve difficult scientific enigmas (Dan. 1:4; 2:30; 5:12, 16). Men of old who sought their Creator diligently have been rewarded with answers to perplexing problems in science and medicine.

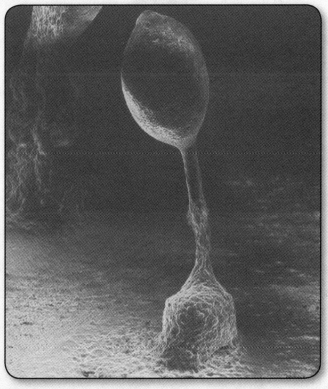

Slime mold of Dictyostellum

Subkingdom Myxobionta
Unusual Protista: Cellular Slime and Water Molds

In this chapter we also describe two fungal-like protozoan phyla, **Acrasiomyota** (cellular slime molds) and **Oomycota** (water molds). Plasmodial and cellular slime molds are small organisms that form abundant amounts of tenacious slime in their habitat. They resemble true fungi in basic physiology and morphology, but have a number of unique characteristics suggesting common design with certain protozoa and some algae. The slime and water molds appear thin, flexible, rod-shaped or spindle-shaped, about 10 μ long. There are no flagella, yet the organisms show active bending movements and a gliding or creeping type of motility.

Plasmodial and Cellular Slime Molds

The yellow, branching growth on the dead log is a protist called a **plasmodial slime mold.** These are common almost everywhere there is moist, decaying organic matter. They exist as solitary single cells and as organisms that grow to several centimeters in diameter. Large and branching as it is, the organism is not multicellular; it is a plasmodium, a single mass of cytoplasm, undivided by membranes and containing many nuclei. This is an amoeboid life stage extending pseudopodia for feeding on bacteria, yeasts, and bits of dead organic matter. Its web-like form is an adaptation that enlarges the organism's surface area, increasing its contact with food, water, and oxygen. Within the fine channels of the plasmodium, cytoplasm streams one way and then the other, in pulsing flows which are beautiful to watch with a microscope. The cytoplasmic streaming probably helps distribute nutrients and oxygen. (This "plasmodium" is not to be confused with the malaria-causing protozoan genus *Plasmodium*.)

Cellular slime molds form abundant amounts of tenacious slime where they are found living. They somewhat resemble bacteria in physiology and morphology, but also have a number of characteristics common to protozoans and even algae. They are a true "mosaic," like the duck-bill platypus (part mammal, bird, and reptile). The most studied cellular slime mold is *Dictyostellum*. It is a useful model for researchers studying the genetic mechanisms and chemical changes underlying cellular differentiation.

The most remarkable feature of these microbes is their habit, at a certain phase of their growth — the so-called swarm stage — to aggregate into large, flat, spreading masses of active cells (a pseudoplasmodium). In most species, this is followed by the appearance of fruiting bodies at different points in the slimy colony. These bodies may be nothing more than rounded, heaped-up mounds, while in other species an elaborate, pigmented, branched structure develops. The rods within the fruiting bodies become transformed into rounded, resting forms or oval, thick-walled microcysts resembling the chlamydospores of molds. After a period, in the presence of moisture, active vegetative cells emerge to form another swarm stage. Slime molds are present in surface soil, dung, compost, decaying leaves, wood, and other kinds of decomposing animal and vegetable matter. Some varieties have been recognized in natural waters. Their activity as saprophytes is important. Certain species can break down the cellulose in dead plant material or the chitin from the exoskeletons of insects. The slime bacteria can kill and digest other bacteria and grow on suspensions of living or heat-killed bacteria or other microbes. It is only in the past few years that slime molds have been studied intensively; their classification is tentative due to their puzzling traits.

Water Molds (Phycomycetes)

Phycomycetes are the common water molds that sometimes appear in goldfish aquariums and the related forms that parasitize water plants and fish. Water molds (Oomycota) share a common design with yellow-green and brown algae. Most of the 580 known types are key saprobic decomposers in aquatic habitats. Of these, many are free-living species that get nutrients from plant debris in ponds, lakes, and streams. Others live inside necrotic tissues of living plants. Some water molds parasitize aquatic organisms. The pale, cottony growths you may have seen on some aquarium fish are *Saprolengia,* mycelia of a parasitic type.

Most species of water molds produce an extensive mycelium, and some of its filaments differentiate into gamete-producing structures. At fertilization, a male and female gamete fuse, thus forming a diploid zygote that develops into a thick-walled resting spore. After germination, a new mycelium develops from the spore. Water molds also produce flagellated, asexual spores. Some water molds are major plant pathogens. For example, grapes with downy mildew have been attacked by *Plasmopara viticola*. Another pathogen seriously influenced human affairs. Over a century ago, Irish peasants grew potatoes as their main food crop. Between 1845 and 1860, growing seasons were cool and damp, and conditions encouraged the rapid spread of *Phytophthora infestans*. This water mold causes late blight, a rotting of potato (and tomato) plants. Its abundant spores were dispersed unimpeded through the watery film on the plants. Destruction was rampant. During a 15-year period, one-third of the Irish population starved to death, died during the secondary typhoid outbreak, or fled to the United States and other countries.

Algae and Its Divisions
The Algae: Subkingdom Phycobionta

Algae are classified, along with the protozoans and slime molds, in that complex group of Protista that are photosynthetic and aquatic. Most algae differ from true fungi and bacteria in that they contain chlorophyll, through which they carry out photosynthesis. Algae might be viewed as the Master's jewels of the sea — the Creator's filamentous, photosynthetic food for fish and ocean life.

Algae are widely distributed in nature, in sunny places on land and in water both fresh and salty, from the Arctic to the tropics. Algae vary from familiar green scum on the surface of quiet ponds to leafy weeds along the seashore and scaly film on tree trunks. Bulky seaweeds called kelp are found on large rocks along the Pacific coast. Algae have many scientific uses, like the Jell-O-like agar used in bacteriological culture media. Agar is derived from an algal seaweed of the genus *Gelicleum*.

Phytoplankton and Productivity

The importance of unicellular algae to society cannot be overstated. As the major type of simple sea life, unicellular algae comprise the microbial population known as phytoplankton (*phyto* refers to plants, and *planktos* is Greek for "wander," thus a "wandering community of plant life"). The phytoplankton live near the ocean surface and use solar energy during photosynthesis to generate most of the molecular oxygen available in the atmosphere. Virtually every animal on land or in the sea depends directly or indirectly on phytoplankton for food, and every animal on land and in the sea depends on the oxygen these algae produce to carry out metabolic activities. Phytoplankton species are among the most important members of oceanic food chains. Indeed, about half the world's organic matter is produced by phytoplankton.

Algae are photosynthetic eukaryotes; only a few phyla have heterotrophic members. Traditionally, Cyanobacteria were classified as blue-green algae and have been placed in the classification chapter because of their distinctiveness in kind, sharing features with Eubacteria and algae (kingdom Protista). They do have ecological and other features in common with eukaryotic algae. In some fresh-water springs, lakes, and oceans, they grow in abundance and account in part for the prolific, teeming aquatic life. The most productive of all ecosystems in the world are coral atolls, where algae grow in symbiotic association with coral zooxanthellae.

In their diverse colors, they are the Creator's colorful provision for ocean life. Like plants, all algae have **chlorophyll A**. Their classification reflects their designed relationships among algal phyla. Although they share a lot in common, they differ in:

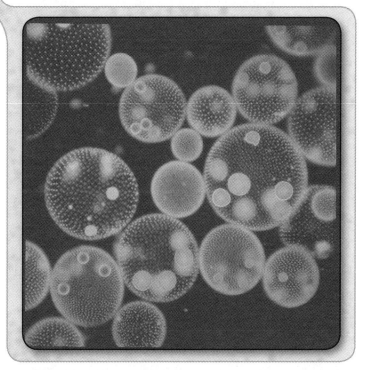

Colony of Volvox

1. Accessory pigments like carotenoids, xanthophylls, phycobilins, and other forms of chlorophyll.
2. Chloroplast structure.
3. Cell-wall chemistry.
4. Number, type, and position of flagella.
5. Food-storage product.

Algae are relatively simple, photoautotrophic, aquatic organisms. These organisms have been classified in various kingdoms including Monera, Protista, and Plantae. Because botanists have traditionally made algal classification, major algae groups will be called **division(s),** the equivalent to the zoological term **phylum** (plural **phyla**). Divisions, the taxonomic equivalent of phylum, are used by botanists more than by zoologists (see Table 4.1).

Greatly significant ecologically, algae account for about 50 percent of global photosynthetic production of organic material. They are the Sustainer's provision for the base of the food chain. Algae come in different forms, including fresh water and marine plankton, and intertidal seaweeds that form the basis of aquatic food webs. They are commonly classified according to chlorophyll pigments and cellular composition. Many algae are unicellular, some are filamentous, others live in colonies such as *Volvox* (previous page), others are multicellular. Dinoflagellates, golden-brown algae (diatoms), and some green algae are generally unicellular. Other green algae are multicellular, but relatively small compared to seaweeds, multicellular marine algae including brown algae (e.g., kelp forests) in cold ocean waters and red algae in warm-water reefs.

Algae are important for more than the oxygen they produce. They are also a major food source for many aquatic organisms. In addition, humans have found many uses for algae. Japanese people cultivate it as a food crop. In New England and Hawaii, certain types of marine algae are eaten as vegetables. Other algae are used as food additives. For example, a substance extracted from a species commonly called Irish moss is used to thicken such things as Jell-O, pudding, and ice cream. In addition, algae can be used as a natural fertilizer. Finally, many useful products like potash, iodine, nitrogen, vitamins, and minerals can be made from processed algae.

The cells making up plants usually have walls made of cellulose. Since green algae have cell walls similar to plants and chlorophyll like most plants, some biologists actually consider them plants and place them in kingdom Plantae. Most biological classification schemes tend to place them in kingdom Protista, though, because they are microscopic and tend to exist as individual cells or simple colonies of cells. (Though many algae exist as individual cells, most form simple colonies held together with slime). A few species form highly complex colonies. A colony of algae is often called a **thallus** (plural is thalli), but that term actually has a much broader definition. A thallus is the body of a plant-like organism not divided into leaves, roots, or stems. Algal colonies are called thalli because they function like a big plant, but with no distinct parts, just one big mass of algae.

Algae, whether in colonies or existing as individuals, have both asexual and sexual reproduction at their disposal. This is one reason for their abundance in aquatic environments. In fact, in ideal conditions, algae reproduce so rapidly that they essentially "take over" their habitat, making the water appear the same color as the algae itself. This is referred to as an algal bloom. Now that you've had a general introduction to algae, let's examine each individual phylum so we can learn more about this interesting subkingdom of Protista.

Division Chlorophyta (Green Algae)

Members of division Chlorophyta are mostly found in fresh water, though some marine species do exist. The most visible feature of these algae is their green chlorophyll pigment. Thus, they are often called green algae. Just like *Euglena*, members of this phylum store their chlorophyll in organelles called chloroplasts. Despite their name, most Chlorophyta also have a yellowish pigment called carotenoid, making them appear yellowish-green.

The other distinguishing feature of this phylum is that its members have cell walls made of cellulose, a substance composed of certain types of sugar and common in the cell walls of many organisms.

Chlamydomonas

A small, actively moving little alga, *Chlamydomonas* (next page) commonly inhabits quiet, fresh-water pools and typically represents green algae (Chlorophyta). *Chlamydomonas* is unicellular, with a slightly oval cell surrounded by a complex, multi-layered wall partially composed of glycoproteins. Two whiplike flagella at one end pull the cell rapidly through the water. The flagella are difficult to see with ordinary light microscopes. The cell itself is usually less than 25 μm long, which is, however, more than three times larger than a human red blood cell. Near the base of the flagella are two or more vacuoles that contract and expand, apparently regulating the water content of the cell.

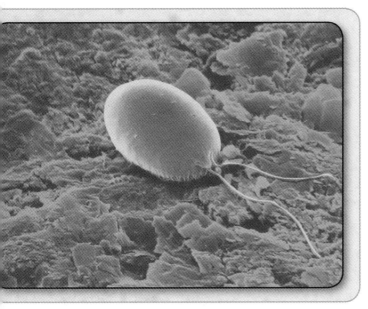

Chlamydomonas

A dominant feature of each *Chlamydomonas* is a single, usually cup-shaped chloroplast at least partially hiding the centrally located nucleus. One or two roundish pyrenoids are located in each chloroplast. Pyrenoids are protein structures thought to contain enzymes associated with synthesizing starch. Most species also have a red eyespot on the chloroplast near the base of the flagella. The eyespot is sensitive to light; it is, however, merely part of an organelle within a single cell and is in no way complex and multicellular like an eye.

Asexual Reproduction

Before a *Chlamydomonas* reproduces asexually, the cell's flagella degenerate and drop off or reabsorb. Then the nucleus divides by mitosis, and the entire cell contents become two cells within the cell wall. The two daughter cells develop flagella, escape, and swim away as the parent cell wall breaks down. Once grown to full size, they may repeat the process. Sometimes mitosis occurs more than once, so that 4, 8, or up to 32 little cells with flagella are produced inside the parent cell. Occasionally, flagella do not develop, and the cells remain together in a colony. When growth conditions change, however, each cell in the colony may develop flagella and swim away. This type of reproduction brings about no changes in the number of chromosomes present in the nucleus, all cells remaining haploid.

Sexual Reproduction

Under certain combinations of light, temperature, and other unknown environmental forces, many cells in a *Chlamydomonas* population may congregate together. Careful study has revealed that pairs of cells appear to be attracted to each other by their flagella and function as gametes, sometimes of two types. The cell walls break down as the protoplasts slowly emerge and mate, fusing together and forming zygotes. A new wall, often relatively thick and ornamented with little bumps, forms around each zygote. This may remain dormant for several days, weeks, or even months, but under favorable conditions, a dramatic change occurs. The cell contents, now diploid, undergo meiosis, producing four haploid zoospores (motile cells that do not unite with other cells; many different kinds of algae produce zoospores). When the old zygote wall breaks down, the zoospores swim away and grow into full-sized *Chlamydomonas* cells.

Spirogyra

A distinctly designed green algae is called *Spirogyra*. Members of this genus get their name and unusual appearance from their spiral chloroplasts. They form colonies of slender, chain-like threads of cells. These colonies, called **filaments,** can become up to two feet long surrounding the filaments. Examination with a microscope reveals a beautiful alga with some of the most striking chloroplasts known. These common freshwater algae, consisting of unbranched filaments of cylindrical cells, frequently float in masses at the surface of quiet waters. Each cell contains one or more long, frilly, ribbon-shaped chloroplasts that look as though spirally wrapped around an invisible pole (vacuole) occupying most of the cell's interior. Some species of *Spirogyra* have as many as 16 of these chloroplasts in each cell. Every one of these elegant green ribbons has pyrenoids at regular intervals throughout its length.

Asexual reproduction. Unlike the two algae just discussed, no zoospores or other cells with flagella are produced by *Spirogyra*. Any cell is capable of dividing, but the only **asexual reproduction** resulting in new filaments occurs through the breakup, or fragmentation, of existing filaments. This is frequently a result of a storm or other ocean disturbance.

Sexual reproduction. In *Spirogyra* colonies, the filaments usually are produced so close to each other that they may actually touch. When **sexual reproduction** begins, the individual cells of adjacent filaments form little, dome-shaped bumps, or papillae (singular, papilla), opposite each other. As these papillae grow, they force the filaments apart slightly, then the papillae fuse at their tips, forming small cylindrical conjugation tubes between each pair of cells. The condensed protoplasts then function as gametes. Usually, those of one filament seem to flow or crawl like amoebae through the conjugation tubes to the adjacent cells, where each fuses with the stationary gamete, forming a zygote. Each moving protoplast is considered a male gamete; the stationary ones function as female gametes.

Thick walls usually develop around the zygotes, which remain dormant for some time, often over the winter. Thick-walled zygotes are characteristic of most freshwater green algae. Eventually, their cell contents undergo meiosis, producing four haploid cells. Three of these disintegrate, and a single new *Spirogyra* filament grows from the interior of the old zygote shell. The type of sexual reproduction seen in *Spirogyra* is called **conjugation.** Would any evolutionist say that these green algae descend from bacteria that undergo conjugation? Unlikely! It is a parallel design by the One who has intelligently designed diverse, discontinuous kinds.

Phylum Chrysophyta (Golden Algae)

Though green algae are responsible for a large portion of the photosynthesis on the planet, the greatest oxygen producers are in phylum *Chrysophyta*. This phylum contains many different species collectively called diatoms, a unique type of algae with a cell wall composed of silicon dioxide, the principal component of glass. This makes their cell walls very hard, providing excellent protection. The cell wall is so hard that it remains long after the diatom dies. When the cell-wall remains of many dead diatoms clump together, they form a crumbly, abrasive substance called **diatomaceous earth.** The silica walls act as microscopic shells or "glass houses" for the tiny organisms. The cell wall is made

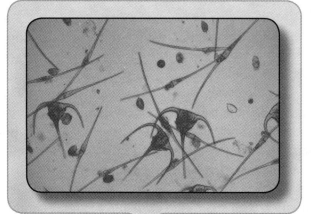

Dinoflagellates

of two almost-equal halves called **valves** (*diatom* is Greek for "cut in two"). Diatoms have an almost infinite variety of shapes and sizes, like snowflakes, and have intricate designs. Their design is evidence that the Creator is a Divine Artist painting beauty in the earth's rivers, lakes, and oceans.

Huge deposits of diatomaceous earth exist in most of the world. Many creation scientists think these deposits were laid down in the worldwide flood described in the Bible (Gen. 6–9). This makes sense, because the catastrophic nature of the Flood would have killed huge numbers of organisms, including diatoms. The currents caused by the flood would then have tended to sweep the remains of the diatoms together in one place. Interestingly enough, scientists who do not believe in the Bible have no real explanation for these huge deposits of diatomaceous earth.

Diatomaceous earth is actually quite useful. Large amounts are used by industry to filter liquids. It is also used as an abrasive, including in toothpaste as a cleaner and polisher.

Although diatoms make up a large part of phylum Chrysophyta, other organisms belong to this phylum. The genus *Dynobryon*, for example, is an alga that forms colonies typically containing a few special cells called **holdfasts** designed to hold onto objects in the water such as rocks. A holdfast is a special structure used by an organism to anchor itself by forming long strands that attach to a surface in the water and act like an anchor. The colony is then not at the mercy of the currents. A colony using holdfasts is called a **sessile colony**.

Phylum Pyrrophyta (Dinoflagellates)

Phylum Pyrrophyta contains a group of single-celled creatures often called dinoflagellates. Their name is derived from the fact that most species have two flagella of unequal length. The image on the previous page shows a magnified image of a dinoflagellate. Notice the two flagella of unequal length on the bottom of the organism. Some of these organisms are heterotrophic and some photosynthetic, and mostly inhabit marine waters. Like green algae, their cell walls are composed of cellulose. Photosynthetic dinoflagellates are an important source of food for many aquatic organisms, including other forms of plankton. The most important thing to remember about the dinoflagellates, however, is that certain species (*Gymnodinium brevis*, for example) frequently bloom in nutrient-rich waters. Because the species are reddish-brown, their bloom tends to turn the sea red around them. As a result, these blooms are often called red tide.

Non-motile dinoflagellates are interwoven with mollusks, sponges, and corals. They live symbiotically, providing each other important benefits. These dinoflagellates lack cellulose plates and flagella, and are called **zooxanthellae**. The most ecologically important zooxanthellae are those living with corals. Coral atolls are among the most productive areas of the world in terms of energy and bioenergetics in an ecosystem. This is mainly due to the zooxanthellae living inside of corals. The nutritive needs of coral are supplied in part by the prey on which it feeds and by its algal symbionts. A large portion of the carbon fixed by algae in photosynthesis is passed to the coral. The food caught by the coral probably supplies both coral and algae with nitrogen, which is then cycled back and forth between the two.

The zooxanthellae can also obtain inorganic nutrient ions directly from sea water. But in nutrient-poor water characterizing most coral reefs, the contribution of coral feeding to the zooxanthellae is probably important. The symbiosis also facilitates the deposition of the coral skeleton, because corals deprived of algae or kept in the dark deposit calcium carbonate much more slowly than under normal conditions. The degree to which the coral depends on the algae varies by species and even within species populations. The nutrients supplied by zooxanthellae make it possible for the corals to grow and reproduce quickly enough to create reefs. Zooxanthellae provide the corals with food in the form of photosynthetic products. In turn, the coral protects the zooxanthellae and gives them access to light. Because of the need for light, corals containing zooxanthellae only live in ocean waters less than 100 meters (328 ft.) deep. They also only live in waters above 20°C (68°F), and are intolerant of low salinity and high turbidity. The most common zooxanthellae are the species *Symbiodinium microadriaticum*.

Red tides are deadly to other marine creatures. Hundreds of thousands of fish can be killed in a single bloom of *Gymnodinium brevis*, because these organisms emit a toxin. Under normal conditions, there are few enough dinoflagellates that the toxin never reaches levels dangerous to marine creatures. During a dinoflagellate bloom, however, the toxin reaches deadly proportions. Interestingly enough, though fish and most other marine life find red tides deadly, the toxin does not affect some invertebrates like clams, oysters, and mollusks. Unfortunately, the toxin does build up in their bodies. As a result, heterotrophs that eat clams, oysters, or mollusks exposed to a red tide can become poisoned. Many human deaths can be attributed to eating clams, oysters, or mollusks exposed to red tides. This is why seafood restaurants refuse to serve these dishes when a red tide occurs in the area from which they get their supplies.

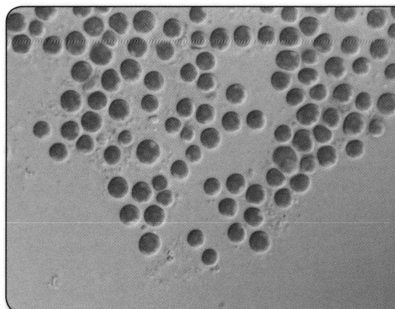

Red Algae

Rhodophyta (Red Algae)

The Rhodophyta (red algal phylum) are mostly marine seaweeds (above), but a few live in fresh water or on land. They often occur at greater depths than the brown algae. Most are multicellular and attached to the substratum, but a few species are unicellular. No red algae attain the large sizes often seen in brown algae. These algae are red because they contain a unique light-absorbing pigment called **phycoerythrin**. In addition to chlorophyll A, found in all photosynthetic organisms except photosynthetic bacteria, Rhodophyta often possess chlorophyll D, not found in any other group of plants. They also contain phycocyanin and phycoerythrin.

The phycoerythrins give many of these algae their characteristic reddish color. It should be emphasized, however, that "red algae" are not always red; many are black.

Rhodophyta are often called red algae because of their strikingly red color. People often confuse these algae with dinoflagellates because they know that dinoflagellates cause red tides. The only thing the red algae have in common with dinoflagellates, however, is color. Like brown algae, members of phylum Rhodophyta are multicellular. Unlike brown algae, however, they tend to live in warm marine waters, not cold. The cell walls contain cellulose and large quantities of mucilaginous material. The reserve product is not starch but a similar polysaccharide. Red algae are an important source of commercial colloids. For example, they are used in culturing bacteria, as a suspending agent in chocolate milk and puddings, and as a stabilizer in ice cream. This compound is often called **floridean starch**, a moisture retainer used in icings, creams, and marshmallows. These algae are a source of agar that is often a food source. Agar has long been used as a thickener in foods such as jellies and ice cream.

Agar is a complex polysaccharide derived from these marine algae. It has some very important properties making it valuable to microbiology; no satisfactory substitute has ever been found. Few microbes can degrade agar, so it remains solid. Also, agar liquefies at about 1,000°C (1,832°F), and at sea level it remains liquid until the temperature drops to about 40°C (104°F). For lab use, agar is held in water baths at about 50°C (122°F). At this temperature, it does not injure most bacteria when poured. Once the agar has solidified, it can be incubated at a temperature approaching 100°C (212°F) before again liquefying. This property is particularly useful when growing thermophilic bacteria. Agar media are usually contained in test tubes (as slants) or Petri dishes (culture plates).

The life cycles of red algae are usually very complex. There is commonly some sort of alteration of generations. Flagellated cells never occur; even the sperm cells lack flagella, and most are carried to the egg cells by water currents. They commonly attach to rocks or other plants, are buried in sand or one's soup, attach to animals, or drift. Still others are epiphytic like *Porphyra nereocystis,* which grows on top of bullwhip kelp (*Nereocystis*). *Porphyra* is served as **nori**, which, when wrapped around sushi, is the seaweed in which uncooked fish is wrapped at a sushi bar.

Phaeophyta (Brown Algae)

Phaeophyta is comprised of multicellular organisms that inhabit cold ocean waters. Members of phylum Phaeophyta, also called brown algae (*phaeo* = dusky), look a lot like plants. In fact, some biologists classify them as such. Most biologists, however, still think they have more in common with algae than with plants, so we classify them in kingdom Protista, subkingdom Algae. Contrary to popular belief, some brown seaweeds are black in color and are often easily mistaken for red algae. A rule of thumb is if it looks brown, then it probably is a brown. If your eyes often deceive you, one way to distinguish a brown from a red is to conduct a quick, rather inexpensive test. Take some alga and rub it on your face. If your face is full of mucilage after ten seconds, it is probably a brown. Brown algae constitute approximately 20 percent of the total number of species along the California coast. In southern and northern California they form extensive bands of rock in intertidal and subtidal areas called kelp forests. They form beautiful forests in the sea.

Giant Kelp Macrocytis

Brown algae are most common along rocky coasts in cooler parts of the oceans, normally growing attached to the bottom in littoral (intertidal) zones. They may be seen abundantly covering exposed rock at low tide along the New England coast. A few species occur in warmer seas, some differing from the majority of brown algae by being able to live and grow when detached from the substratum. Some *Sargassum spp.* form dense, floating mats that cover some 2.5 million square miles of ocean in the Sargasso Sea between the West Indies and North Africa.

All brown algae are multicellular and most macroscopic, some growing as long as 150 feet or more. The **thallus** (plant body) may be a filament or a large, complex 3-D structure. The latter type of thallus has apparently arisen several times independently; in some species developing from interwoven, tightly compacted filaments, and in others resulting from cell divisions in more than one plane. The individual cells are much like those of higher land plants, having cellulose cell walls with pits through which **plasmodesmata** (cell stitching) pass, as well as having large central vacuoles, usually several plastids, and no pyrenoids. However, unlike the cells of most higher land plants, they usually have centrioles.

Like all photosynthetic protists, Phaeophyta possess chlorophyll A. However, they have chlorophyll C instead of the chlorophyll B found in Euglenoids, green algae, and higher land plants. Large amounts of a xanthophyll carotenoid called fucoxanthin are also present. This gives these algae their characteristic brownish color. A variety of unusual carbohydrates are synthesized and used as structural or storage materials.

Reproduction may be either asexual or sexual, the latter often involving specialized multicellular sex organs. These sex organs are called **antheridia** if producing male gametes, **oogonia** if female gametes, or **gametangia** if all the gametes are alike (i.e., the plant is isogamous). In brown algae, the sex organs are ordinarily not enclosed by a protective layer of sterile jacket cells. The life cycle usually features an alternation of **gametophyte** (haploid) and **sporophyte** (diploid) multicellular generations. In forms like *Laminaria*, the haploid gametophyte is reduced, and the diploid sporophyte is much larger and more prominent. In forms like *Fucus*, reduction of the haploid stages has progressed so far that there is no longer any multicellular haploid gametophyte, with the only haploid cells in the life cycle being the gametes. Such a life cycle, very rare in plants, is essentially the sort seen in animals. *Fucus* is an unusual-looking alga growing in upper intertidal zones. The inflated ends are called **receptacles,** which house reproductive parts, eggs, and sperm.

The most commonly known genus within Phaeophyta is *Macrocytis* (opposite page). Species within this genus are called kelp or seaweed, though those terms also seem to be used for many species within phylum Phaeophyta. Kelp and most members of Phaeophyta form holdfasts that allow them to anchor themselves to rocks at the bottom of the ocean. Some kelp can reach lengths of up to 100 feet! Kelp is cultivated as a vegetable in many cultures. Species in genus *Fucus* are often called **rockweed.** These algae are thick and feel leathery. They live in shallow waters along the shoreline, and are generally one to two feet long. One interesting structure on this kind of algae is the air bladder, which can fill with air to allow the organism to float on top of the water. You can see the air bladders on the *Fucus*, they look like brownish bulbs.

Ice cream, pudding, salad dressing, and jellybeans are products made from brown algae. One unique characteristic of the organisms in this phylum is that their cell walls contain alginic acid, commonly called **algin.** This substance is extracted from brown algae and used as a thickening agent in the foods described above. In addition, you can find algin in cough syrup, toothpaste, cosmetics, paper, and floor polish.

DesignFocus 4.4

Algae as the Great Producers of the World's Energy: Algae Energy Flow at Silver Springs

Modern ecology really started with the work of scientist Dr. Howard T. Odum in Florida in the 1950s and 1960s. He was the first biologist to study communities of living things "in the place where they lived." He tried to determine exactly how they interacted, especially trying to find out how energy moved between them. He went to Silver Springs Lake in Florida and directly measured the living material (calories of biomass) developed in a single square meter of the lake in a year for each level:

Level	Amount of Energy	(kCal)
IV	Top Carnivores	21
III	Carnivores	383
II	Herbivores	3,368
I	Producers	20,810

In 1957, he found Silver Springs to be the most productive ecosystem in the continental United States. It is even more productive than the redwood forests of California or the Everglades in south Florida. Other large fresh-water springs in Florida, like Wakulla Springs, have similar productivity measurements. Only coral atolls have higher average productivity. Why such high productivity? The answer may surprise you: algae. Not only is the high productivity in fresh-water springs due to algae, but the base of the food chain in coral atolls is also dependent upon it.

The main reasons for this high productivity are the ultra-clean spring water (visibility greater than 100 feet in some places), abundance of phytoplankton, and the fast-growing algae *Hydrodictyon*. *Hydrodictyon*, the "water net," consists of elongated cells joined at their ends to make polygonal shapes beautifully designed by the Master Weaver. The water net grows on top and is interwoven with large native aquatic plants like *Sagittaria* and exotic plants like *Hydrilla*. *Hydrodictyon* is green algae interwoven with aquatic plants and logs, forming non-motile colonies. Under favorable conditions, it forms large surface blooms in ponds, lakes, and gentle streams. Each colony consists of large, cylindrical cells arranged in the form of a large, lacy, hollow cylinder. Initially uninucleate, each cell eventually becomes multinucleate. At maturity, each cell contains a large central vacuole and peripheral cytoplasm containing the nuclei and a large reticulate chloroplast with numerous pyrenoids. *Hydrodictyon* reproduces asexually by forming large numbers of uninucleate, biflagellated zoospores in each cell in the net. The zoospores are not released from parental cells but, rather amazingly, group themselves into geometric arrays of four to nine (most typically six) within the cylindrical parent cell. Zoospores then lose their flagella and form the component cells of daughter mini-nets. These are eventually released from the parent cell and grow into large mature nets by dramatic cell enlargement. In view of this mode of reproduction, it is easy to see how *Hydrodictyon* forms such conspicuous blooms in nature.

An energy pyramid shows how usable energy diminishes as it flows through an ecosystem. Sunlight enters the pyramid base (first trophic level) and diminishes through successive levels to its tip (the top carnivores). Energy pyramids have a large energy base at the bottom. Energy flows into food webs of ecosystems from an outside source, usually the sun. Energy leaves ecosystems mainly by losses of metabolic heat, which each organism generates. Gross primary productivity is an ecosystem's total rate of photosynthesis during a specified interval. The net amount is the rate at which primary producers store energy in tissues in excess of their rate of aerobic respiration. Heterotrophic consumption affects the rate of energy storage. The loss of metabolic heat and the shunting of food energy into organic wastes means that usable energy flowing through consumer trophic levels declines at each energy transfer.

Energy Flow at Silver Springs

Odum's energy-flow study at Silver Springs became famous. It summarizes the data from a long-term study of a food web in this aquatic ecosystem. Given the metabolic demands of organisms and the amount of energy lost in their organic wastes, only about 6 to 16 percent of the energy entering one trophic level becomes available for organisms at the next level. Because the efficiency of the energy transfers is so low, most ecosystems can support no more than four consumer trophic levels. Sometimes six trophic levels can be observed in aquatic springs in Florida during highly productive years. Most of the primary producers in this small spring are algae, in association with aquatic plants. Most of the carnivores are insects and small fish; the top carnivores are larger fish. The original energy source, sunlight, is available all year long, with a high percentage trapped in the plants due to high visibility in the water — sometimes over 100 feet!

The producers trapped 1.2 percent of the incoming solar energy, and only a little more than a third of that amount became fixed in new plant biomass (4,245 + 3,368). The producers used more than 63 percent of the fixed energy for their own metabolism. About 16 percent of the fixed energy was transferred to the herbivores, most of this being used for metabolism or transferred to detritivores and decomposers. Of the energy transferred to herbivores, only 11.4 percent reached the next trophic level (carnivores). Carnivores used all but about 5.5 percent, which was transferred to top carnivores. By the end of the specified time interval, all 20,810 kilocalories of energy that had been transferred through the system appeared as metabolically generated heat. Bear in mind that this energy-flow diagram is oversimplified, because no community is isolated from others. New individual organisms and substances continually drop from overhead leaves and branches into the springs. Also, organisms and substances are slowly lost by way of a stream that leaves the spring.

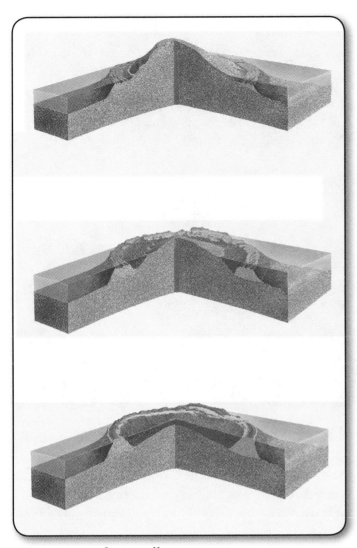

Formation of an atoll

The highest productivity in the world belongs to coral reefs atolls (above). Atolls are sunken volcanic regions. The coral provides an example of a symbiotic relationship, in which neither partner can live without the other. The tiny zooxanthellae living within its tissue help coral make calcium carbonate. Zooxanthellae are dinoflagellates (single-celled algae) within coral tissues. The zooxanthellae also make food for the coral by photosynthesis. The zooxanthellae in turn get both nutrients and a place to live. This association may illustrate the original design for how two different living organisms were meant to live in harmony.

In conclusion, when someone asks you what are the most energy-productive systems in the world, you can tell them it is neither the redwoods of California, nor the crispy-cool Boreal Forests of Canada, nor the forests of the Smoky Mountains. All these are beautiful places with large trees made by the Creator. Yet an unexpected design in God's living creation is among the smallest living organisms. The least are among the greatest. It is algae woven by the Master Craftsman — small, but mighty!

Summary and Conclusions

In summary, the kingdom Protista is made of three major groups of living organisms with no common ancestry. These include protozoans, slime molds, and algae. Protozoans are one-celled, eukaryotic organisms mostly feeding on bacteria and small particulate nutrients. They are classified largely on the basis of their means of motility. These include ciliates, amoebae, flagellates (Euglenoids and Archeazoans), and sporozoans. Slime molds have both fungal and animal characteristics, and are classified as protists. Cellular slime molds resemble amoebae during one stage. When conditions are unfavorable for growth, large numbers of amoeboid cells aggregate to form a single structure called a slug. Plasmodial (acellular) slime molds are a mass of protoplasm called a plasmodium. The entire plasmodium moves like a giant amoeba, engulfing organic debris and bacteria. Cytoplasmic streaming apparently distributing oxygen and nutrients can be observed in these slime molds. Algae are photosynthetic autotrophs — that is, they use light to convert atmospheric CO_2 into carbohydrates for energy. Oxygen is a byproduct of photosynthesis. Productivity on earth depends largely upon algae. In freshwater springs, algae like *Hydrodictyon* contribute greatly to aquatic productivity; in the ocean, plankton and dinoflagellates create high productivity in coral reefs. Algae vary from single cells to kelp 50 meters (164 ft.) in length. Algal types include green algae, brown algae, red algae, dinoflagellates, and diatoms.

In conclusion, it should be obvious that most protists are among the "small but mighty." Most are invisible to the unaided eye, but are ubiquitous. They are mighty in their ecological and economic significance. Due to their irreducible complexity, protists are no longer called simple organisms. Evolutionary biologists suggest that the kingdom Plantae evolved from ancestors of plant-like protists while Animalia evolved from ancestors of the protozoa. However, it is noteworthy that most protists have a cellular structure and metabolism more diversified and complex than any single cell of a complex plant or complex animal.

Chapter Five

Fungi: Recyclers of Nutrients and Sources of Treasures

Fungi are the Creator's recycling bins for decomposition and provide valuable nutrients in the natural world. Nutrients like those involved in the carbon and nitrogen cycle are critical for life to be sustained. Some might see them as Providence's source of antibiotics. Still other creation biologists might view fungi as life designed to digest and decompose organic matter. These relatively large, plant-like organisms make up that division of chlorophyll-free microbes ordinarily referred to when we use the term fungi. Fungi include the varieties of mushrooms, yeasts, and molds. Fungi are heterotrophic and generally derive their nutrition by extracellular digestion and then absorption of organic matter. Heterotrophic decomposers include lichens, those that live in partnership with other life forms, and those that are parasitic. Detailed study of these microbes is the science of mycology. A disease caused by a fungus is called a mycosis, or a mycotic disease, also a fungous disease. The great practical importance of the fungi, in nature, in industry, and in medicine, will become clear in this chapter.

Fungi Are Different from Plants

Historically, John Ray, Carolus Linnaeus, and others considered fungi as plants. This classification system was used until the 1960s. Plants, as recorded in Genesis 1, may have included fungi (fungi are not mentioned); however, the definitions of fungi and plants have changed since the 1970s due to cellular and molecular distinctions. About 100,000 species of fungi have been named and identified, and scientists estimate another 200,000 are waiting to be discovered. After the 1660s, when fungi were first described by Robert Hooke, a creation scientist, these microbes were collected and studied by botanists who considered them simple plants. In fact, until the late-1900s, those wishing to study fungi typically enrolled in botany, though it was clear fungi do not have photosynthetic pigments. Although fungi have traditionally been included in the plant kingdom, they lack chlorophyll and resemble plants only in their general appearance and lack of mobility. Significant differences between fungi and plants include at least the following five features:

1. Fungi are heterotrophs. Perhaps most obviously, a mushroom is not green. Virtually all plants are photosynthesizers, while no fungi have chlorophyll or carry out photosynthesis. Instead, fungi obtain their food by secreting digestive enzymes onto the substrate,

and then absorbing the organic molecules that are released by the enzymes.

2. Fungal cell walls are made of chitin, the same tough material an arthropod (grasshopper or crab) shell is made of and polysaccharides. The cell walls of plants are made of cellulose, also a strong building material.

3. Fungi have unusual reproductive modes. Some plants have motile sperm with flagella. No fungi have this feature. Most fungi reproduce sexually with nuclear exchange rather than with gamete exchange the way plants do.

4. Fungi have nuclear mitosis. Mitosis in fungi is different from that in plants or most other eukaryotes in one key respect: the nuclear envelope does not break down and reform. Instead, mitosis takes place within the nucleus. A spindle apparatus forms there, dragging chromosomes to opposite poles of the nucleus (not the cell, as in most other eukaryotes).

5. Fungi have filamentous bodies. Fungi are basically filamentous in their growth form (that is, their bodies consist of long slender filaments called hyphae), even though these hyphae may be packed together to form complex structures like the mushroom. Plants, in contrast, are made of several types of cells organized into tissues and organs.

There are more cellular differences between these two kingdoms, but already the message is quite clear: Fungi are not plants. The many morphological and molecular distinctions of each group are strong evidence that fungi are different from plants; they are therefore not related to plants or any other group of organisms. DNA studies confirm significant differences from other eukaryotes.

Classification of Fungi

In their systematic classification of the fungi, mycologists do not recognize "yeasts" or "molds" as distinctly separated fungal groups. Everyone, however, knows what is meant by a mold, in the popular sense of the term. Common molds are the most familiar of all the microbes to the layman. Who has not seen moldy food, or moldy grain? To the naked eye, molds may appear like a tuft of cotton, or a sooty black patch, or a fuzzy or powdery mass, variously colored. Most often fungi are found growing on old, moist bread, jellies, fruits, or other foods. They often develop branched filaments, and they characteristically multiply by budding.

TABLE 5.1 Divisions of the True Fungi (Eumycota)

1. *Zygomycota*	asexual spores (sporangiospores) formed in a closed structure (sporangium); produce zygospores (a kind of sexual spore). Septate mycelium (when present). Examples include *Rhizopus* and other bread molds.
2. *Ascomycota*	reproduce most commonly by asexual spores (conidia), but all are capable of forming sexual spores at times (ascospores) in a specially developed little sac (ascus). Examples include sponge mushrooms and yeasts.
3. *Basidiomycota*	sexual spores borne on special club-like stalks (basidia). Examples include gill mushrooms, smuts, and rusts.
4. *Deuteromycota* (*Anamorphs*)	no sexual spores; reproduce by various types of asexual spores, including blastospores (budding). These are also called *Fungi Imperfecti*. Examples include *Penicillium, Aspergillus.*
5. *Chytridiomycota* (Uniflagellate water molds)	no sexual spores; reproduce only asexually through the production of zoospores within a spherical cell. The zygote is commonly converted into a resting spore. They have a mixture of fungal and protozoan traits. One example is *Chytridium.*

The classification of the fungi is based largely upon their reproductive structures called spores. In addition, they are classified on the anatomy of these microbes by the character of the hyphae and mycelium (if present). Some of these features are given in Table 5.1.

One of the principal reasons why the terms "mold" and "yeast" are not given the status of distinct taxonomic groups of fungi is the fact that many varieties of the fungi are both yeast-like and mold-like at different phases of their growth. This double form (dimorphism) is especially common among disease-producing fungi of the division *Fungi Imperfecti*. For example, the organism causing blastomycosis occurs at 37° C as thick-walled, budding, yeast-like cells, but at room temperature (23° C) it grows as a mold-like filament.

Spores

In mycology the term "spore" is used in a very general sense to denote any single, rounded structure which, when separated from the parent fungus, is capable of germinating and reproducing the whole organism. All fungi reproduce by spores of one kind or another. (Bacterial spores, by contrast, are not reproductive bodies, since only one spore forms from any single bacterium.) In the more highly organized molds, as noted above, reproductive spores are formed asexually in great numbers on characteristically differentiated fertile hyphae. In other fungi spores develop directly from the growing (vegetative) portion of the fungus without any special reproductive structure. Also, most fungi (except the *Fungi Imperfecti*) occasionally form sexual spores of some kind.

The principal kinds of asexual spores

1. **Blastospores**: the buds formed by a process of sprouting from the surface of the parent cell. Budding is the characteristic method by which the true yeast multiplies (e.g., *Candida*, *Cryptococcus*).

2. **Chlamydospores**: a rounded, swollen portion of a hypha that becomes surrounded by a thick, tough wall. This represents a resting, encysted part of the fungus, capable of resisting unfavorable environment (e.g., *Aspergillus niger*).

3. **Arthrospores**: segments pinched off or walled off directly from undifferentiated hyphae. Often these round or cylindrical, rather thick-walled cells are seen still in position in the segmented filament (e.g., *Coccidioides*).

4. **Sporangiospores**: the spores formed within a sporangium, as in *Mucor*.

5. **Conidia**: asexual spores formed outside of a limiting membrane, borne on specialized hyphae (*conidiophores*) or arising directly from the vegetative mycelium. They are freed from the hyphae by obstruction at the point of attachment. Microconidia are small, single-celled; Macroconidia are relatively large, spindle-shaped or club-shaped bodies, divided into two or more cells by septa. The latter are characteristic of certain of the ringworm fungi (e.g., *Microsporon*). The differences in the number, size, shape, color, the conidia, and of the conidiophores, are utilized as a guide to identification of numerous genera and species of fungi, especially among the *Fungi Imperfecti*.

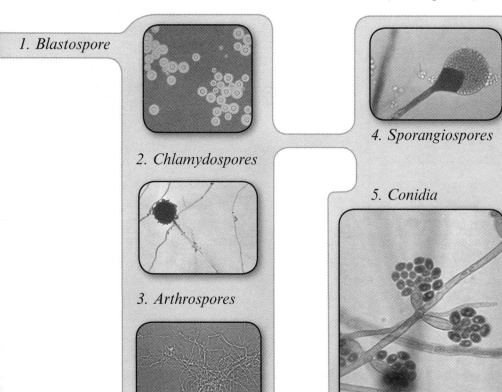

1. *Blastospore*

2. *Chlamydospores*

3. *Arthrospores*

4. *Sporangiospores*

5. *Conidia*

Three major kinds of sexual spores are found in fungi:

1. Zygospores: formed when two undifferentiated hyphae fuse from neighboring growths to make a single, round, pigmented structure, from which new hyphae later develop. Molds of the genera *Mucor* and *Rhizopus* occasionally form zygospores.

2. Ascospores: sexual spores formed within an especially developed closed sac (ascus). A rudimentary sexual process involving fusion of the nuclei of the parent cells precedes the actual formation of the ascospores. This is the kind of sexual reproduction characteristic of the Ascomycetes.

3. Basidiospores: sexual spores formed in groups of four on club-shaped cells known as basidia (singular is basidium). These spores are the result of sexual reproduction between mycelia. This is the kind of sexual reproduction characteristic of Basidiomycetes.

Hyphae and Mycelium

Classification of the common molds and other filamentous true fungi depends, first, on differences in the structure of the filaments. The hyphae are relatively coarse threads, having an average width of about 4 μ. In most fungi the mycelium is septate; that is, the hyphae are divided by cross walls (septa) into a series of cylindrical cells, end to end. But in one order (Zygomycetes), the filaments in the growing organisms are nonseptate. These nonseptate hyphae allow the multinucleated cytoplasm to fuse without interruption throughout the filaments, and consequently the mycelium is said to be coenocytic, (i.e., made up of cytoplasm shared in common by the whole mold).

The part of the mycelium that penetrates into the medium for absorption of food is called the vegetative mycelium. The part of the growth that projects from the surface into the air is the aerial mycelium. It is the mass of aerial mycelium that gives mold their characteristic fuzzy appearance. Under the microscope, the growth is made up of a network of branched threads, called hyphae, which grow to form a tangled mass (the mycelium). Usually there are also present small, round bodies, which are the reproductive elements or spores. This filamentous, web-like structure and the abundant spores are distinct morphological characteristics of these organisms.

In the common saprophytic molds, some of the aerial hyphae become differentiated into special structures, characteristic for each type of mold, from the tips of which reproductive spores are eventually formed. The terminal group of filaments on such a fertile hypha, from which the spores emerge, is called a fruiting body, or sporophore. In the Zygomycetes the tip of each fertile hypha becomes an enlarged head, called the columella. The sporangium, a round sac, surrounds the columella, is the structure where spores form. In other common molds (Aspergillus, Penicillium) the terminal portion of fertile hyphae branches in a characteristic way and finally forms short, finger-like stalks, called conidiophore, containing hundreds of conidia. The conidia, naked, asexually produced spores, have grown from the finger-like tips and into chains that often have a floral pattern or design. They are some of the most emerald-colored (or teal green) and beautiful creations in the fungi world.

Zygomycota
Rhizopus, Bread Mold

The most well-known members of this division come from genus *Rhizopus*, which contains most of the common bread molds. Because these fungi have so many reproductive modes at their disposal, their spores are in the air virtually everywhere. If you leave bread out in the open, bread mold spores will eventually land on it and, within a matter of days, the growing mold will be noticeable. Most molds that grow on bread and other baked goods are harmless if consumed in small quantities. *Rhizopus* also commonly grows on strawberries and gives older fruit the "warm fuzzy" appearance.

There are three ways that these molds can reproduce. They can reproduce asexually when a stolon lengthens and forms new filaments. The new filaments become a new mycelium and thus a new fungus. Another form of asexual reproduction involves the production of sporangia (from aerial hyphae) that release spores. Finally, hyphae can fuse together and sexually reproduce to form a zygospore that can then mature into another fungus. Although the zygospore reproduction is what distinguishes these fungi from ones in other classes, all three means of reproduction are used. The life cycle of *Rhizopus*, a typical zygomycete is illustrated on the following page.

A sequence of drawings showing sexual reproduction in the mold *Rhizopus*. (a) The hyphae of compatible mating types fuse and form a fusion septum. The haploid nuclei within the compatible hyphae have fused at this point to form a diploid zygote. (b) Cells at the septum begin to swell and show early signs of a zygosporangium, the structure that will enclose the zygote. (c) The outer primary wall begins to rupture. (d) The rupturing continues, and (e) the zygosporangium is revealed. The zygosporangium continues to mature as the primary wall separates away. Within the zygosporangium, the zygote is undergoing meiosis to yield one or more haploid spores that will be released to propagate the fungus.

Molds are helpful to man and the environment through the actions of fermentation and decomposition. Those in the soil contribute, along with the bacteria present, to the breakdown of complex organic waste into

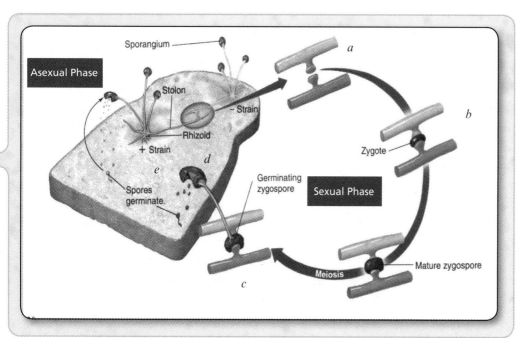

Life cycle of Rhizopus, *a typical Zygomycete*

simpler nitrogenous compounds, which may be utilized by plants for food. Certain varieties are widely used in the Orient for the conversion of rice starch to sugar, as the first step in making alcoholic beverages. The preparation of citric acid from cane sugar by action of molds is an example of the commercial use of these organisms. Some species of *Penicillium* are responsible for the characteristic flavor of certain popular types of cheese. *Penicillium notatum* and related species are the sources of penicillin.

Ascomycota

This is the largest order of fungi, containing numerous important species. Common possession of one characteristic — the capacity to form ascospores — brings together into these taxonomic groups of fungi that represent the opposite extremes of complexity. Ascomycetes include single-celled, true yeasts (genus Saccharomyces) to the complex, highly organized, multicellular molds (e.g., genera Penicillium and Aspergillus). Since the actual process of ascospore formation is much the same in all the many varieties of Ascomycetes, and is very rarely observed in any case, subdivisions among the molds within this great group are based on the appearance, and manner of formation, of the asexual spores (conidia).

The division Ascomycota includes about 30,000 species of ascomycetes, also known as sac fungi. The name ascomycete is derived from the presence of an ascus (pl., asci), a tiny spore-containing sac formed during the life cycle of the fungi. Most ascomycetes are saprobes, but many important plant parasites are found in this division, including the fungi that cause powdery mildew, dutch elm disease, chestnut blight disease, and peach leaf curl disease.

Most species of ascomycetes are composed of filaments, but a few species, such as the yeasts used in fermentation and baking, are single-celled, or unicellular. The septa in the hyphae of ascomycetes have perforations that allow the cytoplasm of one cell to mingle with that of neighboring cells.

The sexual stages of most ascomycetes are less conspicuous than the asexual stages. First, the hyphae of different mating types fuse, a process that brings together the haploid nuclei. Then, the sexually produced ascospores form within the ascus. To form the ascospores, the haploid nuclei fuse to form a diploid cell that undergoes meiosis and gives rise to eight haploid ascospores per ascus. In most ascomycetes, the asci are formed in complex structures called ascocarps, which can be flask-shaped or cup-shaped. In the "cup fungi," the ascocarp is composed of millions of hyphae tightly packed together to form the body of the cup-like container, and asci are exposed on the upper surface. In several species, such as morels and truffles, which are prized as edible fungi, the ascocarp is crowned by bell-shaped tissue that contains the asci.

Life Cycle of Scarlet Cup (*Hygrophorus coccineal*), a Typical Ascomycete

An ascospore germinates to produce a haploid monokaryotic mycelium, which reproduces through the formation of asexual spores (conidia). When monokaryotic mycelia of different mating strains form gametangia, the stage is set for sexual reproduction. A bridge forms between female (color) and male (black) gametangia, allowing the haploid male to enter the female gametangium. The hyphae that proliferate from this gametangium are dikaryotic, that is, each cell contains a pair of haploid nuclei, one of each parental type. These dikaryotic hyphae with interspersed monokaryotic hyphae give rise to the ascocarp. In the ascocarp, the dikaryotic hyphae grow and differentiate to form the asci, within which the haploid nuclei fuse. The resulting diploid nucleus undergoes meiosis producing four new haploid nuclei. These nuclei then divide mitotically, and the mature ascus thus contains eight haploid ascospores. With the release and germination of the ascospores, the cycle begins once more.

Ascomycetes also include various *Penicillium* species, the fungi that produce penicillin and related antibiotics such as ampicillin, amoxicillin, methicillin, and many others. Moreover, some species of *Penicillium* are used to ripen and flavor blue cheese, Roquefort cheese, and Camembert cheese. Also in the division Ascomycota are species of the common black mold Aspergillus. Certain Aspergillus species contaminate house dust and cause allergies and respiratory illness. Aspergillus species can also produce dangerous toxins (called aflatoxins) in foods. These toxins poison the nervous system, and they have been investigated as agents of bioterrorism because they can be produced as bioweapons and added to municipal water supplies. On the positive side, Aspergillus species synthesize citric acid, a major component of beverages. They are also used in the production of soy sauce and vinegar. One species, *A. niger*, is used to produce Beano, the trade name for an enzyme preparation that breaks down galactose, a sugar in cabbage, broccoli, Brussels sprouts, and other "strong" vegetables.

The Yeasts

The yeasts make up a group of fungi whose activities have always been of great practical importance in human affairs. The usefulness of the saprophytic species in the preparation of bread, beers, and wines is well known to all. These microbes are widespread in nature; they are especially abundant wherever much sugar is present. Some varieties are always to be found, for example, in foodstuffs, especially cream and other dairy products, in honey, in the nectar of flowers, in the exuded sap of trees, and on ripe fruits, notably grapes. They occur also in soil, on vegetation, and as symbionts in insects and animals.

In contrast to the somewhat complicated makeup of these familiar molds, the common yeasts, such as those in the ordinary yeast cake, are fungi of much simpler form, for each individual organism exists as a single, independent, microscopic, round or oval cell. The true yeasts stand out from all the other fungi, because they occur constantly as single, budding cells, and do not form the branching filaments (mycelium) which characterize the molds. Certain pathogenic *Fungi imperfecti* (e.g., *Blastomyces dermatitidis*) are dimorphic (i.e., they assume a single-celled, budding form in the body tissues but develop a mycelium in laboratory cultures at room temperature). The yeast-like organisms of the genus Candida form a pseudomycelium, made up of elongated budding cells which have failed to detach. But the true yeasts remain as single cells.

The typical yeast cell is a colorless oval or round body, usually about 10 to 15 µ in diameter (next page). The size varies greatly. Many yeasts have thick walls, giving the cells a double contour or outline. Each organism has a nucleus (though this is not often visible). The cytoplasm commonly contains many granules and vacuoles that often contain large fat droplets. Reproduction occurs by budding (blastospores). Two main groups are recognized among the yeasts: (1) the common, harmless bread and wine yeasts (mostly placed in the genus *Saccharomyces*), which occasionally form ascospores in addition to reproducing by budding; and (2) the *Cryptococcus* yeasts that multiply by budding, but do not form ascospores. Among the latter there are both harmless and highly pathogenic species.

Saccharomyces yeasts have been extensively studied because of their great importance in the manufacture of wines and bakery goods, as well as their value in other industries that depend on a process of fermentation. The relation of the yeasts to fermentation was discovered as early as 1837 by Schwann, but the complete demonstration of the fermenting powers of yeasts was first given by Pasteur, about 1865. The studies of Hansen, about 1880, led to the now universal practice of using pure strains of yeasts in fermentation industries and in the laboratory. The most important of the fermentative changes

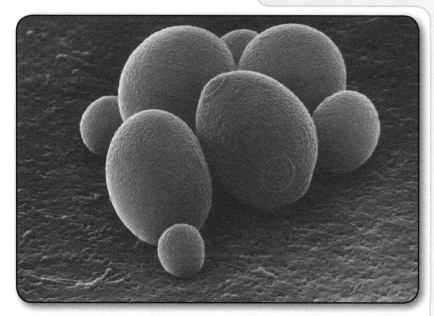

Scanning electron micrograph (SEM) of cells of brewer's yeast

produced by yeasts is the breaking down of sugar to form alcohol. The actual transformation of sugar to alcohol occurs through the action of the enzyme "zymase," which may be expressed from the yeast by pressure.

Saccharomyces cerevisiae is the name most often applied to the common bread yeasts. The familiar yeast cake is composed of compressed living yeast cells, mixed with a little starch. In the making of bread, the first gentle heating of the dough causes the added yeasts to multiply. They ferment the sugar present and cause the release of carbon dioxide. This harmless gas escapes through the dough, leaving countless small holes. Thus the dough rises and the bread becomes light and porous.

Design Focus 5.1

Yeast: One-Celled Creatures That Have Influenced Molecular Genetics

Yeast has been known and loved by human beings since ancient times. Yeasts are mentioned in the Bible, and the word, "leaven" is usually used as a symbol of influence. Leaven is associated with fermentation, which is the process of a steady, gradual change of food to another form. The Bible uses yeast as a word picture to illustrate

how a small object can highly influence the environment surrounding it. Yeast has been portrayed in both a positive and a negative light. On the positive side, when added to dough, it makes bread or cakes rise. Many other good foods also utilize yeast through the fermentation process. Its warm, slightly fruity smell is the smell of live cells at work. On the negative side, certain yeasts cause disease and "corrupt" the body like *Candida albicans*. This yeast is associated with thrush of the mouth and vagina.

Even a slim package of "active dry" yeast contains roughly 35 billion cells of Saccharomyces cerevisiae (baker's or brewer's yeast), and as soon as these cells find food, they produce fermentation bubbles — the bubbles that cause dough to rise or beverages to foam. Yeast is also plentiful. When you eat grapes, you swallow millions of live yeast cells that were feasting on sugar on the grapes' surface. Yeast is inexpensive and easy to grow. Yeast cells double every 90 minutes when food is available, and billions of them will fit in a few Petri dishes. Not only are these cells alive, they can also do almost everything that human cells do to survive: transmit signals from the cell's surface to its nucleus, manufacture thousands of proteins, create a cellular scaffolding, repair DNA in the nucleus, and so on. And although yeast cannot make tissues and does not have a brain, it is universally recognized as the best model organism for studies of anything that goes on inside a single cell.

Researchers speak glowingly of the "awesome power" of yeast genetics to solve problems in biology. Genetic engineering in yeast has been used during the last 20 years. You can stitch bits of DNA from a normal yeast cell onto a plasmid, the plasmid will carry this DNA into a mutant yeast cell, and the normal yeast gene will replace the mutant one at precisely the right place. It's also very quick. The yeast genome has so few genes — 6,000, compared with the estimated 40,000 genes in mice and humans — and the tools for manipulating these genes are so highly developed that yeast experiments can generally be performed in days or weeks. Similar experiments in mammal models might take years — if they could be done at all. In baker's yeast, these cells that reproduce by budding can produce millions overnight and they can all fit into a few Petri dishes. A lot of research can be conducted in a short time. Only bacteria have a faster growth rate.

Another great virtue of yeast is that its genes have very few of the bothersome introns (intervening sequences of DNA) that interrupt the coding sequences of mammalian genes. This makes it easy to recognize where yeast genes are and where their boundaries are, just by looking at the genome sequence. Approximately 70 percent of the yeast genome codes for protein — a huge amount, compared with only 5 percent of the human genome. Despite these differences, large numbers of yeast genes closely resemble those of mice and humans. They also produce nearly identical proteins. In general, when yeast proteins and equivalent human proteins are superimposed in their 3-D structures, they have the same crystalline form. For example, the protein actin has the same structure and function in yeasts and man. This is expected because the same Intelligent Designer made them both.

Most people do not appreciate how similar yeasts are to mammals. The last ten years of research has shown that all the basic pathways within cells are much more conserved than anybody expected at the time. So if you examine a new human protein involved in a human disease, you can find that it matches a yeast protein; this brings up the entire biochemical pathway. For a biomedical scientist, that's like hitting a jackpot. A decade ago, several international labs decided to cooperate on an ambitious plan: They would decipher DNA in the entire yeast genome.

After they divided up the yeast cell's six chromosomes, each lab agreed to tackle a different chunk of them. In 1996, the yeast community proudly published the result of its work: the complete set of genetic instructions that code for *Saccharomyces cerevisiae*, a major milestone. These instructions were spelled out in 12 million base pairs, or subunits, of DNA encoding roughly 6,000 genes. The code is highly specified. Just like the letters in words of Shakespeare's *Hamlet*, so too is the code for yeast and its function. Biologists know nearly every protein that yeast DNA will manufacture. Take one or more letters out in a mutation and there is chaos. The meaning changes, just like it might if you leave out lines in a Shakespeare play. In the case of *Hamlet*, the story would be ruined, in the case of yeasts, they would not survive. By inference, good drama and functional yeasts need a highly specified language given by a brilliant author. Both must have a remarkable intelligence behind the code.

Until then, no one had ever sequenced the entire DNA of any eukaryote (an organism whose cells have a true nucleus and many other features of animal cells). Many of the genes in these simpler organisms bear an uncanny resemblance to those of humans. Unlike human beings, however, these organisms can be grown rapidly, and their genes can be mutated at will — a quality that researchers find essential, since mutations that stop a particular gene from functioning make it possible for scientists to figure out what the normal gene's function would be. Furthermore, model organisms can be mated in any way that suits an experimenter, and their offspring analyzed with ease. That is how scientists have deciphered several genetic pathways that are also found in human cells.

How Similar Are Humans to Baker's Yeast?

Evolutionists expect us to believe that little creatures such as baker's yeast, worms and flies are "our relatives" in the "tree of life" because people share DNA codes in common. What can we possibly have in common with this humble cell, really just a fungus, which is generally used to make dough rise? The answer is stunning: We are so similar to yeast, in some of our genes, that human DNA can be substituted for the equivalent yeast gene — and it works just as well. More than 70 additional human genes have proved able to repair various mutations in yeast. In summary, what is true for yeast is generally true for humans. Just like a car manufacturer, Ford or Chevrolet, uses similar blueprints (like a steering wheel) to design each of its diverse cars, so too did the Maker of Mankind use similar genetic instructions to make yeast. The high DNA specificity to each protein precludes it as a chance event. Only a brilliant Architect could devise such a structural plan that would be employed by both single celled yeasts and *Homo sapiens*.

Just like human cells, yeast cells go through cycles of growth and division — and the genes that regulate these cycles in yeast are practically identical to ours. In fact, nearly everything man knows about the human cell cycle, and much that we know about human cancer, was originally learned in yeast. Such knowledge used to be gained slowly and painfully. When scientists examined the newly sequenced yeast genome a few years ago, they were shocked to find that even though more was known about yeast than any other model organism, two-thirds of yeast's genes had never been identified before — and nobody had any idea what their functions might be.

One of the great things about the genome sequencing projects is that they make it obvious we're still in the frontier of what will someday occur in molecular biology. At the same time, these projects provide us with a very useful tool that allows us to explore large sets of genes and to discover their properties. God has given us the command to have dominion over the earth. As biologists learn more about yeasts at the molecular level, we have the possibility of better understanding how genes work in our own bodies. Biologists also have the possibility of harnessing the power of this amazing yeast to engineer useful pharmaceutical products. Most of the genes in organisms that biotechnologists study are really not understood at all in terms of their roles. And for humans, it's 90–95 percent of the genes that biologists haven't a clue about. That's just a reminder of how much biologists don't know, keeping us humble, and giving us an appreciation that only an awesome God could design such a sophisticated code of life.

In summary, yeasts are once again being leaven in this world, this time in molecular genetics. They are influential in better understanding how a highly specific genome constructs a whole organism. This factual molecular information may influence how biologists engineer useful products in eukaryotic genomes. Finally, the tiny yeast may also be one of the "weapons" that sling a fatal blow to the dogma of Darwinian assertion that chance events eventually lead to the highly complex genes in yeasts. Perhaps yeasts may extend the kingdom through its influence on creation biology, a small stone being thrown at the Goliath evolutionary community of scientists.

The Common Molds

The molds that most often appear upon food and as contaminants in agar plate cultures that have been open to the air belong to several different genera. The best known of these common contaminants are placed in the genera *Mucor*, *Rhizopus*, *Penicillium*, and *Aspergillus*. Some types of molds will grow on almost any object, including the walls and floors of a building, in the absence of sunlight and in the presence of moisture. In localities where the atmosphere is warm and humid, molds may develop on soiled, damp towels or clothing in the laundry bag, on old shoes stored away in the closet, and on books on library shelves.

Molds sometimes grow extensively in the humid rooms of bakeries, and in creameries they may contaminate the butter churns. Certain kinds cause deterioration of textiles and the dry rot of lumber. Aspergilli and other common varieties cause much economic loss when they grow upon strawberries and other fresh fruits as these are being shipped to market. Foods which are well preserved from decomposition by bacteria may, nevertheless, be spoiled by the growth of molds, because the latter develop (though slowly) at low temperatures in materials with a high concentration of sugar or salt, and in substances that are strongly acidic. So biologists find that such foods as preserved fruit and jellies, butter, pickles, sauerkraut, vinegar, and salted and smoked meats may become moldy, even though kept in a cool place.

Molds Produce Antibiotics by Design

The importance of fungi in the ecological structure of the earth is well founded. They are essential contributors to complex environments such as soil, and they play numerous beneficial roles as decomposers of organic debris and as partners to plants. Fungi also have great practical importance due to their metabolic versatility. They are productive sources of drugs (penicillin) to treat human infections and other diseases, and they are used in industry to ferment foods and synthesize organic chemicals.

Among the best known of the medically important fungi are the *Penicillium* molds, which secrete penicillin, the well-known and widely used antibiotic (a substance produced by a living organism that interferes with the normal metabolism of another living organism). Sir Alexander Fleming of England noticed in 1928 that certain bacteria would not grow in the vicinity of the mycelium of a *Penicillium notatum* mold, and gave the name penicillin to the element in the mold that prevented the bacterial growth.

Fleming understood the implications for penicillin's use, but was unable to purify it and produce sufficient quantities to medical use on a widespread basis. In addition, his findings did not particularly excite the medical profession until the outbreak of World War II some ten years later. The breakthrough in the research came, however, with a different species of *Penicillium* mold,

P. chrysogenum. It yielded 25 times the penicillin produced by *P. notatum*. The new fungus was found on a moldy cantaloupe from a local market. In 1941, Ernst Chain and Howard Florey were successful in producing even more penicillin by purifying the antibiotic from *P. chrysogenum*. Later, when this strain was subjected to X-radiation, still other forms were produced that multiplied the penicillin output to 225 times that of Fleming's mold. Using *P. chrysogenum*, pharmaceutical industries could produce large quantities of penicillin G. Thus, this new wonder drug greatly diminished war casualties for United States and Great Britain. Millions of lives every year, since WWII, have been saved in hospitals around the world due to penicillin. Today, most of the penicillin produced around the world comes from descendants of that cantaloupe mold. Since the early 1980s, organ transplants have been aided by the discovery and production of another "wonder drug" from a mold, *Tolyposporium niveum*, found in soil. The drug is called cyclosporine and suppresses immune reactions that cause rejection of transplanted organs without risking the development of leukemia and other undesirable side effects associated with other drugs. It is used widely by physicians to treat thousands of patients undergoing organ transplants every year.

Focus: War Story

Transporting a Treasure (Antibiotics) in a Coat

According to Dr. Edward Alcamo, an amazing war story that deserves to be told is one that happened during WWII. Howard Florey, Ernst B. Chain, Norman Heatley, and others had "rediscovered" penicillin, refined it, and proved it useful in infected patients. (Fleming's discovery of penicillin was not sufficient to produce enough quantity to treat a person.) But it was 1939, and German bombs would soon be falling on London. This was no time for research into new drugs. There was hope, however.

Researchers in the United States were willing to attempt the industrial production of penicillin, so the British scientists made plans to move their lab across the ocean. There were many problems, to be sure, but one was particularly interesting – how to transport the vital

Penicillium cultures. If the molds were to fall into enemy hands or if the enemy were to learn the secret of penicillin, all their work would be wasted. Then Heatley made a suggestion: They would rub the mold on the inside linings of their coats, deposit the mold spores there, and transport the *Penicillium* cultures across the ocean that way.

And so they did. On arrival in the United States, they set to work to re-isolate the mold from their coat linings, and then they began the laborious task of manufacturing penicillin. One of the great ironies of medicine is that virtually all the world's original penicillin-producing mold may have been derived from those few spores in the linings of the British coats. Few coats in history have yielded so great a bounty.

Note that Sir Ernest Chain, co-holder of 1945 Nobel Prize for developing penicillin, was an anti-Darwinist.

To postulate that the development and survival of the fittest is entirely a consequence of chance mutations seems to me a hypothesis based on no evidence and irreconcilable with the facts. These classical evolutionary theories are a gross over-simplification of an immensely complex and intricate mass of facts, and it amazes me that they are swallowed so uncritically and so readily, by so many scientist without a murmur of protest.

Molds Have Other Uses

Literally hundreds of other antibiotics effective in combating human and animal diseases have been discovered since the close of World War II, and the production of these drugs is a vast worldwide industry. Penicillium molds are also used in other ways. Some are introduced into the milk of cows, sheep, and goats at stages in the production of gourmet cheeses, such as blue (Fig. 5.10), Camembert, Roquefort, Gorgonzola, and Stilton. The molds produce enzymes that break down proteins and fats in the milk, giving the cheeses their characteristic flavors.

Aspergillus is a genus of imperfect fungi whose species produce dark brown to blackish or yellow spores. It is closely related to the *Penicillium* molds and is extensively used in industry. One or more species are used commercially for the production from sugar of citric acid, a substance for flavoring foods and for the manufacture of effervescent salts that were originally obtained from oranges. Citric acid is also used in the manufacture of inks and in medicines, and it is even used in some chewing gum. Aspergillus fungi also produce gallic acid used in photographic developers, dyes, and indelible black ink. Other species are used in the production of artificial flavoring and perfume substances, chlorine, alcohols, and several acids. Further uses are in the manufacture of plastics, toothpaste, and soap and in the silvering of mirrors. One species of Aspergillus is used in the Orient and elsewhere to make soy sauce by fermenting soybeans with the fungus. Fermenting soybeans, salt, and rice make a Japanese food called miso with the same fungus. More than a million tons of miso are consumed annually.

Corrupted Molds Produce Toxins

The fact that they are so widespread also means that they frequently share human living quarters, especially in locations that provide ample moisture and nutrients. Often their presence is harmless and limited to a film of mildew on shower stalls or other moist environments. In some cases, depending on the amount of contamination and the type of mold, these indoor fungi can also give rise to various medical problems. Such common air contaminants as *Penicillium*, *Aspergillus*, *Cladosporium*, and *Stachybotrys* all have the capacity to give off airborne spores and toxins that, when inhaled, cause a whole spectrum of symptoms sometimes referred to as "sick building syndrome." The usual source of harmful fungi is the presence of chronically water-damaged walls, ceilings, and other building materials that have come to harbor these fungi. Such materials contain plant products that serve as a rich source of nutrients. People exposed to these houses or buildings report symptoms that range from skin rash, flulike reactions, sore throat, and headaches to fatigue, diarrhea, and even immune suppression. Because they can mimic other diseases, the association with indoor toxic fungi

Aspergillus

may be missed. Recent reports of sick buildings have been on the rise, infecting thousands of people, and some deaths have been reported in small children. The control of indoor fungi requires correcting the moisture problem, removing the infested materials, and decontaminating the living spaces. In the worst cases, the buildings have been burned down to prevent the spread of fungi to surrounding structures.

A number of diseases of both human and animals are caused by *Aspergillus* species. The diseases, called aspergilloses, attack the respiratory tract after the spores have been inhaled. One type thrives on and in human ears. Other diseases caused by different genera of imperfect fungi include those responsible for the widespread problem of athlete's foot and ringworm, for white piedra (a mild disease of beards and mustaches), and for tropical diseases of the hands and feet that cause the limbs to swell in grotesque fashion. One serious disease called valley fever (coccidiomycosis), found primarily in the drier regions of the southwestern United States, usually starts with the inhalation of dust-borne spores of an imperfect fungus (*Coccidioides immitis*) that produces lesions in the upper respiratory tract and lungs. The disease may spread elsewhere in the body, with sometimes fatal results.

Aspergillus flavus, which grows on moist seeds, secretes aflatoxin, the most potent natural carcinogen known. The toxin causes liver cancer, and no more than fifty parts per billion is allowed in human food. In humid climates, such as the southeastern United States improperly stored grain can become moist enough to support the fungus so that foods such as peanuts, peanut butter, and peanut abased dairy feeds become carcinogenic. Dairy cattle feed is even more strictly controlled because concentrations of aflatoxin can accumulate in milk.

Stachybotrys and Sick-building Syndrome

Recently, another fungus has been implicated in a number of serious illnesses. It is *Stachybotrys*, a wet, greenish-black growth that the media have dubbed "killer mold" and causes "sick building syndrome." Is this merely hyperbole, or does *Stachybotrys* deserve its horrific, bad name? No one really knows. Other fungi may be involved in the reported illnesses. In the 1990s, acute pulmonary hemorrhage struck about 50 infants living in Cleveland, Ohio, and 16 died. Since then sporadic cases have been reported in New York and in Texas. A CDC investigation concluded that significant exposure to *Stachybotrys* growing on and in the walls of many of the homes played a significant role in the development of this severe and often fatal lung disease.

Even if it is not the mass murderer portrayed in the media, *Stachybotrys* does cause myriad symptoms that have come to be known as "sick building syndrome." These include coughing, wheezing, runny nose, eye irritation, sore throat, skin rash, diarrhea, headache, fatigue, and general malaise. Some mycologists have described it as having a bad cold that doesn't go away. As with other fungi, *Stachybotrys* thrives in dark, wet places. Basements, especially those that take in groundwater or become very humid during warm weather, provide a perfect environment for *Stachybotrys*. Well-insulated, airtight buildings that do not "breathe" can exacerbate the situation. Studies have found the killer mold in one to three percent of homes tested. And as *Stachybotrys* grows, it produces powerful toxins that can be found in its spores. Inhaling these poisonous spores in high enough concentration produces the flu-like symptoms of sick building syndrome or more serious lung disease.

Stachybotrys – the cause of sick-building syndrome

Creation Focus 5.2

The Origins of Antibiotic Resistance

Many think that antibiotic resistance is a new phenomenon. In reading the newspapers, you would think that since man invented antibiotics or that some new mutation has caused bacteria to mutate and survive than the onslaught of new chemicals. This is far from the truth. Antibiotic resistance has probably occurred since the corruption in creation. One could speculate that within a few days after the Edenic curse (Gen.3), fungi and bacteria were competing with each other in the soil. Fungi and bacteria frequently occupy similar habitats and may often compete for the same nutrients and molecular substrates. Encounters between fungi and bacteria may vary and result in one or the other "winning" the substrate. Antibiotic resistance did not start in some clinic in WWII, nor did it start in a man's laboratory. Antibiotic resistance started in the wild!

The Creator made bacteria and fungi to be extremely prolific as we have already learned. The Master Designer established a balance of fungi and bacteria in the soil so that one would not totally take over the entire soil ecosystem. Each was given a niche, to work side by side together in harmony when first created. But after the corruption of creation, it is likely that some bacteria became pathogenic and perhaps started to compete with fungi. Fungi fought back. They were endowed by their Creator to naturally produce antibiotics. These fungal chemicals inhibit bacteria growth (bacteriostatic), and some produce substances that kill bacteria (bactericidal).

Competitive Interactions between Fungi and Bacteria

A number of natural products, penicillin for example, have been discovered that are antibiotics suitable for therapy. They were originally discovered as secretions of fungi or soil bacteria.

Soil is home to complex ecosystems, and it is not surprising that its inhabitants have adapted to the chemical defenses against each other. In this focus section, bacteria are compared with fungi according to how they compete with each other. Some inherent differences include 1. Size — bacterial cells are much smaller and are able to occupy finer irregularities of the habitat, 2. Bacterial cells can occur in the "hyphosphere" of the fungus, 3. Fungal cells are probably capable of producing a greater variety of enzymes as well as greater quantities, 4. Filamentous vs. unicellular growth, 5. Single cells are very efficient in fluids, 6. Hyphae are most effective in solid environments, and 7. Toxic metabolites, such as antibiotics.

Both fungi and bacteria produce antibiotics. About 2/3 of antibiotics come from bacteria and 1/3 from fungi and artificial sources. Some toxic end products that serve in the bacteria's chemical warfare production include ammonia, CO_2, nitrite, H_2S, methane, and ethylene. A lot of toxic substances are a result of their normal metabolism. Here are some examples of parasitism or lyse of fungi by bacteria: *Streptomyces, Nocardia, Bacillus*, and *Pseudomonas* all may cause hyphae to lysis and sometimes spores. Melanin strongly protects fungal walls against bacterial lysis by "shielding" susceptible polysaccharides (i.e., chitin). Examples of fungi that produce toxic chemicals warding off bacteria (in competition for space and food) include, *Penicillium sp. Aspergillus, Acremonium, Cephalosporium, Cladosporium, Fusarium*, and *Tolyposporium*. Those that produce useful antibiotics for manufacture include *Penicillum spp.* (produces penicillin), *Cephalosporium spp.* (produces cephalosporin), and *Tolyposporium niveum* (produces cyclosporin). On the other side, lysis of bacteria by fungi may occur when wood-rotting fungi produce inhibitory or lethal chemicals for bacterial colonies.

Fungi and bacteria frequently occupy similar habitats and may often compete for the same nutrients. Encounters between fungi and bacteria may vary and result in one or the other "winning" the substrate. This can actually be observed this in the lab by inoculating media with a variety of fungi and bacteria and observing the result. Competitive encounters will be carried out on nutrient agars. It has been suggested that nutrients add a significant extra factor into competition experiments and that non-nutrient media are closer to situations on the natural habitat. Five bacteria that actively demonstrate this competition include *Bacillus subtilis, Micrococcus luteus, Pseudomonas fluorescens, Serratia marcescens*, and *Streptomyces spp.*

Basidiomycetes

Members of the division Basidiomycota are called basidiomycetes, as well as "club fungi" because of the club-shaped basidia they form. There are about 25,000 named species in the division, including puffballs, shelf fungi, earthstars, stinkhorns, jelly fungi, and the familiar gill fungi, among which are the mushrooms purchased at the local supermarket. Basidiomycetes include the most common large, fleshy fungi, such as the toadstools, puffballs, and mushrooms. Basidiomycetes also include some smaller forms that are important plant parasites, known as rusts and smuts. Many of the latter type have complicated life cycles, involving a sexual phase in one plant host and asexual phases in a different plant host. None of these fungi are infectious for man or animals. Basidiomycetes form four spores (called basidiospores) on club-shaped cells known as basidia (singular is basidium). These spores are the result of sexual reproduction between mycelia. The cap and stipe (stalk) of the mushroom is actually only the fruiting body of a vast network of mycelia that exist below the surface upon which the mushroom grows. Most of these fungi are saprophytic, but a few are parasitic.

The basidiomycetes also include certain plant parasites that cause rust and smut diseases. Rust diseases are so named

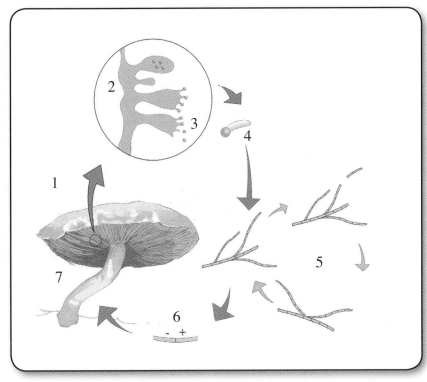

The life cycle steps of a typical mushroom

The best-known members of the division Basidiomycota are the mushrooms. Mushroom is the common name for the spore-producing body of the fungus, a structure called the basidiocarp. The basidiocarp is composed of densely packed hyphae. In its formation, the mycelium of the fungus forms underground, and the mushrooms develop at the outer edge of the mycelium where growth is most active. Sometimes mushrooms appear in rings, the "fairy rings" that seem to sprout overnight in meadows after heavy rains. The figure on the left illustrates this life cycle.

The Life Cycle Steps of a Typical Mushroom

1. On the underside of the mushroom cap, the channels (gills) are lined with club-shaped, sexual reproductive structures called basidia. Nuclear fusion within the basidium give rise to the zygote, a diploid cell.

2. The zygote undergoes a chromosome-halving process called meiosis, and haploid basidiospores form on projections called sterigmata.

3. Basidiospores are released from basidia.

4. Basidiospores germinate hyphae.

5. Basidiospores form sexually opposite hyphae, the (-) and(+) strains. Growth results in the primary mycelium.

6. Later, hyphae of the sexually opposite strains unite and form a secondary mycelium.

7. The hyphae of the secondary mycelium wind together and emerge from the soil as a basidiocarp, which is the mushroom. Basidia form on the underside of the cap to complete the cycle.

The life cycle of the club fungi is rather interesting, and it is illustrative of the complex nature of most fungi. A mushroom begins life as a small mycelium that grows from spores, which have come from another mushroom. As the mycelium begins to grow, it might encounter the mycelium of another mushroom nearby. As the two mycelia begin to intertwine, their hyphae will sexually reproduce. They accomplish this by aligning themselves parallel

because of the distinct orange-red color on the infected plant, a color derived from pigments in the sporangia of the parasitic fungi. Wheat, oat, and rye plants, as well as lumber trees such as white pines, are susceptible. Smut diseases get their name from dark-pigmented fungi that infect and give a black sooty appearance to plants such as corn, blackberry, and various grains. These diseases bring about untold millions of dollars of damage each year. Another basidiomycete produces a unique enzyme that destroys the tough polymers of wood, causing white rot disease. Scientists are investigating this enzyme for its ability to destroy such toxic substances as DDT, dioxin, and other pollutants.

The hyphae of basidiomycetes are divided by perforated septa. The basidiomycetes, however, have a more lengthy dikaryotic stage in their life cycle, a stage during which they have cells with two haploid nuclei. The basidiocarp is a dense mass of dikaryotic hyphae. Eventually, some of the nuclei fuse to form diploid nuclei; the cells then undergo meiosis and form sexually produced basidiospores. The latter form on a specialized hypha called a basidium (the Greek basis means "base"). Each basidiospore is haploid and develops at the tip of a spikelike process. It has been estimated that the average mushroom can contain 15 billion spores.

to each other and forming a small junction, where hyphae are fused. Once fused, the hyphae exchange DNA and form more mycelia. Eventually, through some process that we do not understand, a group of the hyphae will form a complex web and enclose themselves in a membrane.

This membrane-enclosed web of hyphae (often called a "button") is the beginning of the mushroom's fruiting body. When the hyphae are formed in the membrane, the mushroom has reached the button stage of its existence. At that point, the hyphae begin filling with water quickly, and eventually the stipe and cap of the mushroom break through the membrane. The hyphae fill with water so quickly during the button stage, that the stipe and cap of a mushroom can literally "pop up" out of the membrane overnight. Since many mushrooms are hard to see in their button stage, it gives the illusion that a mushroom formed itself overnight, when in fact, the mushroom that you see is the result of many days' growth.

Since the stipe and cap of a mushroom form the fruiting body of a fungus, their main function is that of reproduction. The cap is full of gills, small plates that are lined with basidia. The basidiospores contained on the basidia are flung from the mushroom, where wind and water carry them to a new location, starting the process all over again. Once the fruiting body of the mushroom releases all of its spores, it withers and dies. The fungus is still very much alive, because the mycelium is still digesting and absorbing nutrients below the surface. Eventually, more mycelia will sexually reproduce, clump together, and form another fruiting body.

The fruiting body of the mushroom, of course, is the part that people eat. Although most mushrooms are tasty and nutritious, there are some that are quite toxic. The genus *Amanita*, for example, contains mushrooms that are commonly called "destroying angel" mushrooms. These pure white mushrooms carry a poison that is deadly to humans. If you eat one of these mushrooms, it tastes quite normal. However, once you eat one you will die in about 16 hours. There is virtually nothing that can be done to treat a person who has eaten these deadly mushrooms. Because there are no truly distinguishing marks that can separate poisonous mushrooms from non-poisonous ones, the only place that you should hunt them is in the grocery store. Many people who try to hunt wild mushrooms end up in a hospital or a coffin because the mushrooms that look tasty are, instead, toxic.

Mushrooms often grow in characteristic "ring" patterns in lawns and in forests (right). Sometimes, you can find mushrooms that grow in an almost perfect circle. Inside or outside of this ring of mushrooms, no other mushrooms grow. These rings, often called fairy rings, are believed by some to have magical properties because of their unique appearance. Of course, there is no magic associated with a fairy ring. Instead, it is just a result of the saprophytic nature of the fungus. When a fungal mycelium begins to grow in an area, it eats the remains of dead organisms. As it eats, it grows and reproduces. Eventually, the mycelium will spread out in all directions, making a relatively circular patch of hyphae. Once the hyphae in the center of the circle eat up all of the remains of dead organisms, there is no more food for them, and they die. The hyphae at the edge of the mycelium, however, still have food, because they haven't existed for as long and therefore have not used up the food in their area. As a result, they continue to live, and the mycelium becomes ring-shaped. When it is time to reproduce, the ring produces fruiting bodies, forming a fairy ring. (Note: Ringworm diseases, like Athlete's foot

Fairy ring

and other superficial mycoses grow on our skin, nails, and hair in a similar pattern.)

As time goes on, the mycelium continues to grow outward, and the inner hyphae continue to die because they use up their food. As a result, the mycelium retains its ring shape, but the ring gets larger in diameter. When the reproduction cycle comes again, a new ring of stipes and caps are formed, and this ring is larger than the old one. Some fairy rings have been found in which the ring of mushrooms is only a few inches wide, but has a diameter of nearly 20 feet!

Basidiomycetes is also include puffball fungi. Puffballs, which are also saprophytic, produce their spores on basidia inside a membrane, rather than in the gills of a cap. When disturbed by a passing animal or a heavy wind, the membrane breaks and the spores are released. The spores, which are as fine as dust, are often carried on the wind for several miles before they hit the ground. As a result, you are unlikely to find dense patches of puffballs. They tend to be spread out over vast distances.

The shelf fungi are generally found either on dead wood or on living trees. If you find them on dead wood, they are obviously one of the saprophytic species of shelf fungi, while those found on living trees are the parasitic species. Although parasitic fungi are uncommon, they do exist, and class Basidiomycetes is home to some of them. The spores of the shelf fungi are formed in the pores of the shelves. These spores are also very fine, so that when they are released, they can travel great distances to find another tree on which to grow. Once again, the shelves are just the fruiting bodies of these fungi. The mycelia are inside the wood of the tree. In fact, some parasitic shelf fungi actually add a new layer to the fruiting body each year, resulting in huge shelves growing out of the tree trunk.

Deuteromycota: The *Fungi Imperfecti*

In this division, those fungi that do not form ascospores or other types of sexual spores that have not been observed are placed in this category. Hence, these organisms have an imperfect — or imperfectly known — life history. Traditionally, they have been classified as *Deuteromycetes*. We encounter numerous irregularities in form and development; many have an abundant mycelium at times, while at other times they grow as yeast-like cells, and reproduction occurs through asexual spores elaborated in a variety of ways.

The fungi prior to this section are teleomorphs; that is, they produce both sexual and asexual spores. Some ascomycetes (and other fungi) may have lost their ability to reproduce sexually. These asexual fungi are called anamorphs. *Penicillium* and *Aspergillus* are examples of anamorphs. Many speculate they arose from a mutation in a teleomorph. Perhaps at the time of Creation these fungi reproduced sexually but due to the degenerating genetic code, lost their ability to form spores and only reproduce through asexual methods. Historically, fungi whose sexual cycle had not been observed were put in a "holding" category called *Deuteromycota*. Now mycologists are using tRNA sequencing to classify these organisms. Most of these previously unclassified as *Deuteromycetes* are anamorph phases of *Ascomycota* and a few are basidomycetes. Many textbooks still retain this category of *Deuteromycota* or the *Fungi Imperfecti*.

It is no accident that biologists find many of the fungi pathogenic for plants, animals, and humans among the *Deuteromycota*, for it is a general principle that, with the adoption of a parasitic existence, microbes regularly lose those specialized reproductive and protective structures which characterize related, free-living, saprophytic species. Hence these dangerous fungi are not so easy to identify. Those who are qualified to identify pathogenic fungi usually have training in medical mycology.

Chytridiomycota

The Chytrids – Uniflagellate Water Molds

If you were to immerse dead leaves or flowers, onion bulb scales, dead insects, or other organic material in water that has been mixed with a soil, within a day or two thousands of microscopic chytrids probably would appear on the surfaces of the immersed objects. These simple, mostly one-celled organisms include many parasites of protists, aquatic fungi, aquatic flowering plants, and algae. Some parasitize pollen grains, and many other species are saprobic (feed on nonliving organic material). Some of the most common chytrids consist of a spherical cell with colorless, branching threads called rhizoids at one end. The rhizoids anchor the organism to its food source. Other chytrids may develop short hyphae or even a complete mycelium whose hyphae contain many nuclei. Such multinucleate mycelia without crosswalls are said to be coenocytic. The cell walls of a few chytrids have been reported to contain cellulose in addition to chitin.

Many chytrid species reproduce only asexually through the production of zoospores within a spherical cell. The zoospores, which each have a single flagellum, settle upon release and grow into new chytrids. Some species undergo sexual reproduction by means of the fusion of two motile gametes with haploid nuclei or by the union of two non-motile cells whose diploid zygote nuclei undergo meiosis. The zygote commonly is converted into a resting spore.

The taxonomy of chytrids is debatable, but the presence of a flagellum on the motile cells once excluded it from the fungi. Like water and slime molds, the chytrids have both protozoan and fungal characteristics. In recent years, molecular studies on DNA have led most authorities to suggest they are best associated with the fungi. They do have mycelia and have chitin in their cell wall, thus grouping them with fungi. Their taxonomy may be in a state of flux, but most biology texts now include them with the fungi.

Fungi Cause Important Plant Diseases

Fungi are responsible for many serious plant diseases, including epidemic diseases that spread rapidly and often result in complete crop failure. All plants are apparently susceptible to fungal infection. Damage may be localized in certain tissue structures of the plant, or the disease may be systemic and grow throughout the entire plant. Fungal infections may affect a string of plant parts or of the entire plant, they may cause warts, or they may kill the plant. A plant often becomes infected after hyphae enter through stomata in the leaf or stem or through wounds in the plant body. Alternatively, the fungus may produce an enzyme called cutinase that dissolves the waxy cuticle and covers the surface of leaves and stems. After dissolving the cuticle, the fungus easily invades the plant tissues. As the mycelia grow, they may remain mainly between the plant cells or they may penetrate the cells. Parasitic fungi often produce specialized branches called haustora (sing. haustorium) that penetrate host cells and obtain nourishment from the cytoplasm.

The *Ascomycetes* may be the most important group of fungi that cause plant disease and food spoilage. Most of the blue-green, red, and brown molds that cause food decay are members of *Ascomycota*. This includes the salmon-colored bread mold *Neurospora sp.*, which has played an important role in the development of modern genetics. Many *ascomycetes* are the cause of serious plant diseases, including powdery mildews that attack fruits, chestnut blight, and Dutch elm disease (caused by *Ceratocytis ulmi*, a fungus native to certain European countries).

Brown rot attacks apples, cherries, peaches, plums, and cots and is caused by *Ascomycetes*. Certain imperfect fungi also cause plant diseases. Examples include verticilli that wilt on potatoes, which is caused by the deuteromycete *Vertlium sp.* Some fungal parasites, such as the stem rust of wheat, have complex life cycles that involve two or more different host plants and the production of several kinds of spores. For example, wheat rust must infect a barberry plant at one stage in its life cycle. Since this fact was discovered, the eradication of barberry plants in wheat-growing regions has reduced infection with wheat rust. Wheat rust has not been eliminated by eradication of the barberry, however, because the fungus overwinters on wheat at the southern end of the Grain Belt and forms asexual spores. During the spring, wind blows these spores for hundreds of kilometers, reinfecting northern areas of the United States and Canada.

Maize showing damage caused by the corn smut fungus, Ustilago maydis.

Athlete's Foot and Other Dermatophytoses

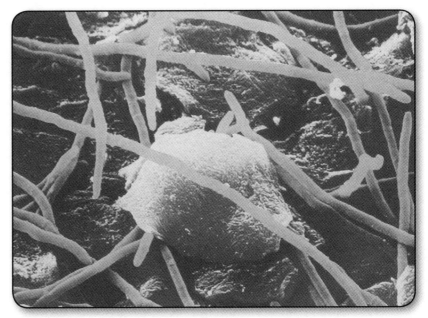

*This fungus causes athlete's foot (*tinea pedis*) in humans.*

Fungal infections strictly confined to the nonliving epidermal tissue (stratum corneum) and its derivatives are called dermatophytoses (a type of mycosis). Common terms used in reference to these diseases are ringworm, (because they tend to develop circular, scaly patches,) and tinea. They form a circular ring on the skin just like mushrooms grow in a ring on your lawn. These fungi belong to the genera *Trichophyton*, *Microsporum*, and *Epidermophyton* in most dermatophytoses. The causative agent of a given type of ringworm differs from person to person and from place to place.

Tinea pedis (right) is known by a variety of synonyms, including athlete's foot and jungle rot. The disease is connected to wearing shoes, because it is uncommon in cultures where the people customarily go barefoot. Conditions that encase the feet in a closed, warm, moist environment increase the possibility of infection. *Tinea pedis* is a known hazard in shared facilities such as shower stalls, public floors, and locker rooms. Infections begin with small blisters between the toes that burst, crust over, and can spread to the rest of the foot and nails.

Pneumocystis carinii and Pneumonia

Pneumocystis pneumonia is caused by *Pneumocystis carinii*. The taxonomic position of this microbe has been uncertain ever since its discovery, when it was thought to be a developmental stage of a protozoan trypanosome. Since that time, there has been no universal agreement about whether it is a protozoan or a fungus. It has some characteristics of both groups. Recent analysis of RNA and certain other structural characteristics indicate that it is more appropriately classified with the yeasts. The disease occurs throughout the world and can be endemic in hospitals. The pathogen is found in healthy human lungs but causes disease among immunosuppressed patients. This group includes people receiving immunosuppressive drugs to minimize the rejection of transplanted tissue and those who have a compromised immunity because of cancer. People with AIDS are also very susceptible to *P. carinii*, probably by the reactivation of an asymptomatic infection.

Before the AIDS epidemic, *Pneumocystis* pneumonia was an uncommon disease; perhaps 100 cases occurred each year. By 1993, it was the indicator of AIDS in more than 20,000 cases. In the human lung, the microbes are found mostly in the lining of the alveoli. There, they form a thick-walled cyst in which spherical cystic-like bodies successively divide as part of a sexual cycle. The mature cyst contains eight such bodies. Eventually the cyst ruptures and releases them, and each body develops into a trophozoite. The trophozoite cells can reproduce asexually by fission, but they may also enter the encysted sexual stage.

Symbiosis in Fungi Lichens

Before we leave our discussion of kingdom Fungi, we must mention the different forms of symbiosis in which its members participate. The most well-known form of symbiosis in which you will find a fungus is the lichen. Lichens are produced by a symbiotic relationship between a fungus (usually of class *Ascomycetes*) and an algae. The algae in the relationship produces food for itself and the fungus by means of photosynthesis, while the fungus supports and protects the algae. As a result of this symbiotic arrangement, you can find lichens where other organisms just cannot survive.

They are commonly found growing on dry rocks, brick walls, fences, and trees. In certain cold, snowy regions, lichens grow so large that they cover a few square miles!

The colorful lichens, common on the bark of trees or on bare rocks, are growths in which algae and a fungus (usually Ascomycetes) are living in a symbiotic relationship. It is thought that the alga is able to survive in what would otherwise provide an unfavorable environment because of the moist medium, while the fungus, for its part, receives some carbohydrates or other nutrient materials from the alga. Many lichens are able to grow at the low temperatures of arctic regions; reindeer mosses are lichens that furnish forage and fodder for animals in polar regions. Lichens are often considered pioneer "plants" in that they exist on dust-covered rocks and eventually thrive on top of rocks after laying down a mat. They can also live in hot, sandy soils that are desert-like in the piney forests of Florida. The well-known indicator litmus is obtained from lichens.

Despite the fact that the algae that make up the known species of lichens can live independently, the fungi that make them up cannot, because the algae produce the food. Thus, they can live with or without the fungus. The fungus just makes their survival easier. The fungus, on the other hand, cannot live without the food that the algae produces. Since the fungus of a lichen cannot live without the algae, one might wonder how lichens reproduce. Actually, it is rather fascinating that two unrelated life forms are highly woven together in complete harmony. Most lichens reproduce by releasing a dust-like substance called a soredium. The soredium contains spores of both the algae and the fungus in a protective case. Thus, the soredium is like a spore that contains two different spores. Wherever the soredium lands, then, both the fungus and the algae can grow. Isn't that amazing? The two separate species work together not only to survive, but also to reproduce!

Like *E. coli*, their association is mutualistic and the fungi provide a structural home, as well as water and minerals for the algae. The alga pays its rent with food in terms of its photosynthetic products, like carbohydrates and oxygen. The mutualistic relationship of totally different species gives us a glimpse of what life was meant to be before the Edenic curse. It points to a harmonious design that the Creator desired when he declared the creation as "good." The chances of two unrelated forms are highly unlikely. There appears to be purpose in the members of two separate kingdoms becoming one in the lichen. Isn't this a wondrous, interwoven design?

A specific example of a lichen is the "deer moss." These sponge-like lichens are extremely common in the

Fungus root

sand of Florida piney forests. They cover much of the forest floor, like an embroidered rug laid over a hard-wood floored dining room. They provide decoration and color to an otherwise bland environment. These sponge-like deer moss of piney forests are classified as fruticose types because they have a shrubby form. Other lichen forms include the crustose (crusty) and folliose (leaf-like) that embroider and decorate old trees and stumps in a forest. The fungi and algae living together in perfect harmony were designed for each other. They are very complex and quite colorful. They are so successful they are found from pole to pole, growing in the cold and hot, as well as desert-like and aquatic environments.

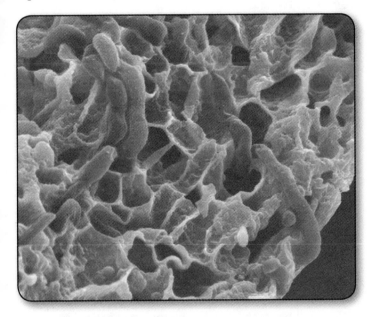

A mycorrhiza is a symbiotic association between a soil fungus and the roots of a vascular plant. The majority of vascular plants roots are mycorrhizal.

Mycorrhizae

A more prevalent (but less well-known) symbiotic relationship in which fungi participate is called a mycorrhizae, or a "fungus root." Nearly 80 percent of all plants with root systems participate in this symbiotic relationship with a fungus. In mycorrhizae, the fungus forms haustoria that penetrate the cell walls of the root system's cells. The fungus absorbs food from the roots as it is transported to the plant. In return, the plant takes in certain needed minerals that it cannot absorb efficiently from the soil without the help of a fungus.

In order to absorb minerals from the soil, an organism must be wide and thin. This is how the mycelium of a fungus grows. This is not, however, the way that a root system grows. Roots usually grow thick and long, trying to go deep within the soil. Since the mycelium of the fungus has the ideal structure for absorbing minerals, it does so in exchange for food. In laboratories, it has even been demonstrated that fungi absorb the minerals when they are plentiful and store the excess. These excess minerals are then released slowly into the roots of the plant when the minerals are scarce in the soil. This nutrient recycling is the Sustainer's plan for maintaining a balance and harmony of materials in nature.

The importance of mycorrhizae first became evident when horticulturists observed that orchids do not grow unless an appropriate fungus lives with them. Similarly, many forest trees, such as pines, decline and eventually die from mineral deficiencies when transplanted to mineral-rich grassland soils that lack the appropriate mycorrhizal fungi. When forest soil containing the appropriate fungi or their spores is added to the soil around these trees, they quickly resume normal growth. Similar results were reported for tall prairie grass plant species with and without mycorrhizal fungi.

Summary and Conclusions

In summary, in this chapter we have examined the beneficial and destructive aspects of fungi. Most fungi are saprophytes and obtain their nutrition from dead organisms. Without fungi, bacteria, and other microbes, life on earth as we know it would be impossible. Decay is essential for recycling. When living things die, fungi secrete digestive enzymes to break down complex molecules into simpler ones. The simple molecules are then used by living organisms to build up cells and tissues. Saprophytic fungi and bacteria continuously recycle the organic chemicals. Only in the new heavens and the new earth will there be no more death and decay. Although some fungi are parasitic and cause such diseases as athlete's foot, ringworm, Dutch elm disease, potato blight, and wheat rust, other fungi in the Creator's providence are extremely helpful to mankind. Without certain fungi, many cheeses would lack their distinctive flavors, for example. Millions of human lives have been spared from bacterial diseases thanks to antibiotics from molds and other fungi.

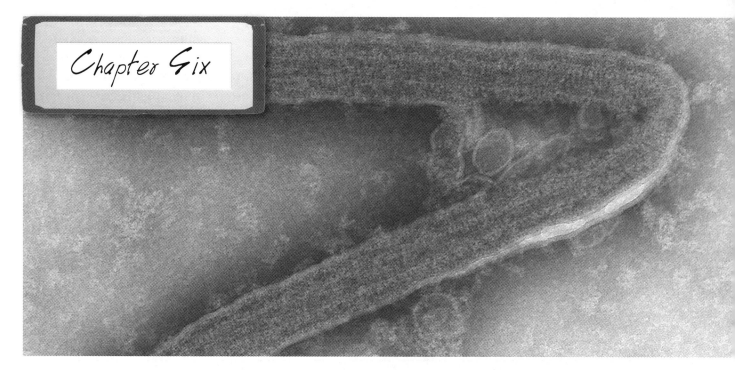

Chapter Six

Viruses: Fallen Genes Coated with Protein

Most of us have experienced waking up and not being able to get out of bed because an alien has invaded our body! We feel run down and dizzy, even though we have had adequate rest. To make matters worse, a sore throat, runny nose, and cough soon accompany these tired feelings. We complain that a "germ" has invaded! We ask our doctor, "What do I have?" The doctor explains that most colds are caused by viruses, such as rhinoviruses, coronaviruses, Coxsackie viruses, respiratory syncytial viruses, adenoviruses, reoviruses, echoviruses, and influenza viruses. The cold is the most common communicable and infectious disease known to mankind. Only dental cavities, caused by bacteria, exceed the number of infections caused by microbes.

Viruses are genes in protein packages. Like bacteria, they work under the direction of a genetic code. Due to their relatively simple structure and fast reproductive rate, viruses make ideal models for understanding molecular mechanisms of disease and how the Creator designed life in its most basic form. In this chapter, we describe viruses (along with related life forms called viroids and prions) and bacteria in terms of their genetics, their role in disease, and their contribution to the environment.

Viruses: Living or Nonliving?

The question of whether viruses are living organisms has an ambiguous answer. Life can be defined as a complex set of processes resulting from the actions of proteins specified by nucleic acids. The nucleic acids of living cells are active all the time. Because viruses are inert when outside living host cells, they are not considered in this context to be living organisms. However, once viruses enter a host cell, the viral nucleic acids become active, and viral multiplication results. In this sense, viruses are alive when they multiply in the host cells they infect. From a clinical point of view, viruses can be considered alive because they cause infection and disease, just as pathogenic bacteria, fungi, and protozoa do. Depending on one's viewpoint, a virus may be regarded as an exceptionally complex aggregation of nonliving chemicals, or as an exceptionally simple living microbe. Virus traits are puzzling; on one hand they can crystallize like sugar cubes, but on the other hand they cause infectious diseases with similar features to some bacterial diseases.

How, then, do we define a virus? Viruses were originally distinguished from other infectious agents because they are especially small (filterable) and because they are obligatory intracellular parasites — that is, they absolutely require living host cells in order to multiply. However, certain small bacteria, such as some rickettsias, share both of these properties. Viruses and cells are compared in Table 6.1.

Table 6.1 Comparison of Viruses and Cells

Trait	Viruses	Typical Cells
1. Structure	Virus particle: nucleic acid core surrounded by protein coat	Cells contain nucleic acids, lipid-protein membrane, ribosomes, cytoplasm, etc.
2. Nucleic Acids	DNA or RNA,	Both DNA and RNA
3. Enzymes	One or a few polymerases	Many enzymes and lysozymes; diverse functions
4. Metabolism	Relies on host-cell metabolism of proteins, nucleic acids, etc.	Makes own ribosomes and enzymes needed for synthesis
5. Reproduction	Relies on host nucleic acids and proteins produced separately, then assembled into whole virus particles	Division into two similar cells following growth. Binary fission or mitosis and meiosis

Characteristics of Viruses

Viruses are infectious particles that probably represent what were once cell parts before the Edenic curse. Perhaps they are renegade cell parts returning "home." Some creationists speculate that after the curse and the Flood, mutations accumulated and once-friendly genes became parasitic in nature. Since viruses, viroids, and prions are all life forms that are dependent on host cells, they represent the ultimate parasites.

Viruses invade cells. Unlike bacteria, a virus lacks the materials necessary for its own growth and reproduction. It must take over a living cell to survive. A virus is simply a core of RNA or DNA surrounded by a protein coat; some viruses also have an outer envelope. A human virus particle, like the common cold virus, encounters a body cell that carries a chemical receptor for that virus. It attaches to the surface of the cell, enters the cell's cytoplasm, and there sheds its protein coating. Now the particle seizes its host's building blocks and machinery to replicate its own nucleic acid and its protein coat. New viruses form within the host cell. Infected cells may burst open, releasing thousands of fresh viruses, or viruses may exit particle by particle through a budding process in which a portion of the cell membrane wraps around the virus core particle. It actually becomes a part of the new, complete viral envelope. The viral particle, or virion as it is now called, floats free and can go on to invade other cells. By commandeering these host cells, viruses can make our lives miserable.

Viruses differ from bacteria, protozoans, and fungi by their ultramicroscopic size and in that they cannot be grown in artificial, cell-free media. They require the presence of living, susceptible cells. In short, they are recognized to be a special class of obligatory intracellular parasites. Table 6.2 lists the major properties and characteristics of viruses. They vary in size, architecture, and function.

Table 6.2 An Overview of Virus Architecture and Properties

SIZE: 20-200 nm in diameter (electron microscope needed to visualize); some 4,500 nm long.

CLASSIFICATION: Neither prokaryotes nor eukaryotes; acellular; classified into multiple families depending on structure and physiology.

ARCHITECTURE: Segment of nucleic acid (RNA or DNA) called the genome; enclosed in a sheath of protein called the capsid; combination of genome and capsid called the nucleocapsid; some viruses surrounded by an envelope (membranous covering); nucleocapsid can be icosahedral (20-sided geometric figure) or helical (spiral) or complex (bricklike); herpes viruses. Adenoviruses and retroviruses are icosahedral, orthomyxoviruses are helical, and poxviruses are complex.

PROPERTIES (Five major characteristics are given priority):

1. The type of nucleic acid — either RNA or DNA — and whether the nucleic acid is single- or double-stranded, linear or circular, in one or more pieces.

2. The symmetry of the nucleocapsid, whether cubic, helical, or complex.

3. The presence or absence of an envelope. Since host-derived envelopes contain lipid, this property is determined by sensitivity to ether.

4. The number of capsomeres with icosahedral viruses, or the diameter of the nucleocapsid with helical viruses.

5. In addition, the size of the virion and the molecular weight of the nucleic acid viral genome.

An Overview of Virus Architecture and Properties

Virus Size

Viruses are among the smallest agents able to cause disease in living things. We measure their size in nanometers (nm, or 10^{-9} m). Most viruses are less than 0.3 nm, or 300 nm, in diameter. They range from 250 nm for poxviruses to 20 nm for rhinoviruses. At the upper end of the spectrum, some viruses approximate the size of small bacteria; at the lower end, they are not much larger than the diameter of a double-stranded DNA helix. A few viruses, such as poxviruses and some of the larger insect viruses (baculoviruses), can be seen with a light microscope, though barely at that. Most viruses must be observed with an electron microscope. Through special staining techniques, their architecture may be determined. Generally, viruses are much smaller than bacteria.

Sizes are estimated principally (1) from the results of ultrafiltration experiments, (2) from the rate of sedimentation of the virus materials in an ultracentrifuge; and (3) from pictures made with the electron microscope. They vary from the relatively large vaccinia, through the viruses of intermediate size (including herpes, measles, mumps, and influenza), to the extremely small ones, among which are found the viruses of encephalitis, poliomyelitis, the common cold (rhinoviruses), and yellow fever. The smallest viruses are just slightly larger than a eukaryotic ribosome.

For comparison, it is helpful to remember that most individual staphylococci have a diameter of 800 to 1,000 nm, and their mass is several thousand times that of the smaller viruses. Some of the smaller ones have diameters of only about four times those of single protein molecules, such as serum albumin (5 nm). The individual units of vaccinia virus and related poxviruses are the largest of the typical viruses. They consist of cubical, brick-like bodies, about 200 to 250 nm across, with a complex internal structure. Other human and animal viruses are roughly spherical.

Influenza virus particles may be described, for example, as spheres with a diameter of about 120 nm. The same virus occurs, however, in the form of rather long filaments. The particles of the equine encephalomyelitis virus are also spherical and have a relatively dense inner zone surrounded by a vaguely outlined peripheral portion; the whole particle is only about 20 to 50 nm in diameter. Some of the plant viruses are spherical, but others have an elongated, rectangular form. The highly purified tobacco mosaic virus appears as needle-shaped or rod-shaped particles, 15 nm wide by about 280 nm long. Bacterial viruses (bacteriophages) have round or hexagonal heads about 100 nm in diameter, and tailpieces often 100 to 200 nm long (opposite page).

Shape and Structure

To make sense of the world, the human mind relies heavily on its perception of shapes and patterns. Spatial patterns can be represented by a fairly small collection of fundamental geometric shapes. Although real viruses never perfectly match geometric figures, they approximate them enough that what is known about geometric figures and their relationship to their environments can be applied to viruses. For these exercises, it is sufficient for one to be familiar with the triangle and the icosahedron. Both shape and scale have important consequences for the stability and growth potential of viruses. Triangular connections usually maximize rigidity, smooth surfaces minimize turbulence, and icosahedral structures maximize both stability and the ability to pack efficiently inside cells.

Viruses are made of complex chemicals, and when viewed under an electron microscope, have a beautiful symmetry and design. For example, most viruses that cause the common cold have a shape based upon the icosahedron. This means the virus coat, or capsid, comprises 20 equilateral triangular faces that provide a stable protein structure consistent with long-term survival. Icosahedral particles pack well in small spaces. In fact, more than 10,000 rhinoviruses could fit into their host cell! Adenoviruses look like balls with spikes sticking out on all sides. Coronaviruses appear to be surrounded by a crown. Rhinoviruses, the most frequent cause of the common cold, have a symmetrical shape like a miniature geodesic dome (like the shape of a large professional sports stadium).

Historically, studies of the tobacco mosaic virus gave the first insight into the intimate structure of viruses. It was found that the particles of this virus may be precipitated from solution in the form of regular, needle-like crystals. Later it was established that the rod-shaped particles consist of a relatively large mass of protein, which forms a coating around a tiny central core of RNA. The virus protein is not itself infectious, but the RNA is. Now, we know that all viruses have the same fundamental makeup — tiny virus particles consisting essentially of a core containing a single nucleic acid (either RNA or DNA) enclosed within a protein coating called the capsid. The complete infectious virus constitutes a virion.

When the smaller spherical viruses, such as those of poliomyelitis, herpes, and the adenoviruses, are enlarged several hundred thousand times under an electron microscope, they are found to have a high degree of structural symmetry. The capsid appears to be made up of many subunits, called capsomeres, packed together around the nucleic-acid core in a regular manner to form a simple geometrical structure. This structure is in the form of a polyhedron with cubical symmetry, or a helix, or variations and combinations of these. Thus, the adenovirus and herpes virus particles have cubic symmetry, and the tobacco mosaic and the internal components of mumps and influenza viruses have helical symmetry. In the larger animal viruses, such as those of smallpox and vaccinia, the geometry is usually more complex, and a structure of greater flexibility, more like that of familiar living cells, begins to appear.

When separated from living cells, as in the laboratory or in the natural environment, a virus is inert. It can even form into crystals, like a sugar cube does. It does not show metabolic activity and does not multiply. It reproduces only within the invaded host cells, where

it utilizes the enzyme systems available there, changing the cells' metabolic processes so as to produce more viral particles like itself. None of the microorganisms discussed in later chapters can be so described.

All known plant viruses contain RNA; the animal and bacterial viruses may contain either RNA or DNA. The nucleic acids are extracted from certain intracellular development. Although in its extracellular phase a virus particle is metabolically inert, it does have the power to attach itself to the surface of a susceptible living cell and then to penetrate into, and thus infect, the cell. The pivotal event is the entrance of the virus' nucleic acid into the host cell, because this material can block the ordinary metabolic activities of the cell and literally take command, converting the cell's metabolism to its own use. Thus begins the intracellular phase of the life cycle of the virus. For example, influenza viruses have en-

zymes that break down host-cell membranes, aiding the adsorption of the virus particles to the surface of epithelial cells in the respiratory tract. Soon, new nucleic-acid material of the same kind is synthesized. More of the viral protein is also independently formed. In the final stages of the infection process, nucleic acid and protein are reassembled in infectious units similar to those in the original virus. In many instances, this series of events results in the death (lysis) of the infected cell, and the new virus particles are all released at approximately the same time. However, in some virus infections — influenza, for example — the newly produced virus particles are released continually as they are formed.

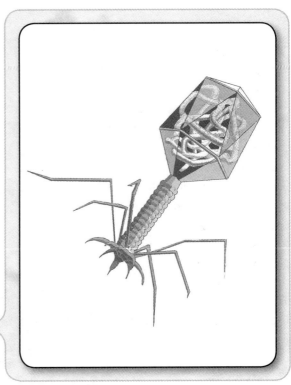

Bacteriophages

Virus Architecture: Virion Anatomy

The virion always contains, at minimum, both nucleic acid and protein. Their arrangement within the virion involves the treatment of intact virions with protease enzymes that degrade exposed proteins and remove important attachment proteins, so that the viruses can no longer infect the cells and begin their replication cycle. Photomicrographs of the virions of two typical viruses, a plant virus (tobacco mosaic virus) and an animal virus (adenovirus), illustrate that the architecture of virions, regardless of their host, is usually based on two simple themes: the helix and the sphere. Currently, high-resolution electron microscopy has made some astounding revelations in the fine structure of viral capsids.

The tobacco mosaic virus consists of an RNA helical genome surrounded by a protein assembly that is reminiscent of a spiral staircase. The term capsid, from the Latin word *capsa*, meaning "box," is given to the protein shell around the nucleic acid; nucleocapsid refers to the entire nucleic acid-protein complex. The morphological units visible in photomicrographs are called capsomeres. The suffix "-mer" is derived from the Greek word *meros*, meaning "part" and usually referring to a subunit or building block of a larger structure.

Helical Viruses

Viruses are classified into several different morphological types on the basis of their capsid architecture. The structure of these capsids has been revealed by electron microscopy and a technique called x-ray crystallography. One of the earliest viruses studied was the plant virus, tobacco mosaic virus, which is based upon a helical structure. Helical viruses resemble long rods that may be rigid or flexible. The viral nucleic acid is found within a hollow cylindrical capsid. The viruses that cause rabies and hemorrhagic fever also display helical symmetry.

Icosahedral or Polyhedral Viruses

Many animal, plant, and bacterial viruses are polyhedral (many-sided) viruses. The capsid of most viruses is a special type of polyhedron called an icosahedron. An icosahedron is a regular polyhedron with 20 triangular faces and 12 corners. The capsomeres of each face form an equilateral triangle. An example of a polyhedral virus in the shape of an icosahedron is the polio virus. Another icosahedral virus is the adenovirus. This virus has spikes projecting from each of the 12 vertices. These are carbohydrate-protein complexes that project from the surface of the envelope. Some viruses attach to host cells by means of these spikes.

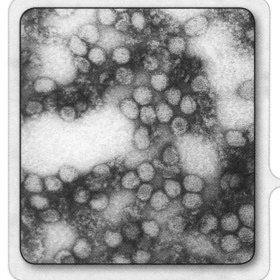

Influenza virus

Enveloped Viruses

An envelope covers the capsid of some viruses. Enveloped viruses are roughly spherical. When helical or polyhedral viruses are enclosed by envelopes, they are called enveloped helical or enveloped polyhedral viruses. An example of an enveloped helical virus is the influenza virus. An example of an enveloped polyhedral (icosahedral) virus is the herpes simplex virus. The anatomy of HIV includes an envelope, but not all virologists agree on its exact structure.

Complex Viruses

Some viruses, particularly bacterial viruses, have complicated structures and are called complex viruses. One example of a complex virus is a bacteriophage. Some bacteriophages have capsids to which additional structures are attached. On the previous page, notice that the capsid (head) is polyhedral and the tail sheath is helical. The head contains the nucleic acid. Later, we will discuss the functions of other structures, such as the tail sheath, tail fibers, plate, and pin. Other examples of complex viruses are poxviruses, which are large and pleomorphic.

History of Virology

Discovery of Filterable Infectious Agents

The invention of filters that do not allow the passage of ordinary bacteria led to one of the most important of all discoveries in biology. It was found that the specific causative agents of certain diseases of plants, animals, and human beings would pass through such filters in invisible form. Iwanowski was the first to observe this, in

1892, when he showed that the agent responsible for the mosaic disease of tobacco leaves is filterable. Beijerinck (1898) demonstrated that the clear filtrate from an emulsion of diseased tobacco leaves, visible under an ordinary microscope, could cause the typical mosaic disease when rubbed into healthy tobacco leaves. Beijerinck described the filtrate as a "contagious living fluid" and referred to the ultramicroscopic infectious factor as a "virus." The word virus, from the Latin meaning "poison," had been used for centuries in this literal sense; but also, in the early days of microbiology, it was loosely applied to various microorganisms (e.g., the "chicken cholera virus," a bacterium studied by Pasteur). With Beijerinck, the term became equated with a filterable, disease-producing agent too small to be seen with an ordinary microscope. This was the beginning for the modern use of the word virus.

In 1898, Loeffler and Frosch described the first filterable animal virus, one that causes foot-and-mouth disease in livestock and sometimes in man. Soon a large number of other conditions, including some of the most common and serious human diseases, were found to be due to infection of the same general kind. It has been established beyond doubt that all viruses are particulates — not merely "poisonous

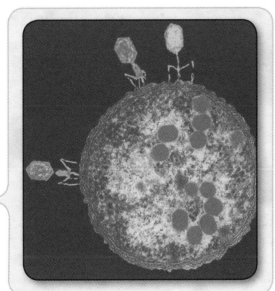

T2 bacteriophage viruses attacking an Escherichia coli *bacterium*

fluids." Each variety consists of solid particles, having a characteristic size, shape, and internal structure. The viruses are recognized as a distinct class of infectious agents with unique properties. The term virus has as explicit a meaning as does bacterium, fungus, or protozoan.

Bacterial Viruses (Bacteriophages)

The viruses perhaps most studied during the past century are those that attack bacteria — known as bacteriophages. From 1915–17, two investigators, Twort and d'Herelle, were the first to call attention to a remarkable phenomenon. They discovered that bacteria themselves could suffer a filterable virus disease. They found that the clear filtrate (free of any visible microbes) contained an agent of some kind that would destroy dysentery germs. If a trace of this filtrate was added to a young broth culture of dysentery bacilli, all or nearly all of the organisms were dissolved (lysed), and the previously cloudy culture became clear in a few hours. Moreover, if a trace of this culture was placed in another young broth culture of dysentery organisms, the same thing occurred, and successive transfers could carry along the mysterious bacteria-dissolving agent indefinitely. When a drop of a filtrate containing the unknown agent came in contact with a young growth of dysentery germs on a solid medium, such as an agar, the growth became glassy and transparent, and the organisms in these transparent areas (called plaques) were found to have been killed. D'Herelle thought he was dealing with an invisible living microbe that was a parasite upon bacteria. He called this living particle a bacteriophage (literally meaning "bacteria-eating agent"). Often a bacteriophage is referred to simply as a phage.

Structure of Phages

A so-called virulent bacteriophage will produce a characteristic lytic infection. The virus particles originally become attached to the bacterial cell by their tails. The nucleic acid of the phage passes into the cell through the attached tail, while the protein coat is left outside. Then the intracellular phase of phage development occurs when the threads of DNA are first broken. It is a fact that lysogenic bacteria are immune to infection by a phage of the type already present in the cell as a prophage.

Life Cycle of Bacteriophage

When a completely healthy cell becomes infected with a bacterial virus (center), the subsequent series of events may follow either of two paths: B or C. Ordinarily, the virus, after entering the cell, goes through its characteristic developmental cycle (C), making many copies of itself, until the cell bursts, releasing the fully infective virus particles. But this destructive infection is not inevitable. Instead the virus may develop only to the provirus form,

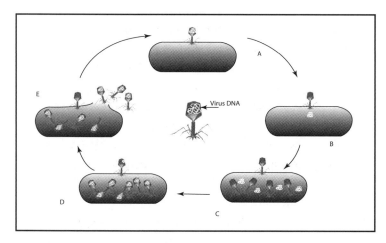

Illustration of the life cycle of a bacteriophage

and the bacterium thus becomes lysogenic; the cell lives and continues to multiply, carrying along the virus genes that have become attached to the nuclear material of the bacteria (B). The provirus is sometimes lost during cell division, returning the cell to the normal (non-lysogenic) state. Ultraviolet light or some other stimulus may dislodge the provirus, inducing again the active intracellular development of the virus and the lysis of the cell.

The Bacteriophage as a Tool in Basic Biological Research

The remarkable phenomena associated with interactions between phages and living bacteria are, in themselves, obviously of great interest. In addition, intensive studies of these relationships have yielded information of immense importance concerning the details of fundamental hereditary processes, not only in microorganisms, but also in higher plants and animals, and in man as well. Later in this chapter we will examine how phages can carry genetic information for toxins, hence making harmless bacteria into virulent ones. Bacteriophages (e.g., *lambda* phage) can also be used as vectors for storing DNA sequences in a gene library and in genetic engineering. This is done by restriction enzymes — cutting the desired gene from foreign DNA and then inserting it into the deleted area. For example, when the recombinant phage DNA is introduced into an *E. coli* cell, the phage replicates itself inside the bacterial cell. Each new phage particle carries the foreign DNA "passenger."

Viruses and Cancer

Peyton Rous was the first person to identify a retrovirus (in the same family as HIV) that could transmit tumors among chickens. This was the first suggestion that viruses may cause cancer in animals. The cancer-causing DNA affected parts of the genome called oncogenes. Oncogenes were thought to be part of the normal viral genome. However, in 1976, Bishop and Varmus proved that the cancer-inducing genes carried by the viruses are actually derived from animal cells. Bishop and Varmus showed that the cancer-causing SRC gene in avian sarcoma viruses is derived from a normal part of chick genes.

Creation Scientist Focus 6.1

Walter Reed and Yellow Jack: The Story of How a Christian Physician Conquered Yellow Fever

Walter Reed Hospital, in Washington, DC, is the best known military hospital by the average American citizen. How many of us know anything of the Christian man after whom it was named — a doctor of quality and grit who freed the United States and Cuba of one of the most dangerous plagues that ever troubled mankind? Yellow fever was a seasonal scourge to the nation, a semitropical nightmare that left up to 85 percent of its victims dead. During the Spanish-American War, it killed more men than bullets did. By a well-conducted series of experiments, Walter Reed demonstrated that the *Aedes aegypti* mosquito was the carrier of the disease. In doing so, he confirmed the key point of the theories suggesting mosquitoes as the carrier. God employs willing hands as His own. From early childhood, Reed, already a practicing Christian, prayed to be used by God in some capacity by which he might better the lot of others.

Courageous Experiments Relied on the Evidence, Not Evolution

In the first series of experiments, female mosquitoes that had already bitten patients with well-marked cases of yellow fever bit 11 volunteers. Of 11 persons, only 2 developed the disease. Dr. Lazear, while collecting blood for study from yellow-fever patients in a Cuban hospital, had a mosquito settle on the back of his hand. He allowed it to stay there until it had drunk its fill. Five days after the bite, he came down with yellow fever. On the evening of September 25, 1900, he died at the age of 34 and *"in dying,"* in Major Reed's own words, *"added one more name to that imperishable roll of honor to which none others belong than martyrs to the cause of humanity."*

Major Reed returned to Cuba and carefully studied Dr. Lazear's notes on the connection between mosquitoes and yellow fever. These notes convinced Major Reed that "the mosquito serves as the intermediate host for the parasite of yellow fever." In the medical community, there was some doubt. And rightly so, because it is the duty of good scientists to withhold acceptance of any new theory until there is adequate evidence and it can be proved beyond a shadow of doubt. To demonstrate that the mosquito is the only carrier of yellow fever, it was necessary to conduct experiments in such a way as to make it impossible for the men experimented on to get yellow fever accidentally. Major Reed and his associates took a piece of ground close to Havana and built a camp there. The campsite was well drained and freely exposed to sunlight and winds. In this camp were quartered men who had never had yellow fever and who were therefore called non-immunes. These men were the American soldiers who had volunteered for the experiments. The first volunteers were John Kissinger and John Moran. Major Reed talked the matter over with them, explaining the risk of suffering and even of death. They held to their purpose. Kissinger volunteered, to use his own words, *"solely in the interest of humanity and the cause of science."* Major Reed's comment on this young man was: *"In my opinion this exhibition of moral courage has never been surpassed in the annals of the Army of the United States."*

Reed proposed to attempt the infection of non-immunes with yellow fever in three ways: (1) by the bites of mosquitoes that had previously bitten yellow-fever patients; (2) by the injection of blood taken from yellow-fever patients; and (3) by exposure to the most intimate contact with fomites. All three sets of experiments were carried on at approximately the same time. Experience had shown that if a person is going to contract yellow fever, he develops it within six days after exposure. Therefore, if the men were kept in quarantine for two weeks without developing the disease, this fact would show they had not become infected before they entered camp. Things were now so arranged that if any man developed yellow fever, the board would know that the disease was the result of the experiment in which he had taken part, and nothing else.

To test the fomite theory, a small frame house called "the infected-clothing building" consisting of one room was erected at Camp Lazear. It was tightly built, and the doors and windows were so placed as to admit as little sunlight and air as possible. The room was kept like the hold of a ship in the tropics — warm, dark, and moist. Three large boxes filled with sheets, pillowslips, blankets, and clothing contaminated with the excretions of yellow-fever patients were placed inside the building. All non-immune young Americans entered the building. They then made the beds with the soiled bed clothing and slept in them. Various contaminated articles were hung about the bed. For 20 nights this room was occupied by these brave men who slept every night in the soiled garments and on the bedding used by yellow-fever patients throughout their illness. They remained perfectly well. The experiment was repeated a third time with the same results. This series of experiments denied the fomite theory. Fomites were proven innocent.

Mosquitoes Proven Guilty

The mosquito-biting experiments began and the mosquitoes that had bitten yellow-fever patients from 15 to 20 days before bit Kissinger. Four days later he had a well-marked case of yellow fever, from which he recovered. Four more positive cases developed in one week. In all, 13 men at Camp Lazear were infected by means of the bites of contaminated mosquitoes, and the disease developed in 10. Fortunately, they recovered. No one else in the camp became ill. As a result of these experiments it was found that yellow fever could be carried from one person to another by the bite of a female mosquito that had previously bitten a yellow-fever patient. In general, people bitten would come down with the disease within six days. It now became clear as to why it took so long for a case of yellow fever to infect a house. Mosquitoes had to bite the patient during the first three days of his illness. Then 12 days had to go by before they could pass on the disease by biting another person in the household. But after that interval of 12 days they were a menace to every non-immune who entered the house or its immediate neighborhood.

By the end of the year 1900, the experiments at Camp Lazear had left no grounds for doubting that one of the greatest medical mysteries of all time had been solved.

Mosquitoes — and mosquitoes only — were the carriers of yellow fever. Major Reed was so moved by the results of the work at the camp that on New Year's Eve he wrote the following beautiful letter to his wife:

"Only ten minutes of the old century remain. Here I have been sitting reading that most wonderful book, 'La Roche on Yellow Fever,' written in 1853. Forty-seven years later it has been permitted to me and my assistants to lift the impenetrable veil that has surrounded the causation of this most wonderful, dreadful pest of humanity and to put it on a rational and scientific oasis. I thank God that this has been accomplished during the latter days of the old century. May its cure be wrought out in the early days of the new! The prayer that has been mine for twenty years, that I might be permitted in some way or at some time to do something to alleviate human suffering has been granted! A thousand Happy New Years . . . Hark, there go the twenty-four buglers in concert, all sounding 'Taps' for the old year."

Cause of Yellow Fever

During later experiments, blood drawn from yellow-fever patients revealed that the specific agent, or germ, of yellow fever is present in the blood of its victims. Major Reed and Dr. Carroll recognized that the production of yellow fever by the injection of blood serum that had previously been passed through a laboratory filter capable of removing all bacteria was a matter of extreme importance. It seemed logical to them to conclude that the specific agent of yellow fever is of such minute size that it passes readily through the pores of a filter. They had, in other words, discovered that the cause of yellow fever is a filterable virus.

Fruits of Victory

Walter Reed passed sentence on the mosquito carriers of yellow fever in these words: "The spread of yellow fever can be most effectually controlled by measures directed to the destruction of mosquitoes and the protection of the sick against these insects." Major William C. Gorgas, Chief Sanitary Officer of Havana, accomplished this work. Practically no one thought that it could be done! Gorgas was able to get rid of the mosquito by draining the swamps near human habitations. Gorgas determined where the female mosquitoes could get the meals of human blood, which they must have in order to lay their eggs. Moreover, they preferred to lay their eggs in clean standing water in artificial containers — rain barrels, pails, pitchers, tin cans, broken bottles, flower vases, pans, and other household utensils.

"Yellow jack," once a major cause of death in the United States, is now under control. Vaccination is the only way of controlling yellow fever. It is impossible to get rid of its forest mosquito carriers by any known anti-mosquito measures. There is as yet no cure for yellow fever. But this ancient foe is surely on the way out, thanks to the gallant men who solved its mystery and to all those who have added to, and applied, the knowledge they won.

Lazear (and others working with Dr. Reed) should be honored, too, for he gave his life in the search. These men and the other noble volunteers saved the world incalculable misery and, as a bonus, eased the building of the Panama Canal. Walter Reed was ever a man of faith (Graves, 1999). Major Reed's brilliant scientific achievement — what entitles him to be called "the conqueror of yellow fever" — is that he produced that evidence and proof! Oh, if only Darwinists would learn from this lesson. Reed's biographer wrote that Christian principle was a distinguishing trait of the conqueror of yellow fever (Graves, 1999). The greatest lesson to be learned from Reed's life is that happiness and usefulness lie in giving what we can to life rather than getting what we can from it. In the book *Microbe Hunters* (1926), Paul De Kruif called Reed a blameless man, "mad to help his fellowmen." Indeed, our national hospitals should be named for such men.

In short, the detection of mosquitoes carrying a virus has helped to alleviate suffering from yellow fever, just as it did for Sir Ronald Ross when he discovered that mosquitoes carried *Plasmodium*, the parasite that caused malaria. The process of detecting causes of disease is often tedious and time consuming, but the outcome of saving lives makes this effort worthwhile. Likewise, learning to detect design in nature and telling others about one's findings may ultimately help people discover their Creator. By eliminating mosquitoes, millions of lives have been spared. By discovering the Creator who is also Savior, millions of souls may be saved from eternal death.

Viruses and Cancer (continued)
Table 6.4 — T4 Bacteriophage Characteristics.

Virus Architecture: This virus has a naked polyhedral head with a helical tail. The head contains double-stranded DNA. The head is an elongated icosahedron, whereas the tail is helical with spikes. It has a complex viral structure.

Table 6.4 continued

Virus Host: *Escherichia coli* (lytic and/or lysogenic relationship)
Virus Classification: *Myoviridae* (bacteriophage), double-stranded DNA, 225 nm in height.
Virulence: The T4 virus does not infect humans; it only infects bacteria. Infection of a bacterial cell by T4 results in the eventual lysis and death of the cell. The virus only affects certain strains of *E. coli*.
Variation: There are many variations of bacteriophages, of which the T4 virus is a specific strain.
Miscellaneous: The T4 injects its DNA into bacteria. Transcription and translation of the phage DNA takes place, leading to the synthesis of phage proteins. The phage building blocks are made and assembled inside the cell, and enzymes are released that lyse the bacterial cell wall. When the bacterial cell wall bursts, many newly formed phages are released to invade other bacteria.

The first real proof of human cancers being caused by viruses came by accident in a transplant case involving the Epstein-Barr virus. Typically, in the United States, EBV causes mononucleosis, and in Africa, two human cancers: lymphoma and nasopharyngeal carcinoma. Nasopharyngeal carcinoma, a cancer of the nose, is found worldwide. Some researchers have also found the virus to be involved in some forms of Hodgkin's disease. About 90 percent of the U.S. population probably carries a latent stage of the EBV in their lymphocytes but has no signs of disease. This latent stage is indicated by the presence in blood serum of antibodies to the virus. Although infection with this virus leads to mild symptoms in healthy children, later it can cause infectious mononucleosis, mostly in teenagers.

EBV was isolated from Burkitt's lymphoma cells in 1964 by Michael Epstein and Yvonne Barr. The proof that EBV can cause cancer was accidentally demonstrated in 1983 when David Vetter, a 12-year-old boy, received a bone-marrow transplant. David was born without a functioning immune system and was kept inside a sterile "bubble" his entire life to isolate him from all microbes. In light of David's living quarters, the news media named him "the bubble boy." Several months after the transplant, he developed signs of infectious mononucleosis, and a few months later he died of cancer. An autopsy revealed that the virus had been unwittingly introduced into the boy through the bone-marrow transplant. The case supported suspicions that EBV can induce cancer in immunosuppressed individuals.

Emerging Viruses

In recent years, new diseases have emerged on the scene, resulting in sensational news stories. These new or changing diseases seem to be increasing, and have the potential to increase in incidence. Viral traffic is central to the origin of most flu epidemics. Emerging viruses may be the result of changes in "traffic" that give viruses new "highways." There is evidence that the changing relationship between influenza and human society is a result of changes in the relationship between humans and their environment. Consequently, antigenic shifts in influenza can be attributed to a reassortment of genome segments, where the frequencies may oscillate from year to year. There are about 23 influenza A viruses that come and go through the years. The observation that 23 viruses fluctuate in their frequency from year to year may indicate there is a limitation to the change, but clearly the diversity of virus strains keeps medical workers investigating and altering vaccines for effective immunization against the flu. Some other emerging viruses include those listed below.

Table 6.5 Examples of Emerging Diseases Caused by Viruses

Emerging Virus	Year Discovered	Disease Caused
HIV	1983	AIDS
Dengue fever virus	1984	Dengue fever
Hepatitis C virus	1989	Hepatitis
Hepatitis E virus	1990	Hepatitis
Hanta virus	1993	Pulmonary syndrome
Ebola virus	1995, 1979	Hemorrhagic fever
West Nile Virus	1999	Encephalitis

Among those emerging viruses that have received much national attention are Ebola (cause of hemorrhagic fever) and HIV (cause of Acquired Immune Deficiency Syndrome, or AIDS). We will examine these two as examples of new viruses that are life-threatening.

Ebola and Hemorrhagic Fever

In 1995, a hospital laboratory technician in the Democratic Republic of the Congo (formerly Zaire), who had a fever and bloody diarrhea, underwent surgery for a suspected perforated bowel. Subsequent to surgery, he started hemorrhaging, and his blood began clotting in his blood vessels. A few days later, health-care workers in the hospital where he was staying developed similar symptoms. One of them was transferred to a hospital in a different city; personnel in the second hospital who cared for this patient also developed those symptoms. By the time the epidemic was over, 315 people had contracted Ebola hemorrhagic fever (EHF), and over 75 percent of them died. The epidemic was controlled when microbiologists instituted training on the use of protective equipment and on educational measures. Human-to-human transmission occurs when there is close personal contact with infected blood, other body fluids, or tissue.

Microbiologists first isolated Ebola viruses from humans during earlier outbreaks in the DRC in 1976. In 1994, a single case of infection from a newly described Ebola virus occurred in Cote d'Ivoire. In 1989 and 1996, outbreaks among monkeys imported into the United States from the Philippines were caused by another Ebola virus but were not associated with human disease. Microbiologists have been studying many animals but have not yet discovered the natural reservoir (source) of the Ebola virus.

Human Immunodeficiency Virus

HIV is the virus that causes AIDS. It is one of several medium-sized retroviruses. It is slightly smaller than a *Mycoplasma*, the smallest of living cells. Its genome consists of single-stranded RNA. When the HIV virus infects cells, it ends up killing the cells. Thus, the human body ends up with an immune deficiency. HIV attaches to a cellular receptor called the CD4 receptor. Once inside the cell, the reverse transcriptase enzyme packaged inside the virus particle makes a double-stranded DNA copy of the RNA genome, which is subsequently transferred to the cell nucleus, where it is integrated into the host cell chromosome and thus becomes part of the cell genome. The viral genome replicates, and eventually the T-cell is killed.

The primary components of HIV include RNA, glycoproteins, reverse transcriptase and a lipid-containing envelope. As mentioned earlier, its genome consists of single-stranded RNA. When the HIV virus infects CD4+ T-cells (often called T-4 lymphocytes), it ends up destroying the immune system. This leads to immune deficiency. In addition to nucleocapsid proteins and the virally coded attachment glycoproteins on the envelope, retroviruses such as HIV contain internal proteins that are often tightly bound to the nucleic-acid genome. Some of these proteins are enzymes necessary for initiating viral replication. Others may be virally coded proteases important in processing viral proteins during the maturation process. It is important to know and understand the anatomy of the AIDS virus because medical workers must be able to recognize specific proteins in the virus in order to properly detect and diagnose HIV disease in a Western Blot electrophoretic pattern. Bands for both an inner and an outer protein must be generated on the gel to positively identify HIV.

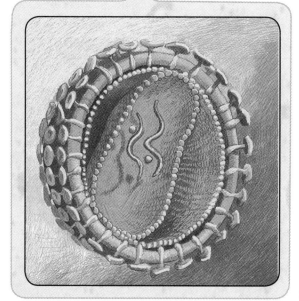
Human Immunodeficiency Virus

HIV enters T-cells, where it sheds its protein coat. New HIV DNA is produced in the T-cell, along with new protein coats, and then released. The T-cells are ultimately destroyed. Because HIV is a retrovirus, the way it replicates is different than most other viruses. HIV uses reverse transcriptase to synthesize new DNA from RNA. The new DNA then replicates, and double-stranded DNA is formed. However, before transcription can take place, the viral DNA must be integrated into the DNA of the host-cell chromosome. In this integrated state, the viral DNA is called a provirus. Unlike a prophage (in a bacteriophage), the provirus never comes out of the chromosome. As a provirus, HIV is protected from the body's immune system and antiviral drugs. Sometimes the provirus stays in a latent state, replicating when the DNA of the host cell replicates. In other cases, the provirus state is expressed, producing new viruses that may infect adjacent cells. Then it completes the cycle through budding, a process by which HIV matures at the membrane of a host cell at the completion of the replication process. Host-cell membranes become part of the HIV infectious virion at this stage. Further structural modifications may occur following release from the cell.

Since the CD4 receptor is also present on other cells in the human body, HIV can get into them, too, but the virus remains latent, essentially hiding out in the cell chromosome without replicating. Later, DNA begins replicating new virus particles that can enter uninfected T-cells and continue the disease process. Because there is always a latent source of HIV DNA in the infected host, it is difficult to cure the infection. In addition to some nucleocapsid proteins and the virally coded glycoproteins on the envelope, retroviruses like HIV contain internal proteins. Some of these proteins are enzymes necessary for initiating viral replication. Others may be virally coded proteases important in processing viral proteins during the maturation process. Infection with this virus is called HIV disease. It is not AIDS until the CD4+ count is less than 200 cells/cc, and infections such as Kaposi's sarcoma and/or Pneumocystis pneumonia are present. Many people confuse the distinction between HIV infections and AIDS itself. AIDS is a continuum of a severe HIV infection.

Prions: Proteins Can Be Infectious

Other infectious diseases that have not been found to have a viral cause might be caused by prions. In 1982, American neurobiologist Stanley Prusiner proposed that infectious proteins caused a neurological disease in sheep called scrapie. The infectivity of scrapie-infected brain tissue is reduced by treatment with proteases but not by treatment with radiation, suggesting that the infectious agent is pure protein. Prusiner coined the name prion for this proteinaceous infectious particle.

Several animal diseases now fall into this category. The most notable prion infection is the "mad-cow disease" that emerged in cattle in Great Britain during 1987. All prion-based neurological diseases are called spongiform encephalopathies because large vacuoles develop in the brain. Two human prion diseases are kuru and Creutzfeldt-Jakob disease, or CJD. These diseases run in families, which indicates a possible genetic link. However, they cannot be solely inherited, because mad cow disease arose from feeding scrapie-infected sheep meat to cattle, and the new

(bovine) variant was transmitted to humans who ate undercooked beef from infected cattle. Additionally, CJD has been transmitted through transplanted nerve tissue and contaminated surgical instruments.

Viroids

Some plant diseases are caused by viroids — short pieces of naked RNA, only 300 to 400 nucleotides long, with no protein coat. The nucleotides are often internally paired, and the molecule has a closed, folded, three-dimensional structure that presumably helps protect it from attack by particular enzymes. The RNA does not code for any protein. Thus far, viroids have been conclusively identified as pathogens only in plants. Annually, infections by viroids, like the potato spindle tuber viroid, result in losses of millions of dollars from crop damage. This once devastated the potato crop in Ireland, causing millions to starve. Current research on viroids has revealed similarities between the base sequences of viroids and introns. Recall that introns are sequences of genetic material that do not code for polypeptides. This observation has led to the hypothesis that viroids microevolved from introns, leading to speculation that future researchers may discover animal viroids.

Neo-Darwinian Evolution and Variation in Viruses

What does this variation look like up close? Probably the easiest examples for observing variation over many generations are in the viruses that cause respiratory diseases (colds and flu). This is because their changes can be observed annually, there are large numbers of cases involved, and good records are kept to monitor and control the spread of these diseases. In this section, by showing the diversity of flu viruses and their changing, but oscillating patterns, we show an example of variation.

The influenza virus has eight chromosomes in its genome. When there is a mixing of "foreign" RNA into its genetic material — a process called reassortment — the virulence of the infection can change. The major chromosomes, HA and NA, when changed, may cause a new strain of virus to emerge in a major way. For example, when infection of the same cells by human and duck influenza viruses mix, a totally new set of genetic instructions may be given. This mixed set of chromosomes is an example

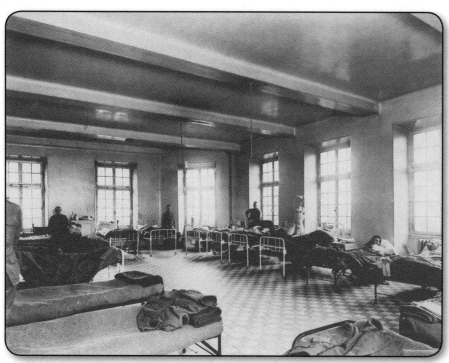

Influenza Ward, 1918

of an influenza virus that can cause several problems in non-immunized humans. This virus is known as a pandemic strain. Infection of one cell with both a human and a foreign genome, such as a human virus from a different population as well as a duck virus, can result in a reassortment of viral chromosomes, followed by selection for a virulent progeny virus not previously present in the human population. Animal reservoirs, which harbor influenza viruses with distinct chromosomes, produce a wide variety of HA and NA antigenic subunits and are a source for new viral genes.

Over the past hundred years, there have been great pandemics, beginning in 1890, 1900, 1918, 1957, and 1968. The so-called Spanish flu of 1918–19 killed between 20 and 40 million people and crippled the U.S. Armed Forces at the end of World War I. About 80 percent of army deaths during that span were due to influenza. What caused so many deaths and severe infections? First, there is evidence that mutation under natural conditions is a common phenomenon among viruses. The sudden appearance of new antigenic variants of influenza virus, for example, has been frequently noted in recent years, and occasionally these mutant viruses have possessed an extraordinarily increased infectivity. This apparently was the kind of variant that appeared in 1918 and brought about a pandemic. Antibodies against old strains did not provide protection against the new variant. To cite another example, the emergence of another strain of this

virus caused the Asian influenza (A1 A2) epidemics in 1957–58.

How Genetic Changes Take Place

Many biologists believe that a mutation-selection model explains most variation. We will describe this mechanism but show that it is inadequate to explain the big changes in flu viruses. We will then examine how changes are believed to occur. Influenza viruses appear to have several mechanisms that lead to antigenic change: 1) a high mutation rate, 2) a rapid replication cycle, and 3) a reassortment of genome segments. Generally speaking, viruses have a well-designed genetic inheritance. The RNA acts like a blueprint that actually points the protein molecules in the correct predetermined direction. In most cases, each virus generation gives in its RNA blueprint the same directions as the parent virus. This means that the genetic code is conservative. However, in a few cases, viruses can change, or mutate, their nucleotide sequences with time. During the duplication of genetic information, mistakes are made, and nucleotide sequences are altered. Sometimes new viruses emerge in adaptation to changing environments. These new environments select from among the available strains of virus.

Influenza viruses have an RNA genome, whereas almost all other living organisms store their genetic information as DNA. Most importantly, replicating RNA, unlike DNA, lacks "proofreading" enzymes that check that the correct bases have been added to the growing chain. Since RNA lacks the ability to "proofread" its genetic message, RNA viruses change more rapidly than DNA viruses. As RNA replicates, it averages about one mistake per 10,000 nucleotides copied. As DNA replicates its complementary strand, it makes one mistake in every one to ten million nucleotides. It is estimated that 0.03 to 2 percent of the nucleotides in the genome of an RNA virus are altered every year. Consequently, antigenic drift of rhinoviruses and influenza can be attributed, in part, to point mutations. In contrast, a very powerful source of genetic change can be introduced by the reshuffling of genes according to the changing environment. There is evidence that certain strains of virus recycle about every 20 years — an occurrence of a major antigenic shift. The mechanism for this periodic emergence of strains appears to be a reassortment of genes; thus, the emergence of different flu serotypes. The emergence of new influenza patterns may not demonstrate a recent mutation, but rather selection among already-existing kinds. Thus, the important event in generating pandemic strains of influenza has not been mutational evolution but rather the reshuffling of existing genes.

Boundaries to Influenza Changes

The variation we observe in influenza viruses has limits; boundaries to change are inherent by the number of rearrangements that can occur among each virus's eight chromosomes. The story of influenza viruses is like that of rose breeds. Although there are many different breeds descending from a distant, common ancestor, roses are still roses. We see this in flu viruses, as well as plants and animals. DNA and RNA allow for many variations on a common theme. Although there may be great diversity to influenza viruses, there are boundaries to their change. The genetic "blueprint" in all living things has limits set by the disastrous consequences that inevitably happen when too many mutations add up. There are boundaries to a given gene pool. This fits with the concept of stasis, or limited change, seen in nature. The principle that "like begets like" seems to be corroborated. Variation has its limits; there are boundaries to how far the changes can occur. This variation of flu viruses is an example of recombination and stasis, not a model of common descent with modification. In other words, despite their many minor changes, those pesky viruses that cause the flu will not mutate into HIV or the Ebola virus. So although you may keep catching the flu, there is no need to worry that someday your disease will turn into AIDS or hemorrhagic fever.

The Origin of Viruses, Prions, and Viroids

Several hypotheses have been brought forward to explain the possible evolution of viruses. A traditional hypothesis from virologists is that intracellular parasitism is by no means an uncommon phenomenon. Other infectious agents besides viruses adjust to an intracellular existence — for example, malaria parasites and other protozoa, all the rickettsiae, and even certain bacteria

such as the leprosy bacilli. The viruses, however, seem to have carried dependence on other living cells to the nth degree. Perhaps the ancestors of our present-day viruses were larger, living microbes that adopted an exclusively intracellular life and then, in the course of time, became increasingly completely dependent on their host cells. In consequence, they lost to some degree their original forms and structure, so that some of them now consist of no more than a few molecules. At the same time, their original physiological activities were largely given up. Now they have no independent metabolism, depending on taking control of the vital activities of their living host cells to furnish the necessary elements they need to maintain and reproduce themselves. This conception would be in line with the principle that the assumption of a fully parasitic existence always involves some loss of substance and of physiological independence. This principle is well illustrated among the protozoa, spirochetes, and fungi. One attractive model regards the viruses as a group of "superparasites," essentially foreign to the tissues they invade, that have evolved from larger intracellular parasites and now are reduced to extremely simple forms, existing only at the expense of the very cells they damage.

Quite apart from the problems of the human and animal diseases that viruses create, their real nature is a topic of great interest. The intimate association of the viruses, particularly their nucleic acid, with the genetic material of infected body cells gives them special significance. The normal components of tissue cells susceptible to a particular virus seem to accept the nucleic acid of the virus as its controlling influence in preference to the nucleic acid of the cells themselves. Many scientists seriously entertain the idea that viruses may be among the chief factors causing normal tissues to become cancerous.

From a biblical creation perspective, we cannot know with certainty the origin of viruses, but it is difficult to imagine them as part of God's original design, all things being "good" at the end of week one (Gen. 1). We might consider viruses as "cursed" or "corrupted" cell parts, or "renegade" agents of the body. There is strong evidence that viruses are more related to our own cells than to other viruses. In their nucleic acid and protein/glycoprotein components, there is greater similarity to their host cells than to other viruses. We can only infer that maybe after the Fall, as man's body began to decay, some viruses started to emerge. However, no one knows for sure.

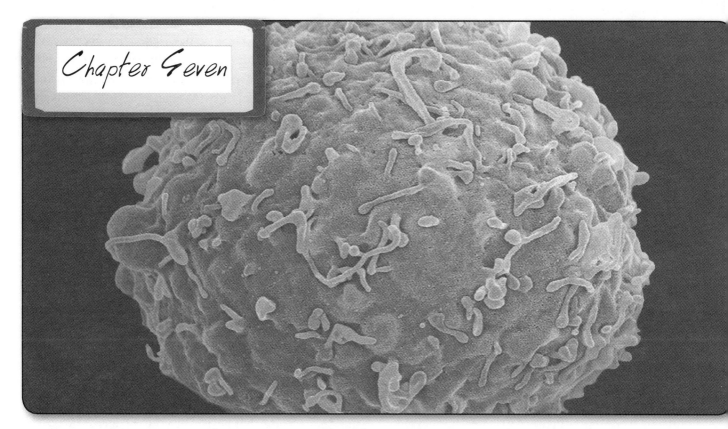

Chapter Seven

The Immune System: Created to Interact with Microbes

Immunology is the branch of biology involving how the body is designed to protect itself from agents of disease called pathogens. The word immune comes from a Latin word meaning "freedom or protection from taxes or burdens." This amazing system battles disease in a manner so complex and intricate that the most gifted imagination could not envision such incredible functions. The primary role of our immune system is to recognize pathogens and destroy only them. Methods of destruction include baths of caustic digestive enzymes, rapid perforation with submicroscopic holes, an overwhelming flood of sticky proteins, and ingestion by amoeba-like cells. In addition, the immune system is designed to prevent the proliferation of mutant cells, such as cancers. But when this system malfunctions or when a boundary is breached, it could result in localized or systemic infections — or worse.

The vital functions of the immune system can be illustrated through the case study of David Vetter, a young man born in 1971 who lacked a functional immune system from birth. He was the first long-term survivor of what biologists call severe combined immunodeficiency syndrome, or SCID. This is an autosomal recessive disease leading to failure of the B- and T-lymphocytes to develop properly. This in turn causes the failure of the immune system, much like the condition of AIDS. Faced with what was at the time a fatal condition, doctors placed David in a sterile environment on the third floor of the Texas Children's Hospital. He was first put into a sterile "bubble" crib — and he was dubbed the "bubble boy" by the media. The doctors then determined what to do for a more extended time. After receiving generous donations, a unique, germ-free room was built. Later, an additional room was built, along with an exclusive "space suit" of transparent polyvinyl chloride film for David to walk in.

A second bubble room was constructed in the Vetter home where David could spend time with his family. After 12 years of this required confinement, doctors cautiously hoped that with new technology they could attempt a bold, new procedure involving David receiving specially treated bone marrow from his sister. Eighty days after the transplant and still in a germ-free environment, David developed some of the clinical signs of mononucleosis. Doctors removed him from isolation for more efficient treatment. They hoped his sister's marrow cells had by then established themselves and would protect David from the common microbes the rest of us encounter daily. Unfortunately, her cells had been infected with Epstein-Barr virus, which produced Burkitt's lymphoma, a rare form of cancer. He died in February 1984, about four months after the transplant. David's death provided a clear link between the Epstein-Barr virus and cancer. The immediate failure of the transplant did not kill him — it was rather the proliferation of the Epstein-Barr virus that caused cancer. Without a working immune system, David was unable to defend against this normally low-risk virus. Besides David, thousands of other children have been born with this syndrome, now routinely and effectively treated by bone-marrow transplants. David's life was medically significant because he was the first long-term survivor, and in his death a great deal was learned about the immune system.

Immune System: Designed to Interact with Microbes

David Vetter's life shows that the immune system acts like a protective physical and biochemical bubble around the human body, protecting against everyday germs. It provides an invisible barrier to nonspecific and specific

David Vetter, "The Bubble Boy"

pathogens. Diseases such as West Nile virus, SARS, invasive "flesh-eating" bacteria, HIV, bird flu, and malaria all threaten people in today's corrupted world. The immune system has been designed as the body's major defense not only against bacteria and viruses, but also fungi, parasites, and toxins. It serves as an invisible boundary of mucous membranes, strong chemicals, and proteins, defending us against new and old diseases. We might also think of it as an umbrella over us, protecting against the constant "rain" of bacteria, fungi, parasites, and toxins. Stages of the immune system include the skin and mucous membranes as the first level of defense, white blood cells as the second line, and antibodies as third level. The immune system includes critical structural features like the lymph glands, lymph nodes, spleen, bone marrow, tonsils, and appendix.

According to Genesis 1, all creation was declared good or very good. It is clear that there were no pathogens and parasites before the Edenic curse in Genesis 3. So did the Creator create the immune system after the fall of man, when the curse was implemented? According to Scripture, the answer appears to be no. It seems God completed His creation at one specific time and is not engaged in a continuous creation, as some maintain. An immune system was undoubtedly included in man's original design. Though no one knows for sure, it seems the immune system would be useful to the body even in a perfect world, because without an immune system, even microbes not normally disease-causing became dangerous.

Did God create the immune system knowing we would need it to battle pathogens after the Fall? Was it inevitable we would encounter germs? These are questions pondered by creation scientists. Creationist immunologist Dr. Joseph Francis suggests that rather than viewing the immune system as we know it today — a defense system against microbes — we should view it as a sensory system designed to interact with beneficial microbes. Granted, our immune system currently deals with the corrupted, cursed world around us; parts of the immune system, like other body systems, are no longer perfect. However, we do see what we believe are remnants of the original very good design. For example, creation scientists hypothesize that our immune system was originally designed to interact with beneficial bacteria and other microbes.

In order to appreciate this refreshing non-Darwinian perspective, we should understand that most bacteria are beneficial to the environment and us. The news media glorifies devastating pathogen-induced diseases, even though over 95 percent of all bacteria are not classified as causing diseases. Likewise, a vast majority of protozoans are mostly free-living or mutualistic. Without large mutualistic populations of beneficial bacteria in our intestines, we would be unable to digest and absorb compounds properly. Occasionally, we read or hear about *E. coli* outbreaks that have caused serious illness, and yet of the nearly 170 strains that exist, less than a dozen are actually classified as pathogenic. The other 150-plus strains are beneficial. In fact, most of them are doing valuable work, as in vitamin-B synthesis. The B-complex of niacin, riboflavin, and vitamin K all come from the *E. coli* population in our gut. In addition, intestinal bacteria help us break down macronutrients and aid in their assimilation into the body.

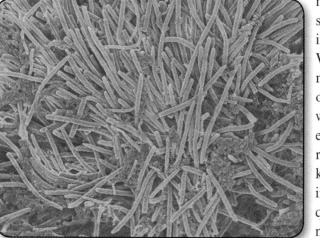

Scanning electron micrograph (SEM) of bacteria on the surface of a human tongue.

Research indicates that beneficial bacteria (normal flora we receive at birth) may even help in the normal development of our gut. Studies using germ-free animals raised without bacteria and other microorganisms, including protozoa normally found in the intestines, show that those creatures do not develop normally. In one study, researchers eliminated bacteria from mouse intestines at a young age. Their intestines did not develop properly, and these "germ-free" mice experienced atypical growth. Also, the circulatory system did not perfuse the intestines properly, strongly suggesting that bacteria may guide development of the gastrointestinal tract.

The normal flora have a symbiotic relationship with the individual. Perhaps the immune system operates in our intestinal ecosystem by protecting some of the bacteria in a symbiotic fashion. The immune system may very well aid in keeping out the deleterious microorganisms that constantly compete with these beneficial bacteria. This is termed microbial antagonism — active opposition between two microbe populations. A related field of study in microbiology is called probiotics (the administration of live microorganisms in adequate amounts), which may very well boost immune function, inhibit the growth of pathogens, and increase resistance to infection. Probiotics mainly concerns repopulating the large intestine with *Lactobacillus* and other beneficial species of bacteria. The surface of your skin, which is mostly dry, is populated with salt-tolerant bacteria inhabiting a specific ecological niche. What would happen if these normal bacterial populations of *Staphylococcus* on the skin were eliminated through, for example, a high antibiotic regimen? As any dermatologist knows, fungal spores resulting in a stubborn infection would quickly occupy the vacated niche. There are several other examples of the important, beneficial work of bacteria and protozoa.

Creation biologist Dr. Joseph Francis describes bacteria and viruses as the biomatrix, or "organosubstrate of life." From this perspective, bacteria and viruses are seen not so much as distinct organisms but as "extra-organismal organs" — that is, the means by which "higher" organisms meet their needs. Indeed, the entire ecosystem is supported by this elaborate maintenance-and-repair substrate. In the biomatrix model, Dr. Francis views the minority of disease-causing bacteria and viruses as having come about by mutations. The original symbiotic function of these organisms was corrupted after the Fall, and they are now pathogens.

It appears from creation research that the immune system may have been originally designed to be a sensory organ. The pre-Fall immune system may have, in sensing our environment, allowed us to interact with microbes originally provided to benefit us, perhaps as nutrients. In addition, viruses may be remnants of "mobile" genes designed to interact with us under certain conditions. Today, viruses can be assimilated into our cells and modify the DNA as a provirus. Perhaps in the past, as people went into a new environment, they needed to adapt to that environment rapidly via viral "inoculation."

Viruses may have been a designed mechanism for genetic change. The immune system might have been involved with this important viral recognition and assimilation into the cell. But after Adam's sin, everything changed, including the mobile genes bound in a virus (Latin for "poison"). It is possible that viruses can modulate organisms at the genome level, but have the potential to promote non-genetic-based phenotype changes. For example, viruses display ability to remodel tissues by promoting apoptosis (programmed cell death) or influencing how cells interact with one another. Perhaps viruses may have been created as mobile extrachromosomal agents of genes for cell regulation. After the Curse, these structures began to harm us. Due to their subsequent corruption, the body had to begin defending itself against viruses. So the system once designed to interact with microbes in a beneficial manner now has to maintain separation from the deadly ones to ensure survival of the host. The immune system was not invented after the Curse, but rather took on a new role, for which it probably had a built-in adaptability.

One specific example of this corruption may be seen in how the immune system interacts with retrotransposons — short, repetitive DNA fragments similar to the retrovirus HIV. Recently, molecular biologists found that on human chromosome 22, human endogenous retrovirus (retrotransposons) turns off the immune system during pregnancy. This design prohibits the mother's immune system from damaging the child's body. These retroviruses cannot fully replicate, only infecting local immune cells (such as macrophages) of the uterus, thereby preventing them from initiating a full-blown immune response. Thus, the mother's immune system remains competent to respond to other infections but is specifically prevented from mounting an immune response to the developing embryo. So in creation, the selective ability to turn off the immune system for protection would be a "good" design. However, since the corruption of creation, the corrupted retrovirus HIV and various leukemia viruses turn off the entire immune system, leaving the body open to devastating infections.

The Impressive Immune System

Immunologists study various cellular and molecular mechanisms the body uses against invading microbes and foreign matter. Several early immunologists saw purpose in the clear design of the immune system. It encompasses not only the study of defense against infectious agents, but also cancers and the acceptance or rejection of transplanted tissues. Immunologists also study effects of immune responses gone awry, such as **autoimmunity**. This occurs when the immune response is inappropriately directed against the cells of the very body they are supposed to protect. Allergic reactions or hypersensitivity (altered reactivity to an antigen) are other well-known autoimmune conditions.

Three body systems form "boundaries" protecting our body from invading pathogens and harmful chemicals. These systems include the **integumentary, immune,** and **lymphatic** systems. The immune system and lymphatic system are being covered in this chapter. Anatomists generally refer to the lymphatic system as that system composed of a network of lymphoid channels transporting lymph through organs and tissues, assisting in our body's defense. In addition, the integumentary system provides a first line of defense against pathogens. The functional portion of our body's defenses is generally referred to as the immune system. This refers to specific cells, antibodies, and other proteins that defend us against disease. These systems overlap in both structure and function, and when functioning properly, provide more than adequate protection. Along with these impressive body defenses come disease symptoms.

The Creator has designed a number of fascinating body defenses that protect us from disease. Traditionally, immunologists recognize three levels of body defense, designed to interact with microbes (Table 7.1). Two of these are nonspecific defenses, meaning they do not distinguish one infectious disease from another. The first line of nonspecific defense is an external barrier consisting of intact skin and mucous membranes. This includes epithelial tissues that cover and line our bodies, as well as the secretions they produce. The second line of nonspecific defense is internal. It triggers chemical signals and involves phagocytic cells and antimicrobial proteins, indiscriminately attacking invaders that have penetrated the body's outer barriers. Inflammation is a sign that this second line of defense has been activated. The third line of defense is the specific (adaptive or acquired) immune response. It is activated as the body encounters pathogens, toxins, and allergens. It works simultaneously with the second line of defense, but responds specifically with T- and B-lymphocytes to specific antigens, and develops immunological memory.

Humans have innate resistance to certain illnesses. For example, all humans are resistant to many infectious diseases of other animals, such as canine distemper. Even resistance to human diseases can vary from person to person. For example, the effect of measles is usually relatively mild for individuals of European ancestry, but the disease devastated the populations of Pacific Islanders first exposed to it by European explorers. The reason may lie in natural selection. For the Europeans, many generations of exposure to the measles virus presumably led to selection of genes conferring some resistance to the virus. On the other hand, Europeans arriving in Africa in the 1700s were devastated by malaria, to which sub-Saharan people groups were relatively resistant, producing only mild symptoms in most native Africans. These are generalizations, with exceptions within various racial or people groups. An individual resistance depends on many factors, including genetics, gender, age, nutritional status, and general health.

Non-specific immunity refers to the restance protecting us against any pathogen, regardless of species. Non-specific resistance includes the first and second lines of defense. The first line of defense, discussed in Chapter 14 in *Body By Design*, includes the skin, mucous membranes, lachrymal apparatus (tears), and the normal flora. The second line of defense includes phagocytes, inflammation, fever, and complement. Other natural antimicrobials include lysozymes, interferon, sebum, gastric juices, and other acid secretions.

The natural internal defenses also include the limited power of normal blood to destroy microbes. The capacity of normal body fluids to kill bacteria is feeble, however, and has little value in protecting us against virulent and invasive organisms. Saliva, nasal secretions, and intestinal mucosa, as well as the tears and other body fluids and tissues, contain varying amounts of lysozyme (see Design Focus 7.2). Lysozyme, a basic protein acting as a mucolytic enzyme at acid pHs, is capable of destroying the outer membranes of some bacterial cells. These substances are similar in chemical structure to polypeptide antibiotics (e.g., bacitracin) and can destroy a variety of bacteria.

Table 7.1 The Multiple Layers of Body Defense

Non-Specific Resistance of the Immune System (Innate Immunity)		Specific Resistance of the Immune System (Adaptive Immunity)
First line of defense	Second line of defense	Third line of defense
• Intact skin	• Phagocytic white blood cells	• Specialized lymphocytes: B-cells and T-cells
• Mucous membranes and their secretions	• Inflammation	• Antibodies
• Normal flora	• Fever	• Memory cells
	• Complement	

Design Focus 7.2

Purposeful Function of Tears with Lysozyme: The World View of Alexander Fleming

A chemical inhibitor of nonspecific nature is the enzyme lysozyme. Alexander Fleming described this protein in 1921. Later he gained recognition for discovering penicillin. Lysozyme is found in human tears and saliva. It disrupts the cell walls of Gram-positive bacteria by digesting peptidoglycan. Fleming's most significant observation about lysozymes was some bacteriophage-type effects on *Staphylococcus* from his nose on blood-agar plate. Within five minutes a drop of the diluted, turbid mucus had become clear. He successfully repeated this many times.

Fleming's first paper on lysozyme was titled "On a Remarkable Bacteriolytic Element Found in Tissues and Secretions." The lysozyme was first noticed during some investigations made on a patient suffering from a common cold. The nasal secretion from this patient

Alexander Fleming

was cultivated daily on blood-agar plates, and Fleming grew a staphylococcal colony. He described how drops of diluted nasal mucus placed on cultures of this organism inhibited their growth and visibly cleared its thick suspensions.

These two preliminary experiments clearly demonstrated the powerful inhibitory and lytic action of nasal mucus upon coccus bacteria. It will be shown later that this power is shared by most of the tissues and secretions of the human body, by the tissues of other animals, and to a marked degree by egg whites. Fleming provided data on the natural distribution of lysozyme, its simple chemical and physical properties, and the list of susceptible organisms. He then allowed himself to speculate — a rare indulgence for him — on the possible biological importance of lysozyme. Fleming predicted that a function of tears, saliva, sputum, and mucus secretions was to rid body surfaces of bacteria by washing them away.

He also demonstrated that 75 percent of the 104 strains of airborne bacteria were destroyed by lysozyme, suggesting that these organisms could not be pathogenic, precisely because they were susceptible to lysozyme. By inference, he suggested that

organisms resistant to lysozyme were pathogenic precisely because of this resistance. He further supported his developing belief that lysozyme was in the front line of natural defense against bacteria. Such defenses are literally a vital function. As soon as a person dies and active defense ceases, bacteria invade the body and destroy it.

Purposeful Function as World View

The argument that lysozyme must have a biological function because it is so widely distributed in living things is, of course, teleological, and Fleming was always searching for facts to support this hypothesis. In modern biology circles this is not considered scientific because it assumes purposeful function. Yet great scientists like Harvey, Pasteur, Lister, Virchow, Ehrlich, and Fleming all used teleology. Many design proponents today once again use teleology because they believe the Creator is not capricious. Could there indeed be a purpose to life? During the 1920s and '30s, Fleming continued his work on lysozymes, finding many clinical applications to his discovery, along with many other blood serum components and body fluids containing lysozymes. It had great predictive power in his day, maybe even contributing to his discovery of penicillin. Though teleology may not be politically correct in secular scientific circles today, it has been a very useful paradigm to great biologists of the past in explaining biological functions.

Humans have been designed with several defense mechanisms. First, the body is covered with skin and mucous membranes that prevent the entry of most foreign material, including microbes. Sensory systems are ready in case the body barriers are violated. These systems can detect dangerous molecules (antigens), such as compounds unique to bacteria (endotoxins) or molecules released only when tissues are damaged. Organic biosensors can direct and assist other host defenses, facilitating the destruction of the foreign material. Also lying in wait are host cells designed to ingest and digest foreign material. If needed, reinforcements can be recruited to the site of the breach. The protection provided by these systems is termed innate immunity (i.e., we are born with it). Innate immunity differs from adaptive immunity (described shortly) in that all invaders are dealt with using a limited set of biochemical weapons. Though the number of copies of the various weapons can be modulated in response to an invader, their mechanisms cannot be modified to enhance the reaction.

The components of innate immunity have been called non-specific defenses, but recent discoveries have shown that most of these components are far from unfocused, instead relying on the recognition of certain molecular patterns of invading microbes or secretions from damaged tissues. This is called pattern recognition. Molecular patterns associated with pathogens include various compounds unique to bacterial cell walls, peptidoglycan, and other biomolecules. Those associated with damage include various proteins (enzymes) normally intracellular and now outside cells, and substances produced during tissue necrosis and damage.

In addition to innate immunity, humans have been created with a more specialized response, termed the adaptive immune response. It develops throughout life and substantially increases the body's ability to defend itself. Each time the body is exposed to foreign material, the adaptive defense system "learns," then "remembers," the most effective response to that specific material, reacting accordingly if the material is encountered again. The foreign material to which the immune system responds is called an antigen. On first exposure to an invading microbe or other antigen, the response develops relatively slowly; the antigen may cause damage if the innate defenses cannot contain it. Successive exposures, however, lead to swifter, greater repeat responses, generally eliminating the invader before it causes obvious additional harm.

The immune system can discriminate between healthy "self" cells (i.e., your own body cells) and dangerous, "non-self" cells. The adaptive immune response uses two general mechanisms to eliminate an invader. If the antigen is within one of the body's own, then the immune system will not attack these cells. If the antigen is from outside the body (like a germ), hence dangerous, then the body responds by making antibodies — complex molecules with two functional regions. One region binds specifically to the antigen; the other functions as a "red flag" alerting other host defenses to remove or destroy the antigen. This design helps prevent the body from attacking itself and avoids self destruction (i.e., an autoimmune disease).

Phagocytosis

One of the early observations regarding the immune system was the ability of the immune system to recognize "self" from "non-self." In animals with either open or closed circulatory systems, phagocytes monitor tissues as they travel through the body. Special white blood cells

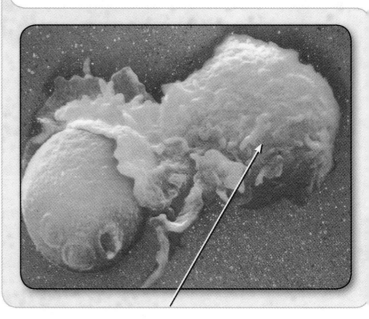

A cultured lymphocyte phagocytosing (engulfing) a yeast cell

called phagocytes are designed to engulf and digest invaders. The discovery of the protective role of phagocytes, a milestone in immunology, was first made in echinoderms. In 1882, Russian biologist Elie Metchnikoff collected transparent starfish larvae on a European beach, pierced them with rose thorns, and waited to see what happened. A day later, he saw that **phagocytes** had collected at the injury site. The thorn in a starfish larva is not unlike a splinter piercing human skin, in terms of the immune system rapidly responding to an antigen.

Phagocytosis is the process by which cells engulf particles in a manner similar to the way an amoeba eats. The particle becomes surrounded by cytoplasmic extensions called pseudopods, which ultimately fuse. The particle thus becomes surrounded by a membrane derived from the plasma membrane and contained within an organelle analogous to an amoeba's food vacuole. This vacuole then fuses with lysosomes (organelles containing digestive enzymes), so that the ingested particle and digestive enzymes still are separated from the cytoplasm by a continuous membrane. Often, however, lysosomal enzymes are released before the food vacuole has completely formed. When this occurs, destructive lysosomal enzymes are released into the infected area, contributing to inflammation.

The body cells that participate in two principal kinds of phagocytosis are neutrophils (Metchnikoff called them **microphages**) and the **macrophages** of the blood. Phagocytic action is often readily apparent on microscopic examination of inflamed tissue. The phagocytes are attracted to invading microbial cells or other foreign particles by a process called **chemotaxis**. Once in contact with microorganisms, leukocytes engulf many of them just as an amoeba surrounds and digests a food particle. When pus is examined under a microscope, many organisms are seen to be within the white cells' cytoplasm. Some bacteria may be engulfed only to escape again, perhaps destroying the phagocyte. Other organisms, like *Mycobacterium tuberculosis*, may survive and even multiply inside phagocytes and be carried by them to lodge in internal organs, like the lungs. But most often, the phagocytized bacteria are destroyed immediately within the leukocyte or when the white cell itself dies.

Nonspecific Cellular Components

The defensive action of lymphocytes is reinforced by macrophages, which have a nonspecific role in that they engulf not only bacteria and other foreign particles, but also leukocytes as well. These phagocytic cells are the scavengers that, when the infection is conquered, clear away the remains of bacteria, leukocytes, and polysaccharide antigens. T-cells, which are generally directed at specific antigens, are the primary warriors in cell-mediated defense. Activated macrophages are phagocytic cells usually found in a resting state. Their phagocytic capabilities are greatly increased when stimulated to become activated

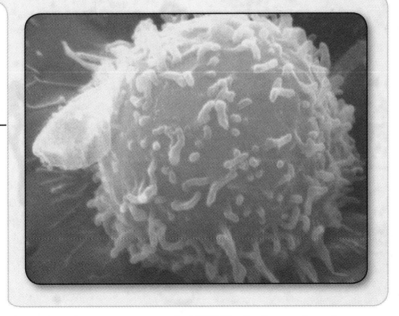

Scanning electron micrograph (SEM) of a human lymphocyte

macrophages. This stimulation is primarily by ingestion of antigenic material. However, cytokines from antigenically activated helper T-cells may also activate macrophages. Activated macrophages are more effective, their appearance becoming recognizably different as well; they are larger and become ruffled. Activated macrophages are especially valued for their enhanced ability to eliminate certain virus-infected cells, and pathogenic intracellular bacteria like *Mycobacterium tuberculosis*. Of great importance is their ability to attack and destroy many cancerous cells. Furthermore, they function well as antigen-presenting cells, or APCs.

Interferon

This is a protein designed to be released from viral-infected cells. It stimulates the proliferation of macrophages and killer T-cells, diffusing to other cells to stimulate their production of antiviral proteins. Interferons are a group of cellular proteins known as cytokines, providing natural protection against a number of viral diseases. Interferon may destroy cancer cells directly and indirectly by activating cytotoxic T-lymphocytes and natural killer cells, along with interfering with viral replication. Dr. Alick Isaac (a British virologist) and Jean Lindenmann discovered this naturally occurring antiviral in 1957. Like lysozymes, interferon is one of the few compounds in the body that has a profound effect on pathogens. Is it any wonder that interferon sales worldwide exceed $1 billion?

Interferons are very important in recovery from many viral diseases, including the common cold. Interferons are produced by various body cells on stimulation by some viruses. They trigger production of antiviral proteins that protect us against the stimulating virus. RNA viruses such as influenza and rhinovirus are better stimulators of interferon than DNA viruses. There have been several attempts to use interferons in treating the common cold, but these have had limited success as "cures." However, the information learned about how interferon "interferes" with viral replication has given pharmacologists ideas for designing antivirals. Recent studies have suggested that interferon may be effective in the treatment of hepatitis C, several types of leukemia, genital warts, AIDS, Kaposi's sarcoma, multiple sclerosis, and others.

Complement Marks Pathogens for Destruction

Complement is a nonspecific group of serum proteins involved in phagocytosis and lysis of bacteria, involving maybe over two dozen interdependent reactions. Complement is a series of nearly 30 proteins circulating in the bloodstream. This system "complements" antigen-antibody activity. Though complement is better known for its relationship to the immune system, the protein series also nonspecifically deters disease. If a parasite causes an infection, complement proteins become active through a cascade of steps assisting in the inflammatory response and phagocytosis. They also help destroy invading parasites through cell lysis.

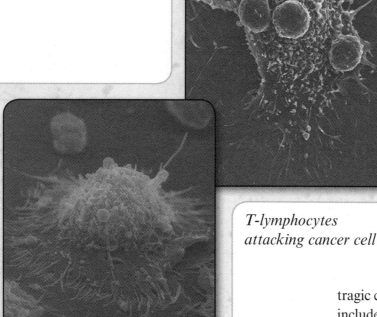

T-lymphocytes attacking cancer cell

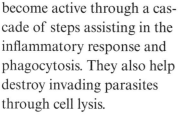

B-lymphocyte

Specific Immunity (The Adaptive Immune Response)

Specific immunity is the third line of defense of the body, providing specific resistance against particular pathogens or toxins. Specific defenses are based on specialized cells of the immune system called lymphocytes, and the production of proteins called antibodies. They are adaptive to specific antigens found in the environment. Creation scientists see this finely tuned system as having been designed from the beginning, not naturalistically explained.

In contrast to nonspecific immunity, specific immunity is ready to respond using both T- and B-lymphocytes to provide immunological "memory" — a greatly enhanced response to re-exposure. The adaptive immune response matures through the growth of the immune system arsenal, which develops the most effective responses against specific invaders as each is encountered. An important hallmark of the adaptive immune response is this "memory." Individuals who survive diseases such as measles, mumps, or diphtheria generally never develop these acute diseases again. Vaccination prevents these diseases by exposing a person's immune system to weakened or killed forms of the causative microbe or its products. While some diseases can be contracted repeatedly, this phenomenon is generally due to the causative agent's ability to evade the host defenses. The adaptive immune response also has molecular specificity. The response that protects an individual from developing symptoms of measles does not prevent the person from contracting a different disease, like chicken pox. The immune system can also discriminate between healthy "self" (your own "normal" cells) and "non-self," such as invading bacteria and toxins. Without this, the immune system would routinely turn against the body's own cells, attacking them just like an invading microbe.

Indeed, this is just what happens with the tragic condition called autoimmune disease, which may include tissue injury due to a person's own (i.e., autoreactive) T-lymphocytes and autoantibodies.

The adaptive or acquired immune system is extraordinarily complex, involving an intricate network of cells and the specific selection of lymphocytes. In fact, as with the immune system in general, immunologists continue to work out many adaptive immune system secrets. In recent years, the discovery of toll-like receptors, or TLR, has provided insight into how the body learns to distinguish substances meriting an adaptive response from those that do not. Scientists now recognize that the innate immune response, for many years viewed as a non-specific, relatively static participant in the host defenses, alerts critical cells of the adaptive response upon discovery of generic patterns associated with microbes.

The High Specificity of the Adaptive Immune Response

The course of an infection may be separated into several separate phases. After about a week or more of first exposure to a given microbe or antigen, clonal selection of lymphocytes is generated. During this delay, the host depends on the protection provided by innate immunity, a critical prerequisite for the adaptive immune response. This first, highly specific response to a particular antigen is called the **primary immune response.** As a result of that initial encounter, the adaptive immune system is able to "remember," via immunological memory, that specific antigen. When the same antigen is encountered later in life, there is an enhanced antibody response called the **secondary immune response.** The efficiency of the secondary response reflects the immunological memory of the immune system "learned" from the first encounter.

The adaptive immune response uses two basic strategies for countering antigens. One response, **humoral immunity,** works to eliminate extracellular antigens via specific immunoglobulin antibodies — bacteria, toxins, or viruses in the blood plasma, lymph, or fluids surrounding tissues, for example. The other response is called **cellular immunity** or **cell-mediated immunity**, or CMI, and involves specifically sensitized T-lymphocytes and macrophages (APCs). Cellular immunity deals with antigens residing within a host cell, such as a virus that has infected a cell by way of the major histocompatibility complex, or MHC. Humoral and cellular immunity are both powerful and if misdirected, can cause great damage to the body's own tissues (autoimmune response). Because of this, the adaptive immune response is tightly regulated; each B- and T-lymphocyte, the primary participants in the adaptive response, requires a "second opinion" from a different type of cell before it can unleash its power.

The Development of the Specific Immune System

The cornerstone of specific immunity is a set of primed or specifically sensitized lymphocytes, along with antibodies. The **lymphocytes** are distributed throughout the body, comprising the lymphoid or lymphatic system. Lymphocytes are small cells, about 7 to 12 μm in diameter, each with a large ovoid-to-round nucleus taking up almost the entire cytoplasm. Electron microscopy reveals that villi cover most of the surface. Under a light microscope, all lymphocytes look similar, varying in cytoplasm. On the basis of developmental history, cellular function, and unique biochemical differences, two types of lymphocytes can be distinguished. They are **B-lymphocytes** and **T-lymphocytes** (opposite page). B-lymphocytes are largely responsible for humoral immunity, while T-lymphocytes are primarily responsible for CMI. In humoral immunity, antibodies provide resistance to disease, while in cell-mediated immunity (CMI), specifically sensitized T-lymphocytes provide resistance through direct cell-to-cell contact via APCs.

The immune system arises in the fetus about two months after conception. Lymphocytes originate from "primitive" cells in the yolk sac, fetal liver, and bone marrow. These unspecialized cells are known as **stem cells** (above). Scripture alludes to healthy body and bone (Prov. 14:30; 15:30; 16:24; 17:22). This is interesting because bone marrow produces lymphocytes, essential for good immunological health. Stem cells differentiate into two types of cells: **erythropoietic** (myeloid), which become red blood cells; and **lymphopoietic,** which become lymphocytes. The Greek word poien means "to make"; thus, lymphopoietic cells are "lymphocyte-making." During the early stages of development, lymphopoietic cells take one of two courses. Some proceed to the thymus, where they are processed via negative and positive selection, emerging as T-lymphocytes (T for "thymus").

The grainy, triangular thymus is large at birth, increasing in size until puberty and attaining a maximum weight of 30–40 grams. Thereafter, it begins to slowly shrink and undergo involution, a fibrous condition. Within the thymus, stem-cell maturation and differentiation occurs, modified by the addition and disappearance of specific surface receptor proteins termed CD antigens. Mature, antigen-specific T-lymphocytes, or T-cells, are ready to engage in **cell-mediated immunity** and are said to be **immunocompetent.** The fully developed T-lymphocytes enter the systemic circulation and colonize the lymph nodes, spleen, tonsils, and other lymphoid organs. The T-cells provide the basis for cell-mediated immunity.

The B-lymphocytes, or B-cells, mature and become immunocompetent in the bone marrow, the bursa equivalent in mammals, though some immunologists favor the liver, spleen, or gut-associated tissue as the maturation site. In the embryonic chick, this area has been identified as the bursa of Fabricus. For this reason, the lymphocyte is known historically as the bursa-derived or B-lymphocyte (the letter B may also stand for bone marrow). Once mature, the B-lymphocytes (B-cells) move through the circulation to colonize organs of the lymphoid system, where they join the T-lymphocytes. B-cells provide the basis for humoral immunity.

Cell-Mediated Immunity

The body's defense against microorganisms infecting its cells is centered in **cell-mediated immunity,** or CMI, which responds with specifically sensitized T-lymphocytes to cells infected with pathogens such as viruses, rickettsiae, and bacteria. T-lymphocytes are further subclassified into **helper T-lymphocytes** and **cytotoxic T-lymphocytes** (also known as killer T-cells). Helper T-lymphocytes (also called CD4 T-cells) carry the co-receptor protein CD4 that recognizes peptide antigens and acts an alarm to the rest of the immune system. T-lymphocytes identify the antigen and migrate to the cortex of lymph nodes, where they stimulate the production of other cells and activate important cells such as cytotoxic T-cells. The action of antigen-presenting cells secreting interleukin-2, or IL-2, activates cytotoxic T-lymphocytes. They also destroy cells that have become cancerous. The process continues with macrophages, large monocytes that can "eat" pathogens and consume other members of the immune system overcome in the struggle. Macrophages clean up the

Illustration of antibodies attached to a cancer cell

debris after helper-T, killer-T, and B-lymphocyte cells have stopped the invaders. Phagocytosis, or "cell eating," occurs when the pseudopods of a macrophage engulf harmful parasites or microorganisms. This is one way that blood serves to cleanse the body of waste and foreign material.

A third type of T-cell, the **suppressor** or **regulatory T-lymphocyte** (also called T-cell) expresses the CD8 co-receptor, and can recognize antigens — even those viral antigens produced in the cytoplasm. They can also slow down or stop the responses of B-cells and other T-cells. Suppressor T-cells play a major role in calling off the attack after an infection has been conquered. This is a simplified version of how our body defenses work at the cellular level. In short, this cell team, working in conjunction with natural defense chemicals like interferon, keeps our bodies protected against harmful invaders.

Humoral Immunity

This is the antibody-mediated defense found in blood plasma, lymph, and other body fluids (*humors* is Greek for "fluid"). It is immunity attributable to specific antibodies in blood plasma. B-cells act as the "biological arms factory," designed to produce millions of potent, specific antibodies. The two classes of B-cells reside either in the pleural and peritoneal cavities, or the bone marrow and lymphoid tissues. Antibodies and helper T-cells often work together during immune responses. Upon activation by an antigen, B-cells undergo differentiation, each producing hundreds of specific antibodies, proteins made in response to specific antigens, then recognizing and binding tightly to them. Antibodies can therefore help neutralize or destroy antigens. Antibodies belong to the soluble-proteins collectively known as immunologlobulins, or Igs. Five classes of **immunologlobulins** are designated IgG, IgM, IgA, IgE, and IgD. Antibodies have at least two identical sites that bind to antigenic determinants. These sites are known as **antigen-binding** or **antibody-combining.** The number of antigen-binding sites on an antibody is called the **valence** of that antibody. For example, most antibodies have two binding sites, so are said to be bivalent. By design, each class plays a different role in the immune response and has a distinguishing size and shape.

Table 7.2. Five Types of Antibodies

TYPE	PROPERTY
IgG	Most abundant; circulates in blood, lymph, and intestine; most pronounced in immunization; first and main antibody produced in fetus; crosses placenta; neutralizes viruses and toxins; principal component of 2° response from vaccine; enhances phagocytosis.
IgM	Largest of antibodies; circulates in blood, lymph, B-cell surface; principal component of 1° response from vaccine; complement fixation; effective in agglutinating antigens.
IgA	Found mainly in secretions such as mucus, tears, saliva, milk; numerous in respiratory infections.
IgD	Found on the surface of various cells; facilitates maturation of the antibody response; antigen receptor on B-cells.
IgE	Involved in hypersensitivity and allergy reactions; also involved in multicellular parasitic infections.

Antibodies are comprised of light (L) and heavy (H) chains attached by disulfide bonds. The most common antibody is IgA, composed of four polypeptide chains: two identical heavy chains and two identical light chains.

These chains are arranged in a Y shape. The two tips of the Y vary from antibody to antibody, and these tips allow the antibody to specifically attack one kind of antigen. These tips, called the **variable regions** or **antigen binding sites,** are the point where the antibody binds to the antigen with the specificity of a key fitting its lock. The rest of each chain in the antibody is called the constant region. The characteristics of the **constant region** determine the class of antibody.

Each class fights antigens slightly differently; IgG helps promote phagocytosis, for example. They bind to the antigen with their variable regions and to macrophages with their constant region, and then macrophages engulf the antigen. IgM groups to form a five-antibody complex, also binding to the antigens with their variable regions and using their constant regions to activate complementary proteins. Interestingly, IgG can also fight antigens this way. IgE helps initiate the inflammatory response, first attaching to basophils with their constant regions. Then, when attached to antigens with their variable regions, the basophils are stimulated to release inflammatory agents. IgA is found in saliva, tears, and mucous membranes. It is also found in breast milk to provide immunity to infants. IgD typically inactivates antigens by simple binding.

Antibodies, then, have several means of fighting antigens:

1. **Bind directly to the antigen**
2. **Bind the antigens together in groups**
3. **Activate complement**
4. **Stimulate phagocytosis**
5. **Stimulate inflammation**

The variable region of an antibody determines the specific antigen it will fight. The constant region determines the method by which it will fight the antigen.

Antibodies are produced by **B-cells** — specialized lymphocytes. Antigen-antibody binding causes these B-cells to divide rapidly. This process is called clonal selection because the resulting population of cells is composed of replicates selected to multiply by the presence of particularly invasive antigens. When exposed for the first time to the antigen for which they are specific, these sites bind to the antigen, and the B-cells begin to proliferate. The proliferation produces two types of B-cells: **plasma B-cells** and **memory B-cells.** The activated plasma cells are large, ellipsoidal or spherical cells that may reach 20 μm in diameter. They undergo morphologic change mainly due to the endoplasmic reticulum, which must expand to provide increased surface area for active protein synthesis. The clumped chromatin of the eccentrically located nucleus looks something like a wagon wheel. The antibodies are released into the plasma so the antibodies can attack the antigens to which they can bind. The memory B-cells are long-lived cells that do not release their antibodies. Instead, they circulate in the body waiting for the next attack by the antigen, allowing the body to respond quickly to subsequent infection by the same antigen. These cells give the immune system its amazing memory.

Variation on a Theme

Antibody diversity is a result of gene rearrangement. There may be an estimated million or more different antibody types. For decades, immunologists were puzzled over how an enormous variety of antibodies could be generated by the limited number of genes associated with the immune system. Because, like all proteins, genes specify antibodies, it would be reasonable to assume that an individual must have a million or more antibody genes. However, genomic experts point out that human cells have only about 35,000 genes. The answer to this antibody diversity mystery is elegant and simple, pointing clearly to intelligent design.

Embryonic cells contain about 300 genetic segments that can be shuffled and combined in each B-lymphocyte as it matures. The process, known as **somatic recombination** or **rearrangement**, is a random mixing and matching of gene segments to fashion unique antibody genes. Information encoded by these genes is then expressed on the surface receptor proteins of B-lymphocytes and in the antibodies later expressed by the stimulated clone of plasma cells. Susumu Tonegawa, winner of the 1987 Nobel Prize for Medicine, described the process of somatic recombination and the discovery of immunoglobin gene D, V, J, and C regions. According to the process, the gene segments coding for the light and heavy chains of an antibody are located on different chromosomes. The light and heavy chains are synthesized separately, and then joined to form the antibody. One of eight constant genes (C), one of four joiner genes (J), one of 50 diversity genes (D), and one of up to 300 variable genes (V) can be used to form a heavy chain. One of 300 variable genes is selected and combined with one of five joiner genes and a constant gene to form the active light-chain gene. After deletion of intervening genes, the new gene can function in protein synthesis.

Tonegawa's discovery was insightful because it questioned two dogmas of biology: that the DNA for a protein must be one continuous piece (for antibody synthesis, the gene segments are separated from each other, then assembled together), and that every body cell has identical DNA (the antibody genes for different B-lymphocytes can differ). Current evidence suggests that more than 600 different antibody gene segments exist per cell. Additional versatility is generated through imprecise recombination and somatic mutation. Therefore, the total antibody diversity produced by the B-cells ranges from 100 to more than 1,000 immunoglobulin possibilities.

This system of producing enormous numbers of antibody types is clearly one of intelligent design. One analogy to this is the principle of variation, as found in classical music. For example, J.S. Bach composed selections such as *Jesu, Joy of Man's Desiring*, and *Variations on a Theme* for church choirs. Bach would make a musical "statement" in his theme, then augment it, diminish it, or use a retrograde (backward looking). Sometimes the theme is varied by a change in an instrument, or sometimes the music changes from a major to minor key. Perhaps you have heard Bach performed by bell choirs at Christmas. You might hear a basic pleasant melody, then re-encounter it in a different way and conclude this is a detailed, masterful arrangement of music. Nature also selects from "successful" structures and varies them in many wondrous ways for survival, even in this fallen world. Just as Bach composed beautiful music, the Creator has composed a variation on an antibody theme that defends the body.

Vaccinations

Vaccination may be described as the deliberate introduction of an antigenic substance to the body to induce adaptive immunity by stimulating production of specific antibodies. Vaccination is based upon the principle of immune cells "remembering" the antigen encountered. There are two basic types of vaccines. The first type contains a live (attenuated) or killed pathogen or products from it. In this kind of vaccine, the pathogen has been weakened so it cannot overtake your body's immune system, but the pathogen's antigens stimulate production of T-cell immunity and protective antibodies. As a result, the lymph system recognizes it, makes antibodies to kill it, then makes immunocompetent B- and T-lymphocytes to "remember" the infection should the individual be exposed to the pathogen again. Since the pathogen is weakened, the body's immune system will destroy it before it can overtake the body. Thus, even though the vaccine actually contains a disease-causing pathogen, the vaccine is safe because the pathogen is so weak that your immune system will both destroy and remember it.

The other type of vaccine contains a synthetic chemical that makes the body react in the same manner as if a certain pathogen has entered the body. This type of vaccine "mimics" a real pathogen, causing the immune system to produce antibodies as well as memory B-cells. Regardless of the type of vaccine, the effect is the same. The vaccine causes your body to form B-cells which in turn produce antibody-making plasma cells, and also produce memory B-cells. The memory B-cells remember the pathogen and provide a quick response to any future infections. Vaccines have virtually eliminated many of the childhood diseases that have claimed the lives of millions of children over the years. Because of the smallpox vaccine, the causative smallpox virus exists only in laboratories. It has been wiped out because the vaccine stopped its ability to reproduce by infecting people.

Even though memory B-cells are long-lived, they do not last the individual's lifetime. Thus, some vaccines require a booster to boost the memory of the infection. When the body is first exposed to a pathogen, the B-cells produce a primary response. This response, as stated above, fights the infection and produces memory B-cells. The memory B-cells then produce a secondary response if the pathogen infects the body later. For example, if you have the influenza (flu) shot, your body will manufacture antibodies against the influenza virus. If you encounter a strain of the flu closely related to the original virus, your body quickly mounts a response that will spare you re-infection, or at least its more severe effects, in some cases sparing your life. Thus, your lymphatic system identifies your blood type and "knows" how to spot specific antigens versus those of the flu virus, like neuraminidase and hemagglutinin.

Thorns, Thistles, and Antigens

Antigens are chemical substances capable of mobilizing the immune system and provoking immune responses. Antigens include protein-polysaccharide complexes that are part of bacteria, viruses, and protozoans. Most antigens are large, complex molecules not normally found in the body and consequently referred to as "non-self." Antigens exhibit two important properties: **immunogenicity,** the ability to stimulate immune-system cells; and the ability to react with products of those cells, or with the cells themselves. Antigens are often called **immunogens.** From a creation world view, they are the "thorns and thistles" of the unseen microbial world.

The list of antigens is as enormously diverse as thorns and thistles in the plant world. Antigens include milk proteins, bee venom, hemoglobin molecules, bacterial toxins, and chemical substances found in bacterial flagella, pili, and capsules. The most common antigens are proteins, polysaccharides, and chemical complexes formed between these substances, and lipids or nucleic acids. Proteins are the most important antigens because their amino acids have the greatest array of building blocks, leading to a huge variety of combinations and thus diversity in 3D structures. Polysaccharides are less potent antigens than proteins because they lack chemical diversity and rapidly break down in the body. Lipids can also be antigenic, as exemplified by the cell-wall lipids of tubercle bacilli (bacteria that cause tuberculosis).

The Lymphatics: Awesome, Distinct, and Interwoven

The lymphatic system consists of the major underlying anatomical structures facilitating the immune response (left). The lymphatic organs are awesome in structure and distinct in function. The anatomy of the diverse lymph nodes is marvelously interwoven, providing further evidence of an intelligent design by the skilled Craftsman. Each lymph node contains leukocytes that defeat highly specific pathogens and toxins. The lymphatic and cardiovascular systems share closely intertwined structures joined by capillaries. The lymphatic system was once thought to be part of the circulatory system since it consists of lymph, a moving fluid coming from the blood and returning to it by way of vessels. Lymph nodes with their capillaries are the most obvious interlacing fabric in the body's primary defense base. The nodes are small, oval structures interweaving with lymph capillaries, blood capillaries, and reticular connective fibers and tissues. A capsule of dense connective tissue with strands covering each lymph node is called a trabercula. These extensions divide the node into compartments, provide support, and interlace with blood vessels into the node interior. The superficial region

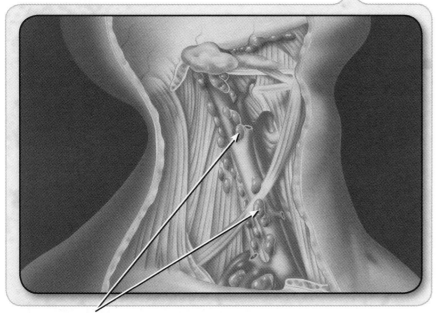

Lymph Nodes

of a lymph node, the cortex, contains many follicles. The deeper region of a node is the medulla. Lymph nodes are a "military base" deploying soldier cells, B- and T-lymphocytes, to locations where "cell wars" occur. Once a bacterium, virus, or toxin invades the body, T- and B-cells quickly go into "battle" from the interwoven, reticular fibers, traveling with lymphatic flow to the "war" zone. Other leukocytes warn the body of danger, assisting in filtering and cleansing the lymph to keep it pure.

There are more than 100 tiny lymph nodes, mainly in the neck, groin, and armpits, but scattered all along the lymph vessels. They act as barriers to infection by filtering out and destroying toxins and germs. The

largest lymph gland in the human body is the spleen. The cervical lymph nodes, located in the neck, are divided into two sets: superficial and deep. The deep cervical glands are large glands situated near the pharynx, esophagus, and trachea. When you have a sore throat, white blood cells mass together in these nodes to fight the infection, which is why your throat often feels swollen and tender.

Lymphatic Nodes: An Interwoven Fabric of Body Defense

Lymph nodes, the most obvious interwoven fabric in the defense system, are small oval structures (left). Lymph nodes are the size of kidney beans and generally are located in clusters near veins at strategic points along medium-sized lymph vessels at the knee, elbow, armpit, groin, neck, abdomen, and chest. Blood is cleaned and filtered in the lymph nodes, and germ-fighting cells gather there during illness. This carefully designed filtration process prevents bacteria, cancer cells, and other infectious agents from entering the blood and circulating through the system. The lymph nodes are the centers for production and storage of some white blood cells, namely the lymphocytes and monocytes, important elements of the body's immune mechanism. During any kind of infection, the nodes enlarge their drainage, due to the multiplication of lymphocytes in the node.

The lymphatic system is a network of interwoven lymphoid channels transporting lymph. Normally, the flow of lymph in a 24-hour period is about three liters. Extracellular fluid is collected from the periphery of the body and directed via the thoracic duct to the general circulation. At strategically located areas, lymph nodes, Peyer's patches, and other lymphoid structures trap and retain antigens. The lymphatic system is designed to collect antigens (including cancer cells spread for the most part along the lymphatics) from the body and concentrate them into lymphoid structures. This is why cancer patients have lymph nodes removed from areas stricken by cancer. Physicians are attempting to lessen the chances the collected cancer cells will spread (metastasize). Lymph-node biopsy analysis also gives doctors an idea about the appropriate therapy for the patient. Unfortunately, with the

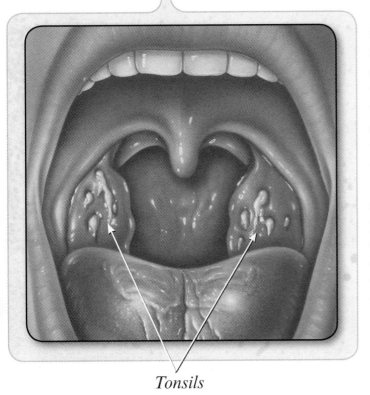

Tonsils

cavity and the nasopharnyx. Tonsils form a protective ring of lymphatic tissue around the nasal and oral cavities and the pharynx, protecting against bacteria, viruses, and other potential pathogens. Unfortunately, tonsils have long been overlooked as immunologically active lymphoid tissue. Seen from the creation perspective, one can see that the tonsils are not a "useless" vestige of evolution, but have been created for our defense.

Anatomists recognize three types of tonsils located in the back of the pharynx: **palatine, lingual**, and **pharyngeal (adenoids)**. The palatine and lingual tonsils comprise two pairs, as well as a cluster of **adenoids** (making up one pharyngeal tonsil). For hundreds of years, the five tonsils were thought be vestigial organs no longer functional, a throwback to our alleged evolutionary ancestors. Anatomists and physiologists now agree that this lymphatic tissue is very important, no longer extracting them when they become inflamed.

The palatine tonsils were once thought to give more trouble than service to the body. Today, creation scientists believe they help contain respiratory infections by maintaining lymphatic boundaries. Tonsils keep infections local and limit their possibility of becoming systemic. They contain germ-killing cells that help protect against upper-respiratory-tract infections such as strep throat.

Adenoids (also called pharyngeal tonsils) are a mass of lymphatic tissue similar to the palatine tonsils, attached to the back wall of the nasal pharynx (i.e., the upper part of the throat opening into the nasal cavity proper). An individual fold of such nasopharyngeal lymphatic tissue is called an adenoid. The surface layer of the adenoids consists of ciliated epithelial cells covered by a thin film of mucus. The cilia, microscopic hair-like projections from the surface cells, move constantly in a wavelike manner, propelling the blanket of mucus down to the pharynx proper. From there the mucus is caught by the swallowing action of the pharyngeal (throat) muscles and sent down to the stomach. The adenoids also contain glands that secrete mucus to replenish the surface film. The function of the adenoids is protective. The moving film of mucus carries infectious agents and dust particles inhaled through the nose to the pharynx, where the epithelium is more resistant. Immune substances, or antibodies, are thought to form within the lymphatic tissue, which, combined with phagocytic action, tends to arrest and absorb infectious agents.

lymphatic vessels removed, lymph begins slowly collecting, causing significant swelling of the affected area. Not only do they have the interlacing design in capillaries, but they also contain bundles of irreducibly complex biochemical packages. The complement system, T-cell and B-cell maturation, and cellular defenses are all irreducibly complex. So in the lymphatic system we see intricacy, complexity, interdependence, and clear purpose.

Not only does lymph play a critical role in the immune system, but it also is designed to absorb fats (cholesterol and long-chain fatty acids) from the intestines, and aid in homeostasis. It transports excess fluid to the terminal vessels. Lymph also helps distribute fluids and nutrients in the body, draining excess fluids and protein so that tissues do not swell up. *Limf* (lymph) means "clear spring water" in Latin. Therefore, lymph keeps other body fluids pure and in balance with the rest of our cells. The lymphatic system absorbs fats from the digestive tract via the lacteals of the small intestine. The fats have entered the lacteals from intestinal villi. Lymph transports fatty content to the venous circulation, eventually distributed or metabolized elsewhere in the body.

Tonsils by Design: A Unique Body Defense

Tonsils are unusually large groups of lymph nodules and diffuse lymphatic tissue located deep within the oral

Diseases, Disorders, and Disruption to the Immune System

Stress and the Immune System

Medical science today now confirms what Greek physicians and biblical writers believed. In experiments with laboratory animals, injury to certain areas of the brain can lead to immune-system changes. These changes affect specific resistance to disease — the immune system's ability to recognize, attack, and remember particular foreign molecules such as viruses and bacteria. Specific resistance to disease is carried out by lymphocytes, called B-cells and T-cells. The "thinking on good things" phenomenon has been known for years — positive attitude assists the immune system's activities, while stress burdens the system. In the 1990s, several research studies showed a direct link between mental state and disease. Some demonstrated a correlation between level of psychological stress and susceptibility to infection by a common cold virus. It was shown that stress and psychological factors could affect immune function. In one study, volunteers received measured doses of a cold virus — five different viruses were tested — or a placebo, a non-infectious "dummy" shot. As expected, some of the volunteers came down with colds and some did not. But among the volunteers injected with any of the five different viruses, the chance of getting a cold (or respiratory infection) was directly proportional to the amount of stress the volunteers said they had experienced during the past year. The study was the first well-controlled demonstration that stress can increase the risk of infection.

These physiological discoveries, along with clinical studies of illness ranging from the common cold to AIDS, have given rise to the rapidly growing field of psychoneurimmunology, or PNI, an outgrowth of more than half a century of research on the physiology of stress. Medical scientists at Ohio State University identified physiological mechanisms responsible for these findings. Providing proof of this phenomenon has been difficult, but researchers are determined to show a correlation between stress and reduced immune activities. Already, they have demonstrated reduced activity in natural killer cells in blood taken from students during exam weeks. It also has been shown that in herpes-infected students, the virus is more active during exams — a reflection of reduced body defense.

Researchers gave Ohio State students hepatitis B vaccinations and then tested for antibody response. Not surprisingly, the more stressed-out and anxious students were, the more they consistently responded with lower antibody levels. Lower antibody levels lower the specific defenses against hepatitis and would leave them prone to infection. Perhaps these students might have contracted hepatitis B more readily if the virus were present. In summary, this line of medical research has demonstrated that both general and specific defenses against disease are lowered when we allow stressful situations to get the best of us.

Acquired Immunodeficiency Syndrome (AIDS)

AIDS, one of this century's most formidable health threats, is now the leading cause of death among Americans ages 25–44. At the turn of the century, almost a million Americans had been diagnosed with AIDS, and more than 60 percent have died of the disease. During 2004, AIDS has continued to rise among young American adults, women, and minorities. According to National Institute for Health figures, the number of Americans with AIDS is expected to reach more than a million in the near future. According to the World Health Organization, there are about 38–40 million human immunodeficiency virus, or HIV, infections worldwide. The fastest growing segments of HIV infection and AIDS are in sub-Saharan Africa, China, and Asia.

AIDS is progression of an HIV infection. The immunodeficiency means a progressive loss of body defenses. Each of the defenses outlined and discussed in this chapter decline until there are effectively none left. In a sense, people with AIDS have a type of "bubble boy" disease, effectively losing all defenses against disease. HIV is a retrovirus that enters T-cells, where it sheds its protein coat. New HIV DNA is produced in the T-cell along with new protein coats, and then released. As HIV multiplies, T-cells are ultimately destroyed. The earliest signs and symptoms of infection are fever, fatigue, rash, headache, joint pain, sore throat, and swollen lymph nodes with infection. Progression to AIDS occurs because of reduced numbers of T-cells and resulting immunodeficiency. AIDS lowers the body's immunity by decreasing the number of helper T-cells; the result is progressive collapse of the immune system, making the person susceptible to opportunistic infections.

The Stages of HIV Infection

The Center for Disease Control classification divides the progress of HIV infection in adults into three clinical stages, or categories. Category A is the where the infection may be asymptomatic or cause persistent swelling in lymph nodes. Category B is characterized by persistent infections by the yeast *Candida albicans* appearing in the mouth, throat, or vagina. Other conditions may include shingles, persistent diarrhea and fever, whitish patches on the oral mucosa, and certain cancerous or precancerous conditions of the cervix. Category C is clinical AIDS. Important AIDS-indicator conditions are *Candida albicans* infections of the esophagus, bronchi and lungs; tuberculosis; Pneumocystis pneumonia; toxoplasmosis of the brain; and Kaposi's sarcoma.

The CDC also classifies the progress of HIV infections based on T-cell populations. The purpose is primarily to furnish guidance for treatment, such as the administration of drugs. The normal CD4 T-cell population of a healthy individual is 800–1000/mm^3. A count below 200/mm^3 is considered diagnostic AIDS, regardless of the clinical category observed. The progression from initial HIV infection to AIDS typically takes about ten years in adults. Cellular war on an immense scale occurs during this time. About 100 billion HIVs are generated every day, each with a remarkably short half-life of about six hours.

These viruses must be cleared by the body's defenses, which include antibodies, cytotoxic T-cells, and macrophage. Most HIV is produced by infected CD4 T-cells, which survive for only about two days (T-cells normally live several years). Every day, about 2 billion CD4 T-cells are produced to compensate for losses. Over time, however, there is a daily net loss of at least 20 million CD4 T-cells, a major marker for tracking the progression of HIV infection. Recent studies show that the decrease in CD4 T-cells is not due entirely to retroviral destruction of the cells, but primarily the shortened life of the cells and the big failure to compensate by increasing production of placement T-cells.

Survival With HIV

HIV infection devastates the immune system, which is unable to respond effectively to pathogens. Success in treating these conditions has extended the lives of many HIV-infected people. As the historical record of the AIDS epidemic lengthens, it has become apparent that not all HIV-positive individuals progress inexorably to AIDS and death. A significant group — about five percent of all those infected — are long-term non-progressors. These infected individuals remain free of AIDS and even symptoms, their CD4 T-cell counts remain stable, and survival exceeding 25 years is predicted. In some cases, the virus seems less virulent, but in most, the immune system, especially cytotoxic T-cells, is apparently more effective. A surprising aspect of the AIDS epidemic is that certain people are subjected to multiple HIV exposures yet never become infected at all. The evidence is that their CD4 T-cells are innately resistant.

Effects of AIDS

The first stage of AIDS is an acute HIV infection. Its first signs are swollen lymph nodes (next page). Frequently, people with an acute HIV infection experience fever, diarrhea, rash, lymphadenopathy, night sweats, and general fatigue similar to acute infectious mononucleosis. When

Scanning electron micrograph of human immunodeficiency virus (HIV), grown in cultured lymphocytes. Virions are seen as small spheres on the surface of the cells.

the CD4 T-cell count in blood is less than 200/μL, the CDC defines this condition as AIDS. When the immune system is seriously compromised in this way, the body becomes susceptible to many microbial opportunistic infections.

Many Opportunistic Diseases

Once the body becomes immunocompromised, many diseases can emerge. If any of them go untreated, they will cause a serious challenge to the AIDS patient. Even a common cold can be serious. Some of the more common opportunistic diseases include Herpes, tuberculosis, *P. carinii* pneumonia, cryptosporidiosis, severe thrush, toxoplasmosis, histoplasmosis, and

A) Swelling in the lymph nodes

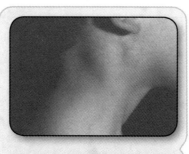

B) Candida albicans appearing in the mouth

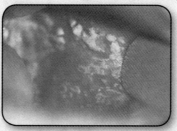

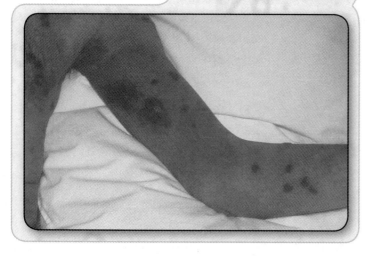

C) Kaposi's sarcoma in an AIDS patient

others. A comprehensive list of other opportunistic diseases infecting AIDS patients would take an entire page to list. Many of these potential pathogens develop from the body's normal flora. Almost any virus, bacterium, protozoan, fungus, or multicellular parasite that can act as a human pathogen is a serious threat to an AIDS patient. This is why most AIDS patients take over two dozen drugs on a regular basis to combat these diseases. Sooner or later, HIV-infected individuals end up at a hospital for treatment for one or more infections from opportunistic organisms.

There are approximately 50 million cases of HIV worldwide. If trends continue at the current rate, the number of AIDS cases could easily double by the year 2010! AIDS has swept across sub-Saharan Africa on an extraordinary scale. Two-thirds of the world's AIDS cases are here. Half of these cases are found in what is called the "AIDS Belt" — a chain of countries in eastern and southern Africa. Heterosexual intercourse serves as the main vehicle for spreading HIV in Africa. In contrast, in the United States the most frequent transmission of HIV is by homosexuals and IV drug users. In parts of Africa, nearly 25 percent of the population is HIV positive. It is suggested that lack of circumcision of men in this region make them particularly susceptible to HIV infections. Now an even greater epidemic is growing in China and much of Asia.

New HIV Drugs

Treatment of HIV infection with reverse transcriptase inhibitors and protease inhibitors has been shown to delay the progression of HIV infection to AIDS. Promising results from clinical trials involving several new AIDS drugs have created new optimism in AIDS research. There is also a growing consensus that combinations of these drugs are better than any single agent alone. This concept, known as a drug "cocktail," has been used by physicians to treat people infected with HIV for only a few months. HIV was not detectable in the blood of these patients after one year of therapy. The researchers think that combination therapy is the most effective because it attacks HIV through two different mechanisms. AZT and 3TC are in a drug class known as reverse transcriptase inhibitors. These drugs work by blocking reverse transcription of cDNA from the viral RNA genome. Thus, no double-stranded DNA is made for transport to the cell nucleus and subsequent integration into the host-cell chromosome.

Saquinavir, indinavir, and ritonavir, in contrast, are protease inhibitors, a new class of drugs that block the maturation of infectious particles from HIV infected CD4 T-cells. Both regimens have provided significant long-term benefits compared with monotherapy. This new cocktail combination was the most impressive, producing significant delays in the progression of disease and improved survival in patients with HIV. However, these treatments are currently incredibly expensive. In addition, subsequent findings indicate significant toxicity with these drug combinations. There is also concern that their continued use will lead to increased mutation rates in HIV. However these promising findings now give hope to HIV-infected people that their life span may be significantly longer than they had thought possible.

Summary and Conclusions: A Design Perspective on Immunity

In summary, a creation-science viewpoint predicts that all living organisms were originally good and the human body likely had a symbiotic relationship with microbes. A remnant of the pre-Fall environment, which was free of disease, suggests the immune system was originally designed to interact positively with microbes. After corruption and the Curse, the immune system's interaction with microbes had to change, and now it has become a defensive body system, screening for dangerous pathogens and toxins.

Evolution declares that the living world evolved slowly over millions of years; the immune system is no exception to that dogma. However, we know from Scripture and science that God created everything in six days (Gen. 1); our immune system is no exception to that truth. The nature of the immune system is such that it must be fully formed and functional — ready to engage with microbes and products of the environment. It makes no biological sense to have a slowly, gradually evolving immune system! Either it works (survival) or it does not (death). Either white blood cells are successful in engulfing pathogens or they are not. So we must have an immune system fully formed and functional from the start. This sounds like creation.

Table 7.3. Anibodies: Soldiers of the Immune System Analogy

Type	Analogy	Analogy
IgM	Marines, Men	Largest of Antibodies; Principal component of 1° response; First to arrive; shortest stay.
IgG	GI, Army	Most abundant; Stays longest; Principal component of 2° response from vaccine; enhances phagocytosis.
IgA	Aqua, Navy	Found mainly in secretions, such as mucus, tears, saliva, milk. Numerous in respiratory infections.
IgD	Defends the President	Assist B-Cell response facilitates maturation of the Secret Service antibody response; Antigen receptor on B-Cells. Some functions of IgD are not known; it is a "secret."
IgE	Elevate, Air Force	Involved airborne allergens: allergy reactions; Also involved in multicellular parasitic infections.

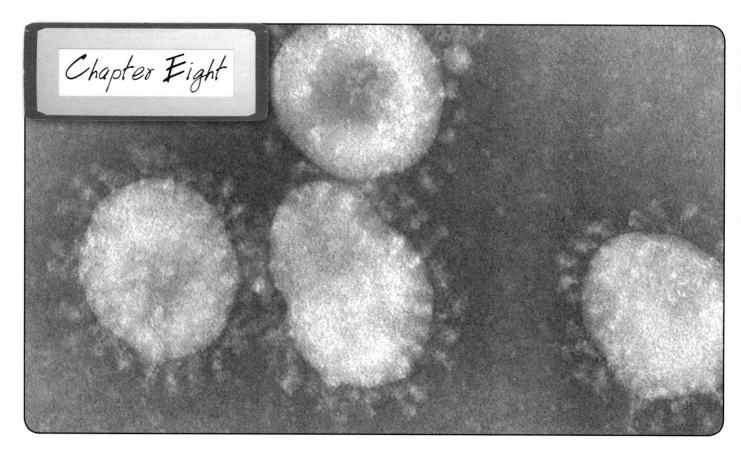

Chapter Eight

Emerging Diseases: Plagues of the Present and Future

New Diseases and Plagues in Headlines

With each passing year, news headlines reveal some new disease outbreak or plague. The outbreak of severe acute respiratory syndrome, or SARS, has caused world-wide panic. A new form of the virus that causes the common cold in humans was behind the rapidly emerging SARS phenomenon, according to the National Centers for Disease Control and Prevention, or CDC. The number of people thought to have SARS grew to more than 8,000 worldwide, including hundreds of deaths during the spring of 2003.

The CDC presented strong evidence that this highly contagious coronavirus was, if not the primary cause of the illness, at least a major contributor. The CDC is part of a network of 11 leading international laboratories formed by the World Health Organization, or WHO, that determined a cause as well as treatments for SARS. CDC researchers were able not only to grow the virus in the laboratory based on cultures from two SARS patients, but they also found evidence of the previ-

ously unknown strain in tissue samples from affected patients. It appears to be a mixture of duck and human coronavirus.

Scary stuff! How could a common cold virus lead to such terrible consequences? When terrible diseases come our way, believers in Jesus Christ can take refuge in the shadow of the Almighty. Psalm 91:3 says, "Surely he shall deliver thee from . . . the noisome [deadly] pestilence." Although Christians are not exempt from terrifying diseases, it is true that they can and will find refuge in their Creator as pestilence and plagues destroy those around them. Christians are not called to fear these diseases, but to study and apply all known biblical principles (such as quarantine), employ effective hygiene measures, and seek professional medical help in times of crisis.

Deadly plagues are not new to man. We read of deadly pestilence and infectious disease outbreaks throughout the Bible. In the Old Testament, we read about laws that Moses gave and principles for controlling disease, such as washing of hands, quarantines, and facemasks. In Exodus 15:26, *Jehovah Rapha* states that He would put *none of these diseases* upon those who obeyed Him. It is interesting that when God's people have followed these health principles, fatalities have been minimized. For example, in 1665, bubonic plague was negligible among Jews. To date, SARS has caused no deaths in the United States, in part because of vigorous practice of quarantining. We read in Leviticus 13:46 about controlling infectious diseases by quarantining those who have them, and the idea of controlling the spread of droplet infections through facemasks first appears in Leviticus 13:45.

For years, physicians, priests, pastors, and laymen have been asking, "Why are there new diseases?" Critical questions that medical scientists are asking and trying to answer are:

1) What diseases are truly new?
2) Why do new diseases keep popping up?
3) What is the origin of these new, emerging diseases?
4) How do secular biologists differ from those with a biblical world view in explaining infectious diseases?
5) When did disease ultimately originate in the first place?

New and Emerging Diseases

SARS may have dominated the headlines during early 2003, but it wasn't the only emerging disease on the WHO's radar screen that year. In central Africa, an outbreak of the dreaded Ebola fever had stretched into its fifth month. In Belgium and the Netherlands, a virulent new strain of avian flu was wiping out entire chicken farms. Dutch farmers recently slaughtered 18 million birds in hopes of stopping the outbreak. Yet the bird flu has spread to several provinces and jumped from poultry to pigs and even people, causing 83 known human cases. Most of the infected people have suffered only eye inflammation, but some have developed respiratory illness. One of them, a 57-year-old veterinary surgeon, died of pneumonia. Bird flu virus was found in the lungs, and no other cause of death could be detected.

SARS, Ebola, and Avian flu — the parade of frightening new maladies continues, each one confirming that our species, for all its cleverness, still lives at the mercy of microbes. In fact, over 30 new or emerging diseases have occurred since the 1970s. It didn't seem that way 30 years ago — not with smallpox largely defeated, AIDS still undreamed of, and medical science emerging at an unprecedented clip. Even as optimists proclaimed victory over germs, our large urban areas, factory farms, jet planes, and blood banks were opening broad new avenues for infection!

The Historical Fight Against Disease

About the time that spontaneous generation was finally disproved to everyone's satisfaction, the Golden Age of medical microbiology was born. Between 1875 and 1918, most disease-causing bacteria were identified, and early work on viruses had begun. Once people realized that some of these invisible agents could cause disease, they tried to prevent their spread from sick to healthy people. The great successes in human health in the last 100 years have resulted in the prevention of infectious diseases with vaccines and treatment of these diseases with antibiotics. The results have been astounding!

Perhaps new plagues have surprised the Western world in the last two decades because of the progress made in preventing and treating infectious diseases over the last century. In 1900, emphasis was placed on childhood diseases. Until about 1870, over one-third of the world's children died from such diseases as measles, mumps, whooping cough, diphtheria, typhoid, and scarlet fever. Although adults commonly lived to ripe old ages, the average age at death in 1900 was 47 because so many people died in childhood. However, after the turn of the 20th century, the fight against disease began meeting with more success. Since 1940, medical science has found a defense against so many childhood diseases that the average life expectancy in America has risen by nearly 30 years. In 1915, when almost one baby out of ten died in early childhood, the emphasis in medicine was on prevention of high infant mortality. Although the number of infant deaths is still high in some underdeveloped countries, by the early 1990s the infant mortality rate in America had dropped to less than 1 in 100. Upon entering the new millennium, drastic shifts in life expectancy and causes of death in the United States caused a change in emphasis from infectious diseases to "adult" conditions like heart disease and cancers.

Most childhood diseases once concerning society are seldom seen today. Because many children grow to adulthood, more elderly people live today than 100 years ago. As people live to be old, we see more diseases associated with the process of steady decline in body function, which starts during the early to mid-20s. With lower body reserves and lower resistance to disease, the elderly are less able to cope with infections and other illnesses. Senior citizens' tendency to have disabling conditions comes at a time of decline in standards by which families help their aged parents. Western countries are also experiencing sharp increases in cases of renal disease, as well as conditions related to alcohol, tobacco, other drugs, and obesity.

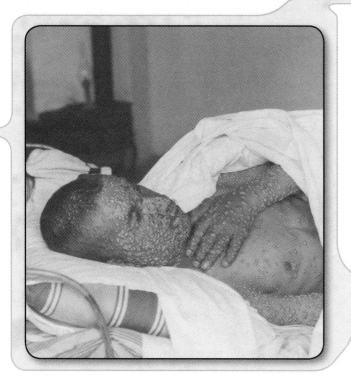

Patient infected with the smallpox virus

By the year 2000, the average life span of Americans had extended to the 80s. Thanks to modern sanitation, asepsis, antiseptic surgery, vaccination, and effective antibiotic treatments, medical science has reduced the incidence of some of the worst diseases — such as smallpox, bubonic plague, and influenza — to a small fraction of their former numbers. No longer do we see mass numbers of people dying from infectious diseases like they did for centuries. For example, prior to flu vaccines, more Americans died of influenza in 1918–1919 than were killed in World War I, World War II, the Korean War, and the Vietnam War combined. The most serious global pandemic at the time killed an estimated 40 million people. But by the early 1970s, with the advent of numerous vaccines and antibiotics, people felt safe against such epidemics recurring.

Past Triumphs

The viral disease smallpox was one of the greatest killers the world has ever known. It is estimated that ten million people have died from this disease over the past 4,000 years. It was brought to the New World by the Spaniards and made it possible for Hernando Cortez, with fewer than 600 soldiers, to conquer the Aztec Empire, with subjects numbering in the millions. During a crucial battle in Mexico City, an epidemic of smallpox raged, killing only the Aztecs, who had never been exposed to the disease.

In recent times, an active worldwide vaccination program has resulted in no cases being reported since 1977. Although the disease will probably never reappear on its own, its potential use as an agent in bioterrorism is raising great concern.

Bubonic plague has been another great killer. One-third of the entire population of Europe — approximately 25 million people — died of this bacterial disease between 1346 and 1350. Now, generally less than 100 people in the entire world die from it each year. In large part, this dramatic decrease results from controlling the population of the black rats that harbor the bacterium. Further, the discovery of antibiotics in the early 20th century made the isolated outbreaks treatable, so the disease is no longer the scourge it once was. In general, by the mid-1970s medical scientists were predicting the eradication of most deadly infectious diseases.

Present and Future Challenges

By the mid-1970s, surprises came when new diseases began popping up. Though progress has been very impressive against bacterial diseases, a great deal remains to be done, especially in treating viral diseases, as well as conditions prevalent in developing countries. Even in wealthy developed countries with sophisticated health-care systems, infectious diseases remain a serious threat. For example, about 750 million cases of infectious diseases of all types occur in the United States each year. These diseases lead to 200,000 annual deaths and cost tens of billions of health-care dollars. Respiratory infections and diarrheal diseases cause most illnesses and deaths in the world today. In addition to the well-recognized diseases, 30-plus seemingly "new" diseases have emerged and continue to arise. In the last several decades, they have included the diseases listed in Table 8.1 (pg. 137).

Recent History of Emerging Infectious Diseases

The increasing incidence of new plagues indicates that infectious diseases are not only not disappearing, but also seem to be re-emerging and increasing. The infectious diseases cropping up in recent years are either new or changing, and either are increasing or have the potential to increase in incidence in the near future. Some of the factors contributing to the emergence of Ebola, for example, are minor changes in existing organisms, the spread of known diseases to new geographic regions or populations, and increased human exposure to new and unusual infectious agents. Exposure to new germs results mainly from ecological changes like deforestation and construction. Many recent incidents highlight the extent of the problem.

Lyme Disease

In 1975, the Connecticut Health Department received hundreds of calls about cases of what appeared to be arthritis in children in Lyme, Connecticut. Despite assurance from physicians that arthritis was not infectious, the callers were not satisfied. A state epidemic investigation was begun. Public health officials began trying to locate all those who had a sudden onset of swelling and pain in the knees or other joints.

This odd disease seemed to cluster in late spring and summer and last from a week to a few months. Most patients had symptoms in the following stages, the first one typically beginning with a skin rash. The rash began as a red spot or bump and slowly enlarged. In the second stage, symptoms were influenza-like fatigue, chills, fever, headache, stiff neck, joint, and muscle pains, and backache. Joint pain, swelling, and tenderness, usually of a large joint (e.g., the knees) characterized the third stage. These symptoms developed beginning about six months after the rash, and slowly disappeared over years.

Later it was found that the disease spreads when bacteria injected by an infected tick multiply and spread across the skin, the bacteria disseminates into body tissues by the bloodstream, then immune reaction produces tissue damage. In the 1970s, this disease became known as Lyme arthritis.

The clustering of cases was most reported in wooded areas along lakes and streams. This suggested that the disease was transmitted by an arthropod. It was found that affected people were more likely to have a household pet than those without pets. Pet owners are more likely to come into contact with ticks picked up in the woods by those pets. The importance of this finding was emphasized when most patients reported that their arthritic symptoms were preceded by an unusual bull's-eye skin rash that spread to a six-inch ring. Concurrently, scientists found spirochete bacteria

in the guts of many of the ticks sent from Connecticut. The spirochete, named *Borrelia burgdorferi,* was later determined to be the cause of Lyme disease.

Legionnaires' Disease

This condition came from nowhere during the U.S. Bicentennial. From July 21–24, 1976, the Bellevue-Stratford Hotel in Philadelphia hosted the 58th annual convention of Pennsylvania's chapter of the American Legion. Toward the end of the convention, 140 conventioneers and 72 other people in or near the hotel became ill with fever, coughing, and pneumonia. Eventually, 34 individuals died of what came to be called Legionnaires' disease. In January 1977, CDC investigators announced the isolation of a bacterium from the lung tissue of one of the patients. They called it *Legionella pneumophila.* Legionnaires' disease was found to spread unlike other airborne diseases. *Legionella* exists where water collects, and it apparently becomes airborne in wind gusts and breezes. Cooling towers, industrial air-conditioning units, humidifiers, stagnant pools, and water puddles have been identified as sources of the bacteria.

AIDS

Acquired immunodeficiency syndrome (AIDS) first came to public attention in 1981 with reports from Los Angeles that a few young homosexual men had died of a previously rare type of pneumonia known as Pneumocystis pneumonia. These men had experienced a severe weakening of the immune system, which normally fights infectious diseases. Soon these cases were correlated with an unusual number of cases of a rare form of cancer, Kaposi's sarcoma, among young homosexual men. Similar increases in such rare diseases were found among hemophiliacs and intravenous drug users.

Researchers discovered that AIDS was caused by a previously unknown virus. The virus, now called human immunodeficiency virus, or HIV, destroys certain white blood cells in the immune system called CD4 lymphocytes. Sickness and death result from microorganisms or cancerous cells that might otherwise have been defeated by the body's natural defenses. So far, once symptoms develop, the disease has been inevitably fatal.

By the end of 1999, nearly 700,000 people in the United States had been diagnosed with AIDS, with more than 60 percent dying as a result. A great many more people had tested positive for the presence of HIV in their blood. As of 2002, health officials estimated that nearly a million Americans carried the virus. In 2003, the WHO estimated that over 47 million people world-wide had become infected with HIV.

By studying disease patterns, medical researchers found that HIV could be spread through sexual activity, by contaminated needles, from infected mothers to their fetuses before birth, and by blood transfusions — in short, by transmission of body fluids from one person to another. Since 1985, blood used for transfusions has been carefully checked for the presence of HIV, and it is now quite unlikely that the virus can be spread by this means.

West Nile Virus

West Nile virus is the cause of West Nile encephalitis, or WNE, a disease that can produce an inflammation of the brain. WNE was first diagnosed in the West Nile region of Uganda in 1937. In 1999, the virus first appeared in North American humans in New York City. By 2002, 3,559 people had been infected in 37 states. The West Nile virus is now established in non-migratory birds in 42 states, and WNE has occurred in horses in 15 states. The virus, carried by birds, is transmitted between and to horses and humans by mosquitoes. West Nile may have arrived in the United States through an infected vector or by a mosquito or bird onboard a ship.

E. coli Turns Deadly

Escherichia coli is a normal inhabitant of the large intestine of vertebrates, including humans, and its presence is beneficial because it helps produce certain vitamins and breaks down otherwise indigestible foodstuffs. However, a strain called *E. coli 0157:H7* causes bloody diarrhea when it grows in the intestine. This strain was first recognized in 1982, and since then has emerged as a public health problem. It is now one of the leading causes of diarrhea worldwide. In 1996, some 9,000 people in Japan became ill and seven died. The recent outbreaks of *E. coli 0157:H7* in the United States, associated with contamination of undercooked meat and un-pasteurized beverages, have alerted public health officials that new methods of testing for bacteria in food must be developed.

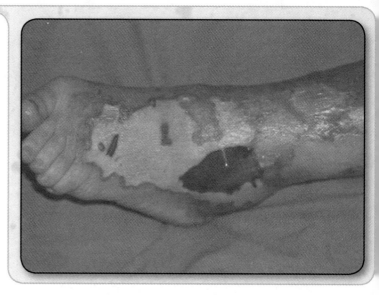

Streptococcal Gangrene *or* Necrotizing Fascitis *of the foot and ankle, caused by so-called flesh-eating Group A Streptococcus bacteria*

Flesh-eating Bacteria

In 1995, so-called flesh-eating bacteria were reported on the front pages of major newspapers. The bacteria are more correctly named "invasive group A Streptococcus." There has been a trend toward increasing rates of flesh-eating bacteria in the United States, Scandinavia, England, and Wales. The reasons for the recent increase are unclear.

Ebola

Microbiologists first isolated Ebola viruses from humans during earlier outbreaks in Congo in 1976. (The virus is named after Congo's Ebola River.) In 1994, a single case of infection from a newly described Ebola virus occurred in the middle of Africa. In 1989 and 1996, outbreaks among monkeys imported to the United States from the Philippines were caused by another Ebola virus but were not associated with human disease. Microbiologists have been studying many animals but have not yet discovered the natural reservoir (source) of Ebola virus.

Hantavirus

Hantavirus pulmonary syndrome brought public attention in 1993 when two people in the same household became ill and died within five days of each other. Their illnesses began with a fever and cough rapidly progressing to respiratory failure. Within a month, 23 additional cases, including 10 deaths, were reported in the Four Corners area of the American Southwest. Worried tourists began canceling vacations to the area, and residents wondered who would get the disease next. Using techniques that only became available in the 1990s, microbiologists determined that the cause was a newly recognized Hantavirus called the Sin Nombre virus, which is carried by deer mice. Researchers developed a test to rapidly identify the virus, making recommendations to help people reduce their risk of exposure to potentially infected rodents. It is probably not a new virus. Comparisons of Hantavirus genes suggest that the virus probably came to North America with the first rats from the Old World.

Giardiasis

Since the 1970s, giardiasis has emerged to become the most commonly detected protozoal disease of the intestine in the United States. Though not reportable to the CDC, the disease is estimated to attack thousands of Americans annually. The causative agent is named *Giardia lamblia*, a member of the protozoan class with flagella. Giardiasis is commonly transmitted by water containing Giardia cysts stemming from cross-contamination of drinking water with sewage. In the 1970s, for example, 38 cases in Aspen, Colorado, broke out after a sewer line was obstructed, causing sewage to leak into the town's water supply. In recent years, outbreaks in day-care centers and schools have resulted from contact with feces. In addition, the disease has become common among wild animals, from which it can be obtained via contaminated water. In 1989, a notable cluster of 22 cases in Albuquerque, New Mexico, was related to contamination of water used to wash lettuce for tacos.

Cryptosporidium

Also in 1993, an outbreak of cryptosporidiosis transmitted through the public water supply in Milwaukee resulted in diarrheal illness in an estimated 403,000 persons. The microorganism responsible for this outbreak was the protozoan *Cryptosporidium*. First reported as a cause of human disease in 1976, it is responsible for up to 30 percent of diarrheal illness in developing countries. In the United States, transmission has occurred via drinking water, swimming pools, and contaminated hospital supplies.

Disease Focus 8.1:

Putting a New "Light" on Cholera
The Genesis of Disease–Causing Vibrio
A Variational Change in Vibrios turn a Mutualistic Relationship into Parasitism (Disease)

Cholera is classified as an emerging disease because new strains are constantly infecting different parts of the world in devastating ways. However, it is really an old disease and is thought to have originated in the Far East, thousands of years ago; Sanskrit writings indicate that it existed in India, many centuries before Christianity. With the increased movement of goods and people during the 1800s, cholera spread from Asia to Europe and then to North America. Cholera was a major epidemic disease of that time and has killed millions over the millennia. Some people called it "lingering consumption" because it consumed the body like chronic tuberculosis. It was not until 1883 that Robert Koch isolated *Vibrio cholerae*, the comma-shaped bacterium that causes this disease. It secretes a powerful exotoxin (a poisonous protein) that causes severe and lasting diarrhea. Where and how did this horrible disease originate?

Creation scientists think that today's pathogenic bacteria were beneficial or at least mutualistic in the world before man fell into sin. In other words, beneficial bacteria changed into disease-causing bacteria as a result of the Fall and God's cursing of the earth (along with thistles, thorns, and harmful mutations). *Vibrio cholera* causes the human intestinal disease, cholera, because of the toxin protein that the bacteria secrete. What if – prior to the Fall – this protein had an alternative positive function? Recent research has shown there might be some evidence to this creation suggestion.

A "cousin" of the cholera bacteria is *Vibrio fischeri*, a non-pathogenic, bioluminescent bacterium. This species of *Vibrio* can emit light. This phenomenon, bioluminescence, plays an important role in the symbiotic relationship between some of these bacteria and specific types of flashlight fishes and squids. For example, certain types of squid have a specialized organ within their ink sac that is colonized by *Vibrio fischeri*. The light produced in the organ is thought to serve as a type of camouflage that helps obscure the squid's contrast against the light from above and any shadow it might cast. The bacteria therefore helps protect the animal from predation and perhaps in attracting a mate. In return, the squid provides nutrients to the symbiotic bacteria, facilitating their growth. This mutualistic relationship typifies the symbiosis of organisms originally designed by the Creator. Note that the bioluminescence is catalyzed by the enzyme luciferase. The genes encoding this enzyme are only expressed when the density of the bacterial population reaches a critical point of hunger. This regulated expression is called quorum sensing and is now recognized as an important communication means used by a variety of different bacteria.

When the *Vibrio fischeri* get hungry, they secrete a protein that does not sicken the squid but rather informs it. There is also an "erosion" of epithelial lining. The erosion causes no harm, but rather it sends a communication signal. This protein signals that the bacteria need food, which the squid then provides. Maybe microbiologists who study cholera pathogenesis have been studying an aspect of "normal conversation" between organisms that has gone wrong. Creation scientists would suggest that this corrupted message is a result of the Curse. Perhaps, over time, the genome of the original *Vibrio* type changed and this "good" bacterium, which produced a non-poisonous protein (called ToxR – the cholera homolog toxin), decayed into one that produced a poisonous protein (i.e., the cholera toxin).

This is consistent with the creation theory proposed by biologist Dr. Joseph Francis. He has suggested the Biomatrix of Life theory which views the world of viruses and microbes from a creation perspective. Dr. Francis proposed that microbes were created as a biomatrix; a link between macro-organisms and a chemically rich but inert physical environment, to provide a substrate upon which multicellular creatures can thrive and persist. (There is a similar symbiotic relationship between plant roots and fungi.) Indeed, many bacterial cells communicate and function as a symbiotic community, and a growing number of these relationships are constantly being discovered. Pathogenesis resulting from the Fall and Curse is both a rare and recent divergence from the original creation intent. The *Vibrio fischeri* and *V. cholera* microbes are just such an example. In summary, the good symbiotic design of protein production needed to produce bioluminescence in *Vibrio fischeri* changed (a "light corruption") to the production of a pathogenic toxin in *Vibrio cholera* (causing "lingering consumption"). A once mutualistic symbiotic relationship between bacteria and animals has now been corrupted in man. The effects of sin seem to always turn what was once "light" into "darkness."

Mad Cow Disease

In 1996, countries worldwide were refusing to import beef from the United Kingdom, and the U.K. had to kill hundreds of thousands of cattle born after 1988, because of an epidemic of bovine spongiform encephalopathy, or BSE, but better known as mad cow disease. BSE first caught the attention of microbiolo-

Examination of a cow showing uncoordinated movements characteristic of BSE *"mad cow disease"*

gists in 1986 as one of a handful of diseases caused by an infectious protein called a prion. Studies suggest that the source of the disease was cattle feed prepared from sheep infected with their own version of the disease. Cattle are herbivores (plant-eaters), but their growth and health are improved by adding protein to their feed. Creutzfeldt-Jakob disease, or CJD, is a human disease also caused by a prion. The incidence of CJD in the United Kingdom is similar to the incidence in other countries. However, by 2000, the U.K. reported 46 human cases of CJD caused by a new variant related to the bovine disease.

Ecological Disturbances

One of the major contributors to new and emerging diseases is urban sprawl into previously wilderness, jungle, or desert environments. Man and his livestock coming into contact with wild animals and their "germs" results in a mixing of genetic information between the pathogens of domestic animals and wildlife. Man then comes into contact with his pets and livestock carrying these new "germs," and new strains of disease are born.

The dark side of progress is now unmistakable; many of the advances that have made our lives more comfortable have also made them more dangerous. So what's to be done? As the SARS outbreak has shown, surveillance is critical. By spotting new infections wherever they occur and working globally to contain them, we can greatly reduce their impact. But is preparedness our ultimate weapon? Do we know enough about the genesis of new diseases to prevent them? Could we avert the next SARS? Or could we stop the next Ebola or AIDS? What would a reasonable strategy look like?

Man is unable to control many new disease outbreaks in rural, jungle, and desert environments. Most new diseases begin when a person catches something from an animal — a transaction shaped by chance or even weather. When healthy young adults started dying of a respiratory syndrome in New Mexico in 1993, it took health experts several weeks of intensive lab work to identify the culprit. To the scientists' amazement, it wasn't a human pathogen at all. It was a novel member of the Hantavirus family, a group of rodent viruses that sometimes spread through the air after rats or mice shed them in their urine. The previous outbreaks had occurred in Asia. So why were people dying in New Mexico? Scientists now believe the American mice had harbored the virus all along but had never been populous enough to scatter infectious doses in people's tool sheds and basements. What changed the equation that year was El Niño. This ocean disturbance caused an unusually warm winter in the Southwest. The mouse population exploded as a result — and the Hantavirus got a free ride.

Until someone harnesses the jet stream, such accidents are sure to happen, but quirky weather isn't the greatest threat we face. Along with the 30-plus new diseases that have cropped up since the mid-1970s, causing tens of millions of deaths, forgotten scourges have resurfaced with alarming regularity. Many experts feel infectious diseases will continue emerging, warning us that complacency and inaction could lead to a "catastrophic storm" of contagion. Ecologists studying the causes of disease emergence find that human enterprise is a significant force. Almost any activity disrupting a natural environment can enhance the mobility of disease-causing microbes.

The point is not that rain forests or wilderness areas are dangerous — it is that unexpected rearranging of ecosystems can be hazardous to our health. This is true in both the Amazon Basin and the woods of Connecticut. This is where Lyme disease emerged, and it, too, is a product of the way we use our land. *Borrelia burgdorferi*, the bacterium causing Lyme, lives in the bodies of deer and white-footed mice, passing between those animals in the heads of biting ticks. People have crossed paths with all these critters for generations, yet the first known case of Lyme disease dates back only to 1975. Why did we suddenly become vulnerable?

An animal ecologist has tied the event to suburban development. In open woodlands, foxes and bobcats keep a lid on the Lyme agent by hunting the mice that carry it. But the predators vanish when developers chop woodlands into subdivisions, and the mice and their ticks proliferate unnaturally. In a recent survey of woodlots in New York, biologists found that infected ticks were some seven times more prevalent on half- and 1-acre lots as on lots of 10 to 15 acres. The bottom line: You are more likely to get Lyme disease in the suburbs of big cities and golf courses than in wilderness and woods.

Just as microbiological techniques helped researchers fight sexually transmitted diseases and smallpox, they will help scientists discover the causes of new, emerging infectious diseases in the 21st century. Undoubtedly there will be more new diseases. Ebola virus and Hantavirus are examples of viruses that may be changing their abilities to infect different host species.

Infectious diseases may re-emerge because of the development of resistance to antibiotics. The breakdown of public health measures for previously controlled infections has resulted in unexpected cases of tuberculosis, whooping cough, and diphtheria.

The diseases mentioned are caused by viruses, bacteria, protozoa, and prion types of microorganisms. This book introduces you to the enormous variety of parasites and pathogens ("germs"). You are also learning about the origins of disease from a biblical perspective and seeing that most of these new diseases are not really new, but rather variants of old diseases.

Germs have been around since the Edenic curse and corruption of the created world. Gene-flow patterns change over the years, mutations alter original design in various ways and environmental conditions change, so consequently we see new variants to older diseases.

Factors Encouraging New Diseases

Many of these diseases are not really new, but an increased occurrence and wider distribution have brought them to the attention of health workers. Using the latest techniques, biomedical scientists have

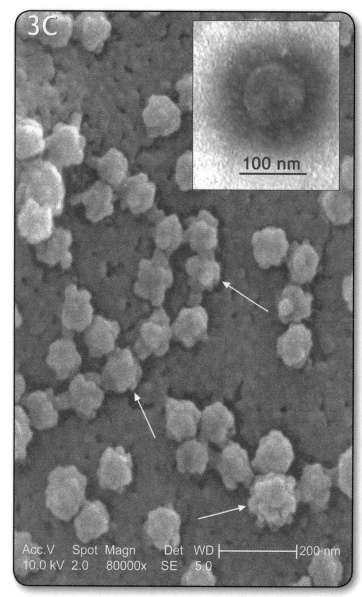

3C

100 nm

Acc.V Spot Magn   Det WD |——————————|200 nm
10.0 kV 2.0 80000x   SE   5.0

This scanning electron micrograph reveals the "rosettelike" appearance of the matured SARS-CoV (coronavirus) particles (arrows)

Hantavirus. This virus infects rodents, usually without causing disease. The infected animals, however, shed the virus in urine, feces, and saliva; from there, humans can inhale it as an aerosol. The Hantavirus and Lyme disease are only two of many emerging human diseases associated with small-animal reservoirs.

Some emerging diseases arise because the infectious agents change abruptly and gain the ability to infect new hosts. It is possible that HIV, the cause of AIDS, arose from a virus that once could infect only monkeys. Some bacterial pathogens, organisms capable of causing disease, differ from their non-pathogenic relatives in that the pathogens contain large pieces of DNA that confer on the organism the ability to cause disease. These pieces of DNA may have originated in unrelated organisms.

Since 1976, many new infectious diseases of humans and animals have appeared. Are there other agents out there that may cause "new" diseases in the future? The answer is undoubtedly yes!

Resurgence of Old Diseases

Not only are "new" diseases emerging, but many infectious diseases once on the wane in the United States have also begun to increase again. Furthermore, many of these diseases are more serious today because the causative agents resist the antibiotics once used to treat them. One reason for this resurgence is that thousands of foreign visitors and U.S. citizens returning from travel abroad enter this country daily. The two diseases that most threaten us are tuberculosis and malaria. Growing antibiotic resistance, international travel, and new emerging strains make these major global health threats. One in three people have antibodies to tuberculosis, which mean they have been exposed, and there have been about 10 million in the United States and 1.5 billion cases worldwide. Most of the new cases are from those foreign born, but in second are those cases associated with AIDS. The WHO reports 300 new cases of malaria every day and 500 million cases worldwide. In addition, malaria is making a comeback in the United States.

The re-emergence of some diseases, like cholera, is due to the natural selection of bacteria. For example, a new serotype of *Vibrio cholerae*, designated *0139*, appears to be nearly identical to the strain most commonly causing cholera epidemics, *V. cholerae*

isolated, characterized, and identified these agents of disease. Now methods need to be developed to prevent them.

A number of factors account for these emerging diseases arising even in industrially advanced countries. One reason, as discussed earlier, is that changing lifestyles bring new opportunities for infectious agents to cause disease. We gave the example of suburban cities expanding into rural areas, bringing people into closer contact with animals previously isolated from humans. Consequently, people become exposed to viruses and infectious organisms that had been far removed from their environment. Besides the Lyme disease example already mentioned, another good example of this is the

0139, except that it has gained the ability to produce a capsule. This is not evolution, but a structural variation found in many bacteria, including *Streptococcus pneumoniae*, the major cause of pneumonia. The consequence of the new serotype is that even people with immunity against the earlier strain are susceptible to the new one. Resistance to the effects of antimicrobial drugs contributes to the growing number of cases. A major cholera outbreak in Latin America occurred from 1991 to 1993.

About one in five outbreaks come from a country where such diseases as malaria, cholera, plague, and yellow fever still exist. In developed countries these diseases have been eliminated largely through sanitation, vaccination, and quarantine. An international traveler incubating a disease in his or her body, however, could theoretically circle the globe, touch down in several countries, and expose many people before becoming ill. As a result, these diseases are recurring in countries where they had been virtually eliminated.

A second reason that certain diseases are on the rise is that in both developed and developing countries, many childhood diseases have been so effectively controlled by childhood vaccinations that some parents have become lax about having their children vaccinated. The unvaccinated children are highly susceptible, and the number of those infected has increased dramatically. These diseases include measles, polio, mumps, whooping cough, and diphtheria.

Also contributing to the rise in infectious diseases is the increasing proportion of elderly people, who have weakened immune systems and are susceptible to diseases that younger people readily resist. In addition, HIV-infected individuals are especially susceptible to a wide variety of diseases, such as tuberculosis and Kaposi's sarcoma.

Mutations and Mechanisms of Change

The most likely germs to mutate are viruses; then, in order of likelihood of change, come bacteria, protists, fungi, and multicellular parasites like worms.

Viruses can be classified by genetic code, either DNA or RNA, but not both. Those viruses with RNA as their blueprint mutate much faster than DNA viruses, due to their single-stranded nature and lack of a good "proofreading" mechanism. The diversity of colds can be attributed, in part, to various coronaviruses and

other RNA viruses such as influenza that have been modified over time. There may be two reasons why SARS has been shown to have a fast mutation rate. First, the technology that sequences genetic codes (DNA and RNA) has improved dramatically. Nearly all 26 countries where SARS has been reported have produced a sequence in a matter of weeks, and the rate of reporting subtle changes in viral genomes has gone from years to days. The technology is so good that virtually any high-tech lab can sequence genomes weekly and observe subtle differences. Never before in biology has such a technological feat been accomplished.

The SARS coronavirus has an RNA genome, whereas living organisms usually store their genetic information as DNA. Most importantly, since RNA lacks the ability to "proofread" its genetic message, to check that the correct bases have been added to the growing chain, RNA viruses change more rapidly than do DNA viruses. As RNA replicates, it averages about one mistake per 10,000 nucleotides copied. As DNA replicates its complementary strand, it makes one mistake in every one million to ten million nucleotides. It is estimated that up to two percent of the nucleotides in the RNA genome of a virus are altered every year. Consequently, antigenic drift of coronaviruses can be attributed in part to point mutations. In layman's terms, RNA viruses lack a good spellchecker in their word-processing program. Many errors go undetected and repeat many times.

When an RNA mutation occurs within a virus, a change may also occur on the viral protein coat. This coat contains antigens eliciting varying antibody responses in the human body.

Other pathogens mutate and varieties are selected from the environment. Some have tremendously diverse changes, while others have more stable genetic codes. In each case there is no additional genetic system (though a single or a few nucleotides may be added) to make them a fundamentally different kind of germ (or pathogen). Coronaviruses are still coronaviruses, Ebola is still Ebola, malarial parasites are still *Plasmodium sp.*, etc. "Like breeds like," but with variation within a kind.

Traditional Ideas Challenged

This idea of mutation and environment bringing about new diseases sounds a lot like evolution, but it is not real evolution. It is nothing more than *variation within a kind* of pathogen or germ. There is horizontal transfer of information or a net loss of information — a reshuffling of the deck of gene cards. Evolutionists have been quick to jump on this as a fact of evolution, proposing Darwinist solutions to this growing health concern.

In *Discover* magazine, Lori Oliwenstein describes a revolution taking place in biology and medicine. She suggests that Charles Darwin and his theory of natural selection have something to offer today's medicine. She affectionately refers to "Dr. Darwin" because modern neo-Darwinists like Paul Ewald have successfully predicted outcomes of hemorrhagic fever and the changing Ebola virus using evolutionary theory. On one hand, Ewald has done us a favor by making observations concerning virus emergence and changing virulence patterns. Creationists and evolutionists make the same observations, but see them through different glasses. We have a different world view, or perspective, on where the disease is going. Creationists see that germs do have boundaries in how far they can mutate and do have limits on their devolution.

No creationist would deny Ewald's contributions to biology and the understanding of new and re-emerging pathogens (including HIV and AIDS, Helicobacter and ulcers, and heart disease and Chlamydia). This is a variation within specific virus and bacteria kinds. No one debates his observations or changing within kinds. What is disturbing is the suggestion that "Dr. Darwin's" philosophy of survival of the fittest be applied in medicine, and the idea that we still have a Stone Age body in this new age. Darwinists want their viewpoint to be the glue not only in all biology, but now also in medicine.

What's next? It is interesting that evolutionists advocate Charles Darwin as "Dr. Darwin," the humanistic physician. He himself suffered from poor health (Chagas' disease) most of his adult life. One concern for Christians is the suggestion that Darwin's philosophy of survival of the fittest be applied in medicine. The suggestion of linking Charles Darwin to your family physician is like having your local high school biology teacher diagnose and prescribe medications for SARS. The biology teacher may excel at teaching about cold viruses and their infection mechanisms, but you would probably rather have an infectious-disease doctor prescribe and monitor your health condition.

A Judeo-Christian world view of disease is now giving way to Darwinian medicine and New Age philosophy in the mainstream. For 200 years in the United States, there was a Christian consensus about issues of disease and their cause, but now few biologists and physicians look for biblical solutions to the plagues of mankind. Instead, they are looking to Charles Darwin and his theories to explain disease, developing humanistic solutions to solving man's illnesses. Secular scientists, however, do not even consider a biblical or creation perspective on disease.

Darwinian Medicine Introduction

Most Christians and Jews had little notion of the moral changes affecting American society in the 1960s. These changes would abolish the Christian consensus on which our civilization and its medical services rested, and permit us to drift back into pagan indifference or outright cruelty toward the chronically sick, elderly, and handicapped. But in this post-modern world, the secular attitude is again indifference toward the handicapped, the poor, and those "unfit" in Darwinian terms. For instance, as we write this, Darwinian medicine is gaining a foothold in many major medical schools. No wonder national governments have sought absolute control of the medical field. Those who hold the reins of the health system hold the ultimate power of life itself.

Medicine at its best has been the *by-product* of Christian ideals — the modern hospital, nursing, and the caring bedside manner. Epidemiology, and the myriad techniques and instruments of modern surgery were for the most part developed within Christian lands, often by committed Christians. Unfortunately, in recent triumphs of medicine, the Christian spirit has too often waned. To prevent the Christian ideals forming modern medicine from dissolving away, we need to pause and reflect upon the Christian roots of modern medicine as exemplified in some of it greatest practitioners. This chapter is written with that purpose in mind. Although Darwinian medicine is increasingly fashionable, with many now asserting that nothing makes sense in medicine except in the light of evolution, we propose that medicine and human biology should be based upon the evidence.

Many secular biologists and physicians are applying Darwinian ideas of natural selection, chance, biological fitness, competition, macromutations, and changing environmental conditions to explain their naturalistic view of disease. As Christians, we look for answers in the Bible starting with Genesis, searching for clues in epidemiology and medical sciences.

Solutions to Coming Plagues

Christians have the possibility of knowing ultimate answers because they know God, the Creator. It has been said that the greatest philosophical questions are "Why is there terrible sickness in this world?" and "Is there any hope for relief?" Apart from the conviction that God is the Lord described in the Bible, there is no answer. At best, the distinguished biologist may be able to describe *what* has happened in order to explain how something came to be. But why it should have happened remains unanswered, apart from the revelation our Creator gives man in Scripture. As Christians, and students of the Bible, we are not left in doubt. God made all things for His own glory and purposes. That is why the Scriptures tell us that "the heavens declare the glory of God" (Ps.19:1) and "the whole earth is full of his glory" (Isa. 6:3).

In the gospels, we observe the healing miracles of Jesus. These miracles are early glimpses of restoration and healing that the Great Physician will perform.

Christ will provide the cure. The Great Physician and Savior himself, Jesus Christ, has promised great deliverance from disease. In addition to the curse being removed, in Revelation we read about healing from the Tree of Life (Rev. 22:2). An interesting observation is that the leaves of the tree of life have great value also, bringing healing to the nations. This implies a *cure* for all the sickness and plagues of the world. In this case, the passage might be read: "The leaves of the tree were for the cure of the

nations." The chemical ingredients of the rich foliage of the trees might be available for multiple uses as medicine for all people for all ages. Not only will the Curse be removed, but also any remnant of pathogens will be destroyed — our bodies healed through the life-giving fruit from the Tree of Life from the Great Physician.

Table 8.1 Selected Emerging Diseases

Bacteria	Year	Disease
Borrelia burgdorferi	1975	Lyme disease
Legionella pneumophila	1976	Legionnaires' disease
Staphylococcus aureus	1978	Toxic shock syndrome
Escherichia coli 0157:H7	1982	Hemorrhagic diarrhea
Bartonella henselae	1983	Cat scratch disease
Vibrio cholerae 0139	1992	New serotype of cholera
Corynebacterium diphtheriae	1994	Diphtheria epidemic

Fungi	Year	Disease
Pneumocystis carinii	1981	Pneumonia
Coccidioides immitis	1993	Coccidioidomycosis

Protozoa	Year	Disease
Cryptosporidium parvam	1976	Cryptosporidiosis
Plasmodium spp.	1986	Malaria
Cyclospora cayetanensis	1993	Severe diarrhea

Viruses	Year	Disease
HIV	1983	AIDS
Dengue fever virus	1984	Dengue fever
Hepatitis C virus	1989	Hepatitis
Hepatitis E virus	1990	Hepatitis
Hantavirus	1993	Pulmonary syndrome
Ebola virus	1979, 1995, 2014	Hemorrhagic fever
Epstein-Barr (Herpes-type)	1984	Chronic fatigue syndrome
West Nile virus	1999	West Nile encephalitis
Coronavirus	2003	SARS
Monkeypox	1970, 2003	Monkeypox disease

Prions	Year	Disease
Bovine spongiform	1996, 2003	Mad cow disease

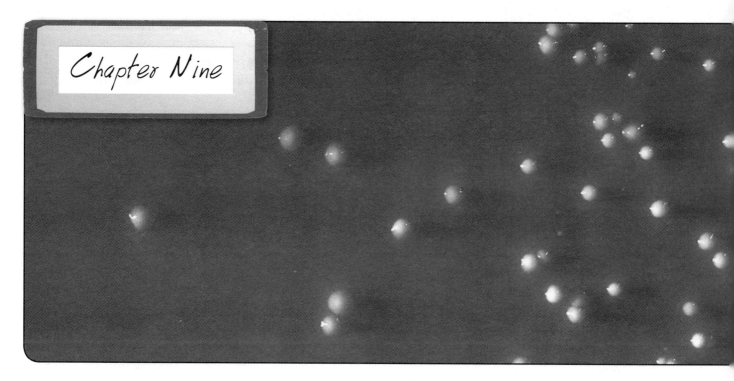

Chapter Nine

The Origin of Disease: A Creation Perspective

Throughout the ages, billions of people have suffered and died of infectious disease. Global pandemics of Spanish influenza, tuberculosis, smallpox, bubonic plague, typhus, leprosy, and other pestilences have wiped out whole villages and as much as a fourth of entire continents at a time. New plagues of West Nile Virus, malaria, cholera, measles, AIDS, SARS, and now avian flu presently threaten entire populations. Colds, the flu, ulcers, cavities, chronic sickness, and daily diseases — why are we plagued with such common misery? We know that sin interfered with God's "very good" creation in the beginning, but just how did infectious diseases arise? This is an important topic for us to understand because more deaths during man's existence (thousands of years) have been due to infectious disease than from any other cause.

Creation, Corruption, and the Edenic Curse

Infectious diseases had no place in the original creation. According to Genesis, everything was not only good as God pronounced it to be, but after the creation week He pronounced it very good.

Within that definition we find no allowance for death, suffering, disease, or major catastrophe. Therefore, it is evident that disease has no origin in the beginning; furthermore, disease itself was not created, because that would not be consistent with God's nature and the perfect creation.

Genesis 1 describes a good God making a very good creation. It was God's intent for man to live in Paradise. Bacteria and other microorganisms were originally designed to manufacture vitamins in man and animals, fix nitrogen, serve essential functions in soil maintenance, recycle elements, and assist in purification processes in nature. However, when man chose to sin, God cursed the earth. The earth included the soil and all that was within it, including millions of microbes.

"And unto Adam he said, Because thou hast hearkened unto the voice of thy wife, and hast eaten of the tree, of which I commanded thee, saying, Thou shalt not eat of it: cursed is the ground for thy sake; in sorrow shalt thou eat of it all the days of thy life; Thorns also and thistles shall it bring forth to thee; and thou shalt eat the herb of the field; In the sweat of thy face shalt thou eat bread, till thou return unto the ground; for out of it wast thou taken: for dust thou art, and unto dust shalt thou return" (Gen. 3: 17-19).

Microbes in a Fallen World

Most likely, bacteria and other microbes underwent mutation and other degenerative processes.

Thorns and thistles appeared and everything began to decay. To mirror this degeneration, some bacteria have now become the "thorns and thistles" among otherwise beneficial bacteria. With the loss of genetic information, bacteria began to use a host for functions that they could no longer do themselves; this marked the emergence of infectious disease.

Since the worldwide flood of Noah, only in this century has man been enabled to live longer. That, in part, is due to vaccinations, asepsis in surgery, and antibiotics. What factors have led to this widespread suffering, misery, and death from infectious disease? In this chapter, a mechanism and model on the genesis of germs is presented from a creation perspective.

A Creation Model of Infectious Disease

The Devolution of Microbes, Man, and Mobile Genes

There is no written historical record of how, when, where, or why infectious diseases began. The Bible does not say precisely when contagious diseases began either; so creationists and evolutionists alike have formulated their ideas regarding the origin of diseases based upon limited evidence. After a review of the medical, evolutionary, and creation literature, a multifaceted model is given at the end of this chapter. This model attempts to explain the origin of many infectious diseases, especially those caused by bacteria. As one studies the Bible and current microbiological research, one can conclude that the cause of the deadly microorganisms can be attributed to the fall of man and its subsequent curse that lead to an overall decay of the originally good creation of man, microbes, and mobile genes. The genesis of germs, also known as the origin of infectious disease, appears to be explained by three major decay factors: man's defenses (i.e., the human body and its immune response), the microbe, and "mobile" genes.

Man's Body Deteriorates

Beside the decay of microorganisms, the deterioration of the human body is another explanation for how illness became a part of life. For example, Adam, Eve, and their immediate descendants may not have been susceptible to the effects of typhoid that is produced by Salmonella. According to microbiologist, Dr. Kevin Anderson, their bodies probably were not susceptible to the effects of the molecule that those bacteria contained. Many people in the 21st century think that the human body is superior because the average person is living longer than those in the past few centuries. However, there is increasing evidence that we are physically degrading. There was a time when man commonly lived to ages much greater than the average life span today (see Gen. 1-11). The human body appears to have degraded enough over the generations that it suddenly appears to be susceptible to microbes with which it was once able to safely interact. We are physically very inferior (based upon life span) to the humans that lived at the time of the flood of Noah's day.

Body Boundaries Blur and Break since the Beginning

The Creator made the world and the human body with boundaries. However, since sin entered the world, these natural barriers have been comprised; the original function is blurred, and then some barriers break. Soon, an infection (colonization by bacteria) becomes disease. Varying susceptibility to diseases can be seen today. Genetic factors also play an important role in individual susceptibility to infection. Some people may have genes that are similar to those of Adam and have very few problems with infectious disease. Their body defenses, barriers to infection, and boundaries are still intact. But others, like David Vetter (the "bubble boy"), have very few body defenses. There is reasonable evidence that the body defense variation involving the blood, enzymes, and cell membranes has been maintained by relative resistance to different diseases. Varying genetics may reflect varying susceptibility to bacterial, viral, and yeast infections. There is increasing evidence that some people are "born" with innate immunity to various diseases, such as dental caries, gastritis, and typhoid fever. Bacteria cause cavities, ulcers, and typhoid, but not everyone has bad symptoms.

As far as human health, microorganisms are actually interwoven with the human body's immune system. The skin is covered with good microorganisms that serve a beneficial purpose. The microorganisms provide a protective layer on the skin against pathogens. The pathogens cannot easily become established because competing skin microflora kills it. For instance, the mouth, throat, and sinus cavities have native micro-organisms that make an unfavorable environment for pathogens. Other protective boundaries in the human body are likely to have undergone decay, such as weaker enamel on teeth.

The Decay of Teeth

One structural example of devolution in the human body is teeth and their susceptibility to dental caries (the most common infectious disease in the world). The number of dental caries (cavities) that a person develops during their lifetime appears to be related to the enamel strength, pits and fissures in teeth, food type, and pH of the oral cavity. Some people rarely get cavities and seem to have the "genetics" that might have typified Adam and Eve. The structure of their enamel remains strong throughout their life. Others constantly get cavities in spite of good hygiene habits. What accounts for the difference in susceptibility? Perhaps, the answer can be found in the amount of "decay" in their genes that code for tooth enamel and their tooth anatomy (e.g., pits and fissures versus an even surface).

Disease Focus 9.1

Typhoid Mary – A Picture of How the Human Body May Have Once Interacted with "Deadly" Bacteria

Infection by microbes does not necessarily mean disease. Microbiologists call the former, "colonization" and the latter, "infectious disease." Over the years, many people have had pathogenic bacteria colonize their bodies without causing disease. Information about these people that never get sick from such "germs" provides a picture of how the body's original design was made to handle mutations (i.e., deadly bacteria). The most famous example of a convalescent carrier was Mary Mallon. Mary Mallon (1869-1938), also known as "Typhoid Mary," was an Irish immigrant who was the first known healthy carrier of typhoid fever in the United States. Ms. Mallon may represent a picture of how the human body previously interacted with *Salmonella typhi*. She contracted the bacteria that caused typhoid fever at some point, but she had no noticeable symptoms.

Her body was apparently designed to safely handle the *Salmonella typhi* and remain healthy; however, she was still capable of spreading the disease to others. Mary worked as a cook in the New York City area between the years 1900 to 1907. During this part of her working career, she infected more than fifty persons with the disease, some of whom died. Mary was a cook in several homes in New York when the residents showed symptoms of typhoid. Mary spent months helping to care for the people whom she made sick, but her care may have unwittingly worsened the victims' illness. She changed employment many times, and people were infected in every household in which she worked. A dessert of iced peaches, one of Mary Mallon's favorite recipes, frequently transmitted the disease.

It was not until a sanitary engineer, named George Soper, made a careful investigation of the typhoid

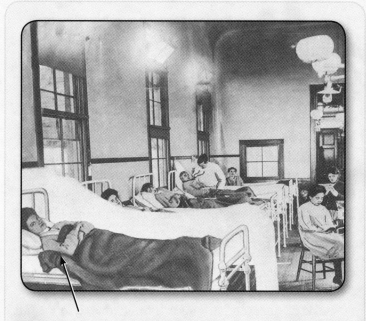

Typhoid Mary in Hospital Bed
New York, NY – Mary Mallon, known as "Typhoid Mary." She was the first person identified as a carrier of typhoid bacilli in the United States. Her-self immune to the disease, she spread typhoid while working as a cook in the New York City area. She is pictured here after having been institutionalized on Brother Island where she stayed from 1914 until her death in 1938.

epidemic that Mary was identified as a carrier. He approached her with the news that she was spreading typhoid. She protested his request for urine and stool samples. Soper later published his findings in a prominent medical journal in 1907. This persuaded a New York

City health inspector to investigate and find Mary to be a carrier. This information caused the inspector to put Mary in isolation for three years at a hospital located in New York. After a series of isolation and release, the result was the same each time. She remained a healthy carrier of typhoid; she felt fine, but then she transmitted the deadly bacteria to others. Finally, she was seized after a decade of transmission and confined in quarantine for life. She became something of a celebrity, and was interviewed by journalists who were forbidden to accept as much as a glass of water from her. She died in 1938 of pneumonia, and was buried in Bronx, NY. The autopsy of her body revealed that her gallbladder was still actively shedding typhoid bacilli.

Today, Typhoid Mary is a term for a convalescent carrier of a disease who is a potential danger to the public because they refuse to take certain precautions or cooperate with the authorities to minimize the risk. However, in her defense, it should be pointed out that gall bladder surgery was very risky at that time and she may have saved her own life by refusing the operation. Today, we know about people with immunity to a variety of infectious diseases because their body is able to "handle" the microbe. It is very likely that in the beginning, man's body (like Adam and Eve) was designed to interact with a variety of microbes. Boundaries were intact and able to handle corrupted bacteria and other microbes. Mary Mallon represents a type of early humans who had bodies that could successfully "handle" potentially pathogenic bacteria, thus explaining how people before the great flood could live for centuries.

When understanding how and why diseases emerged, another factor to consider is the one of God's absence. When God physically left the Garden of Eden and put into place a "natural" means of maintenance, deterioration and decay would happen at a more rapid rate. We can imagine that in the beginning the Creator, who is orderly, was taking a more proactive role in sustaining the earth and the body of Adam, in case an "accident" was to happen. The same Creator who walked with Adam daily was the one who healed the blind man, cleansed the leper, made the mute talk, and helped the lame man walk.

Microbes Decay

Many people ask, "*Why is there such suffering and death? Why were there plagues and pestilence throughout history, and why do they still exist in modern times?*" It was not until after sin entered the world that some microorganisms became pathogenic, or harmful, to man. One explanation is that the good bacteria began to deteriorate or degenerate into the pathogenic bacteria. Genomic decay is one of the most likely theories for explaining the origin of bacterial pathogenicity. It is consistent with the creation idea of a degenerating creation; but the minor changes in the genetic code could have changed the course of human history. When a bacterium degenerates, it loses valuable information and must find other sources to survive. Bacteria generally are made as one cell; and as they lose information from their genetic hardware they consequently can no longer produce their own needed materials to synthesize cell parts. And so, as they lack information they have to gain that same information or the same materials that come from the information from some other creature (an animal or a person) and in doing so they cause disease symptoms.

So, what about evolutionary arguments? Since bacteria can add information, could this process be used as evidence for evolution? The answer is no. Evolutionists may argue that this is acquiring information, but the acquisition of small DNA segments is still leading to disease. A parallel process, for example, is how rust forms: rust is the addition of oxygen plus iron. This added information is not progressive evolution, but rather it is a deteriorating process (i.e., corrosion). The organization is going downhill!

The Genesis of Germs: From Mutualism to Parasitism

There is a fine line between wellness or health and disease. A distinction should be made between the infection itself, that is, the entrance or colonization of the microbe and the primary injury to the body tissues, and the clinical disease which it may bring. Over the millennia, the ability of man's body to keep bacteria in check via anatomical boundaries and immune response, in general, has diminished. Today, we still see varying degrees of colonization of microbes, infection, and disease among people. The infection may occur for hours, days, months, or even years before disease symptoms are felt, and some symptoms are not noticed at all. The word **infection** is derived from Latin origins meaning, "to mix with or corrupt." Infection refers to the relationship between two organisms, the host and the microbe, and the competition for supremacy that takes place between them. A host whose resistance is strong remains healthy, and the microbe is either removed by the host or assumes a benign relationship with the host. By contrast, if the host loses the competition, then disease develops. The term disease *(dis [against] ease)* is from Latin that means, "living apart," a reference to the separation of ill individuals from the general population. Disease may be viewed as any change from the general state of good health. It is important to note that the words "disease" and "infection" are not synonymous; a person may be infected without becoming diseased.

Beneficial colonization and infection occurs today. Perhaps when looking at the numbers of these events and microbes involved, beneficial colonization can be seen as a much more frequent event than pathogenesis. The concept of infection in the host-microbe relationship is expressed in the body's normal flora. The **normal flora** is a population of microorganisms that infect the body without causing disease. The relationship between the body and its normal flora is an example of symbiosis. In some cases the symbiosis is beneficial to both the body and the microorganisms; this relationship is called **mutualism**. For example, species of *Lactobacillus* live in the human vagina and derive nutrients from the environment while producing acid to prevent the overgrowth of other organisms. *Escherichia coli* is generally presumed to live in a mutualistic manner in the intestine of the body, because it pays us "rent" with the vitamins that are derived from the bacteria.

Pathogenicity refers to the ability of a parasite to gain entry to the host's tissues and bring about a physiological or anatomical change resulting in a change of health and thus disease. The word "pathogenicity" is derived from the Greek term *pathos*, meaning suffering. The term pathogen has the same root and refers to an organism having pathogenicity. The symbiotic relationship between host and parasite is called parasitism. The word virulence is derived from the Latin term, *virulentus*, meaning full of poison, and it is often used to express the degree of pathogenicity. It is a matter of degree. An organism such as the *Yersinia pestis*, the agent of Black Death (bubonic plague) is said to be hypervirulent. Another highly virulent bacterium is the typhoid bacillus.

By comparison, an agent such as rhinovirus that causes common colds, or *Streptococcus mutans* that causes dental caries, has a low virulence. However, it should be noted that a genetic change could make an organism, like *E. coli*, turn from a beneficial bacterium to a highly virulent pathogen, *E. coli 0157H7*.

Disease Focus 9.2
Diseases in the Bible

Two diseases found in the Bible, leprosy (Hansen's disease) and plague, are discussed in this chapter because of their frequency and the genomic decay that has taken place in both germ agents. Plague and leprosy are used more times than any other disease in the Bible. Their use in modern times is different than biblical times, yet there is no doubt that they overlap and still illustrate important points today. The term *plague (plague, plagued, plagues)* (Hebrew = *deber, maggephah, makkah, nega, and negeph*; Greek = *mastix, plege*) occurs 128 times in the KJV Bible. However, these numerous mentions of the word actually include many different infectious diseases of today, such as bubonic plague. A plague may be any form of

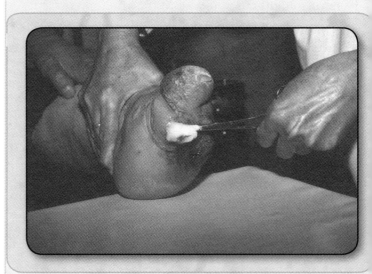

Leprosy. Cleaning the deformed foot of a person suffering from leprosy (Hansen's disease) with an antiseptic. Leprosy is a chronic inflammatory disease caused by the bacterium Mycobacterium leprae.

trouble or harassment, but the term most often has a reference to a disease of epidemic proportions. Also, it is used to refer to a disease's occurrence and especially when it is fatal in its effects. The Book of Revelation speaks of many plagues in the last days.

The term leprosy (including leper, lepers, leprosy, leprous) occurs 68 times in the Bible: 55 times in the Old Testament (Hebrew = *tsara'ath*) and 13 times in the New Testament. In the Old Testament, the instances of leprosy that were mentioned most likely meant a variety of infectious skin diseases (including Hansen's disease) and even mold and mildew when mentioned on clothing and walls.   In the New Testament (Greek = *lepros, lepra*), it is then likely to be discussing Hansen's disease. The precise meaning of the leprosy in both OT and NT is still in dispute. It is a comprehensive term that probably includes the modern Hansen's disease (esp. in the NT) and infectious skin diseases. The term, "Hansen's disease" was not given until 1873, when A. Hansen described the leprosy bacillus. Only at this point was a precise definition for leprosy made available. Word meanings do change; for instance in the days of Pasteur, the terms virus, bacterium, and fungus were used interchangeably. Meanings today are used because specific causes for infectious diseases were determined.

The Origin of Hansen's Disease (Leprosy)

Leprosy has terrified humanity for thousands of years, and was reported as early as 600 B.C. in India, China, and Egypt. Hansen's disease is still a major health problem in many parts of Africa, Asia, and Latin America. For many centuries, leprosy was considered a curse of God, often associated with sin. It did not kill, but neither did it seem to end. Instead, it lingered for years, causing the tissues to degenerate and deforming the body. In biblical times, victims were required to call out "Unclean! Unclean!" and usually they were also ostracized from the community. Many have thought this to be a disease of the skin. It is better classified, however, as a disease of the nervous system because the leprosy bacterium attacks the nerves. The agent of leprosy is *Mycobacterium leprae*, an acid-fast rod related to the tuberculosis bacterium. The Norwegian physician, Dr. Hansen, first observed this organism in 1873 and thus it was referred to as

Hansen's bacillus. Hence, leprosy is now referred to as Hansen's disease. Leprosy is spread by multiple skin contacts, as well as by droplets from the upper respiratory tracts.

The disease has an unusually long incubation period of three to six years, a factor that makes its identification very difficult. The bacteria are also heat sensitive; therefore, the bacillus lives in the cooler regions of the body. Its symptoms start in the skin and peripheral nervous system, then spread to various cooler parts like the hands, feet, face, and earlobes. Severe cases also involve the eyes and the respiratory tract. Patients with leprosy experience disfigurement of the skin and bones, twisting of the limbs, and curling of the fingers to form the characteristic claw hand. Facial features accompany thickening of the outer ear and collapse of the nose.

It was Dr. Paul Brand's (the late world-renowned orthopedic surgeon and leprosy physician) work with leprosy patients that illustrated, in part, why God permitted there to be pain in this world. The leprosy bacillus destroys nerve endings that carry pain signals; there is a total loss of physical pain in advanced leprosy patients. When these people cannot sense touch or pain, they tend to injure themselves. Tumor-like growths called **lepromas** may form on the skin and in the respiratory tract, and the optic nerve may deteriorate. The largest number of deformities develops from loss of pain sensation due to extensive nerve damage. For instance, inattentive patients can pick up a cup of boiling water without flinching. Many patients accidentally let hot objects burn their fingers. In fact, some leprosy patients have had their fingers eaten by rats in their sleep because they were totally unaware of it happening; the lack of pain receptors cannot warn them of the danger.

According to Dr. Brand, the best example in the Bible of a person with Hansen's disease is the man with the withered hand (Mark 3:5; Matt. 12:13; Luke 6:10). The man with the "withered hand" most likely suffered from tuberculoid leprosy. The deterioration and shriveling of limbs is indirectly due to leprosy bacillus. Hansen's disease causes poor circulation and the loss of control that provides life-sustaining materials (oxygen and nutrients) from the blood. Without blood there will be deterioration and a lack of harmony, order, symmetry, and design. The people suffering from Hansen's disease injure themselves due to a lack of pain. The withered hand is due in part to the leprosy bacillus attacking the peripheral nervous system. This indirectly cuts the flow of blood to the hand; this results in atrophy. No touch and no pain in the skin lead to a lack of proper muscle use: misuse of limbs, injuries, and muscle paralysis.

Mycobacterium leprae: A Decaying Creation

The best example of a bacterium undergoing genomic decay is *Mycobacterium leprae* (Disease Focus 9.3). The leprosy bacillus has a long incubation time and a total dependence upon living in animal or human tissue. The sequencing of *M. leprae* bacillus has given us insight into why this is the case. The sequencing of *M. leprae* has revealed that approximately 25 percent of functional genetic information has been lost. The extreme genomic decay that it has undergone has resulted in extensive metabolic constraints and an unusually slow growth rate. God has given people the understanding to discover many of the secrets of the mycobacterial genome that may be used to restore health.

This acid-fast bacillus has an incredibly slow doubling time of about 12 days and cannot be cultured in any standard medium; it can only be cultured in armadillos and the hind footpads of mice. Since 30°C is the optimum growth temperature for *M. leprae* (most of the human body is 37°C), it grows only in cooler regions of the body, such as the peripheral nerves, skin, testes, and mucous membranes of the upper respiratory tract, primarily the nose. It is transmitted via aerosol, droplets, and prolonged direct contact. It resides within the macrophages and Schwann-cells, and cannot survive in the extra-cellular environment. The destruction of the Schwann-cells is what causes the nerve damage resulting in an accompanying loss of sensation that is characteristic of Hansen's disease.

Disease Focus 9.3:

Mycobacterium leprae: The Details of Decay

Comparative genomics have contributed to a greater understanding of the leprosy bacillus. Major breakthroughs occurred by comparing the genomes of *Mycobacterium leprae* and its closest relative, *M. tuberculosis*. Gene clones from *M. leprae* in *M. smegmatis* (i.e., a nonpathogenic *Mycobacteria*) were used to determine the functionality of similar genes. The evaluation of the genomes of *M. leprae*, M. *smegmatis*, and *Mycobacterium tuberculosis* has revealed the necessary biosynthetic pathways. These comparisons have revealed that *M. leprae* has lost well over 2,000 genes (~25 percent of its total genome) since decaying from an original *Mycobacterium* species.

In order to determine the extent of decay of the leprosy bacillus, the genomes of *M. leprae* and *M. tuberculosis* chromosomes were used for comparison. Biologists believe that *M. leprae* has arisen from *M. tuberculosis* or a similar ancestor. *M. leprae* has undergone extensive devolution in metabolic and respiratory functions which then cause serious energy limitations. Compared to the 4.41-megabase (Mb) genome of *M. tuberculosis*, the 3.27 Mb genome of *M. leprae* is quite conserved. *M. leprae* possesses only 1,614 functional genes, compared to approximately 4,000 functional genes in *M. tuberculosis*. The *M. leprae* genes are denser than those of *M. tuberculosis*. *M. tuberculosis* has 4,411,532 base pairs (bp) compared to the 3,268,203 DNA base pairs in *M. leprae*. However, *M. tuberculosis* only contains 6 nonfunctional genes (i.e., pseudogenes), whereas the genome of *M. leprae* consists of 1,133 pseudogenes. *M. tuberculosis* has 4,025,965 protein coding bases; in contrast, *M. leprae* has 1,626,387 protein coding bases.

M. leprae contains 75 percent of the genes required for optimal growth in *M. tuberculosis*. There is only a 27 percent correspondence for genes non-essential to growth, thus *M. leprae* conserves a minimal amount of genes required to reproduce. This minimal genome is the cause for *M. leprae's* inability to be grown in a Petri dish and characteristically slow growth in laboratory animals. Some of the major pathways lacking in *M. leprae* include synthesis of vitamin B-12 (i.e., cobalamin) and cell wall components (i.e., mycobactin and sulfur). Many genes that are central in metabolism are essential for growth. Some of the primary genes include those required for synthesis of amino acids, nucleic acids, and key cellular processes, including cell division, protein synthesis, replication, iron (i.e., siderophore) production, and transcription. Many of the genes required for growth in *M. tuberculosis* are constrained in *M. leprae*.

Cell Wall and Cell Processes Lost

In *M. tuberculosis* there are 751 genes devoted to the cell wall and cellular processes; however, *M. leprae* only possesses 371 genes for these functions. The cell wall (and its components) is essential for growth and survival.

The inner layer of mycobacterial cell wall is composed of peptidoglycan, and the outer layer consists of mycolic acid. Mycolic acid is needed for a firm cell wall, and it performs other functions. The genes that typically code for this are mycolic acid that are both pseudogenes in the leprosy bacillus.

Two specific genes that are critical for coding the enzymes that are necessary for growth have been lost as well. *Mycobacterium smegmatis* (fast growing) and *M. tuberculosis* are found in *M. bovis*, *M. avium*, and *M. leprae*. The portion of the *M. leprae* genome that codes for proteins, sugars (polysaccharides), lipids (fat), peptidoglycan, and other chemicals consists of approximately 260 functional genes and approximately 76 pseudogenes. According to this data, the efficiency of the cell wall construction should be reduced by approximately 25 percent.

M. leprae contains about 110 functional genes devoted to cell functions, which would include: cell division, adaptations to atypical conditions, detoxification, and production of amino acids, fatty acids, efflux proteins, and various ions. Approximately 25 percent of the genes responsible for cell division are non-functional. Over 50 percent of the genes accountable for detoxification are pseudogenes. About 50 percent of the genes that code for adaptations and atypical conditions, amino acids, proteins, and ions have decayed to a non-functional state. There are no functional genes for fatty acid transportation. Though *M. leprae* has decayed significantly, it still possesses enough information to produce its necessary components, such as lipids, amino acids, and DNA. It can also directly obtain these components from the host cell. It appears that the most significant result of the minimal genome is an incredibly slow growth rate.

Energy Metabolism

Intermediary metabolism and respiration is coded for by 895 genes in *M. tuberculosis*, but only 431 genes are present in *M. leprae*. There has been a reduction in the ability to break down sugars through glycolysis (anaerobic respiration) and other metabolic pathways. Two-fifths of the genes coding for the pentose phosphate pathway have diminished to pseudogenes. All of the genes that would be devoted to anaerobic respiration have corrupted into non-functional counterparts, therefore *M. leprae* possesses no anaerobic or microaerophilic capabilities. Furthermore, one-fourth of the bacillus' genes devoted to aerobic respiration have also decayed to pseudogenes.

Jesus Healing the Leper, 1864 (oil on canvas). Musee des Beaux-Arts, Nimes, France

With so many of the major metabolic functions being greatly reduced or even eliminated, *M. leprae* would have a slow growth rate. It takes 12 days for one bacterium to make another. (Recall, most bacteria take 20 minutes for binary fission, a type of asexual reproduction.) Also, the malic enzyme, which has been connected to fast growth in Mycobacteria, is lacking in *M. leprae*. It takes 3 months to 20 years (and the record is 40 years) for an infection to cause disease. However, once the leprosy bacillus is established in the body, it is difficult to eradicate. The growth is slow, but steady and sure.

Mycobacterium leprae has undergone extensive decay compared to other Mycobacteria species. *M. leprae* possesses the minimal essential genes necessary for the biological and structural properties in the Mycobacteria kind. It possesses the "essential'" gene set to survive, but little else. This is in contrast to *Pseudomonas aeruginosa* that has a large genome of over six MB, making it the largest known set of genes for a bacterium — and it grows on everything. The deterioration is likely due to the Edenic curse, which is consistent with a degenerating creation.

After 1981, the World Health Organization recommended multi-drug therapy (MDT) for those infected with *M. leprae*. This therapy consisted of the antibiotic trio of clofazimine, rifampicin, and dapsone. They were found very effective in curing Hansen's disease in as few as six months. The world has seen dramatic reduction of the infection. Since 1985, the prevalence rate has dropped 90 percent, and 14 million people have been cured. Leprosy has been eradicated from 113 countries. Since 2001 there has been a 20 percent annual decrease in new cases detected. This cleansing of leprosy in the modern world may be a picture of how someday The Great Physician will restore our bodies in heaven. Just as Jesus restored the man with the withered hand, He will also restore His decaying creation to good state once again (Luke 6:6).

Disease Focus 9.4

Biblical Leprosy and Hansen's Disease

Biblical leprosy and Hansen's disease have in common that both are dreaded and people were shunned because of them. The noun *tsara'ath* appears about two dozen times in the Hebrew Bible. It is most frequently seen in Leviticus, where it is used to describe a state of defilement manifested as a scaly condition of the skin, a condition of cloth, leather, and the walls of houses. In the Septuagint, the Greek translation of the Hebrew Bible, *tsara'ath* was translated as *aphe lepras*. These words in Greek implied a skin condition that spread over the body. *Tsara'ath* has continued to be translated as "leprosy," even though this term is broader; as there was no leprosy as we know it in the Middle East during the time period the Hebrew Bible was written. Others have suggested that the translation of *tsara'ath* includes "molds." The recent discovery of a highly, toxic mold (*Stachybotrys sp.*) that contaminates buildings and causes respiratory distress, memory loss, and rash lends support to the translation of *tsara'ath* to include "mold." Most likely *tsara'ath* incorporates a "collection" of contemporary terms, including Hansen's disease, infectious skin diseases, and mold (or even mildew) diseases.

Biblical leprosy is a broader term than the leprosy (Hansen's Disease) that we know today. The scholars who first translated the Bible from Hebrew to Greek used the term *lepra* when faced with the untranslatable Hebrew word *tsara'ath*. The writers were not medical students but good observers who recorded what they saw. The Hebrew *tsara'ath* included a variety of ailments. It referred primarily to uncleanness or imperfections according to biblical standards. A person with any skin blemish was *tsara'ath*. The symbolism extended to rot or blemish on leather, houses, and woven cloth. Other Old Testament references to leprosy are about punishment or consequences of sin. Balance these passages against others where God sent different afflictions for disobedience: the plagues on Pharaoh and Egypt, the Bubonic plague of the Philistines, the foot disease of King Asa of Judah. Leprosy is not singled out from other afflictions.

References to leprosy have a different emphasis between the Old and New Testaments. The Hebrew word *tsara'ath* and references to leprosy throughout the Old Testament have two particular contexts: 1) reference to ceremonial laws and ritual uncleanness, and 2) punishment or for consequences of sin. All New Testament references to leprosy are in the Gospels and in the context of healing and social well-being. Jesus touched people with leprosy. People with leprosy traditionally have suffered banishment from family and neighbors. Jesus broke with the tradition; He treated people with leprosy by touching and cleaning them. Jesus had compassion on those who had leprosy.

Gene Swapping: Horizontal Gene Transfer Among Bacteria

Bacteria are quick-change artists. They have to be. Without warning, a person consumes a bacterium living in the dressing on a salad bar, and then it is transported to the stomach, which is highly acidic. Or a bacterium about to be injected into a human arm by an insect will soon encounter an environment very different from the one inside the insect. Only the adaptable survive. Bacteria change, not only by mutating their genomes but also by receiving and incorporating DNA segments from members of other species.

How can one define a single bacterium species if large portions of that bacterium's genome are cobbled together in gene segments acquired from a mixture of other bacterial species that are not its direct ancestors but its contemporaries? Bacteria are using this capacity for acquiring genes from other organisms to allow them to adapt to rapidly changing environments and to become resistant to antibiotics. This rapid-change ability makes them capable of causing new, emerging, and re-emerging diseases. It facilitates and increases their options for survival.

Bacterial reproduction is usually described as asexual, because bacteria have no equivalent of the genetic fusion of two different cells that is characteristic of sexual reproduction in eukaryotes. Nonetheless, bacteria do have the ability to exchange segments of DNA with other bacteria. Because these segments can become fixed in a bacterium's genome and confer new traits, gene exchange among bacteria could be considered to be a form of bacterial sex. DNA exchange between bacteria is called horizontal gene transfer to differentiate it from vertical gene transfer, the inheritance of a gene(s) from a progenitor. It is now known that many infectious diseases are due to the horizontal transfer of not just one gene, but many genes in clusters called cassettes, or pathogenicity islands.

The packages of genes frequently are transferred via plasmid DNA that code for enzymes, toxins, virulence factors, and proteins that lead to misery in the host recipient of germ-causing microbe. They are a corruption of the original good plan of the Creator. Corruption is the the act of changing, or of being changed, for the worse; departure from what is a good, or the ideal design by the Creator in Genesis 1 and 2. Additional information contaminates an otherwise good message.

For decades, bacteria have been known to be capable of horizontal gene transfer in the laboratory. In fact, information about horizontal gene transfer was the foundation of the genetic engineering revolution. Only when biotechnologists were able to insert foreign DNA into bacteria in the laboratory did cloning (via transformation) become possible. Until recently, however, many biologists have downplayed the importance of horizontal gene transfer as a form of bacterial variation in nature. However, new research on bacterial genomes and the discovery of what makes them pathogenic have provided evidence that the horizontal (not vertical)

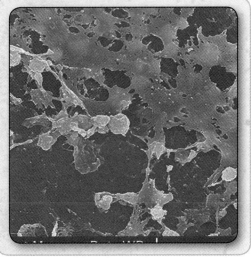

Scanning electron micrograph (SEM) of Staphylococcus aureus *bacteria the sticky-looking substance woven between the round cocci bacteria, and is known as "biofilm." This biofilm has been found to protect the bacteria that secrete the substance from attacks by antimicrobial agents such as antibiotics.*

changes are what make bacteria different. In addition, the evidence is accumulating to support the contention that not only does horizontal gene transfer occur frequently in nature but that it plays a significant role in bacterial cell variation, corruption, and devolution (a form of variation).

The Origin of "Super Staph"

Methicillin Resistant *Staphylococcus aureus* (MRSA)

Staphylococcus aureus is a bacterium that can live harmlessly in the nose and occasionally on the skin in a state known as colonization. Most likely, *S. aureus* was originally designed to live in harmony with man as a harmless, normal flora. Perhaps it played a positive role in the recycling of elements in nose or skin as its "cousin," *S. epidermidis*, did in its original good design. Today, *S. aureus* causes many diseases, including skin boils, infection of leg ulcers and pressure sores. Occasionally, it can cause more serious disorders such as blood poisoning (septicemia) and bone, joint, or heart valve infection. It is the number one hospital acquired (nosocomial) infection. Up until recently, commonly used antibiotics, such as penicillin, killed most strains of *Staphylococcus aureus*.

Now, *S. aureus* is resistant to many antibiotics, including methicillin. Although *methicillin-resistant Staphylococcus aureus* (*MRSA*) can also live harmlessly in the nose or skin, if infections develop they can be more difficult to treat. In addition, some types of *MRSA* appear to spread easily between patients in the hospital who then might become ill as a result. *MRSA* is sometimes called "Super Staph" or the "Superbug" in the press because of its resistance, its ability to cause infections in hospitalized patients and its capacity to cause outbreaks on wards. The reason that hospitals seem to be hotbeds for resistant MRSA is because so many different strains are being thrown together with so many doses of antibiotics, vastly accelerating this natural selection process.

Resist Saying, "This Is Evolution"

Although *MRSA's* antibiotic resistance and toxin genes appear to have been added to its existing plasmids, it has lost some key metabolic functions to survive on its own. *S. aureus* has picked both its resistance (R) genes and toxin genes from a pathogenicity island of *Enterococcus faecalis* (see Focus 9.4). This new information is a corruption of original plasmid DNA. This horizontal transfer does not improve the overall fitness of the bacteria. This change has allowed the bacterium to thrive primarily in hospital environments (number one nosocomial infection in some hospitals). However, it has reduced cellular functions in the wild, altered enzyme activities, and in some *S. aureus* mutations, eliminated expression of the normal genes.

While such changes in MRSA can be regarded as "beneficial" to bacterium because they increase the survival rate of bacteria in the presence of the antibiotic, they involve mutational processes that do not provide a genetic mechanism for real evolution (i.e., molecules to man). You should resist saying "evolution"; there is a loss of total function and *MRSA* will lose its ability to compete with other bacteria in the wild and in a non-antibiotic environment.

The Origin of Bubonic Plague

Although some forms of the bacteria *Yersinia* are harmless, other forms have devastated human populations, with a plague of biblical proportions (Ps. 91:3–7, 9,10). Bubonic plague (also known as the "Black Death" that killed one fourth of Europe's population in the 1300s) appeared as a great pestilence several

times in the Old Testament, including in Psalm 91 and in 2 Samuel 24:14–25. Perhaps the clearest example of such a plague is recorded in 1 Samuel 6:4–19, where there is a specific reference to the tumors on people (*bubos* = the tumors of lymph glands) and to rats (the animal vector that carried the plague bacterium, *Yersinia pestis*). The biblical timeframe for the plagues described in 1 Samuel was about 3,000 years ago. Interestingly, experts on plague "evolution" estimate the emergence of *Y. pestis* about 1,500–20,000 years ago.

Plague's Origin is Multifaceted

Many infectious diseases can be traced back to the decay and corruption of the original created design of microorganisms as a result of the Fall. **Corruption** literally means to destroy (from the Latin, *corruptus*). In biological terms, corruption is a loss of genetic information or an inappropriate addition of genetic material; whether an insertion or a deletion, the result is damage to the original code. The origin of pathogenic (disease causing) bacteria such as *Y. pestis* is both complex and multifaceted, and it may be explained by a combination of genes that were lost, added and moved. The story of *Yersinia's* degeneration into the plague pathogen may serve as a model of "fast" genomic decay and corruption.

It appears that the beginning of pathogenicity in the genus *Yersina* started with a net loss of chromosomal DNA from its original "kind." Later in time, there were minor additions of plasmid DNA as well as viral and bacterial DNA. A few plasmid genes for toxins have been acquired from other existing species, but many chromosomal genes were lost. It takes only a few such gene changes to produce this new, extremely infectious variant, so it may have taken only hundreds or a few thousand years to produce the current bubonic plague strain that has existed for about the last 500 years.

Loss of Chromosomal DNA

Researchers hypothesize that key chromosomal genes (i.e., involved in metabolic pathways) were lost in the change from a soil inhabiting *Yersinia* type to a pathogenic *Yersinia* species. Pathogenic *Yersiniae* have lost the genetic expression of numerous (about 149) genes. Of the genes lost, 58 are the result of frameshift mutations, 32 have undergone deletions, and the rest are nonsense muta-tions — all of which prevented pre-existing genes from being normally expressed.

An important feature of the *Y. pestis* genome is the presence of pseudogenes. Biologists consider that these genes reflect a loss of structural information and function. Dr. Wren, the leading plague expert in the world, suggests that the genes lost in *Y. pestis* affected bioenergetic functions, including dicarboxylic amino-acid metabolism. This reduction of metabolic pathways may allow the bacterium to conserve energy. The newly emerged strains (variants) are streamlined and might contribute to the development of pathogenicity (i.e., plague) due to the genes they lack. The absence of im-portant biosynthetic genes is believed to be a hallmark of genomic decay.

Genes Added and Moved

The corruption by three genes of a relatively benign recent ancestor of *Y. pestis* may have played a key role in the emergence of bubonic plague. A recent report by Hinnebusch and colleagues, a plague expert team at the National Institutes for Health, suggests that the acquisition of two plasmid genes (i.e., just a few dis-crete genetic changes) in recent times changed the fairly harmless *Y. pseudotuberculosis*, which caused mild food poisoning, to the agent of the "Black Death." A third gene (carried on plasmid pMT1) produces mu-rine toxin, an enzyme required for the initial survival of *Y. pestis* bacilli in the flea midgut (Table 9.1). By acquiring this gene from another organism, *Y. pestis* made a crucial shift in its host range. The bacterium now could survive in fleas, and it devolved to rely on its blood-feeding host for transmission. This is just an-other example of the flexibility of many microbes and how they sometimes repackage themselves into more dangerous agents of infectious disease.

This last corruption is one that distinguishes *Yersin-ia pestis* from all closely related, more benign bacteria such as *Y. pseudotuberculosis* and other *Yersinia* (e.g., *Y. entercolitica*). In turn, as *Y. pestis* adapted to rely on its new blood-feeding host for transmission, the emer-gence of more deadly bacterial strains would have been favored. It appears that these minor plasmid additions were the last changes made in an otherwise long series of genetic losses in *Y. pseudotuberculosis'* chromosome.

Table 9.1 Virulence-associated plasmids of *Yersinia pestis*

Plasmid Size	Transferred Factor	<u>Action</u>
pPla (9.6 kb)	Pla surface (protease)	activates plasminogen activator; destroys C3B; C5A (i.e., complement factors)
pYV (70.3 kb)	Yops (proteins)	interferes with phagocytosis and immune system
pMT1 (96.2 kb)	phospholipase D (Murine toxin)	bacterial transmission in fleas

One pathogenicity island was acquired by *Yersinia pestis* from another bacterium. This cassette of genes was not the evolution of new chromosomal DNA; it was an acquisition through lateral gene transfer. It produced a corrupted message that gave bacteria a new "position" in the gut. *Y. pseudotuberculosis* lacks a po-sition gene (i.e., hms locus gene), which encourages the bacilli to remain harmlessly in the midgut of the flea. Plague bacilli, by contrast, have this inserted locus gene. Free from its original control and causing a lack of "good direction" information, the bacteria migrate from the midgut to the foregut and then form a plug of packed bacilli passed on to the victim.

Genes, Germs, and Genesis

Plague bacteria are not the only microorganisms that have degenerated into disease-causing organ-isms. Other pathogenic bacteria that have undergone genomic decay include various mycoplasmas (e.g., *Mycoplasma genitalium* and *M. pneumonia*, the latter causes pneumonia) and *Mycobacterium leprae* (the leprosy bacillus).

Focus 9.5

Pathogenicity Islands and other Prickles

In Genesis 3, the Scripture explains that when God cursed the earth, thorns and thistles appeared. These *"prickles"* came about because of man's sin. From this point onward, we might imagine that genes were corrupted and germs were formed. In a figurative sense, what was previously "round" became sharp. The sharpness of bacteria (and other microbes) in today's terms has to do with pathogenicity factors – namely, genes that code for poisons, toxins, enzymes, proteins, and virulence factors.

What makes a bacterium pathogenic? As mentioned before, bacteria in the body and soil were originally made for beneficial purposes. However, after the Edenic curse, beneficial structures deteriorated into malevolent structures through means of mutation, retrogression, and contamination. Smooth, round leaves

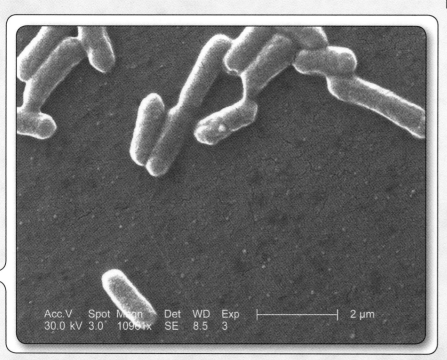

Escherichia coli O157H7

and stems became thorns and thistles. Some of the contaminating processes that lead to pathogenicity include plasmid transfer, transduction, and conjugation.

While studying anthrax, Robert Koch was the first person to discover direct evidence that bacteria caused disease. Robert Koch first defined pathogenic-

ity in 1890, when he extended his germ theory. These "pathogenicity islands" convey the virulence that is necessary for disease to develop. Since then, hundreds of pathogenic bacteria have been associated with disease. Pathogenicity islands have been used to refer to the clusters of genes responsible for virulence (e.g., enzymes and toxins), and they are fairly large segments of the genome of the pathogenic strains that are absent in nonpathogenic strains. These islands have many of the properties of intervening sequences, which suggests that they move by lateral gene transfer. These blocks of genetic information could move from a pathogenic strain into an avirulent organism, and then convert it to a pathogen. Such lateral transfer processes show how the corruption of a pure "kinds" lineage can make quick jumps and a break in the Creator's original plan.

Pathogenic bacteria are defined by the capability of causing disease in a host. What makes a bacterium pathogenic is the set of genes that it possesses. The genes can be distributed on the chromosome, on plasmids (independent extrachomosomal genetic elements) and on a prophage. A prophage is a bacteriophage in which latent viral genes are incorporated into the bacterial chromosomes without causing disruption of the bacterial cell. Recently, blocks of virulence genes in the chromosome have been observed in virulent strains but not in avirulent strains. For example, normal *E. coli* does not possess these blocks whereas pathogenic *E. coli* does. These significant differences (e.g., nucleotide composition) between the chromosome and the pathogenicity island are observed and typical; it suggests that mobile genetic elements may have played a significant role in the devolution of pathogens.

One line of evidence for horizontal gene transfer as a selection force comes from examination of bacterial genome sequences. To find genes with two very similar DNA sequences in two distantly related bacteria suggests that these sequences might have been acquired by horizontal gene transfer. The number of such examples is increasing. The growing appreciation of how much horizontal gene transfer may have contributed to the variation (i.e., microevolution) of bacteria has caused microbiologists to question whether the "standard evolutionary tree," which is characterized by well-isolated branches, should in fact be replaced by interwoven nets of branches. If two species have been differentiated on the basis of differences in their ability to utilize lactose and whether the genes that allow lactose utilization can be transferred by horizontal gene transfer, how firm then is this definition of species? Is this not variation with a "kind" or type? The significance of horizontal gene transfer is that it represents a defilement of the original bacteria types.

Medical Significance of Pathogenicity Islands

Effects of horizontal gene transfer, seen from the viewpoint of diversity analysis of bacterial lineages, may seem a rather abstruse topic. Yet, horizontal gene transfer among bacteria usually has immediate, practical effects on human health. Generally scientific studies have shown that not only is horizontal gene transfer spreading antibiotic-resistant genes, but horizontal gene transfer is also contributing to the evolution of disease-causing bacteria. A commonly seen recent example of a harmless bacteria devolving into a pathogenic one is the intestinal *Escherichia coli O157H7* strain that occasionally causes fatalities. This "killer *Escherichia coli*" causes bloody diarrhea and kidney failure in children. Such strains appear to have been created by a horizontal gene transfer event from *Shigella flexneri.* The pathogenicity island, designated *SHI-2* for *Shigella*, is a less virulent strain of *E. coli* that has acquired genes to enable it to make a new toxin. The toxin is thought to be responsible for kidney failure; a symptom not previously associated with *E. coli* infections.

As we develop a model of the origin of infectious disease from a creationist, biblical perspective, these bacteria may provide us with a glimpse of what has happened to living things over time in a fallen, cursed, and corrupted world. One helpful analogy is a faulty wire in a home. As any homeowner knows, failure to repair frayed electrical wiring is a fire hazard and can be disastrous. Any cut or a break in an electrical line, can be very dangerous. One would suppose that the same holds true for a bacterium. Though electrical lines are safe most of the time, a corrupted line becomes a hazard.

Mobile Genes Pose a Problem of Defilement

The concept of keeping the "seeds" separate and distinct is very insightful on a variety of microbial genetic issues. In Deuteronomy 22:9 and Leviticus 19:19, God tells the Israelites that if they do not keep the cattle separate from "diverse" kinds and seeds separate from "diverse" seeds, they will receive a curse on not only their immediate field, but also their vineyard. You cannot help but wonder if God meant that He knew the natural consequence of diverse gene mixing that leads to disease. It is clear that mixing genes from separate "kinds" (or types) is not the Creator's way.

One application of this principle might render the passage as, "Do not randomly plant two kinds (strands) of genes (DNA/RNA) in your cells; if you do, not only the microbes you 'plant' in the nucleus and plasmid but also the fruit of the entire host (man and animals) will be defiled (with virulence)." The exception to the consequence of diverse gene mixing is genetic engineering, because that is designed and controlled gene mixing. Defilement or corruption can be seen in pathogenicity islands that are added (via horizontal transfer) from one bacteria kind to another. This principle of randomized gene mixing can be seen in the transfer of pathogenicity islands in bacteria and in the origin of avian flu through the mixing of bird and mammal influenza strains.

The Origin of Bird Flu

Bird flu poses one of the greatest threats to human health if a pandemic occurs. Recall from Chapter 8, the Influenza A virus is an RNA virus that can change quickly. This rapid change occurs through the accumulation of small point mutations called antigenic drift, as well as through major genome reassortment called antigenic shift. Viruses rapidly change primarily because of the presence of many error-prone viral enzymes that replicate their genomes. This is especially the case with RNA viruses. Consequently, RNA viruses have mutation frequencies that are several folds higher than the observed mutation frequencies of DNA viruses.

Animal viruses may be degenerate genes coated by proteins that are cobbled together by co-option processes, or they may be decaying products from several genomes and proteins models. Recall from Chapter 7 the specific example of the degeneration of a normal gene (i.e., retrotransposons) to a retrovirus. On human chromosome 22, a gene (i.e., human endogenous retrotransposon) turns off the immune system during pregnancy. This design prohibits the mother's immune system from damaging the child's body. These genes cannot fully replicate, only infecting local immune cells (such as macrophages) of the uterus, thereby preventing them from initiating a full-blown immune response. Thus, the mother's immune system remains able to respond to other infections but is specifically prevented from raising an immune response to the developing embryo. So in Creation, the selective ability to turn off the immune system for protection would be a "good" design. However, since the corruption of creation, the degeneration and corruption of good genes in human and animal hosts have changed.

influenza virus particles are excreted in high concentration in their feces which helps spread the virus between birds and mammals. Besides residing within wild aquatic bird reservoirs such as ducks, two groups of influenza A viruses (the *H5* and other strains) can infect domestic fowl. These strains are responsible for causing avian flu, which lately has received a lot of media attention because of its presence in chickens that are raised for human consumption. As well as infecting birds, two subtypes of influenza A can also be isolated from swine, which may be referred to as swine flu subtypes. These two strains isolated from swine are the *H1N1* and *H3N2* subtypes, with the former being a human pandemic strain.

Influenza in Birds Causes Little Harm

Perhaps these genes then co-opt, or randomly acquire proteins, and then leave the body as pathogenic viruses. These pathogenic viruses then open the world to devastating infections.

Influenza A Viruses

One might imagine that at one time good genes degraded in wild birds (i.e., ducks), but it did not affect them. However, once these deteriorated genes left the birds and transferred to mammals (e.g., pigs) and man, the major problems emerged. The terrible Spanish flu (1918-1919) developed quickly and mysteriously. It probably picked up some key genes from an avian source (possibly a duck or goose). Analysis by Dr. Jeffery Taubenberger and colleagues indicates that the *H1N1* flu virus originated in an avian flu strain but spent time "evolving" in an unidentified host before emerging 1918. It appeared mysteriously out of nowhere, caused tremendous distribution, and went away just as mysteriously when World War I ended. This was a corruption and decay of the originally good design of gene transfer, re-assortment, and recombination.

All known influenza A strains that infect humans are perpetuated in aquatic birds where it appears to cause asymptomatic infections. From these aquatic birds,

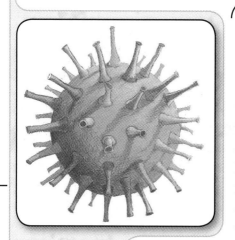

Avian flu virus

Influenza A viruses are brought about in the wild birds of the world, predominantly in waterfowl, in which the 16 subtypes coexist in perfect harmony with their hosts. In these natural hosts, the viruses remain stable in molecular form, showing minimal change (variation) at the amino acid level over extended periods. This fact indicates that the influenza-bird association is ancient; this lack of change is surprising because influenza viruses are segmented, negative-stranded RNA viruses that have no quality-control mechanisms during replication and are highly prone to variation. After transfer to a new type of host, either avian or mammalian, influenza viruses undergo rapid corruption, devolution, or defilement. However, all 16 HA subtypes, including *H5* and *H7*, have, until recently, been considered to be benign in their natural hosts. This benign equilibrium between the influenza virus and its host may have changed.

The Genesis of Bird Flu

Before 1997, no evidence had indicated that *H5* influenza viruses could infect humans and cause fatal disease. The precursor of the *H5N1 influenza virus* that spread to humans in 1997 was first detected in China, in 1996, when it caused a moderate number of deaths in geese. However, it attracted very little attention at the time. This goose virus acquired internal gene segments from influenza viruses later found in quail. It also acquired the neuraminidase gene segment from a duck virus. This all took place before the goose virus became widespread in live poultry markets in Hong Kong and killed 6 of 18 infected persons. Culling all domestic poultry in Hong Kong destroyed this H5N1 virus; the genotype has not been detected since that time. However, different reassortments continued to emerge from goose and duck reservoirs that contained the same *H5 HA* glycoprotein but had various internal genes. The *H5N1 viruses* continued to change, and in late 2002, a single genotype was responsible for killing most waterfowl in Hong Kong nature parks. This genotype of *H5N1* spread to humans in Hong Kong in 2002, killing 1 of 2 infected persons, and was the precursor to the current strain of bird flu (i.e., the Z genotype) which has become dominant. The current strain spread in an unprecedented, first-time fashion across Southeast Asia and is now spreading across Europe, and parts of Africa.

To date, more than 140 million domesticated birds have been killed by the virus or culled to stem its spread; as of spring 2006 more than 150 persons have been infected in Asia, Africa, and Europe. These recent *H5N1 influenza* viruses have acquired the unprecedented and disturbing capability to infect humans. These incremental changes intensify concern about this bird flu virus' potential to cause a global pandemic. These genes were presumably acquired from viruses found in waterfowl in Southeast Asia, but the actual gene donors have not yet been identified. While most *H5N1 influenza* viruses that have been isolated from avian species in Asia since 1997 are highly pathogenic in certain poultry (pheasants and domestic fowls), they show varied pathogenicity in other species.

There is evidence that swine also may be involved in the interspecies transmission by providing an environment where human influenza viruses originate. Pandemic subtypes rarely occur, yet when they do emerge it happens suddenly. Many of these subtypes first appeared in China. It is believed that this is because China's cultural heritage allows considerable domestic exposure to aquatic fowl, such as ducks, as well as a close domestic association with pigs. Influenza viruses can use a process known as genetic reassortment to create new pandemic strains that represent a combination of avian, human, and possibly even swine genomes. In reassortment, parts of individual genomes between closely related strains of

virus are exchanged, creating a viral strain that is capable of infecting a different host, such as humans.

Making the Jump from Chickens to Humans

Currently, there are three potential pandemic influenza A strains (*H5N1*, *H7N7*, and *H9N2*) with all three being recently isolated from domestic fowl. The *H9N2* strain first emerged in Hong Kong in 1999 and recently reemerged in 2003. This particular strain has killed three people and caused the mass killing of chickens in Hong Kong poultry markets to rid the influenza. Similarly, the *H7N7* strain emerged in the poultry industry in the Netherlands. The *H7N7* strain of influenza A has killed one person, and this has also required the slaughter of chickens by the thousands. Ominously, evidence was obtained for *H7N7* human-to-human transmission as well as infection within nearby pig farms. In 2003, the *H5N1* subtype emerged in Asia, and has now proven fatal to people on three continents and caused the culling of over 200 million birds.

As of spring 2006, not one of these viruses appeared to have acquired the necessary characteristics to cause widespread human infections, although experts seem to agree that it is only a matter of time before this happens. Of the three subtypes, perhaps the *H5N1* subtype has the greatest pandemic potential. A *hyper-virulent-H5N1* strain now is endemic to Asia, and unfortunately, China has recently reported that the highly virulent *H5N1* avian flu strain can now be isolated from pigs. These observations make it likely that reassortment with a human strain will occur to produce an H5N1 virus with the capability for widespread human-to-human transmission. Therefore, the United States government and other international agencies have declared the development of a vaccine to protect against the *H5N1* strain a top priority.

Flu Pandemics

The "Spanish" influenza pandemic remains a threatening warning to public health. Many questions about its origins, its unusual epidemiologic features, and the basis of its pathogenicity remain unanswered. The public health implications of the pandemic therefore remain in doubt even as we now grapple with the feared emergence of a pandemic caused by *H5N1* or another virus. However, new information about the 1918 virus is emerging, for example, sequencing of the entire genome from archival autopsy tissues (see Historical Focus 9.5). But, the viral genome alone is unlikely to provide answers to some critical questions. What caused so many deaths and severe infections? Historical Focus 9.5 discusses the 1918 flu pandemic and attempts to provide an understanding for this specific influenza. It also attempts to provide implications for future pandemics that require careful experimentation and in-depth historical analysis.

Mechanisms of Spread

Were the highly pathogenic *H5N1 viruses* transferred within and between countries by persons, poultry, or objects that carry germs (i.e., fomites)? In previous outbreaks of highly pathogenic *H5* and *H7* infection in multiple countries, the spread was directly attributable to humans. The primary means in which influenza virus is spread in poultry is by the movement of poultry and poultry products; establishing good security measures on poultry farms is therefore an important defense. The poultry industry is a huge, integrated complex in Asia. Nonetheless, the supposed involvement of multiple lineages of *H5N1* argues against human-mediated spread from a single source. Live poultry markets are an amplifier and reservoir of infection, and they probably play a role in the maintenance and spread of the virus in the region.

However, a number of other factors unique to affected Asian countries make control difficult. Backyard flocks are common in the region, and these domesticated birds are not subject to any security measures. Fighting cocks are prized possessions and are often transported long distances. Fighting cocks may also play a role in the spread of infection and in transmission to humans. Many of the affected countries have weak veterinary communications and are facing highly pathogenic avian influenza outbreaks for the first time. The migrant ducks that commonly wander through rice fields scavenging fallen rice seeds are another potent mechanism for the spread of infection.

Keep the Seeds Separate and Distinct

"Thou shalt not let thy cattle gender with a diverse kind: thou shalt not sow thy field with mingled seed" (Lev. 19:19, KJV). One modern paraphrase of Leviticus 19:19 might be "Don't mix your domestic livestock (i.e., pigs) with wild birds (i.e., ducks) or they may become virulent." Later, the Bible says *Thou shalt not sow thy vineyard with divers seeds: lest the fruit of thy seed which thou hast sown, and the fruit of thy vineyard, be defiled" (Deut. 22:9, KJV).* This principle of defilement or corruption may explain the origin of avian flu through the mixing of avian and mammal influenza strains. Farmers in areas where bird flu is endemic should be careful about allowing their domestic livestock to intermingle with wild birds. In addition, they should keep a clear separation between human and animal inhabitation.

Historical Focus 9.5
Doughboys Die of the Spanish Flu

America's soldiers of World War I were referred to as doughboys. In 1918, many army privates were destined for the trenches of World War I in France. Some otherwise healthy young men began to bear symptoms of the flu. The Spanish flu was unusual because the most susceptible people were young, strong, and in the prime of life. The 1918 influenza victims were from healthy 20- to 50-year-old age groups (i.e., the age of military service), as opposed to the normally more susceptible age groups of the very young or very old. Uniquely, it produced a deep cyanosis (blue skin) that affected the face, lips, and lungs. Somehow, the virus penetrated the deepest parts of the lung for unknown reasons. It was known to kill some people in as little as 12 hours after contracting the virus. There was also an extraordinarily high mortality rate of 20 times the norm for influenza. In many of the cases that did survive the critical first few days of the influenza attack, death was precipitated by a rampant secondary infection with pneumonia bacteria.

In particular, one 21-year-old complained of chills, fever, headache, backache, and a cough. Within a week, he was dead – 1 of 21 million people worldwide who would succumb to the influenza pandemic of 1918. For almost 90 years, samples of the doughboy's lungs sat in a warehouse run by the Armed Forces Institute of Pathology in Washington, D.C. RNA bearing the solution to an enduring mystery lay hidden in his tissues; this RNA contained the genetic code for the worst pandemic in human history. Dr. Jeffery K. Taubenberger and his associates exhumed the deadly flu strain and fragments of its genes from the frozen tissue of the buried doughboy. Taubenberger and his colleagues had begun their search for the virus's genes by selecting at random 28 of the 70 pandemic victims whose

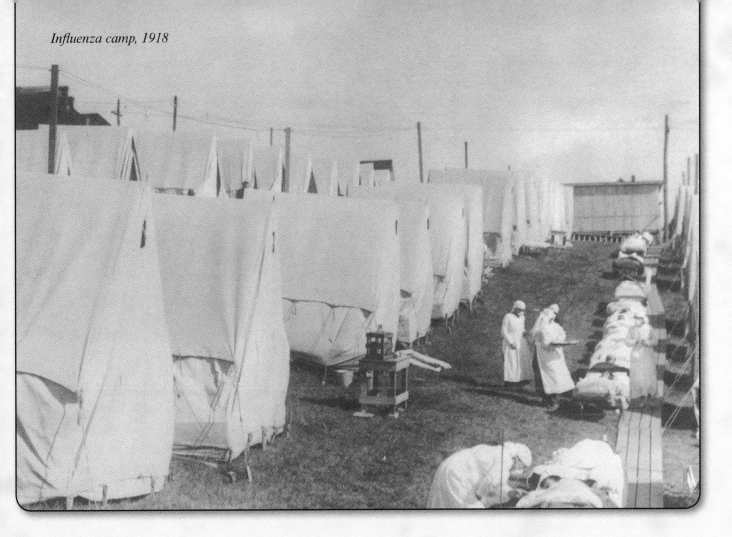

Influenza camp, 1918

lung samples are stored at a government facility. Autopsy reports from 1918 disclosed that seven of these servicemen died soon after becoming ill, which enhances the likelihood that lung tissue might contain intact bits of RNA from the virus's unusual eight-strand genome.

People who live longer are less likely to harbor the virus, because the body's defenses eradicate the microbes, Taubenberger says. In such cases, bacterial pneumonia delivers the fatal blow. But in the seven servicemen who died quickly, the immune counterattack might not have had time to wipe out the virus. The researchers drew a blank in six cases. This Army private, however, was unusual. His left lung had suffered extensive bacterial pneumonia, but his right lung had not. (The most common cause of actual death from influenza was not the virus itself but rather by pneumonia. The most common form of bacterial pneumonia is caused by the bacterium, *Haemophilus influenzae*.) This raised the possibility that the right lung might still harbor the virus. To find out, the researchers removed some tissue from the paraffin in which it was stored. Step by step, they broke it down until only RNA remained. It yielded valuable information and could be helpful if a future pandemic occurs. Dr. Taubenberger believes that it could happen again.

Virologist Robert Webster of St. Jude Children's Research Hospital in Memphis, TN, thinks that the 1918 virus represents the ultimate disease-causing agent. We need to understand as much as possible about this virus because the world will get another pandemic, maybe late in this century or early in the next. One pandemic was one too many. In the 1918 outbreak, nearly 700,000 people died in the United States alone. Over 50 million worldwide died of the Spanish flu over a two-year period. This was the pandemic of the century!

The people who preserved this tissue probably never imagined what might be possible down the road. Dr. Ann H. Reid, who worked with Dr. Taubenberger, made millions of copies of nine RNA fragments of five flu genes. Dr. Thomas G. Fanning then deciphered the sequences of the fragments and compared them to every other known sequence of the flu gene. It is unique and was designated H1N1. The team has also confirmed prior evidence suggesting that the sequences most closely resemble those from swine flu. Researchers are attempting to rebuild the entire genome of the virus, perhaps yielding clues to its hypervirulence. Many researchers feel that its information might help in the making of a vaccine, if needed. According to Dr. Webster, if this virus strain were to reemerge, this information would serve to get a best-match vaccine that would probably protect us quite well. In conclusion, the understanding of the 1918 virus (arguably the worst pandemic of all time) may help us to deal better with epidemics of the future, including avian flu and other virally caused diseases, like SARS. The scary thing about the 1918 influenza epidemic is that it came without warning, then affected young men who were uncharacteristic victims of any flu known and mysteriously went away. Some worry that avian flu may do the same.

Future Flu Pandemics

Over the years, several pandemic viral strains of influenza A have arisen. For example, there was the 1890 flu, the 1918 Spanish flu, and other flu epidemics in 1957 and 1968. Therefore, it appears almost inevitable that the next pandemic strain is currently lurking in some reservoir. Despite considerable knowledge of the genetic structure of the 1918 virus, no one is quite sure why the flu that year was so virulent, and there is still considerable scientific disagreement about where it came from. It is likely that a new surface protein appeared on this virus, one that humans had never encountered before and to which they therefore had no immunity. But there must have been other genetic features of this virus that also contributed, and these remain a mystery, even though complete viral gene sequences of the bug have been developed from the preserved tissue.

So the question arises: Could it happen again? In a sense, it already has happened again, though not in such a devastating form. The "Asian flu" of the winter of 1957–1958 killed 70,000 Americans. The 1968–1969 "Hong Kong flu" killed 34,000. The new subtype that appeared that year, called Influenza A (H3N2), was milder, perhaps because only the hemagglutinin protein changed and the neuraminidase stayed the same, therefore people may have had some residual resistance to it. Still, Influenza A (H3N2) has caused 400,000 deaths in the United States since its emergence in 1968, and 90 percent of them were among people older than 65. In fact, the subtype that caused the 1918 pandemic, Influenza A (H1N1) continued to circulate for years, having undergone antigenic drift. This caused a large number of deaths in 1920 (probably reduced by greater immunity among the population as well as by the attenuated form of the virus), and then periodic outbreaks until it disappeared in 1957. None of the outbreaks, though, was anywhere near the severity of

that of 1918. What made the 1918 strain so deadly has been a longstanding medical mystery. Analysis for those genes and proteins revealed viral features that could have both suppressed immune defenses and provoked violent immune reactions in victims, which contributed to the high mortality. Known bird and mammal influenza hosts are unlikely sources of the pandemic virus, so its origin remains unsolved. In 1977 it reappeared, but again it was without devastating consequences.

In any case, most experts on the flu think that the answer is yes, it could happen again. The reservoir of influenza is believed to be wild waterfowl, and the pandemics of 1957 and 1968 were both produced by changes in the surface proteins of an avian strain of the virus. Such an alteration in the future could produce a pandemic as bad as, or worse than, the 1918 disaster. Of course, circumstances now are a bit different. We have a flu reporting system; we know how to make vaccines against the flu; we have antibiotics to treat the bacterial infections that killed so many in the pandemic of 1918; we even have several antiviral medicines that are helpful. But we also know that microbes are persistent and very adaptable, and that there is always the possibility that one of them will come up with an answer to the most elaborate defenses that have been constructed against it.

The Future of Bird Flu

At the time of this writing, bird flu appears to be imminent to spread into the United States via the Alaskan Aleutian islands. As birds fly naturally across the Bering Strait from Siberia, some birds will inevitably carry with them avian flu. Once it lands in North America, the fear is that it will spread down the west coast. The US government is monitoring it closely. However, the predictability is like forecasting a hurricane when a tropical storm is in the Atlantic Ocean. You know that it is coming, but whether it will be a Category 1, 2, 3, 4, or 5 is known only to God before it actually hits. The heightened monitoring of avian flu will help warn us of a potential epidemic. But, what can we do? Perhaps, regulations on keeping livestock separate from wild animals may reduce "viral" mixing. In addition, we can stockpile antiviral medications and vaccines. Beyond this, it is in the Creator's Hand. Concerns about future outbreaks of avian flu (mutation) and other influenza pandemics will continue. More research needs to be done on the origin of infectious disease from a creation, biblical perspective. There are still many mysteries and challenges ahead.

Figure 9.1

A multifaceted model of factors that have led to the origin of infectious disease

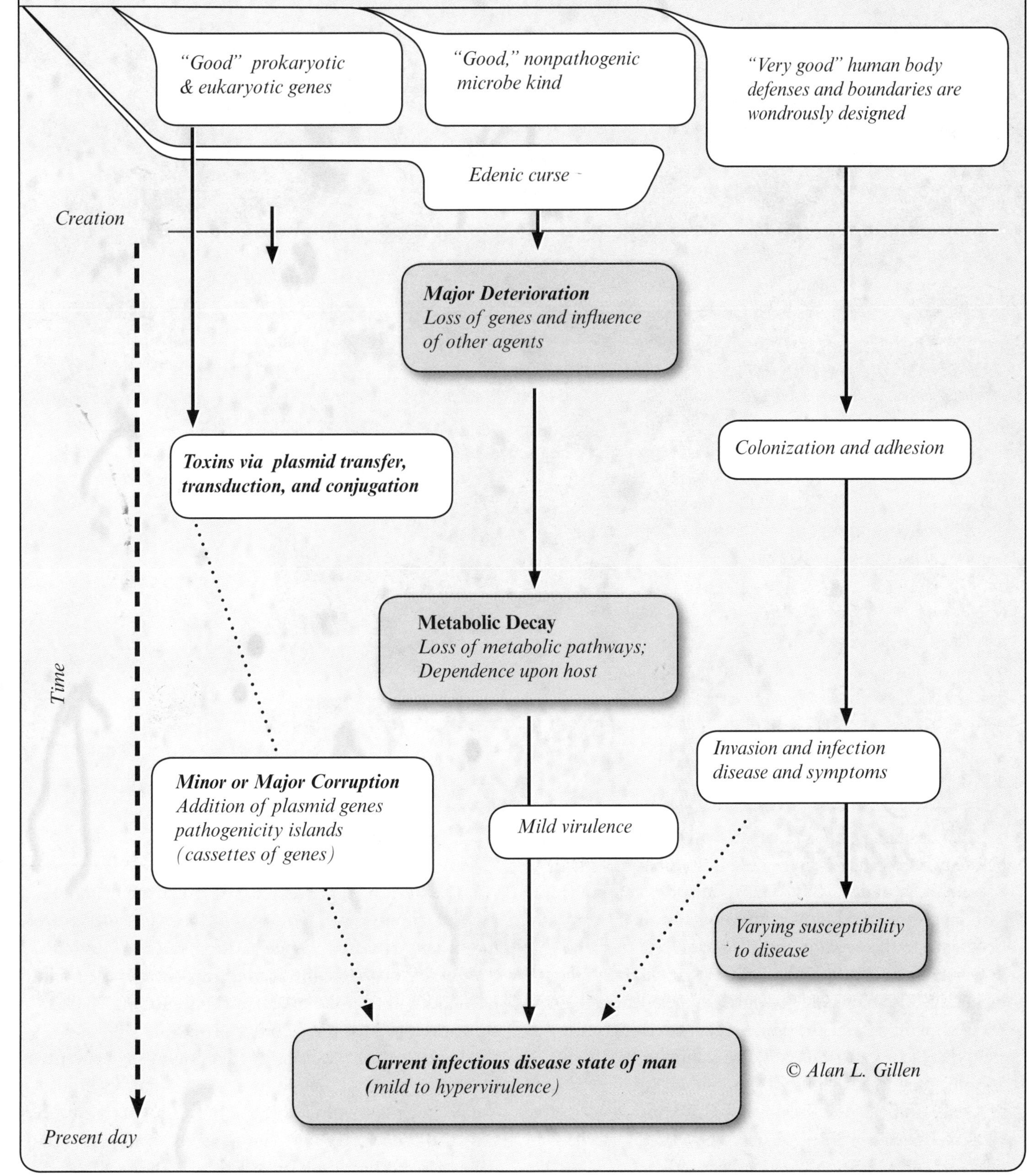

Creation

Time

"Good" prokaryotic & eukaryotic genes

"Good," nonpathogenic microbe kind

"Very good" human body defenses and boundaries are wondrously designed

Edenic curse

Major Deterioration
Loss of genes and influence of other agents

Toxins via plasmid transfer, transduction, and conjugation

Colonization and adhesion

Metabolic Decay
Loss of metabolic pathways; Dependence upon host

Minor or Major Corruption
Addition of plasmid genes pathogenicity islands (cassettes of genes)

Mild virulence

Invasion and infection disease and symptoms

Varying susceptibility to disease

Current infectious disease state of man
(mild to hypervirulence)

© Alan L. Gillen

Present day

Chapter Ten

Plagues and Pestilences of the Future

The Fourth Horseman

Plagues and pestilences are not over. It will get worse before it gets better. There is little doubt that the fourth horseman, pestilence, has saddled up and is charging at us with lance poised. However, we can parry his thrusts with obedience to the Creator and His Word. We read about horsemen (i.e., angels in Revelation) that will bring judgment and this will include plagues and pestilences that will wipe out a quarter of the population. We do not know what disease it may be. It could be influenza, smallpox, bubonic plague, SARS, Ebola, measles. It could be a germ that mankind has never seen before. We just do not know what pathogen it will be. We only know that it will be terrible. There is hope only for the believer.

The Pale Horse of Pestilence

The first three horsemen of Revelation bring religious deception, war, and famine. Disease often travels in tandem with fear. While the first can lead to the death of thousands, the second can unravel the social fabric, disrupting the precarious balance of relationships essential for the stability of nations. Famine weakens the body, especially the immune system, thus lowering the resistance to disease. As plagues come, the people most vulnerable are the very young, the very old, and those starving. The most recent diseases that have invoked fear have been bird flu, Ebola, SARS, and flesh-eating *Streptococcus*. Tomorrow it could be another, even greater plague to sweep across the landscape, leaving death and destruction in its wake. As we examine the four seals in Revelation 6, it is evident that these seals, dramatically depicted by four horsemen, show the effect of false religions, war, famine, and plague among the earth's population in the days leading to the return of Jesus Christ. Each of these seals represents powerful forces that devastate human life on the earth. The cumulative effect will lead to such conditions that if Jesus Christ did not intervene and cut short the time of tribulation, "no flesh would be saved" (Matt. 24:22).

The Ride Of The Fourth Horseman

We now come to the fourth seal, the fourth horseman, and his ride of death by plague. Revelation 6:7–8 mentions this about the fourth seal: "When He opened the fourth seal, I heard the voice of the fourth living creature saying, 'Come and see.' So I looked, and behold, a pale horse. And the name of him who sat on it was Death, and Hades followed with him." The "pale" (*chloros*) color of the fourth horse may indicate a yellow green, the pale green of a dying plant, or the paleness of a sick person in contrast to a healthy appearance. In the process of physiological death, the skin usually becomes pale; there may be signs of blood buildup in the part of the body at lowest elevation. This is known as **livor mortis**. Livor mortis begins on the point of death. The human body becomes distended. The skin color progressively changes from green to blue to purple, and finally to black. Perhaps some people may be pale blue, the color of cyanosis. This was the color of people's skin, face, and lips during the 1918 influenza pandemic. This was also the color of people's skin during the bubonic plague. This horse is the color of death.

In Jesus' parallel prophecy in Matthew 24, He explained that in the wake of religious deception, war and famine would come "pestilences" or disease epidemics (Rev. 6:7). "Plague" in Scripture denotes not only pestilence but also other calamities in nature that God uses to punish a disobedient humanity. Of course, any such calamities make populations much more vulnerable for the spread of disease epidemics.

Revelation 6:8 states: "And power was given to them over a fourth of the earth to kill with sword, with hunger, with death and by the beasts of the earth." By the time the fourth horseman completes his ride, a fourth of earth's inhabitants will experience incredible devastation. The death toll will be unlike any other from plague and disease in human history. To understand how bad it can be, recall from Chapter 9 the history and origin of bubonic plague. Today cases are still reported, and many people die each year. The disease originates in rodents and is usually transmitted to people by fleas. This is a hypervirulent disease. As few as 10 bubonic plague cells can cause a person's death. Perhaps disease transmission from rodents is part of what Revelation 6:8 means by death from "the beasts of the earth." Microbial and viral infection could also be intended. The pale yellowish-green color maybe due to a Staphylococcal infection.

Human-Engineered Germs and Bioterror

Throughout its history, plague, anthrax, and smallpox have been used as offensive weapons against populations. The Mongols would catapult plague-infested corpses over the walls of besieged cities. Thousands would die as the disease spread through the walled-in population. During World War II, Japan dropped plague-infested fleas on China. According to government authorities, American research that grew as a result of the war experience led to a decades-long research project at Fort Detrick, Maryland. This proved that biological warfare was a feasible method of waging war.

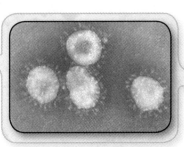

After the first Gulf War in 1991, weapons inspectors confirmed that Iraq had developed biological weapons and had even equipped some warheads with germs to use against Saddam Hussein's enemies. The location of these weapons since that time is part of the unsolved mystery of that regime. Other highly virulent organisms, like tularemia (a tick-borne disease) could be used in an aerosol to cause pneumonia with just a few bacteria. Could some of these diseases be in the hands of a terrorist group, waiting to be used on the West?

Naturally Caused Infectious Disease

Beyond the human-engineered biological warfare, another type of pestilence could be waiting as well. Virologists who study the subject say diseases, like Hanta A virus or SARS, could lurk quietly in the background and could erupt at any time. However, it could take years to develop a viable vaccine to combat these newly emerging viruses. In the meantime, other mutant strains are waiting to jump the species barrier from animals to humans. When they do, the results could be catastrophic. A breakdown caused by war in one part of the world, coupled with an outbreak of influenza, as in World War I, could set in motion a disease pandemic on the scale of those described in the Book of Revelation.

The Antidote to Great Plagues

When we look at the four seals of Revelation, we have to understand the context of God's eternal message to mankind. False religion, war, famine, and disease are the results of man's broken relationship with Him. And when these horsemen make their rides, it will be after repeated warning and pleading from God to turn from sin and to trust Jesus Christ, Savior and Great Physician. What is the antidote to the fourth horseman of disease? In John 3:16, the Bible says "For God so loved the world, that he gave his only begotten Son, that whosoever believeth in him should not perish, but have everlasting life."

When God brought the Israelites out of Egypt, He told them: "If thou wilt diligently hearken to the voice of the Lord thy God, and wilt do that which is right in his sight, and wilt give ear to his commandments, and keep all his statutes, I will put none of these diseases upon thee, which I have brought upon the Egyptians: for I am the Lord that healeth thee" (Exod.15:26). However,

if they disobeyed and broke the covenant, they could expect disease to afflict them and their nation.

The human race is bound to its Creator in a relationship that will reach a conclusion. Mankind eventually will come face to face with God and admit that He is the one and only true God. The book of Revelation shows God's merciful intervention in human affairs to both correct and save man from destruction. God will bring justice to the earth, but first there will be a time of unparalleled tribulation of plagues, pestilences, and pandemics.

The Fifth Horseman and the Great Physician

Indeed, the apostle John saw more than four horsemen in his vision. He saw five. Revelation 19:11–16 shows us the ride of the fifth horseman. It is the appearance of Jesus Christ, on a white horse from heaven, intervening in world affairs at its most crucial point — the future restoration of Eden which will take place when the Great Physician (*Jehovah Rapha*) returns.

God revealed himself as *Jehovah Rapha* in the context of great sickness occurring around His people. *Rapha* means "to cure, to repair, to heal, to mend back together," or restore one to health or usefulness. Usually the word "heal" or "healing" is used in conjunction with *Jehovah Rapha*. In addition, "healing" implies being sewn together, mending, stitching up, binding to, or adhering on. God is involved in the restoration of lives by pulling together things that are out of joint. He stitches our life into a beautiful tapestry, including dark threads (black and gray) mixed with silver and gold threads on the underside and a beautiful cloth picture on the top side. He is the Master Surgeon in our life. He can mend broken strands because He is the Creator who has woven life together from the beginning. This is the nature of *Jehovah Rapha*.

While many Egyptians were suffering from plagues, God protected His people. The Israelites were receptive to God's voice and His instruction of health principles in the Levitical law. Most likely, God's people listened due to the dramatic contrast of Egyptians experiencing plague and sickness, while they experienced good health and blessing. God often gets our attention during times when we or the people around us are sick. It appears that we are receptive to God's prescriptions for life, death, health, and sickness when He has our attention. "And God shall wipe away all tears from their eyes; and there shall be no more death, neither sorrow, nor crying, neither shall there be any more pain: for the former things are passed away" (Rev. 21: 4).

The Exodus of Germs

There is hope for the Christian: some day, Eden will be regained. The Curse will be removed and there will be no more disease! Revelation 21:4 says, "And God shall wipe away all tears from their eyes; and there shall be no more death, neither sorrow, nor crying, neither shall there be any more pain: for the former things are passed away." Christ will provide the cure. This great deliverance from disease has been purchased by the Great Physician and Savior himself, Jesus Christ. Revelation 21:6 says, "It is done." The Greek word for this proclamation is *Gegonan*. This is a statement of divine finality. The genesis of germs will be no more. They will be going, going, gone!

Bacterial Genetics

The Bacterial Chromosome

Bacteria typically have a single circular chromosome consisting of a single circular molecule of DNA with associated proteins. A bacterial chromosome has a circumference of approximately l nm and is about 100 to 1,000 times longer than the bacterial cell it is packaged into. The chromosome is looped and folded, and attached at one or several points to the plasma membrane. The DNA of *E. coli*, the most-studied bacterial species, has about 4 million base pairs and is about 1 mm long — 1,000 times longer than the entire cell. However, because DNA is very thin and tightly packed inside the cell, this twisted, coiled macromolecule takes up only about 10 percent of the cell's volume. This highly twisted DNA is referred to as supercoiled DNA. The complete base sequences of several bacterial chromosomes have been determined. The mapping, sequencing and study of the molecular characterization of genomes is called genomics. The most important genetic questions being addressed concern how cells use the genetic information available to them.

Microbial Genomes

The discovery of prokaryotic and eukaryotic genomes presented scientists with great volumes of data, and, for the first time in history, made available the entire genetic content of a living organism. But it also created the dilemma of what to do with the data. As studies continued and years passed, there emerged the new science of genomics. For the microbiologist, the field of medical genomics offers fresh insights into the disease process. From genome analysis, for example, scientists can deduce the importance of a specific function. For example, *Haemophilus influenzae* lacks the genes for three Krebs-cycle enzymes, a fact that may help microbiologists understand its ability to thrive in the human body. By comparing the genomes of virulent and avirulent strains, molecular clues are revealed concerning what causes a microbe to be pathogenic (disease-causing).

The complete sequence of nucleotides in many genes and in more than 100 microbial genomes has been deciphered. A high percentage of them have medical importance or have utility in the biotechnology industry. On the average, a typical microbial gene has about 1,000 nucleotides. The first genome to be completely determined, in the late 1970s, was that of the bacteriophage ØX174, which infects *Escherichia coli*. This genome contains 5,386 nucleotides, and encodes a small set of genes for capsid proteins and for the proteins required for replication of its DNA. More than half the genome is dedicated to three structural proteins that form the capsid. The other half of the genome might be predicted to encode only two or three genes.

Viral genomes vary in size from a few thousand nucleotides to more than 200,000 nucleotides. The RNA phage, MS2, has only 3,569 nucleotides that code for four genes. HIV has 10,000 nucleotides encoding approximately 10 genes, and human cytomegalovirus (a type of herpes virus) has 230,000 nucleotides that define 208 genes.

Most bacterial genomes contain a few million nucleotides that encode approximately 2,000 to 5,000 genes. An exception is the *Mycoplasma sp.* genome, which has fewer than one million nucleotides and encodes less than 500 genes. *Mycoplasma sp.*, a wall-less bacterium, is believed to have the smallest genome of a self-replicating organism. The ability of microbial pathogens to cause disease results from the expression of key virulence genes that may exist within the genome or on plasmids. Microbial agents may exchange virulence genes (and other genes) by a variety of processes described earlier. Discrete segments of DNA that encode virulence traits are sometimes called pathogenicity islands. A pathogenicity island may consist of several genes or merely one. The virulence genes of some bacterial pathogens reside in genomes of viruses that have become integrated into the bacterial genome. For example, the virulence of *Corynebacterium diphtheriae* is due primarily to a single highly toxic protein that it secretes. Virulence genes often occur in clusters of functionally related groups. For example, a cluster of several genes may be involved in transporting molecules to the bacterial surface that then enable a pathogen to attach to a special cell in the body and invade that cell.

Some of the most important medical microbe sequences include *Borrelia burdorferi* (Lyme disease), HIV (AIDS), *Escherichia coli* (gastroenteritis), *Helicobacter pylori* (ulcers), *M. tuberculosis* (tuberculosis), *Staphylococcus aureus* (boils, skin infections, etc.), and *Plasmodium falciparum* (malaria). Probably the most outstanding achievement in microbiology was the complete sequencing in 1997 of *Escherichia coli*. Studied for decades and a regular on the pages of this book, *E. coli* is the organism of choice for studying how bacteria work. Because there is an enormous amount of biological literature on the organism, a gene and its gene product can be fit into the vast understanding of its biology. A research group identified 4,638,858 base pairs in the 4,288 genes of the *E. coli* genome.

The Institute for Genomic Research was back in the news in 1997, when another germ, *Mycobacterium tuberculosis*, was also sequenced. Tuberculosis is responsible for more deaths worldwide than any other disease. *Mycobacterium* has a complex cell wall that protects it against body defenses and antibiotics. The newly identified genes will help scientists understand this defense. By the end of the 20th century, the genomes of over 50 organisms were known, and by the year 2002 over 100 genomes were known. Some researchers see the genes as mechanisms for diagnosing disease, and they envision DNA as molecular snippets they can use to send patients home cured of their illnesses. In that sense, all the DNA knowledge uncovered in the past half-century is merely a preamble to the startling discoveries waiting to be made in the decades ahead. For many physicians, DNA will be a pharmacological substance of extraordinary potency that can be used to treat disease and its symptoms, while correcting the imperfections that make patients susceptible to disease.

Mechanisms of Genetic Exchange in Bacteria

We have already described how bacteriologists have demonstrated the existence of nuclei in bacterial cells. As bacteria reproduce, these structures function as the carriers of heritable factors from parent to daughter cells, just as in multicellular organisms similar cell nuclei bear genetic determinants. There are a variety of ways that genes carrying pathogenicity (disease-causing) traits. These include transduction, conjugation, and transformation.

The process of reproduction in all kinds of bacteria and in all circumstances is not quite as simple and straightforward as described above. For example, in certain bacilli, elongation of the cell in one direction only, and the formation of a new cell wall and cytoplasmic membrane at the "growing point" (where the elongation originates), have been described. This may be thought of as a kind of budding process, similar to that exhibited by dividing yeast cells. Also, studies of bacterial genetics indicate that transfer of genetic (nuclear) material from one bacterium to another may occur. The exchange involves DNA and can be mediated either by a bacterial virus (bacteriophage), in which case the phenomenon is termed transduction, or by chemically purified DNA, in which case the term is transformation. Conjugation is a mating process in which two bacteria temporarily fuse. This is rare, and its significance in the ordinary life of bacteria is unknown.

Transformation: Evidence That DNA Bears Genetic Information

In 1928, Griffith injected mice with living, but noncapsulated and avirulent, *pneumococci* of type II along with a suspension of killed, capsulated, virulent *pneumococci* of type III. To his surprise, the mice died, and from their tissues Griffith recovered a pure culture of virulent *pneumococci* having type III capsules. Evidently the ability to form type III capsules had been transferred from the dead type III cells to the living, noncapsulated *pneumococci* of type II; the latter were thus transformed to virulent, capsulated, type III *pneumococci*. In 1944, Avery and his associates were able to carry out the same transformation, and their experiments proved that the transforming principle was DNA. A soluble extract of the DNA from one strain of *pneumococci*, when added to another strain of a different type, causes some of the cells of the second strain to acquire one or more of the properties of the first strain, such as its type of capsule. Once acquired, these properties were transmitted to all descendants. It was learned that many different traits may be transformed this way. Transformation is the process by which genes are transferred from one bacterium to another as donor DNA are incorporated into treated cells.

Conjugation

The idea that bacteria might have a form of sexual reproduction was first shown by Tatum and Lederberg in that they demonstrated that a form of genetic recombination could occur between different strains of *E. coli*. Conjugation requires the presence of the fertility (or F) factor in one of the bacteria of a genetic element. The cell containing this factor is called F+ and is regarded as the "male" bacterium. "Female" strains do not contain the F factor and are designated as F-. Actual conjugation of the two strains probably occurs by formation of a bridge between specific pili on the F+ strain

and receptor sites on the F-. During conjugation, genetic material passes only from the F+ to the F- bacterium, later becoming integrated into the latter's chromosome through recombination of genetic material from both strains. The circular bacterial chromosome is opened and becomes linear for transfer across the conjugation bridge. Most antibiotic resistant traits are "exported" to other cells this way in the form of plasmids.

Plasmid

The mechanisms for the transfer of hereditary material not involving transduction and conjugation led to the coinage of a new genetic term: plasmid. Plasmids are small, circular pieces of self-replicating, double-stranded DNA that are accessory genetic elements in the cell. There may be as few as one and as many as a thousand copies in the cell. They are like minichromosomes. Plasmids compose about 1-5 percent of the size of the bacterial chromosome. Plasmids may add to the biological "fitness," or survival ability, of the bacterium. Plasmids are responsible for carrying many different types of information for bacteria, but probably the best known and studied are resistance (R) factors for antibiotics. There are R factors for more than 50 antibiotics. Resistance to penicillin began shortly after World War II, the first time that antibiotics were administered to patients. By the 1950s, resistance to tetracycline and other antibiotics was emerging. Our understanding of plasmid transfer of antibiotic resistance helps physicians deal more effectively with clinical issues when prescribing antibiotics for life-threatening infectious diseases. It is primarily resistance (R) factors transferred in plasmids that makes practicing medicine around the world difficult during times of epidemics.

Many R factors contain two groups of genes. One is called the resistance transfer factor (RTF) that includes genes for plasmid replication. The r-determinant plasmid codes for the production of enzymes that activate certain drugs or toxic substances. Different R factors, when present in the same, can recombine to produce R factors with new combination of genes in their r-determinants. In other cases, the accumulation of resistance within a single plasmid is quite remarkable. For example, one gene carried on this plasmid can demonstrate resistance to sulfonamides, streptomycin, chloramphenicol and tetracycline. Also, genes for resistance to mercury-particular plasmid can be transferred between three enteric (intestinal) species, including *E. coli, Klebsiella*, and *Salmonella*.

Other plasmids code for proteins that enhance the pathogenicity of a bacterium. The strain of *E. coli* causing infant diarrhea and traveler's diarrhea carries plasmids that code for toxin production and for bacterial attachment to intestinal cells. Without these plasmids, *E. coli* is a harmless resident of the large intestine; however with phage in its plasmids, *E. coli* is pathogenic. Other plasmid-encoded toxins include skin stripping toxins of *Staphylococcus aureus, Clostridium tetanus* neurotoxin, and toxins of *Bacillus anthracis*. Still other plasmids contain genes for the synthesis of bacterial toxic proteins that kill other bacteria. These plasmids have been found in many bacterial genera, and they are used as markers for the identification of certain bacteria in clinical laboratories.

Afterword

Ebola and the Genesis of Germs

The latest epidemic of hemorrhagic fever caused by the Ebola virus has captured the international and national news headlines. The Ebola outbreak is currently wreaking havoc in Africa and has scared many in this country since two missionaries returned to the United States for treatment in July 2014. Since then we have had three additional medical evacuations of Americans with Ebola back to the States (another missionary, an unidentified worker for the World Health Organization in Sierra Leone, and a news cameraman); we have had the first patient to come down with Ebola while in the U.S., the first patient to die in the U.S. of Ebola, and the first case of transmission of the disease from one person to another in the U.S. Of all these patients, three were treated successfully; one has died and three remain isolated in treatment.

As of mid-October 2014, estimates from the World Health Organization are that over 8,300 people have contracted Ebola, of which over 4,000 have died[1]. Future estimates have as many as 2 million with Ebola in Africa by January 2015. The numbers of cases reported in West Africa so far this year are more than triple that of any epidemic since the disease was first described in 1976. Ebola infection starts like many other tropical diseases like malaria, with fever, fatigue, muscle aches, and weakness; but then in about ten days massive bleeding, hemorrhaging, and destruction occur.

The spread of scary diseases like Ebola is a cause for concern and leads to questions such as:

1. Where did all these germs come from, and how do they fit into a biblical worldview?

2. How can something so small have such a huge deadly impact on the world around us?

I cannot give a specific "genesis" or origin for Ebola — there is still a lot of mystery surrounding the disease. Bats are a suspect reservoir for Ebola in the rainforest, but no one knows what the virus may be doing in these animals. I do provide a basic perspective for Ebola in *The Genesis of Germs*. Disease was not intended in the original, very good design of creation. Infectious diseases are a secondary state in creation and a result of the Fall, subsequent Curse, corruption, and decay of many microbes, genes, and infectious agents. Many do not realize that some viruses, bacteriophages, are "good" and play a positive role in controlling bacteria in oceans. They recycle many elements in ecosystems.

In this book, I do suggest several major factors that probably led to the origin of disease. These include the modification of original microbe "kinds," mutation, displacement, and decay of genetic material. Ebola is a terrifying disease, like many other biblical diseases and plagues.

For those who do not have hope in Jesus Christ and His future plan for an exodus of germs, it seems hopeless. But Christians do have a hope in the Creator and Great Physician.

Those medical missionary workers like Dr. Kent Brantly and Nancy Writebol who survived Ebola got stronger with experimental serum involving monoclonal antibodies from those who previously survived the disease. The missionaries are very courageous and demonstrate Christian compassion to those in need. I believe Christians should provide treatment to those in need and should also be thinking through and studying the genesis of germs.

---

1 "Texas nurse who had worn protective gear tests positive for Ebola," by Elizabeth Cohen, Steve Almasy, and Holly Yan, CNN Health, http://www.cnn.com/2014/10/12/health/ebola/index.html.

List of related articles:

Gillen, A.L., and Sherwin, F. "Origin of Bubonic Plague." *Journal of Creation*, 20 (1) (2006): pp. 7–8.

Gillen, A.L. 2007. "Biblical Leprosy: Shedding Light on the Disease that Shuns." *Answers Magazine* vol. 2 (3) pp. 77–79.

Gillen, A.L. 2008. "Microbes and the Days of Creation." *Answers Research Journal* 1 (2008): pp. 7–10.

Gillen, A.L., and Sherwin, F. "Louis Pasteur's Views on Creation, Evolution, and the Genesis of Germs." *Answers Research Journal* 1 (2008): pp. 43–52.

Gillen, A.L., and Anderson, S. "Darwin at the Drugstore. The Cost of Antibiotic Resistance in *Serratia marcescens*." Answers in Genesis *Answers In-Depth website*. Posted July 15, 2008.

Gillen, A.L. "The Genesis of MRSA: A Modern Day 'Leprosy' and Hospital Menace." https://answersingenesis.org/natural-selection/antibiotic-resistance/the-genesis-of-methicillin-resistant-staphylococcus-aureus/. Posted July 2, 2009.

Gillen, A.L., and Oliver, J.D. "Creation and the Germ Theory: How a Biblical Worldview Helped Shape the View that Germs Make Us Sick." Answers in Genesis *Answers In-Depth website*. Posted July 29, 2009.

Gillen, A.L., and Oliver, J.D. "Dr. Koch, Creation, and the Constancy of Germs." Answers in Genesis *Answers In-Depth website*. Posted April 7, 2010.

Gillen, A.L., and Oliver, J.D. "The Genesis of Pathogenic E. coli." Answers in Genesis *Answers In-Depth website*. Posted October 6, 2010.

Gillen, A.L., and Gibbs, R. "*Serratia marcescens*: The Miracle Bacillus." Answers in Genesis *Answers In-Depth website*. Posted July 20, 2011.

Gillen, A.L. "Antony van Leeuwenhoek: Creation "Magnified" through His Magnificent Microscopes." Answers in Genesis *Answers In-Depth website*. Posted Aug. 15, 2012.

Gillen, A.L., and Sherwin, F. "The Genesis of Malaria. The Origin of Mosquitoes and Their Protistan Cargo, *Plasmodium falciparum*." Answers in Genesis *Answers In-Depth website*. Posted June 19, 2013.

Gillen, A.L., and Conrad, J. "Our Impressive Immune System: More than a Defense." Answers in Genesis *Answers In-Depth website*. Posted January 15, 2014.

Gillen, A.L. "The Wondrous Weaving of the Skin and its Microbiome." Answers in Genesis *Answers In-Depth website*. Posted July 16, 2014.

Gillen, A., Daycock, W., &. Serafin, A. "High MRSA Carriage Rate among Nursing Microbiology Students." *Advances in Microbiology*, 4, 871–877. http://dx.doi.org/10.4236/aim.2014.413096. Posted 2014.

True or False Questions

1. Bacteria have many variations in their life forms, but there is no hard evidence that one type of bacteria is progressively evolving into another more advanced type.

2. Bacteria are all invisible, potentially harmful little creatures.

3. *E. coli* devotes 98 percent of its energy to swimming from your bladder toward the kidney.

4. The eukaryotic cells of bacteria are generally much smaller and simpler in structure than prokaryotic cells.

5. Throughout history, *Escherichia coli* has had beneficial and also detrimental results in society.

6. A bacterium is said to be motile when it cannot move.

7. Resistance to antimicrobial drugs contributes to the growing number of cases of diseases once thought eradicated.

8. It is possible for germs to mutate and evolve into totally new diseases.

9. It is possible for some normally harmless bacteria, like *Serratia marcescens*, to change slightly, and in turn cause disease in immune compromised individuals.

10. Scientists have correctly applied "survival of the fittest" to make advances in medicine.

Multiple Choice

1. What percentage of bacteria is pathogenic?
   a. 2%
   b. 5%
   c. 25%
   d. 75%
   e. 100%

2. Name the microbiologist who first described synthesis of the red pigment found in bacteria that often cause bread and communion wafers appear to have blood on it.
   a. Joseph Lister
   b. Robert Koch
   c. Louis Pasteur
   d. John Tyndall
   e. Robert P. Williams

3. Give the name of the pigment responsible for the bright red color in the bacteria that appeared as "blood."
   a. tuberculin
   b. chlorophyll
   c. prodigiosin
   d. hemoglobin
   e. rhodopsin

4. In his book, *Darwin's Black Box*, Dr. Michael Behe describes flagella as _____.
   a. being a design paradigm
   b. having irreducible complexity
   c. having the "most efficient machine in the universe"
   d. evidence of evolution
   e. necessary for the survival of bacteria

5. Some evolutionists believe some bacteria are:
   a. evolving into more complex and dangerous forms.
   b. irreducibly complex.
   c. primitive and basic.
   d. unnecessary for life on earth.
   e. a and c

6. Which bacteria produce vitamins for the body?
   a. *E. coli*
   b. *Chlamydia trachomatis*
   c. *Legionella*
   d. *Treponema*
   e. *Rickettsia*

7. Which of the following scientists devised the theory of spontaneous generation by boiling plant infusions in swan-necked flasks that maintained their sterility for long periods of time?
   a. Joseph Lister
   b. Robert Koch
   c. Louis Pasteur
   d. John Tyndall
   e. Anna Roby

8. The idea that microbes "pop" into existence from substances less complex than a living cell is termed:
   a. spontaneous generation
   b. sporulation
   c. binary fission
   d. pleiotrophy
   e. etiology

9. Microbiology is the study of:
   a. small amounts of biology (Yayy!)
   b. organisms too small to seen with the unaided eye
   c. small unaided eyes
   d. small amounts of organisms
   e. small amounts of un-eyed organisms

10. Name the brightly red pigmented bacteria that once thought to cause the "blood of Christ" to appear on communion wafers.
   a. *E. coli*
   b. *Chlamydia trachomatis*
   c. *Legionella pneumophilia*
   d. *Treponema palladium*
   e. *Serratia marcescens*

Chapter Two Questions

True or False Questions

1. The only group of bacteria that have flagellum are the spirilla.

2. The cell walls of Gram-negative bacteria are more complex chemically than those of Gram-positive organisms.

3. Bacteria thrive in cold temperatures, which explains why there is more sickness in winter.

4. The technique of Gram-staining allows a clearer view of the cell wall.

5. When classifying bacteria by shape, it is important to master Latin since all the names come from Latin derivatives.

6. The eukaryotic cells of bacteria are generally much smaller and simpler in structure than prokaryotic cells.

7. Bacteria that are cultivated for some time in the laboratory have the same capacity to produce disease as those in the environment.

8. Bacterial flagella are unique structures not equivalent to the cilia or flagella of protozoa.

9. Bacteria have adapted to more different living conditions than any other group of organisms.

10. At the turn of the 20th century, anthrax was the leading cause of death in the USA.

Multiple Choice

1. The word bacteria comes from the Latin word meaning:
   a. berry
   b. corkscrew
   c. staff or rod
   d. ball
   e. stick

2. Which group moves by rotation of internal, flagellum-like filaments produces a corkscrew-like movement?
   a. *Proteobacteria*
   b. *Chlamydias*
   c. Spirochetes
   d. Gram-Positive Bacteria
   e. *Cyanobacteria*

3. Who was the first known scientist to observe microorganisms, including bacteria?
   a. Louis Pasteur
   b. Joseph Lister
   c. Anton van Leeuwenhoek
   d. Robert Koch
   e. David DeWitt

4. What is the purpose of bacterial spores?
   a. They divide and increase in cell numbers, allowing the bacteria to reproduce.
   b. Spore formation permits cells to survive adverse conditions.
   c. Spores are an important food source for fastidious bacteria.
   d. Spores allow bacteria to disperse to new locations.
   e. b and d

5. When studying and classifying bacteria, it is important to consider which of the following?
   a. growth characteristics
   b. morphology and metabolic way of life
   c. molecular composition
   d. staining characteristics
   e. all of the above

6. Bacteria have thrived due to _____.
   a. varied metabolic abilities
   b. small size
   c. rapid reproductive rate and ability to form resistant spores
   d. producing their own food through spore formation
   e. a, b and c

7. In the group of bacteria called spirilla, you would see _____.
   a. Bacteria shaped like a berry.
   b. Bacteria that were rod shaped.
   c. Bacteria having a helical shape like a corkscrew.
   d. Bacteria with smooth sides and no flagella.
   e. Bacteria that form spores.

8. Which of the following bacteria would be a member of the bacilli group?
   a. A bacterium shaped as a short and thick cylinder.
   b. A bacterium shaped like a long and slender rod.
   c. A bacterium that is not perfectly round, but are flattened on one side or more or less elongated.
   d. A bacterium that is slightly curved and less rigid with blunt ends.
   e. a, b, and d

9. The difference between Gram-positive and Gram-negative bacteria was discovered in the _____ .
   a. late 1800s with more widespread use of microscopes and improved staining techniques.
   b. early 1900s as man began to study bacteria in order to develop antibiotics.
   c. mid-1900s as man began to look for biohazards to use in war.
   d. mid-1900s with the invention of the electron microscope.
   e. late 1900s with the mapping of the genome of many bacteria.

10. The cell wall of a bacterium is best described as _____.
   a. fluid, excreting biofilm
   b. rigid with some elasticity
   c. soft and pliable
   d. closely connected to its cytoplasm
   e. of little importance to the function of bacteria

11. How fast can an *E. coli* bacterium swim?
   a. nearly 5 times the length of its body in one hour inside your urinary tract
   b. nearly 10 times the length of its body in one minute inside your urinary tract
   c. nearly 50 times the length of its body in one second inside your urinary tract
   d. nearly 100 times the length of its body in one hour inside your urinary tract
   e. *E. coli* bacterium do not swim at all.

12. The fastest growth of bacteria happens in which phase?
   a. lag phase
   b. logarithmic phase
   c. stationary phase
   d. motile phase
   e. death phase

Chapter Three Questions

True or False Questions

1. Ulcers are caused by stress and poor diet.

2. A person exposed to *Treponema palladium* will develop a sore throat.

3. Those plants which have mutualistic bacteria associated with their roots (i.e., legumes) include clover, peas, beans, and alfalfa.

4. Archaea are different from bacteria because their cell membranes have unusual lipid composition.

5. The most successful bacteria are the ones that live in harmony with their hosts.

6. Infection of bacteria always leads to disease.

7. A disease is an infection that impairs the normal state of health.

8. Only Gram-positive bacteria, like the anthrax bacteria, produce toxins.

9. *H. pylori* was discovered by Barry Marshall and won the Nobel Prize in Physiology and Medicine in 2005.

10. Anthrax is the likely cause for one of the "plagues of Egypt" that is described in the book of Exodus.

Multiple Choice

1. To develop his famous postulates, Robert Koch first studied what disease?
   - a. tuberculosis
   - b. diphtheria
   - c. cholera
   - d. meningitis
   - e. anthrax

2. What is the correct order for Koch's postulates?
   1. The pure culture must cause the disease when inoculated into an experimental animal.
   2. The causative microorganism must be re-isolated from the experimental animal and re-identified in pure culture.
   3. The causative microorganism must be isolated and grown in pure culture.
   4. The causative microorganism must be present in every individual with the disease.

   - a. 1, 2, 3, 4
   - b. 2, 1, 4, 3
   - c. 4, 3, 2, 1
   - d. 4, 3, 1, 2
   - e. 2, 4, 1, 3

3. Koch discovered which species to be susceptible to cholera?
   - a. guinea pigs
   - b. mice
   - c. cattle
   - d. dogs
   - e. man

4. How long did it take to solve the mystery of Legionnaires' disease?
   - a. 6 hours
   - b. 6 days
   - c. 6 weeks
   - d. 6 months
   - e. 6 years

5. What is important about the species of bacteria called *Rhizobium leguminosarum*?
   - a. They are denitrifying bacteria that add in the decomposition of organic matter.
   - b. They are nitrogen-fixing bacteria that add nourishment through root nodules.
   - c. They are nitrifying bacteria that release ammonia.
   - d. They prosper in high heat and give color to the waters of Yellowstone.
   - e. They are "oil-eating" microbes that clean up oil spills like the Exxon Valdez.

6. What was one laboratory problem that faced the doctors researching Legionnaires'?
   - a. Media pressure to solve the mystery.
   - b. Power failures that interfered with bacterial growth in incubators.
   - c. Failure of equipment
   - d. Determining what the bacteria required as food.
   - e. Too many mice died in the laboratory.

7. What previous experience helped Dr. Fliersman understand *Legionella pneumophila*?
   - a. His father had worked on air conditioning units and he understood bacteria grew in them.
   - b. He had studied soil around nuclear plants.
   - c. He had studied thermophilic bacteria and recognized similarities.
   - d. He had studied diseases that plagued American veterans.
   - e. a and c

9. The Archaean known as *Halobacterium* is characterized by
   _____.
   - a. growing rapidly in fresh water ponds
   - b. its purple light–sensitive pigment
   - c. its red light–sensitive pigment
   - d. living only in cold climates
   - e. none of the above

10. The microorganisms of the hot springs are:
   - a. bacteria
   - b. algae
   - c. protozoa
   - d. a and b
   - e. a, b, and c

11. What are microbes that thrive in hot springs called?
   - a. bacteria
   - b. heat mosaics
   - c. thermobacteria
   - d. thermophiles

Chapter Four Questions

True or False Questions

1. The organelles of protozoa have a "parallel" function to that of organs in complex animals.

2. In malaria parasites, the characteristic reproduction method is sporulation.

3. Schizogony is reproduction by totally asexual means and produces new cells called merozoites.

4. These parasitic forms of protozoans are naturally more common in distribution than the free-living organisms.

5. The findings of Leeuwenhoek were readily accepted by British scientists.

6. Most protozoa are larger than bacteria.

7. All protists are microscopic.

8. Leeuwenhoek is known as the "Father of Biology."

9. An amoeba has no visible internal structures except a nucleus.

10. Malaria parasites reproduce by both sporulation and schizogony depending on where it is in the life cycle.

11. Agar is a complex polysaccharide derived from these red algae.

12. Surgeon-Major Ronald Ross found organisms similar to the malaria parasite in horses.

Multiple Choice

1. Free-living protozoa are found:
    a.   in fresh water
    b.   in salt water
    c.   in the soil
    d.   in decaying organic matter everywhere
    e.   all of the above

2. "Amoeba" is derived from a Greek word meaning
_____.
    a.   "false feet"
    b.   "move"
    c.   "simple"
    d.   "change"
    e.   "life-like"

3. An almost universal characteristic of protozoans is:
    a.   have low energy
    b.   to be parasitic
    c.   locomotion
    d.   a and b
    e.   a and c

4. The protozoan *Euglena* ingests food through its:
    a.   mouth
    b.   gullet
    c.   gill slits
    d.   eyespot
    e.   paramylon

5. The cause of African trypanosomiasis is:
    a.   the tsetse fly
    b.   *Euglena*
    c.   *Trypanosoma brucei*
    d.   *Trypanosoma lamblia*
    e.   *Paramecium caudatum*

6. The protozoan *Giardia* has been known to:
    a.   infect man
    b.   infect wildlife
    c.   possibly have infected Leeuwenhoek
    d.   exist in clear, running springs
    e.   none of the above

7. The disease giardiasis can be avoided by:
    a.   not drinking from streams
    b.   using iodine tablets when camping
    c.   city planners ensuring the water supply is safe
    d.   changing baby diapers
    e.   a, b, and c

8. These organisms are characterized by hundreds of short, hair-like processes on their body.
    a.   Flagellates
    b.   Amoebae
    c.   Ciliates
    d.   Sporozoa
    e.   none of the above

9. Malaria means:
    a.   "*Plasmodium Anopheles*"
    b.   "yellow fever"
    c.   "bad mosquito"
    d.   "swamp fever"
    e.   "bad air"

10. What needs to be present for a definitive diagnosis of malaria to be made?
    a.   Fever of 104 degrees or greater
    b.   Sudden onset of chills and shaking
    c.   Presence of an "O" ring in red blood cells
    d.   A high population of Anopheles mosquitoes
    e.   A dead Anopheles mosquito with malaria parasites in its saliva

True or False Questions

1. Fungi are not considered plants because they contain chlorophyll.

2. Scientist have many more species of fungi to discover.

3. Yeasts and molds are considered distinctly separate fungal groups.

4. Ascus means "tiny" spore-containing sac.

5. Aspergillus can be used to make vinegar and also as an agent of bioterrorism.

6. True yeast has many cells.

7. Bacteria multiply faster than yeasts.

8. The Creator created bacteria and fungi to live in harmony.

9. Alexander Fleming had no idea that penicillin was important when it was discovered.

10. Antibiotic resistance has only occurred recently as patients insisted on antibiotics for non-bacterial infections.

11. Fungi produce 90 percent of the antibiotics used by man.

12. Fungi cells are smaller than bacteria cells.

Multiple Choice

1. Which of the following is not a purpose of Fungi:
   a. to help in decomposition of organic matter
   b. to help prevent wheat rusts in crops
   c. to help in the fermentation process
   d. to help with photosynthesis
   e. b and d only

2. Which of the following is not caused by a fungus?
   a. Mycosis
   b. Tuberculosis
   c. Pneumocystic pneumonia
   d. fungous disease
   e. all of the above

3. Historically, fungi were first considered to be:
   a. plants
   b. microbes
   c. bacteria
   d. blastospores
   e. parasites

4. The scientist who first described fungi was:
   a. Louis Pasteur
   b. Robert Hooke
   c. John Ray
   d. Carolus Linnaeus
   e. Joseph Lister

5. The long, slender filaments of a fungi body are known as:
   a. spores
   b. hyphae
   c. buds
   d. spores
   e. chitin

6. The part of the mycelium that gives molds their characteristic fuzz is the:
   a. vegetative mycelium
   b. sporophore
   c. columella
   d. aerial mycelium
   e. spore

7. Which statement is not true regarding the genus *Rhizopus*:
   a. Bread mold belongs to the division of *Rhizopus*.
   b. Mold in this division also attaches fruits.
   c. *Rhizopus* molds only reproduce asexually.
   d. These molds use stolons in their reproduction.
   e. *Rhizopus* forms a septum during reproduction.

8. Sir Alexander Fleming could not purify or produce large amounts of:
   a. *P. Chrysogenum*
   b. *P. Notatum*
   c. *Tolyposporium niveum*
   d. *Aspergillus flavus*
   e. *Acremonium*

9. This strain was subjected to x-rays in order to produce more antibiotic.
   a. *P. chrysogenum*
   b. *P. notatum*
   c. *Tolyposporium niveum*
   d. *Aspergillus flavus*
   e. *Acremonium*

10. Penicillin was first widely used in:
    a. 1928
    b. World War I
    c. World War II
    d. 1941
    e. 1950

True or False Questions

1. DNA viruses mutate faster than RNA viruses.

2. The term capsid comes from the Latin word *capsa*, meaning "hat."

3. Dental carries are the most common viral infection in humans.

4. Photomicrographs of the virions of tobacco mosaic virus and an animal virus show that the architecture of virions is vastly different between the two.

5. Viruses with the icosahedral shape have 20 equilateral triangular faces that provide a stable protein structure consistent with long-term survival.

6. Once the HIV virus infects CD4+ T-cells (often called T-4 lymphocytes) in large numbers, it leads to a destruction of the immune system.

7. Viruses are adequately described as "poisonous fluids."

8. Viruses change quickly because of their RNA genome instead of DNA genome.

9. Viruses can be classified as either prokaryotes or eukaryotes.

10. The virion always contains at minimum both a nucleic acid and a protein.

11. In 1995, African hospitals first dealt with a new disease caused by the Ebola virus.

12. Modern science has discovered the vector for Ebola.

Multiple Choice

1. Which features do viruses have in common with living cells?
   a. the ability to crystallize
   b. the ability to adapt and change
   c. the ability to reproduce by themselves
   d. the ability to metabolize
   e. none of the above

2. Since viruses are non-living until they enter a host, they are considered to be _____.
   a. virions
   b. renegade cell parts
   c. opportunistic
   d. parasitic
   e. c and d

3. Which of the following is not a characteristic of a virus?
   a. relies on a host-cell metabolism
   b. has a nucleic acid core surrounded by protein
   c. contains only one or a few enzymes
   d. relies on the host's reproductive capabilities to spread
   e. contains both DNA and RNA

4. The size of the smallest viruses can be said to be _____.
   a. approximately the size of small bacteria
   b. larger than 300 nm in diameter
   c. highly visible with a light microscope
   d. not much larger than the diameter of a double-stranded DNA helix
   e. none of the above

5. What is the best example of variation that we have?
   a. potato spindle tuber viroid
   b. colds and flu
   c. bacteria
   d. Epstein-Barr virus
   e. HIV-causing cancer

6. How would you best describe the shape of a helical virus?
   a. It is a regular polyhedron with 20 triangular faces and 12 corners
   b. The capsomeres of each face form an equilateral triangle.
   c. It is spherical in shape.
   d. It resembles long rods that may be rigid or flexible.
   e. The virus is enclosed by an envelope.

7. The word virus comes from the Latin meaning word meaning _____.
   a. "invisible"
   b. "tiny"
   c. "microscopic"
   d. "disease"
   e. "poison"

8. A structural property of HIV is _____.
   a. it displays helical symmetry
   b. the genome is DNA
   c. it contains two molecules of reverse transcriptase
   a. it lacks a lipid-containing envelope
   b. its diameter is around 50 nm

9. How would you best describe the shape of an icosahedral virus?
   a. It is a regular polyhedron with 20 triangular faces and 12 corners.
   b. The capsomeres of each face form an equilateral triangle.
   c. It is spherical in shape.
   d. It resembles long rods that may be rigid or flexible.
   e. a and b

10. Bacterial viruses were first named _____ by_____.
   a. bacteriophages, D'Herelle
   b. bacteriophages, Beijerinck
   c. microbes, D'Herelle
   d. microbes, Beijerinck

True or False Questions

1. The immune system was designed to interact with microbes.

2. The immune system cannot sense anything in the environment; this is the job of the eyes, ears, nose, and throat.

3. An example of a positive interaction between the immune system and microbes is *E. coli* in the intestines that provide nutrients and vitamins for the human body.

4. T-cells are responsible for directly manufacturing antibodies.

5. T-cell receptors are identical to antibodies.

6. The immune response is directed against all the body cells.

7. All bacteria have dangerous antigens (germ molecules) on their surface.

8. Antibody molecules are not flexible; they are very rigid in structure.

9. IgA is the most abundant immunoglobulin found in the fluids of the body.

10. Gene rearrangement is responsible for the variation of a theme in the antibody response and the generation of the various antibody types.

11. IgG are the antibodies to first arrive during an infection.

12. IgM are the largest antibodies.

Multiple Choice

1. The study of host defenses and how they can be mobilized and directed specifically against an invading pathogen is termed:
   a. immunology
   b. genetics
   c. endocrinology
   d. pathology
   e. physiology

2. An excessive, inappropriate, or dysfunctional immune response to germs may be the result of:
   a. stress
   b. allergies
   c. autoimmune diseases
   d. immunosuppressive diseases
   e. being young

3. The human immunodeficiency virus (HIV) that causes the disease known as AIDS selectively infects _____ cells.
   a. CD 8 (suppressor T)
   b. B cells
   c. plasma
   d. helper D
   e. CD 4 (cytotoxic T)

4. The lymphatic system with its branching reticular fibers in the spleen, lymph nodes, and lymph capillaries best illustrates which Intelligent Design principle:
   a. correlation of structure and function
   b. interwoven complexity
   c. homeostasis
   d. order and organization
   e. maintenance of boundaries

5. The body defense systems with their umbrella or bubble-like protection is best illustrated in the life of:
   a. Louis Pasteur
   b. Joseph Lister
   c. Alexander Fleming
   d. Dr. Gillen
   e. David Vetter

6. The immune system with regards to its ability to adjust to new circumstances and where it learns and responds to highly specific pathogens best illustrate which Intelligent Design principle:
   a. correlation of structure and function
   b. interwoven complexity
   c. homeostasis
   d. adaptation
   e. maintenance of boundaries

7. One of the earliest researchers to explore the use of chemicals from tears to kill microbial pathogens was:
   a. Koch.
   b. Hooke.
   c. Fleming.
   d. Ehrlich.

8. Phagocytes are important to the body because they:
   a. patrol the bloodstream and tissues engulfing foreign cells
   b. occupy "fixed sites" within some tissues engulfing foreign cells
   c. kill bacteria infected human cells
   d. a and b
   e. a, b, and c

9. In the organization of your defense system, phagocytic cells are best thought of as:
   a. a first line of defense
   b. a second line of defense
   c. a third line of defense
   d. a site of bacterial growth
   e. a source of antibodies for recognition purposes

10. The structure within phagocytic cells that first meets up with and ultimately results in the digestion of bacterial cells is the:
    a. nucleus
    b. mitochondrion
    c. residual body
    d. cell wall
    e. lysosome

True or False Questions

1. The diseases we face today are exactly the same strains that have always existed.

2. Weather can sometimes play a part in the emergence of a new disease.

3. AIDS came to public awareness through an outbreak of Pneumocystis pneumonia.

4. All people who test positive for HIV have symptoms of AIDS.

5. The presence of *E. coli 0157:H7* in the human intestine is a normal occurrence.

6. The reason for the increase of flesh-eating bacteria has been established.

7. It is possible for common cold viruses to mutate into more deadly viruses, like Ebola.

8. Comparisons of Hantavirus genes suggest that this new virus.

9. In wealthy developed countries with sophisticated health-care systems, infectious diseases are no longer a serious threat.

10. *Cryptosporidium* is responsible for up to 30 percent of diarrheal illness in developing countries.

11. Changes that make our lives more comfortable can also expose us to new diseases.

12. *V. cholerae 0139* is the same strain of cholera that plagued early pioneers in America.

Multiple Choice

1. Medical principles of washing of hands, quarantines and facemasks were first recorded in:
    a. Darwin's *Origin of Man*
    b. the Bible
    c. the writings of Hippocrates
    d. Eastern mysticism
    e. New Age philosophy

2. Many people were proclaiming victory over germs, however, new ones emerge due to:
    a. large urban areas
    b. germs evolving into new diseases
    c. jet planes
    d. blood banks were opening broad new avenues for infection
    e. all but b

3. A 1993 outbreak of *cryptosporidiosis* in Milwaukee was caused by:
    a. contaminated raspberries
    b. unsanitary conditions in a nursery school
    c. contaminated lettuce
    d. contaminated drinking water

4. The increasing incidence of new plagues indicates that infectious diseases are not only not disappearing, but also seem to be: _____.
    a. strengthening by attacking people with compromised immune systems
    b. increasing
    c. mutating into antibiotic resistant varieties
    d. re-emerging and increasing
    e. a and c

5. Some of the factors contributing to the emergence of Ebola are:
    a. minor changes in existing organisms
    b. the spread of known diseases to new geographic regions or populations
    c. increased human exposure to new and unusual infectious agents
    d. a and b
    e. all of the above

6. Lyme disease got its name from:
    a. the green tick that transmits it
    b. the doctor who discovered the cause
    c. the convention where the first outbreak occurred
    d. a bacteria called *Borrelia lymus*
    e. the town where the first outbreak occurred

7. What did the people with Lyme disease have in common?
    a. they all attended the same convention
    b. they all lived in the city
    c. they were all pet owners
    d. they all had Pneumocystis pneumonia
    e. they all developed chronic diarrhea

8. Which of the following is not correct regarding AIDS.
    a. The immune system is overactive due to the alien presence of HIV.
    b. AIDS is transmitted through transfer of body fluids.
    c. Once AIDS develops, it is always deadly.
    d. Over 47 million people worldwide have HIV.
    e. All choices are correct.

9. *E. coli 0157:H7* was first discovered in _____.
    a. 1976
    b. 1981
    c. 1982
    d. 1993
    e. 1995

10. When investigating the cause of a new disease, researchers should consider _____.
    a. weather
    b. disruption of natural environment
    c. development of drug-resistant varieties of disease
    d. infectious agents change abruptly and gain the ability to infect new hosts
    e. germs arriving due to international travel of people and animals

True or False Questions

1. Antimicrobial resistance can be due to spontaneous mutation or gene acquisition.

2. *M. leprae* probably represents a decayed bacterium from faster growing *Mycobacterium* species.

3. The microorganisms found on healthy skin make it vulnerable to pathogens.

4. One structural example of devolution in the human body is teeth and their susceptibility to dental caries.

5. The number one hospital acquired infection is MRSA.

6. It has already been proven that H5N1 can be transmitted from person to person easily.

7. Typhoid Mary presents an example of how God may have intended our human body to interact with potentially dangerous bacteria.

8. Influenza A virus is as virulent in birds as it is in humans.

9. In Hansen's Disease, the largest number of deformities develops from loss of pain sensation due to extensive nerve damage.

10. The information about horizontal gene transfer was the foundation of the microorganisms evolving into more complex forms.

11. Pathogens do not develop resistance against antibiotics through natural selection.

12. The current potential pandemic influenza strains recently isolated from domestic fowl are H5N1, H7N7, and H9N2.

Multiple Choice

1. The 1918 flu epidemic is most likely due to:
   a. antigenic drift of virus
   b. total re-arrangement of chromosomal segments in the influenza virus
   c. evolution of a cold virus into a flu virus
   d. change in global climate
   e. antigenic variation of rhinovirus

2. Bird flu is caused by what strain?
   a. Avian Virus #101
   b. H1N2
   c. H5N1
   d. Duck Virus #202
   e. Spanish Flu Virus

3. The biblical principles (or verses) that might explain the origin of bird flu come from which verses? **(Choose Two)**
   a. Lev. 19: 19
   b. Gen. 3:18
   c. Rev. 21:3
   d. Deut. 22:9
   e. John 3:16

4. What are pathogenicity islands?
   a. special nucleotides that code genes
   b. strands of RNA that cause virulent characteristics
   c. a short piece of naked RNA, only 300 to 400 nucleotides long, with no protein coat
   d. discrete segments of DNA that encode virulence traits
   e. a latent source of HIV DNA

5. What causes the virulence of influenza to change?
   a. infection of different kinds of vectors such as birds or swine
   b. mutations and the reassortment of foreign RNA into the genetic material of the virus
   c. antibiotic resistance
   d. infection of immunodeficient individuals causes the virus to get stronger
   e. the lack of research for anti-viral drugs

6. The origin of infectious disease can be explained by:
   a. man's defenses
   b. the microbe
   c. mobile genes
   d. all of the above

7. The source of variation among microorganisms that were once identical is :
   a. antibiotic resistance
   b. virulence factors
   c. genomic decay
   d. mutation
   e. all of the above

8. *Mycobacterium leprae* has a generation time of:
   a. 20 minutes
   b. 1 hour
   c. 6 hours
   d. 12 days

9. The plague bacillus is known as:
   a. *Plasmodium vivax*
   b. *Pneumocystis carinii*
   c. *Streptococcus pyogenes*
   d. *Yersinia pestis*

10. The bacterium that appears to have picked up a pathogenicity island and causes a common food-borne illness is:
    a. *Yersinia pestis*
    b. *E. coli* O157H7
    c. *E. coli* K 12
    d. *Mycobacterium leprae*
    e. a, b and d

True or False Questions

1. The third horse described in Revelation 6:7–8 is said to be "pale." This refers to the paleness of a sick person or the pale yellow-green of a dying plant.

2. During WWII, Japan used biological warfare on China.

3. As few as ten bubonic plague cells can cause death.

4. Jehovah Rapha means "the Great Physician who cleanses."

5. While the Egyptians were experiencing plagues, the Israelites were protected because they obeyed the heath principles in Levitical law.

Multiple Choice

1. The diseases that have most recently invoked fear have been:
    a.   Ebola
    b.   SARS and bird flu
    c.   flesh-eating *Streptococcus*
    d.   all of the above

2. A plague in Scripture denotes:
    a.   pestilence alone
    b.   pestilence and other calamities in nature
    c.   famine
    d.   war

3. The fourth horseman of the apocalypse represents:
    a.   war
    b.   famine
    c.   religious deception
    d.   pestilence and disease

4. The fifth horseman is:
    a.   war/famine
    b.   religious deception
    c.   pestilence and disease
    d.   Jesus Christ

5. What fraction of the earth's population will see incredible devastation when the fourth horseman completes his ride?
    a.   1/4
    b.   1/2
    c.   1/8
    d.   3/4

6. Livor mortis is when:
    a.   the skin shows signs of blood build up
    b.   part of the physical death process
    c.   skin color progressively changes from green to blue to purple then finally black
    d.   all of the above

Critical Thinking Questions

1. Scott and Linda went on vacation in a third-world country. They had been warned not to drink the water. They were very careful to heed the warning. Scott still got sick, but his wife did not. How is this possible? Explain your answer.

2. Anthrax was a problem immediately after September 11th when it was found in letters placed in the mail system. What other bacteria might potentially be used in a bioterror attack? Outline a plan that could be used to protect us from such an attack.

3. Recently the number of tuberculosis cases has risen with the strain being more antibiotic resistant. Many cases are multi-drug resistant. What might be the cause of these new strains forming? What should be done to combat the problem?

4. Why did God give Adam an immune system?

5. Explain the contribution of one creation biologist. How did the use of both traditional microbiology techniques and his thinking God's thoughts after Him help him achieve his goals? How did his achievements affect the history of microbiology? (For example, think about how Carl Fliermans made the connection between *Legionella pneumophila* and Legionnaires' disease. How did the use of Koch's postulates help his research?)

6. What are the differences between variation and neo-Darwinian evolution? Explain why antibiotic resistance is not an example of Darwinian evolution. What factors lead to minor changes in bacteria? Why is antibiotic resistance an important healthcare issue, as well a vital issue for the Christian faith?

7. Epidemics and plagues are documented back to ancient times. They are also predicted for the future. How should a Christian respond to these? How do we deal with the fear exhibited by society and the media?

8. Provide an explanation for the devolution of *Mycobacterium leprae* (i.e., the cause of Hansen's disease) from faster-growing mycobacteria. How does the idea of a decaying creation fit with the observation that in the soil, there are non-pathogenic *Mycobacterium* species and that grow fairly rapidly, pathogenic *M. tuberculosis* that grows moderately fast, and pathogenic *M. leprae* that grow very slowly?

9. Explain the emergence of pandemic strains of influenza. In your answer, be sure to include a discussion of the how the 1918 Spanish flu and avian (bird) flu viruses represent a change from the original influenza virus strains.

10. HIV is said have originated from a related virus (SIV, Simian Immunodeficiency Virus) in a primate like monkeys and chimpanzees. HIV is thought to have evolved in humans after "jumping" from primates to humans. Based upon the principle of decay, provide an alternative explanation of HIV devolving from human cell parts. (Hint: A "normal" retrotransposon on human chromosome 22 shuts off the immune system during pregnancy.)

11. How does "Typhoid Mary" exemplify the human body (i.e., the immune system) as it might have been in the early Genesis times (i.e., the antediluvian age)?

12. Using the knowledge gained in this book, give possible examples of what plagues are foretold in Revelation.

Photo and Illustration Credits

Science Photo Library: 7, 31, 32, 43, 46, 50, 58, 61, 63, 65, 66, 67, 74, 78, 82, 83, 88, 89, 91, 97, 105, 106, 108, 112, 113, 114, 119, 120, 121, 124, 128, 130, 132, 142, 159

Center for Disease and Control: 4, 13, 15, 20, 22, 34, 36, 40, 49, 74, 92, 96, 123, 126, 134, 138, 147, 150, 159

Bryan Miller: 8, 11, 14, 21, 25, 26, 28, 45, 53, 54, 55, 56, 57, 59, 71, 85, 95, 98, 102, 107, 111, 116, 152, 159

Corbis: 86, 140, 155

Apologia Education Ministries, Inc.: 39, 46, 76

Getty: 145

References

Alcamo, I. E. (1999). *DNA Technology: The Awesome Skill* (2nd ed.). London: Academic Press.

Alcamo, I.E. (1997). *Fundamentals of Microbiology* (5th ed.). Redwood City, CA.: The Benjamin/Cummings Publishing.

Alcamo, I.E. (2003). *Microbes and Society: An Introduction to Microbiology.* Sudbury, MA: Jones & Bartlett Publishers.

Alcamo, E. I. and L.M. Elson. (1996). *The Microbiology Coloring Book.* Harper Collins College Publishers, New York.

Anderson, K. L. (2005, March). "Is Bacterial Resistance to Antibiotics an Appropriate Example of Evolutionary Change?" *CRSQ, 41(4):* 318-326.

Atlas, R. M., & Bartha, R. (1998). *Microbial ecology: Fundamentals and Applications* (4th ed.). San Francisco, CA: Benjamin Cummings.

Behe, M. J. (1996). *Darwin's Black Box: The Biochemical Challenge to Evolution.* New York: The Free Press.

Bergey's, D.H. (1984). *Bergey's Manual of Systematic Bacteriology* Vols. 1, 2, 3, and 4 Williams and Wilkins, Publishers, Baltimore.

Bergey, D.H. *et. al.* (1994). *Bergey's Manual of Determinative Bacteriology.* 9th ed. Williams and Wilkins. Baltimore.

Bergman , J. (1999). "Did God Make Pathogenic Viruses?" *Technical Journal* 13(1):115–125.

Bindle, W. (1995). *A Field Guide to Germs.* New York: Henry Holt and Company, Inc.

Black, J. G. (2004). *Microbiology: Principles and Explorations* (6th ed.). Chichester: John Wiley & Sons.

Brand, P., & Yancey, P. (1980). *Fearfully and Wonderfully Made.* Grand Rapids, MI: Zondervan.

Bryceson, A. & Pfaltzgraff, R. E. (1990). *Leprosy,* 3rd ed. New York.: Churchill Livingstone.

Burdon, K .L., & Williams, R. P. (1968). *Microbiology* (6th ed.). New York: Macmillan Co.

Carmichael, C., Gillen, A. L., Sherwin, F., & Wile, J. (2007). (In Preparation). *Biology: A Search for Design, Order, and Complexity.* Anderson, IN: Apologia Educational Ministries, Inc.

Cartwright, F. F. (1972). *Disease and History.* New York: Dorset Press.

Coppedge, D. (2002). "Microscopic Magnificence: Antony van Leeuwenhoek." *Christian History* (Fall 2002 issue) *76* (10): 42.

Darwin, C. (1859). *The Origin of Species* [Reprint of 1st ed.]. New York: Avenue Books.

Dawkins, R. (1996). *Climbing Mount Improbable.* New York: W. W. Norton and Company.

Dawkins, R. (1996). *The Blind Watchmaker.* New York: W. W. Norton and Company.

De Kruif, P. (2002). *Microbe Hunters.* New York: Harcourt Publishers.

Debre, P. (1998). *Louis Pasteur.* Baltimore: Johns Hopkins University Press.

Dembski, W. (1998). *The Design Inference.* Cambridge: Cambridge University Press.

Denton, M. J. (1986). *Evolution: A Theory in Crisis.* Bethesda, MD: Adler and Adler.

Denton, M. J. (1998). *Nature's Destiny.* New York: The Free Press.

Dixon, B. (1976). *The Magnificent Microbes.* New York: Athenaeum.

Dixon, B. (1994). *Power Unseen: How Microbes Rule the World.* W.H. Freeman and Co, New York.

Dobell, C. (1932). *Antony van Leeuwenhoek.* New York: Harcourt Brace.

Dubos, R. J. (1986). *Louis Pasteur: Freelance of Science.* New York: Da Capo Press.

Eiglmeier, K. (2001). "The Decaying Genome of Mycobacterium leprae." *Lepr. Rev.,* 72: 387–398.

Fisher, R. B. (1977). *Joseph Lister, 1827-1912.* London: MacDonald and Jane's Publishers.

Francis, J.W. (2003). "The Organosubstrate of Life: A Creationist Perspective of Microbes and Viruses," pp.434-444 in: Ivey, R. L. (ed.), Proceedings of the Fifth International Conference on Creationism. Creation Science Fellowship, Pittsburgh, PA.

Garrett, L. (1994). *The Coming Plague: Newly Emerging Diseases in a World Out of Balance.* New York, NY. Farrar, Straus and Giroux.

Garrity, G. M. (ed.) (2001). "Vol. 1: The Archaea and the Deeply Branching and Phototrophic Bacteria." *Bergey's Manual of Systematic Bacteriology* (2nd ed.). Berlin: Springer-Verlag.

Garrity, G. M. (ed.) (2005). "Vol 2: The Proteobacteria." *Bergey's Manual of Systematic Bacteriology* (2nd ed.). Berlin: Springer-Verlag.

Gillen, A. L. (2005). "The Immune system: Designed to Interact with Microbes." *Origins* [*A Journal of the Biblical Creation Society*], *40:* 5-9. Warwicks, Great Britain.

Gillen, A. L. (2006). *Symbiosis: Introductory Microbiology Lab Manual.* Boston: The Benjamin Cummings Custom Laboratory Program for the Biological Sciences.

Gillen, A. L., & Mayor, H. D. (1995). "Why Do We Keep Catching the Common Cold?" *The American Biology Teacher, 57(6):* 336-342.

Gillen, A. L., & Williams, R. P. (1993). "Dinner Date with a Microbe." *The American Biology Teacher, 55(5):* 268-274.

References

Gillen, A. L., & Williams, R. P. (1994). "Pasteurized Milk As an Ecological System for Bacteria." *Labs That Work: The Best of the How-to-dos-its*. Reston, VA: NABT Publications.

Glasser, R. J. (1976). *The Body is the Hero*. New York: Random House.

Gorbach, S.L. (1990). "Lactic acid bacteria and human health." *Annals of Medicine, 22*, 37-41.

Graves, D. (1999). *Doctors Who Followed Christ*. Grand Rapids, MI: Kregel Publications.

Hinnebusch B. J., Perry R. D., & Schwan T. G. (1996). "*Yersinia pestis* Hemin Storage (hms) Locus in the Transmission of Plague by Fleas." *Science, 273*: 367–370.

Hinnebusch, B. J., Rudolph, A. E., Cherepanov, P., Dixon, J. E., Schwan, T. G., & Forsberg, A. (2002). "Role of *Yersinia* Murine Toxin in Survival of *Yersinia pestis* in the Midgut of the Flea Vector." *Science, 296*: 733–735.

Joklik, W. K., et al., (eds.) (1992). *Zinsser Microbiology* (20th ed.). Norwalk, CT: Appleton & Lange.

Lax, E. (2004). *The Mold in Dr. Florey's Coat: The Story of the Penicillin Miracle*. New York: Henry Holt Books.

Lederberg, J. (ed.) (2000). *Encyclopedia of Microbiology* (2nd ed.). Academic Press.

Levine, A. J. (1992). *Viruses*. New York: Scientific American Library.

Lim, D. V. (2003). *Microbiology* (3rd ed.). Dubuque, IA: Kendall/Hunt.

Lorange, E. A., Race, B. L., Sebbane, F., & Hinnebusch, B.J. (2005). "Poor Vector Competence of Fleas and the Evolution of Hypervirulence in *Yersinia pestis*." *J. Infect. Dis., 191*: 1907-1912.

Madigan M. T., Martinko, J. M., & Parker, J. (2003) *Brock Biology of Microorganisms* (10th ed.). Englewood Cliffs, NJ: Prentice Hall Inc.

Marieb, E. N. and Hoehn, K. (2007). *Human Anatomy & Physiology*, Seventh Edition. Benjamin Cummings Company, San Francisco, CA.

Martini, F.H. (2007). *Fundamentals of Anatomy and Physiology*. Seventh Edition. Benjamin Cummings Company, San Francisco, CA.

McMillen, S. I., & Stern, D. E. (2000). *None of These Diseases* (3rd ed.). Old Tappan, NJ: Fleming H. Revell Company.

Morris, H. M. (2006). *The New Defender's Study Bible* (KJV). Grand Rapids, MI: Word Publishing.

Morris, H. M. (1988). *Men of Science, Men of God*. El Cajon, CA: Master Books, Inc.

Needham, C., Hoagland, M., McPherson, K. & Bert Dodson, B. (2000). *Intimate Strangers: Unseen Life on Earth*. Washington D.C.: ASM Press.

Nesse, R. M. & Williams, G. C. (1994). *Why We Get Sick? The New Science of Darwinian medicine*. New York: Vintage Books.

Nester, E. N., Roberts, C. E., Pearsall, N. N., Anderson, D. G., & Nester, M. T. (2007). *Microbiology: A Human Perspective* (5th ed.). Boston: WCB McGraw-Hill.

Paley, W. (1802). *Natural Theology* [Reprinted 1997]. Charlottesville, VA: Lincoln-Rembrandt Publishers.

Parker, G. (1996). *Creation: The Facts of Life*. Green Forest, AR: Master Books.

Parkhill, J. *et al*. (2001). "Genome Sequence of *Yersinia pestis*, the Causative Agent of Plague." *Nature, 413*: 523–527.

Penrose, E. (1998). "Bacterial Resistance to Antibiotics — a Case of Un-natural Selection." *Creation Research Society Quarterly, 35*: 76-83.

Pommerville, J. C. (2004). *Alcamo's Fundamentals of Microbiology* (7th ed.). Sudbury, MA: Jones & Bartlett Publishers.

Postagate, J. (1992). *Microbes and Man* (3rd ed.). Cambridge: Cambridge University Press.

Prescott, L. M., Harley, J. P., & Klein, D. A. (2004). *Microbiology* (6th ed.). New York: McGraw-Hill.

Radot, M. V. (1885). *Louis Pasteur: His Life and Labours*. New York: D. Appleton and Co.

Reid, R. (1975). *Microbes and Men*. New York: Saturday Review Press.

Roberts, L. S., & Janovy, Jr., J. (1999). *Schmidt and Roberts' Foundations of Parasitology* (6th ed.). Boston, MA: WCB McGraw-Hill.

Ryrie, C. (1994). *Ryrie Study Bible* (KJV). Chicago, IL: Moody Press.

Ryrie, C. (1994). *Ryrie Study Bible: Expanded ed.* (KJV). Chicago, IL: Moody Press.

Schaechter, M., Ingraham, J. L., & Neidhardt, F. C. (2005). *Microbe*. Washington D.C.: ASM Press.

Seifert, H. S. & DiRita, V. J. (2006). *Evolution Of Microbial Pathogens*. Washington, DC: ASM Press

Singleton, P., & Salisbury, D. (2002). *Dictionary of Microbiology and Molecular Biology* (3rd ed.). John Wiley & Sons.

Strong, (1948). *Strong's Exhaustive Concordance of the Bible*. Nashville, TN: Royal Publishers.

Tortora, G. J., Funke, B. R., & Case, C. L. (2004). *Microbiology: An Introduction* (8th ed.). San Francisco, CA: Benjamin Cummings.

Tortora, G., Funke, B., & Case, C. (2007). *An Introduction to Microbiology* (9th ed.). San Francisco, CA: Addison-Wesley Longman.

Tortora, G. J. and Grabowski, S. R. (2000). *Principles of Human Anatomy and Physiology, ninth edition*. John Wiley & sons, Inc.. New York.

Wells, J. (2000). *Icons of Evolution: Science or Myth?* Washington, D.C.: Regnry Press.

Williams, R. P., & Gillen, A. L. (1991). "Kitchen Microbiology and Microbe Phobia." *The American Biology Teacher 53(1)*: 10-11.

Wood, T. C. (1981). "Acts and Facts: Genome Decay in the Mycoplasmas." *Impact, 340*: 1–4.

Wren, B.W. (2003). "The Yersiniae — a Model Genus to Study the Rapid Evolution of Bacterial Pathogens." *Nature Micro. Rev., 1*: 55-64.

Zhou, J., Thompson, D. K., Xu, Y., & Tiedje, J. M. (2004). *Microbial Functional Genomics*. Hoboken, NJ: John Wiley & Sons.

Zinsser, H. (1935). *Rats, Lice and History*. New York: Blue Ribbon Books.

A

Acquired immunity – An immune response targeted at a specific pathogen or toxin.

Adaptation – Any heritable characteristic of an organism that improves its ability to survive and reproduce in its environment. Also used to describe the process of genetic change within a population, as influenced by natural selection. Creationists use this term to refer to a short-term change in the response of a body system as a consequence of repeated or protracted stimulation; whereas, evolutionists use this term to mean an adjustment to environmental demand; through the long-term process of natural selection acting on the genotype.

Adaptation package – Biological organisms are more than the sum of individual structures; their ability to function successfully is due to an entire "package of parts."

Aerobic bacteria – Bacteria that require free oxygen to survive in a given environment.

Alveolus – An individual air capsule within the lung; the basic functional unit of respiration.

Anaerobic bacteria – Bacteria that grow in an environment devoid of oxygen.

Analogy (analogous structure) – A body part similar in function to a body part of another organism but only superficially similar in structure, at most. Such similarities are regarded not as evidence of inheritance from a common ancestor, as in homology, but as evidence only of similar function.

Anatomy – The branch of science concerned with the structure of living organisms and the relationship of their organs.

Antibiotic – A chemical secreted by a living organism that kills or reduces the reproduction rate of other organisms.

Antibiotic-resistant – When a microbe is no longer susceptible to an antibiotic. Most frequently it refers to a bacterium that becomes "immune" to an antibiotic due to a mutation, or lateral transfer of a plasmid or transposons.

Antibodies – Specialized proteins that aid in destroying infectious agents.

Anticodon – A three-nucleotide base sequence on tRNA.

Antigen – A protein that, when introduced in the blood, triggers the production of an antibody.

Archaea – prokaryotic cells resembling bacteria that live in extreme environments, such as high temperature, salt or methane. They differ from true bacteria in that they have some cellular features that are like eukaryotic cells.

Asepsis – Freedom from infection; a condition in the body that is free of pathogens, as in wounds or surgical incisions that are free from pathogenic bacteria, fungi, viruses, protozoans, and parasites.

ATP (adenosine triphosphate) – The universal energy-carrying molecule manufactured in all living cells as a means of capturing and storing energy. It consists of adenine with a sugar, ribose, to which are added in linear array, three phosphate molecules.

Avian (bird) Flu – A highly specific type of influenza which is very fatal. It is caused by the H5N1 Influenza A virus.

B

Bacilli – Elongated, rod shaped bacteria observable under a high powered microscope. Bacteria belonging to the *Enterobacteraciae* family are bacillus-shaped.

Bacillus – Genus of Gram-positive spore forming bacilli that are widely distributed in the environment. They produce endospores, making them highly resistant to environmental factors. In spore form they can remain viable for years in a harsh environment. Some species are considered pathogenic. Pathogenic isolates: *B. anthracis* (causative agent of anthrax) and *B. cereus* (causes food poisoning in foods such as rice, potatoes, and meats). Other common isolates include *B. subtilis* and *B. megaterium*.

Bacteria – plural form of the Latin bacterium, meaning "staff" or "rod." Bacteria are prokaryotes and among the most abundant organisms on Earth. The vast majority play a positive role in nature. About five percent are disease-causing (pathogenic).

Bacteremia – The presence of bacteria in the blood.

Biochemistry – The scientific discipline concerned with the study of chemical reactions that occur in organisms (they explain the metabolic processes of life in the language of chemistry).

Black Death – refers to the specific bubonic plague pandemics of the Middle Ages; See "bubonic plague."

Blind Watchmaker – Richard Dawkins' metaphor for non-intelligent, purposeless, natural selection; expressing the idea that design characteristics seen in living things are not like the intelligent purpose and craftsmanship associated with watch-making.

Blood – A modified connective tissue consisting of formed elements that are suspended and carried in plasma (a straw-colored liquid consisting of water and dissolved solutes). These formed elements and their major functions include erythrocytes (oxygen transport), leukocytes (immune defense), and platelets (blood clotting).

B-lymphocyte – Specialized leukocytes processed in the bone marrow (or bursa equivalent); these cells give rise to plasma cells that produce antibodies.

Bone marrow – The soft sponge-like material in the cavities of bones. Its principal function is to manufacture erythrocytes, leukocytes, and platelets (formed elements of blood).

Bubonic plague – A deadly bacterial disease caused by Yersinia pestis, also known as the "Black death." Symptoms include formation of bubos, fever, and blackening of the skin.

Bubos – The tumors of lymph glands.

C

Capillary – A microscopic blood vessel that connects an arteriole and a venule; the basic unit of the circulatory system.

Cascade – A series of chemical reactions, or events, that involve interdependent reactions.

Cell – The basic unit of structure and function in living organisms.

Chlorophyll – A pigment necessary for photosynthesis.

Chloroplast – An organelle containing chlorophyll for photosynthesis.

Chromatin – Clusters of DNA, RNA, and proteins in the nucleus of a cell. The extended form of chromosomes during interphase.

Chromoplasts – Organelles that contain pigments used in photosynthesis.

Chromosome – DNA coiled around and supported by proteins, found in the nucleus of the cell.

Cilia – Hairlike projections that extend from the plasma membrane and are used for locomotion.

Coagulation – Refers to blood clotting. The process by which platelets and soluble plasma proteins interact in a series of complex enzymatic reactions to finally convert fibrinogen into fibrin. It works on a positive feedback cycle.

Cocci (singular, coccus) – Bacteria which are spherically shaped and observable under a high powered microscope.

Coliform – Group of Gram-negative bacilli from the *Enterobacteriaceae* family that produces gas via lactose fermentation. Their presence is commonly considered an indication of fecal contamination. *E. coli* is an example of a coliform.

Commensalism – A relationship between two organisms of different species where one benefits and the other is neither harmed nor benefited.

Cold, Common – mild viral infection involving the nose and respiratory passages (but not the lungs). It may be caused by rhinoviruses, coronaviruses, adenoviruses, and other infectious agents.

Conjugation – A temporary union of two organisms for the purpose of DNA transfer.

Convergent evolution – Evolution of similar appearances in unrelated species.

Corruption – Literally means, "to destroy" (from the Latin *corruptus*). The origin of pathogenic (disease-causing) bacteria is complex and multifaceted, and may be explained by a combination genes that were lost, added and moved.

D

Darwinism – The theory that all living things descended from an original common ancestor through natural selection and random variation without the aid of intelligence or nonmaterial forces.

Design – The purposeful arrangement of parts; a plan, a scheme, a project, or a purpose with intention or aim.

Differential media – media that contains a substance or chemical that can distinguish between different types of bacteria.

DNA (deoxyribonucleic acid) – Nucleic acid found in all cells (except mature red blood cells); the genetic material that specifies protein synthesis in cells.

E

E. coli, Escherichia coli, – An enteric bacterial species used in many biological research projects which inhabits the intestines of humans and other animals. Proliferation can cause newborn meningitis, diarrhea, and urinary infections.

Glossary

Emergent properties – Properties found in living things that show that the sum together is greater than the separate, independent parts.

Endotoxin – A substance that is part of the outer cell wall of all Gram-negative bacteria. Its toxic properties remain even after the bacteria is dead, making it easy to accumulate in dust or other matrices. Inhalation can cause activation of macrophages and other cells in the lung that result in inflammation. Fever, coughing, and other respiratory symptoms can occur.

Enteric bacteria – Bacteria that reside in the intestinal tract. Most of these bacteria are not harmful to the human body and many are mutualistic with humans, providing valuable vitamins and breaking down nutrients. Many of these beneficial bacteria are now called "probiotics bacteria."

Erythrocytes – Red blood cells.

Escherichia – Bacteria genus belonging to the family *Enterobacteriaceae*. *E. coli* is the most common isolate of this genus and is a part of the normal flora of the intestinal tract. It is, however, capable of causing illnesses ranging from mild food poisoning to severe kidney damage, and even death. The pathogenic serovars (types) of *E. coli* are divided into four groups, whose identification usually require serological methods:

Enterohemorrahagic *E. coli* – produces bloody diarrhea and can progress to kidney damage and death. *E. coli O157:H7* is in this category.

Enteroinvasive *E. coli* – causes watery diarrhea with blood and mucus.

Enteropathogenic *E. coli* – characterized by fever, vomiting, and diarrhea.

Enterotoxigenic *E. coli* – characterized by watery diarrhea and dehydration.

Evolution (evolve) – Mere "change in living things over time," but also meaning descent with modification, that is, particular mechanisms to account for change such as natural selection and gene mutation.

Extracellular – Outside of a cell or cells.

F

Fecal Coliform – A sub-group of coliforms. These bacteria are found almost exclusively in the fecal matter of humans and animals. Presence of these in the environment is consistent with fecal contamination.

Fermentation – The anaerobic breakdown of sugars into smaller molecules.

Flagellate – A protozoan that propels itself with a flagellum.

Fungi – These relatively large, plant-like organisms make up that division of chlorophyll-free microbes ordinarily referred to when we use the term fungi. Fungi include the varieties of mushrooms, yeasts and the molds. Fungi are heterotrophic and generally derive their nutrition by extracellular digestion and then absorption of organic matter.

G

Gene – A section of DNA that codes for the production of a protein or a portion of protein, thereby causing a trait.

Gene pool – The total genetic material in the population of a species at a given point in time.

Genome – The total DNA for a given organism.

Genus (plural, genera) – The first part of the scientific name. For example, *Homo sapiens* is the scientific name for man. "Homo" is the genus name. The genus differentiates organisms from each other included within a family.

Germ – A common term for "pathogen." Germ comes from the Latin *germen,* meaning bud — something small that yet contains the beginning of life in it.

Gradualism – The view that evolution occurred slowly over time with transitional forms grading finely a line of descent.

Gram stain – A fundamental bacterial identification method which involves a multi-step staining procedure. The bacteria will generally fall into either the Gram-positive or Gram-negative category. The categories are defined by the resultant color of the bacterium at the end of the staining process.

Gram-negative – A stain that is a pink to red color.

Gram-negative bacilli – This category contains a broad range of bacterial specimens. Two main sub-categories may be considered: enteric and non-enteric. Common isolates are *E. coli* and *P. aeruginosa*

Gram-negative cocci – Most bacteria in this group are considered pathogenic, and isolation from the environment is rare. Some examples include *Neisseria* (Gonorrhea) and *Haemophilus* (bacterial meningitis).

Gram-positive – A stain that is a deep blue or purple color.

Gram-positive bacilli – These are considered envirmental contaminants. They are found in air, swab, bulk, and soil samples. Some species within this group are considered pathogens and can be severe. Common isolates are *Corynebacterium* and *Bacillus*.

Gram-positive cocci – These are most frequently isolated from clinical samples. They are found as normal flora of the skin, mucous membranes, and other areas of humans and animals. These bacteria are considered mainly as opportunistic pathogens. Common isolates are *Staphylococcus, Streptococcus,* and *Micrococcus.*

Great Physician – This is Jesus, the God-Man who heals men/women of physical disability, infectious disease, emotional and spiritual disorder. Restores sick men and women to health, and gives dignity to those who are ashamed of their condition.

H

Hemoglobin – The pigment that gives red blood cells their characteristic red color. It functions in the transport of oxygen and carbon dioxide.

Hemophilia – Refers to several different hereditary deficiencies of coagulation.

Homeostasis – A state of body equilibrium, or the maintenance of an optimal, or stable, internal environment of the body.

Homology (homologous structure) – A body part with the same basic structure and embryonic origin as that of another organisms. In evolutionary theory, it implies the common ancestry of the two. In Creationism, it implies a common design.

Humoral immunity – Immunity which comes from antibodies in blood plasma.

Hypha – A filament of fungal cells.

Hypothesis – In the scientific method, 1) an educated guess, 2) a tentative explanation, or 3) a proposition that is to be confirmed by test.

I

Immunity – A specified defense against a disease.

Immunocompromised – A condition characterized by a decreased function of the immune system. Some examples include AIDS patients, transplant recipients, and the elderly.

Immunodeficiency – An impairment of immunological function which leads to greater susceptibility to opportunistic infections (e.g., SCIDS and AIDS).

Immunological defense – The process by which the body protects itself from pathogenic invaders such as bacteria, fungi, parasites, and foreign substances.

Influenza – also known as the flu, is a contagious disease that is caused by the influenza virus. It attacks the respiratory tract in humans (nose, throat, and lungs).

Innate immunity – An immune response that is the same regardless of the pathogen or toxin encountered.

Intelligent design (cause) – Any theory that attributes the action, function, or structure of an object to the creative mental capacities of a personal agent. In biology, the theory that biological organisms owe their origin to a preexistent intelligence.

Interdependent parts – Body structures that are interdependent on each other. The body is one unit, though it is made up of many different types of cells and tissues. The body parts work together, cooperate, and cannot exist without each other. This resulting condition of these parts working together is that the sum of the actions is greater than the separate, individual actions.

Interferon – Proteins secreted by cells infected with a virus. These proteins stimulate nearby cells to produce virus-fighting substances.

Ions – Substances in which at least one atom has an imbalance of protons and electrons

Irreducible complexity – Interdependent parts of living (and non-living) things that cannot be reduced further without losing their intended function (e.g., mousetrap parts working together).

J

Jehovah Rapha – The God who heals. The God who makes a person whole, and the One who restores a life of calamity to a life of dignity and usefulness.

L

Lactose – A disaccharide of glucose and galactose, or simply, milk sugar.

Lateral gene transfer – Any process in which an organism transfers DNA to another cell that is not its offspring.

Legionella – Genus of Gram-negative bacilli isolated from stagnant water, mud, and other environments where water can collect and remain undisturbed. This is responsible for Legionellosis and is primarily characterized by pneumonia. The common isolate is *L. pneumophila.*

Leprosy – An infectious disease of the nervous and skin systems caused by *Mycobacterium leprae*. In the Old Testament, leprosy also referred to a number of infectious skin diseases.

Leukocytes – White blood cells which perform various defensive functions in blood.

Lipid – Compounds that do not mix with water, including fats, phospholipids, and steroids.

Lymph – A clear, plasma-like fluid formed from interstitial fluid that flows through lymphatic vessels.

Lymph nodes – Encapsulated masses of lymph tissue arranged into compact, somewhat spherical structures that are found along lymph vessels.

Lymph tissue – Groups of lymphocytes and other cells which support the lymphocytes.

M

M. leprae – *Mycobacterium leprae* causes peripheral nerve damage and it is the species of bacteria that is responsible for leprosy (Hansen's disease).

Media – A nutrient-based substrate used to grow bacteria and fungi. Media is available in many different varieties and can range from very basic to highly selective and differentiating.

Membrane – A thin layer of soft, pliable, and often permeable tissue.

Messenger RNA – The RNA that performs transcription.

Metabolism – The chemical changes that occur within the body. The sum total of all processes in an organism which convert energy and matter from outside sources and use that energy and matter to sustain the organism's life functions.

Microbe – Abbreviated term for microorganism. It means, "small life." The term microbe generally includes bacteria, protozoans, small fungi, and sometimes viruses.

Microorganisms – Living creatures that are too small to see with the naked eye.

Mitochondria – The organelles in which nutrients are converted to energy.

Model – A paradigm, or an explanation or representation of something that cannot be seen.

Molecules – Chemicals that result from atoms linking together.

Monocytes – Largest of white blood cells. They are phagocytic and differentiate into tissue macrophages.

Morphology – The form or structure of an organism.

Mosaic – Patterns and designs showing contrasts among colors, pigments, structures, and/or organisms in their environment.

MRSA – methicillin resistant *Staphylococcus aureus*; this bacteria group is very resistant to many types of antibiotics (esp. methicillin)

Mucociliary escalator – The mechanism where cilia of mucous membrane cells move particles along respiratory membranes and down the throat, where they are swallowed.

Mutation – A radical chemical change in one or more alleles. An abrupt and marked change in the DNA of an organism compared to that of its parents. A relatively permanent change in the DNA involving either a physical change in chromosome(s) or a biochemical change in the order or number of nucleotide bases in gene(s).

Mutualism – A relationship between two or more organisms of different species where all benefit from the association.

Mycobacterium – Genus of Gram-positive acid fast bacilli that can be found on decaying material in the soil. However, certain species have adapted to human, birds, and other animals. Mycobacterium are resistant to harsh environmental conditions due to their cell wall and may be found in a variety of places ranging from air droplets to the footpads of armadillos. Some species within this genus cause disease such as leprosy and tuberculosis. Pathogenic isolates are *M. leprae* (leprosy) and *M. tuberculosis* (tuberculosis).

N

Natural selection – Process in nature where one genotype leaves more offspring for the next generation than other genotypes in that population. The explanation is that the elimination of less-suited organisms and the preservation of more suited ones result from pressures within the environment, or competition, or both.

Neo-Darwinism – The concept of Darwinism with the addition of mutation, population, and Mendelian genetics.

Neuron – A nerve cell.

Normal flora – The microorganisms that can be found on or in the body of healthy humans and animals.

Nosocomial infection – An infection contracted as a result of a hospital stay.

Nucleotide – The fundamental structural unit of a nucleic acid, or DNA, made up of a nitrogen-carrying base, a sugar molecule, and a phosphate group.

Nucleus – The region of a eukaryotic cell that contains the cell's main DNA.

O

Opportunistic pathogens – Pathogens that do not usually cause disease unless the individual is immuno-compromised. Such a condition might include chronic illness, AIDS, cancer, and/or trauma. An example of an opportunistic pathogen is *Pseudomonas aeruginosa*.

Order – A fixed or definite plan and system.

Organic molecule – A molecule that contains only carbon and any of the following: hydrogen, oxygen, nitrogen, sulfur, and/or phosphorous.

Organism – The living body that represents the sum total of all its organ systems working together to maintain life.

Organization – A unified coherent group or systemized whole.

P

Parasite – An organism that feeds on a living host.

Parasitism – A relationship between two organisms of different species where one benefits and the other is harmed.

Pathogen – An organism that causes disease. Technical term for germ, or germ-causing microbe, such as virus, bacterium, or protozoan that may be disease-causing.

Pathogenicity island – A cassette of genes involved causing infectious disease. This is not the evolution of new chromosomal DNA, but was an acquisition through lateral gene transfer.

Pellicle – A firm, flexible coating outside the plasma membrane.

Penicillin – An broad-spectrum antibiotic drug used to treat bacterial infections; this was the first antibiotic discovered and one of the most widely used antibiotics with few side effects; however, many bacteria are resistant to its treatment.

Pestilence – Disease that spreads rapidly, causing many deaths; natural disasters such as infectious disease, parasites, locusts, floods, and other such catastrophes.

Phagocytosis – The process by which a cell engulfs foreign substances or other cells; the particle containing vacuole fuses with a lysosome whose enzymes digest the food. An example of this is macrophages eating bacteria and other invaders of the body.

Phenotype – The observable expression of an organism's genes.

Phospholipid – A lipid in which one of the fatty acid molecules has been replaced by a molecule that contains a phosphate group.

Photosynthesis – The process by which green plants and some other organisms use the energy of sunlight and simple chemicals to produce their own food.

Phylogeny – The "evolutionary" history of an animal, person, or plant.

Physiochemical forces – Naturalistic view of how blind, mechanistic forces, through chance and natural selection, over millions of years, may explain the irreducible complexity of anatomical structures and physiological functions of the human body.

Physiology – The study of life processes in an organism. The study of the functions of an organism and its parts. The science of the functioning of living organisms.

Phytoplankton – Tiny floating photosynthetic organisms, primarily algae.

Plague – May be any form of trouble or harassment, but the term most often has a reference to a disease of epidemic proportions. Also, it is used to refer to a disease's occurrence and especially when it is fatal in its effects.

Plankton – Tiny organisms that float in the water.

Plasma – The fluid portion of the blood, which is mostly water.

Plasma cell – A mature antibody-secreting B-cell found mainly in lymph nodes.

Plasma membrane – The semipermeable membrane between the cell contents and either the cell wall or the cell's surroundings.

Plasmids – Small, circular, double-stranded units of DNA that replicate within cells independently of the chromosomal DNA. They function like a mini-chromosome, and confer one or more traits to a bacterium and can be reproduced separately from the main bacterial genetic code.

Plasmolysis – Collapse of a walled cell's cytoplasm due to a lack of water.

Glossary

Plasticity – The ability of the microbes to make adjustments to changes.

Platelets – Cell fragments in blood which help prevent blood loss

Population – A group of interbreeding organisms coexisting together.

Producers – Organisms that produce their own food.

Prokaryotic cell – A cell that has no distinct, membrane-bounded organelles.

Protozoan – One-celled eukaryotic cell (or a few cells) creature; most having a true nucleus, mitochondria and other organelles. Examples include *Amoeba, Euglena, Paramecium,* and *Plasmodium* (the agent of malaria).

Pseudogenes – DNA sequences similar to normal genes that are non-functional.

Pseudomonas – Gram-negative bacilli that are widely found in nature. They are especially prevalent in hot tubs and swimming pools due to the fluctuations in temperature and improper sanitation procedures. Some species such as *P. aeruginosa* and *P. flourescens* can be opportunistic pathogens to plants, humans, and animals. Disease states may range from mild skin infection and swimmer's ear to corneal ulceration and vision loss due to microbial keratitis. The disease conditions may be exacerbated if the host is immunocompromised.

Pseudopod – A temporary, foot-like extension of a cell, used for locomotion or engulfing food.

Pseudostratified columnar epithelium – Tissue that has cells (like bricks on end) with relatively large cytoplasmic volumes.

Pyemia – Pus-forming infection.

R

Resistance – When a microbe is no longer susceptible to a drug, such as an antibiotic. Most frequently it refers to a bacteria that becomes "immune" to an antibiotic due to a mutation, or lateral transfer if a plasmid or transposons.

Respiration – The breakdown of food molecules with a release of energy.

Rhizoid hypha – A hypha that is imbedded in the material on which the fungus grows.

Ribosomes – Non-membrane-bounded organelles responsible for protein synthesis.

S

Salmonella – This genus belongs to the family *Enterobacteriaceae*. It is part of the intestinal flora of birds and other animals such as pigs. It can be found in water, raw animal food products, and animal feces. *Salmonella* is spread through ingestion of contaminated foods and can cause a variety of diseases ranging from mild food poisoning to severe septicemia. Pathogenic isolates: *S. typhi* (Typhoid) and *S. typhimurium* (food poisoning).

Scientific law – A theory that has been tested by and is consistent with generations of data

Selective advantage – A genetic advantage of one organism over its competitors that causes it to be favored in survival and reproduction rates over time.

Selective media – Media that contains a substance or chemical that inhibits the growth of certain microorganisms while permitting the growth of others.

Septicemia – Blood infection, or high levels of virulent microorganisms by bacteria, such as *Streptococcus pyogenes*. A condition characterized by high levels of virulent microorganisms in the bloodstream.

Serological test – Tests which utilize antibody detection methods for disease diagnosis purposes.

Serratia – This genus belongs to the family *Enterobacteriaceae*. Can be found in environments such as on plants, soil, water, insects, rodents, and the digestive tract. Some species are major contributors to nosocomial infection and can also be pathogenic to animals.

Speciation – The development of a new species by reproducing their ancestral population, resulting in the loss of interfertility with isolation of organisms from it.

Species – A unit of one or more populations of individuals that can reproduce under normal conditions, produce fertile offspring, and are reproductively isolated from other such units. Also, the second part of the scientific name. For example, *Homo sapiens* is the scientific name for man. "*Sapiens*" is the species name. The species classification helps to differentiate it from all other organisms included in a genus.

Spirochaete (spirilla) – Bacteria which are "s" shaped (doubly curved rods) and observable under a high powered microscope.

Spore – A reproductive cell with a hard, protective coating.

Staphylococcus – Gram-positive cocci that are found as normal flora of the skin and mucous membranes. Can also be isolated from dust, water, and food products. Several species are considered as opportunistic pathogens to humans and animals. The primary pathogenic species in the genus is *S. aureus*, which causes food poisoning.

Stasis – The constant morphology of a species over a long period of geologic time.

STDs – Sexually transmitted disease(s).

Strains – Organisms from the same species that have markedly different traits.

Streptococcus – These Gram-positive cocci can be found as normal flora to the skin and mucous membranes. Most species are considered as opportunistic pathogens and some species may cause potentially severe diseases in humans and animals. For example, *S. pyogenes* can cause Rheumatic fever and *S. pneumoniae* can cause respiratory illness.

Structural homology – The study of similar structures in different species.

Symbiosis – A close relationship between two or more species where at least one benefits.

Synergism – Usually refers to properties found in non-living things (especially chemicals) that show the sum together is greater than the separate, independent parts.

T

Taxonomy – The science of classifying organisms.

The immutability of species – The idea that each individual species on the planet was specially created by God and could never fundamentally change.

Theory – A hypothesis that has been tested with a significant amount of data.

Tissue – A group of functionally similar cells performing a distinct structure.

T-lymphocyte – Specialized leukocytes processed in the thymus gland; these lymphocytes provide the body with specific cell-mediated immunity.

Total coliform/*E. coli* test – This analysis provides a quantitative assessment of the coliforms and *E. coli* present in a given sample. The presence of these microorganisms is consistent with fecal contamination.

Transduction – The process in which infection by a virus results in DNA being transferred from one bacterium to another.

Transformation – The transfer of a DNA segment from a nonfunctional donor cell to that of a functional recipient cell.

U

Urine – Yellow liquid waste formed from the metabolic breakdown of protein into nitrogenous wastes (urea and water from the excretory system).

V

Vaccine – A weakened or inactive version of a pathogen that stimulates the body's production of antibodies which can aid in destroying the pathogen.

Vacuole – A membrane-bounded "sac" within a cell.

Vestigial structure (organ) – A body part that has no function, but which is presumed to have been useful in ancestral species.

Vibrionaceae – Family of Gram-negative straight or curved rods.

Villus – A minute projection that extends outward into the lumen from the mucosal layer of the small intestine.

Virus – A non-cellular infectious agent that has two characteristics: (1) It has genetic material (RNA or DNA) inside a protective protein coat. (2) It cannot reproduce on its own.

Vitamin K – Fat-soluble vitamin K1 is found in foods, and K2 is produced by E. *coli*. They are needed for the clotting protein, prothrombin to form.

Z

Zooplankton – Tiny floating organisms that are either small animals or protozoa.

Index

Index

Index

plague, 6, 13, 22, 33-34, 37, 49, 60, 126, 128, 135, 138, 142, 146, 148-149, 158-160, 164, 173-174, 176-179, 183

plankton, 42, 64, 67, 71, 183

plasmids, 18-19, 148-150, 162-163, 183

Plasmodium, 37, 52, 58-62, 71, 100, 135, 137, 162, 164, 168, 173, 184

pneumonia, 18, 20, 22, 27, 37-38, 40, 49, 89, 103, 123-124, 127, 129, 135, 137, 141, 149, 154-155, 160, 169, 172, 181

population, 19-20, 35, 44, 47-48, 52, 55-56, 58, 63, 65, 101, 104, 108, 117, 123-124, 128, 132-133, 142, 148, 156, 158-159, 168, 174, 178, 180, 182, 184

prion, 103, 132-133

prodigiosin, 16-17, 165

producers, 66, 69-70, 184

prokaryotic cell, 184

protozoan, 52-54, 56, 58-60, 62, 73, 88-89, 97, 124, 131, 168, 180, 184

pseudogenes, 144-145, 149, 184

Pseudomonas, 29, 84, 145, 183-184

pseudopod, 40, 55, 184

Q

quinidine, 60

R

red blood cells, 53-54, 59-60, 115, 168, 179-181

Reed, W., 4, 98-100

resistance, 6, 17-21, 83, 108, 110-111, 114-115, 122, 127, 133-135, 139, 142, 147-148, 156, 158, 163-165, 169, 173, 175-177, 184

respiration, 25, 34, 70, 145, 178, 184

rhinoviruses, 92, 94, 104, 179

rhizoid hypha, 184

ribosomes, 28, 41-42, 93, 184

RNA, (ribonucleic acid), 20, 28, 41, 89, 93, 95-96, 102-105, 113, 124, 135, 151-152, 154-155, 162, 170, 173, 179, 182, 185

Ross, R., 4, 58, 60-61, 100, 168

S

Salmonella, 13, 27, 37, 139-140, 163, 184

SARS, 107, 126-127, 133, 135-138, 156, 158, 160, 174

Serratia marcesens, 15-16

sexually transmitted diseases, (STDs), 18, 133, 184

speciation, 184

spirochaete, (spirilla), 25-26, 29, 35, 45, 166, 184

spontaneous generation, 10-11, 51, 127, 165

spore, 25, 33-34, 62, 73-74, 87, 90, 166, 169, 178, 184

Stachybotrys, 82-83, 146

Staphylococcus, 6, 18-19, 27, 37, 108, 110, 137, 147, 162-163, 181-182, 184

stasis, 105, 185

strains, 6, 16, 18-20, 23, 29, 32, 60, 77-78, 85, 101, 104-105, 108, 111, 131, 133-134, 147, 149-154, 156, 160, 162-163, 172-173, 175, 185

Streptococcus, 6, 18-19, 26-29, 37, 130, 135, 142, 159, 173-174, 181, 184-185

superbug, 19, 31, 147

symbiosis, 46, 67, 89, 132, 142, 177, 185

T

taxonomy, 88, 185

The Origin of Species, 176

theory, 10-13, 19, 23-24, 33, 36, 38, 41, 47, 99, 132, 136, 150, 164-165, 176, 179, 181, 184-185

tissue, 9, 29, 34, 36-37, 39, 46, 53, 71, 77, 88-89, 102-103, 105, 112-114, 116, 120-121, 126, 129, 144, 154-156, 178, 182, 184-185

T-lymphocyte, 115-116, 185

transduction, 13, 19, 150, 157, 163, 185

transformation, 19, 78, 147, 163, 185

transposons, 18-19, 178, 184

typhoid fever, 27, 37, 139-140

Typhoid Mary, (Mary Mallon), 140-141, 173, 175

U

ulcers, 136, 138-139, 147, 162, 167

urine, 45, 133-134, 140, 185

V

vaccine, 34, 56, 59-60, 117-119, 125, 153, 155-156, 160, 185

variation, 6, 16, 19-21, 101, 103-105, 118, 135-136, 139, 147, 150-152, 170-171, 173, 175, 179

vector, 56, 60, 130, 148, 170, 177

vestigial organ, 38, 121, 185

Vibrio, 26-27, 37, 131-132, 134, 137

viroid, 103, 170

virus, 16, 20, 39, 92-98, 100-107, 109-110, 113, 115, 119-120, 122-124, 126-131, 133-138, 143, 151-156, 160, 162-164, 170-173, 175, 178, 181, 183, 185

vitamin K, 9, 108, 185

W

West Nile virus, (disease), 101, 107, 130, 137-138

white blood cells, 107, 110, 112, 120, 125, 129, 182

Williams, R., 16, 165, 176-177

Y

yellow fever, 94, 98-100, 135, 168

Yellowstone National Park, 40, 42

Yersinia pestis, 13, 37, 142, 148-149, 173, 177, 179

yogurt, 7, 9, 23-24

Z

Zooplankton, 185

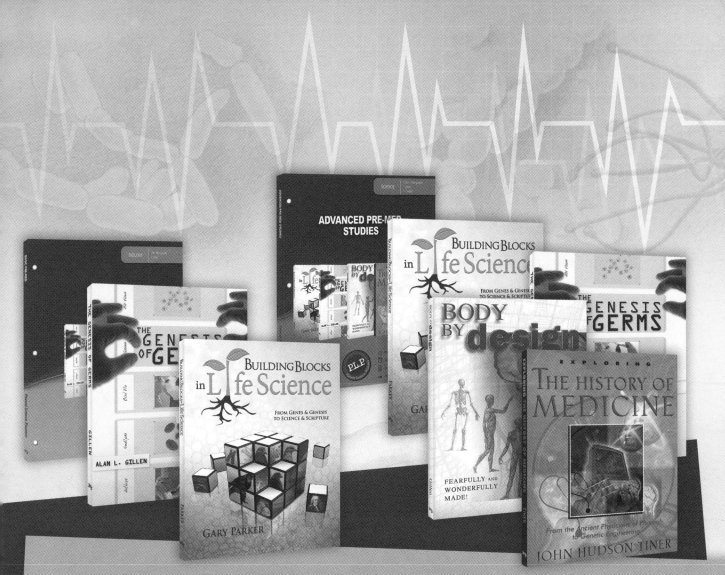

Master Books Parent Lesson Planners (PLP):
We have done all the work for you!

BASIC PRE-MED
1 YEAR COURSE – 8TH TO 9TH GRADE

ADVANCED PRE-MED STUDIES
1 YEAR COURSE – 10TH TO 12TH GRADE

Turn sniffles into a teachable moment! Learn about the history of germs and the mechanisms of life in this two-book course on biology! How diseases mutate, ways science tries to stop them, our natural built-in defenses, human development, genetic functions, patterns in life — all combined for a unique, in-depth exploration encouraging students to learn.

3 book package: *The Genesis of Germs; Building Blocks in Life Science; Parent Lesson Planner*
Now Only $45.99

Get the science basics in this exciting pre-med study! Explore medical history as you discover the intricate design of the human body. Learn about germs as you unlock the code of life with a solid overview of the scope and application of medical and scientific knowledge. From genetics to bones to surgeries, discover a powerful array of sciences and advances!

5 book package: *Building Blocks in Life Science; The Genesis of Germs; Body by Design; Exploring the History of Medicine; Parent Lesson Planner*
Now Only $78.99

From the Center of the Sun to the Edge of God's Universe

Think you know all there is to know about our solar system? You might be surprised!

Master Books is excited to announce the latest masterpiece in the extremely popular *Exploring Series*, *The World of Astronomy*. Over 150,000 copies of the *Exploring Series* have been sold to date, and this new addition is sure to increase that number significantly!

- Discover how to find constellations like the Royal Family group or those near Orion the Hunter from season to season throughout the year.
- How to use the Sea of Crises as your guidepost for further explorations on the moon's surface
- Investigate deep sky wonders, extra solar planets, and beyond as God's creation comes alive!

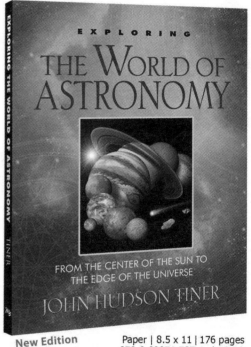

New Edition

Paper | 8.5 x 11 | 176 pages
978-0-89051-787-1 **$14.99**

The book includes discussion ideas, questions, and research opportunities to help expand this great resource on observational astronomy.

Order your copy today to begin *Exploring the World of Astronomy!*
nlpg.com/worldofastronomy

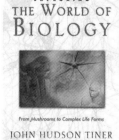

The World of Biology
978-0-89051-552-5
$13.99

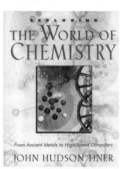

The World of Chemistry
978-0-89051-295-1
$13.99

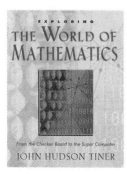

The World of Mathematics
978-0-89051-412-2
$13.99

The History of Medicine
978-0-89051-248-7
$13.99

The World Around You
978-0-89051-377-4
$13.99

Planet Earth
978-0-89051-178-7
$13.99

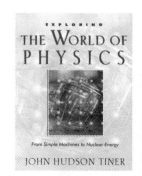

The World of Physics
978-0-89051-466-5
$13.99

Courses for high school and beyond that proclaim the intricate and awesome works of God!

Body by Design defines the basic anatomy and physiology in each of 11 body systems from a creational viewpoint. Every chapter explorers the wonder, beauty, and creation of the human body, giving evidence for creation, while exposing faulty evolutionistic reasoning.

Body by Design
by Alan Gillian
978-0-89051-296-8
$13.99

Flood by Design takes you into a fascinating aspect of the Genesis flood you may never have considered. Examine unusual rock formations and evidence that only the biblical flood model can fully explain.

Flood by Design
by Michael Oard
978-0-89051-523-5
$14.99

From the acclaimed Creation Research Society, this technical study of rock strata, and the fossils found therein, gives a solidly scientific rationale for believing in a young earth. This advanced guide is ideal for upper-level homeschool students, college students, or anyone wishing to explore this fascinating subject in-depth and includes questions for review at the end of each chapter.

Geology by Design
by Carl Froede Jr.
978-0-89051-503-7
$14.99

The universe was created with purpose and reason; and modern science with all of its experiments, exploration, and sophistication has never proven otherwise. In fact, as author Dr. Danny Faulkner makes plain, advanced science argues more for a created cosmology than a big bang.

Universe by Design
by Dr. Danny Faulkner
978-0-89051-415-3
$14.99

Master Books®
A Division of New Leaf Publishing Group
www.masterbooks.net